7/03

B

IN

D0344287

5192
3372

Elspeth Huxley

By the same author

Ed., with E. T. Williams,
The Dictionary of National Biography 1961–1970, 1981

Ed., with Lord Blake,
The Dictionary of National Biography 1971–1980, 1986

The Dictionary of National Biography 1981–1985, 1990

Ed. *The Dictionary of National Biography 1986–1990*, 1996

Ed. *The Dictionary of National Biography:
Missing Persons*, 1993

Ed. *Hutchinson Encyclopedia of Biography*, 1996

Ed. *Power: A Political History*, 1990

AS AUTHOR

The Swahili Coast, 1971

David Livingstone, 1998

*The History of St Antony's College, Oxford,
1950–2000*, 2000

(with Philip Awdry) *Cataract*, 1985

Elspeth Huxley

A BIOGRAPHY

C. S. NICHOLLS

Thomas Dunne Books
St. Martin's Press ≉ New York

THOMAS DUNNE BOOKS.
An imprint of St. Martin's Press.

www.stmartins.com

Library of Congress Cataloging-in-Publication Data

Nicholls, C. S. (Christine Stephanie)
    Elspeth Huxley : a biography / C. S. Nicholls.—1st U.S. ed.
       p. cm.
    Includes bibliographical references (p. 459–465) and index.
    ISBN 0-312-30041-7
    1. Huxley, Elspeth Josclelin Grant, 1907–1997. 2. Authors, English—20th
century—Biography. 3. Radio broadcasters—Great Britain—Biography.
4. Conservationists—Great Britain—Biography. 5. British—Kenya—
History—20th century. 6. Rift Valley Province (Kenya)—Biography.
I. Title.

PR6015.U92Z78 2003
828'.91209—dc21   [B]
                                        R2003046542

First published in Great Britain by HarperCollins*Publishers*

First U.S. Edition: July 2003

10 9 8 7 6 5 4 3 2 1

For Joan Considine, teacher and friend,
and in memory of my parents,
Kit and Olive Metcalfe

CONTENTS

ILLUSTRATIONS

(Unless otherwise stated, photographs are from private collections)

Jos Grant
Nellie and Elspeth, 1907
The grass hut in which the Grants lived while waiting for Kitimuru to be completed, 1912
Kitimuru, 1913
Inside Kitimuru
Elspeth as a child
Elspeth feeding her pet duiker, Twinkle
Kitimuru in 1999 (© *Stephen Taylor*)
Jos and Nellie at Kitimuru, 1920
The Norfolk Hotel, Nairobi, in the 1920s
Two views of Nairobi in the 1920s
Denys Finch Hatton, Jack Pixley, Lady Colvile and Tich Miles
Chania Bridge and the Blue Posts Hotel
Nellie, Jos and Elspeth in the 1920s
Elspeth aged fifteen
Elspeth as a bridesmaid, 1923
Joss Hay, Bobby Roberts, Jos, Lady Idina Hay, Cockie Blixen, Princesse Philippe de Bourbon and Nellie at Gilgil, 1924
Gachehe
Judith and Trudie Denman, Nellie and Jos, and Evelyn Waugh, 1931
Jos in the 1930s (© *British Empire and Commonwealth Museum*)
Elspeth in the 1930s
Rose Cartwright, Nellie and 'Sharpie', 1937

Gervas Huxley, 1914
Elspeth in 1935
Elspeth and Gervas on honeymoon in Cornwall, December 1931

Elspeth (*Photograph reproduced by courtesy of the National Portrait Gallery, London*)

Nellie in the 1930s (© *British Empire and Commonwealth Museum*)

Njombo in the 1930s

Gikammeh (© *British Empire and Commonwealth Museum*)

Woodfolds

Gervas and Elspeth with Charles at his christening, 1944

Harold Raymond, Cleggy, Vera Raymond, Charles and Gervas at Woodfolds, 1947 (© *British Empire and Commonwealth Museum*)

Karanja and Mbugwa (© *British Empire and Commonwealth Museum*)

Elspeth and her dachshund Honey in 1960 (© *Topham/Press Association*)

Nellie in the 1960s

Gervas in 1967

Charles in the 1980s

Cockie Blixen (© *Kathini Graham*)

Ingrid Lindstrom (© *Kathini Graham*)

Elspeth, Holly Aird and Hayley Mills during the filming of *The Flame Trees of Thika*, 1981 (© *Hulton Deutsch*)

Elspeth, Esmond Bradley Martin and Peter Scott at Slimbridge, 1980s (© *Chrysee Bradley Martin*)

Elspeth on her last safari in Kenya (© *British Empire and Commonwealth Museum*)

Elspeth and Michael Blundell with Kenya friends, 1980s (© *Kathini Graham*)

ACKNOWLEDGEMENTS

I am most grateful to Chatto & Windus for allowing me to read and quote from their papers deposited in Reading University Library. Reading University Library, Rhodes House Library in Oxford, Cambridge University Library, the Scott Polar Research Institute at Cambridge, and the British Empire and Commonwealth Museum in Bristol have been most helpful and accommodating – my thanks go to them all. My quotations from Elspeth Huxley's letters and papers are by kind permission of the trustees of the estate.

Many people helped me in a variety of ways when I was writing this book. Some granted me interviews, some allowed me to read their Huxley letters, others lent me books and yet others provided encouragement and support. The list is long, but each of these people went out of their way to be helpful: Carolyn Bateman, Mary Bennett, Mary Blackley, Peter Bostock, Michael Bott, Chryssee and Esmond Bradley Martin, Hugo Brunner, Mary Bull, Freddie Burnaby-Atkins, Anne Carnelly, Michael Carney, Tobina Cole, Deborah Colvile, Joan Considine, Daphne Cross, Robert Cross, Anthony Dyer, Terence Gavaghan, Barbara Gough, Kathini and Donald Graham, Gareth Griffiths, Morna Hale, R.K. Headland, Tuppence Hill-Williams, Michael Holroyd, Adrian House, Alexander Huxley, Frederica Huxley, Hugh Huxley, Heather Jeeves, Richard Johnson, Mrs P. Jones, June Knowles, Robert Lacey, Belinda Leyfield, Alan Lodge, John Lonsdale, Mary Lovell, Andrew Lownie, Mona Macmillan, Geraldine Macoun, Ingrid Maggs, Sir Charles Markham, Peter Meadows,

Miriam and Nigel Nicholls, Lord (John) Oaksey, Cherry Palmer, John Pinfold, Patricia Pugh, Lady (Philippa) Scott, Sir Roger Swynnerton, Stephen Taylor, Vera Tugwell, Bridget Wainwright and Angela Watt. All these people I thank heartily for their kindness and generosity.

Christine Nicholls
Oxford, 2001

PREFACE

'Colonialism,' said Elspeth Huxley in 1990, 'is now a dirty word to many, arousing feelings of indignation in black breasts and guilt in white ones – emotions equally disruptive, in my opinion, to a calm assessment of past history and the profitable conduct of present affairs. The most cogent summing up of colonialism I have seen was handed down by the quarterchief of Wum in Cameroon to the indefatigable traveller Dervla Murphy in the words: "Colonialism is like the zebra. Some say it is a black animal, some say it is a white animal, and those whose sight is good, they know it is a *striped* animal." '[1]

Elspeth Huxley grew up in colonial Kenya, during a time of little doubt about the rightness of the British Empire and its assumed civilising mission. There she began to write about her country and its inhabitants – her first work was published in Nairobi newspapers when she was fourteen. Thereafter her pen never ceased, and her forty-two books included novels, biographies, detective stories and political commentary, indeed any medium that would get her ideas across. She was also a broadcaster and journalist. Her semi-autobiographical *The Flame Trees of Thika* (1959), its chapters Olympian in their strengths and weaknesses, was as delightful and evocative a story as Karen Blixen's *Out of Africa*. It became a best-seller, introducing the sights and sounds of Africa, its hopes and despairs, to thousands who would never set foot in that continent.

Elspeth Huxley's somewhat clipped tones became familiar from her radio broadcasts. For many years she was in favour of a partner-ship of black and white going forward together in Kenya until the country became economically viable. What she said was often unpopular. Whatever the wrongs of colonialism, she wrote of it with compassion and insight, changing her views as she grew older until she concluded that the sooner the whites left Kenya the better. This book traces how she came to that conclusion, which from the personal point of view meant that her mother Nellie Grant, a Kenya farmer, would have to abandon her beloved farm on the western slopes of the Rift Valley, a place Elspeth had visited almost annually after she married and settled in England. The relationship between mother and daughter, detailed in this book, is crucial to the understanding of Elspeth Huxley, and Nellie features largely in the story. She wrote to her daughter more than once a week, in letters so vivid that they gave Kenya a prominent place in Elspeth's mind. Elspeth kept the letters, and they have been used extensively in the writing of this biography. Nellie did not, alas, keep Elspeth's replies for longer than a week, but she commented on all her daughter's activities, thus providing us with an account of Elspeth's life.

In her youth and early middle age all Elspeth's books were about Africa, but in late middle age she turned to Britain and biography. In her eighties she began again to write of her beloved Kenya, and revisited the haunts of her African youth with walking-stick and grandchildren. 'One of the mild surprises of advancing age,' she said, 'is to discover that part of one's lifetime has turned into history, a process which one generally assumes had come to a halt about the time that one was born.'[2] Elspeth Huxley chronicled that lifetime in prose of exceptional beauty and clarity, but she exaggerated and concealed, as autobiographers are wont to do. Here is her true story.

FAMILY TREES
AND MAPS

The Grant Family

Sir Charles Grant
1836–1903
m. [1] Ellen Baillie
d. 1885
dau. of Henry Baillie,
of Redcastle, Inverness-shire
and Philippa Gregory
dau. of 6th Viscount Strangford

m. [2] Lady Florence Lucia Harris
d.1909

Allastair Edward George
1892–1947
m. [1] Elizabeth Montagu-Stuart Wortley

m. [2] Ann Bridget Dominica Herbert

Robert   Mary   Evelyn   Elizabeth Anne

Josceline Charles Henry
1874–1947
m. 1906
Eleanor Lilian Grosvenor
1885–1977
dau. of Richard de Aquila Grosvenor,
Baron Stalbridge

Elspeth Josceline
23 July 1907–10 January 1997
m. 12 December 1931
Gervas Huxley
1894–1971

ELSPETH JOSCELINE
23 July 1907–10 January 1997
m. 12 December 1931
Gervas Huxley
1894–1971

Charles Grant
b. 10 February 1944

m. [1] 1968
Frederica Lispenard Huxley

m. [2] 1997
Louise Garvey

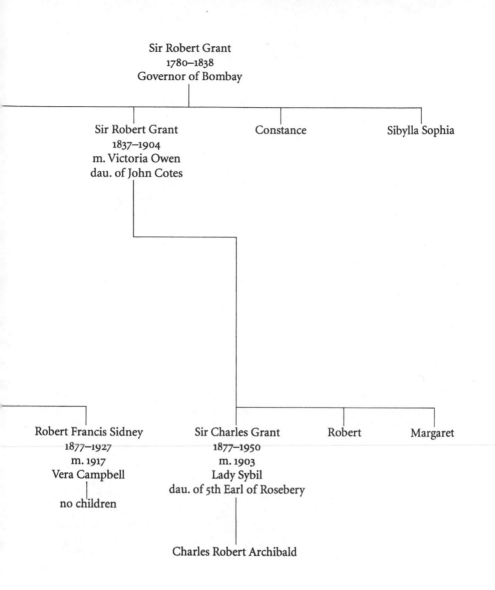

Sir Robert Grant
1780–1838
Governor of Bombay

Sir Robert Grant
1837–1904
m. Victoria Owen
dau. of John Cotes

Constance

Sibylla Sophia

Robert Francis Sidney
1877–1927
m. 1917
Vera Campbell

no children

Sir Charles Grant
1877–1950
m. 1903
Lady Sybil
dau. of 5th Earl of Rosebery

Robert

Margaret

Charles Robert Archibald

The Grosvenor Family

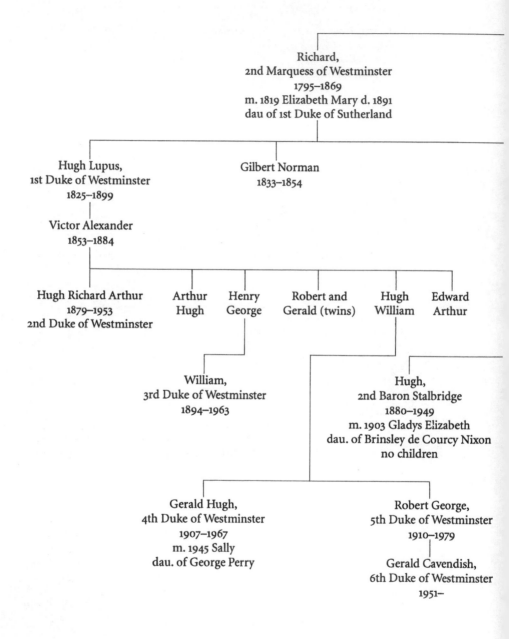

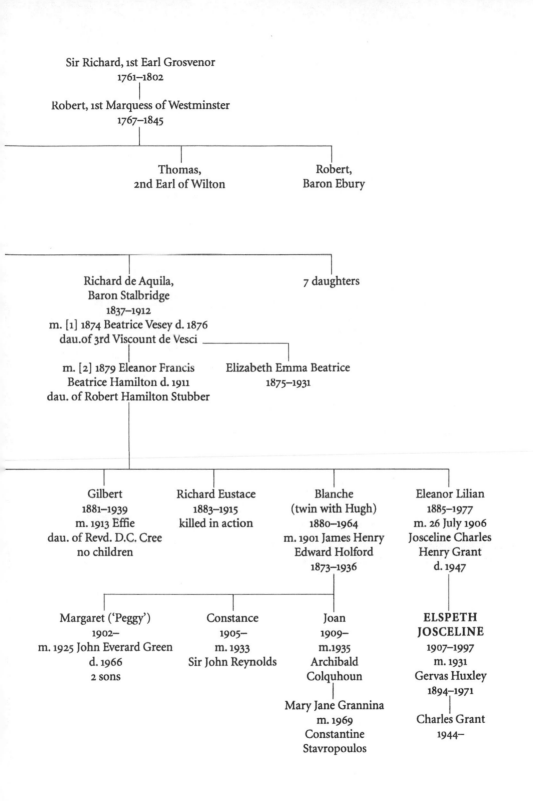

Sir Richard, 1st Earl Grosvenor
1761–1802

Robert, 1st Marquess of Westminster
1767–1845

Thomas,
2nd Earl of Wilton

Robert,
Baron Ebury

Richard de Aquila,
Baron Stalbridge
1837–1912
m. [1] 1874 Beatrice Vesey d. 1876
dau.of 3rd Viscount de Vesci

7 daughters

m. [2] 1879 Eleanor Francis
Beatrice Hamilton d. 1911
dau. of Robert Hamilton Stubber

Elizabeth Emma Beatrice
1875–1931

Gilbert
1881–1939
m. 1913 Effie
dau. of Revd. D.C. Cree
no children

Richard Eustace
1883–1915
killed in action

Blanche
(twin with Hugh)
1880–1964
m. 1901 James Henry
Edward Holford
1873–1936

Eleanor Lilian
1885–1977
m. 26 July 1906
Josceline Charles
Henry Grant
d. 1947

Margaret ('Peggy')
1902–
m. 1925 John Everard Green
d. 1966
2 sons

Constance
1905–
m. 1933
Sir John Reynolds

Joan
1909–
m.1935
Archibald
Colquhoun

ELSPETH
JOSCELINE
1907–1997
m. 1931
Gervas Huxley
1894–1971

Mary Jane Grannina
m. 1969
Constantine
Stavropoulos

Charles Grant
1944–

The Huxley Family

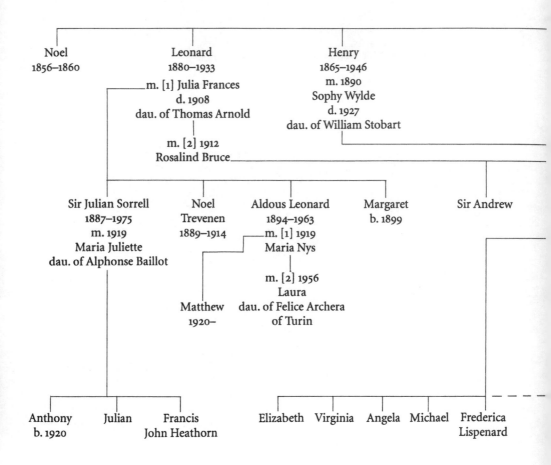

Noel
1856–1860

Leonard
1880–1933
m. [1] Julia Frances
d. 1908
dau. of Thomas Arnold

m. [2] 1912
Rosalind Bruce

Henry
1865–1946
m. 1890
Sophy Wylde
d. 1927
dau. of William Stobart

Sir Julian Sorrell
1887–1975
m. 1919
Maria Juliette
dau. of Alphonse Baillot

Noel
Trevenen
1889–1914

Aldous Leonard
1894–1963
m. [1] 1919
Maria Nys

m. [2] 1956
Laura
dau. of Felice Archera
of Turin

Margaret
b. 1899

Sir Andrew

Matthew
1920–

Anthony
b. 1920

Julian

Francis
John Heathorn

Elizabeth   Virginia   Angela   Michael   Frederica
Lispenard

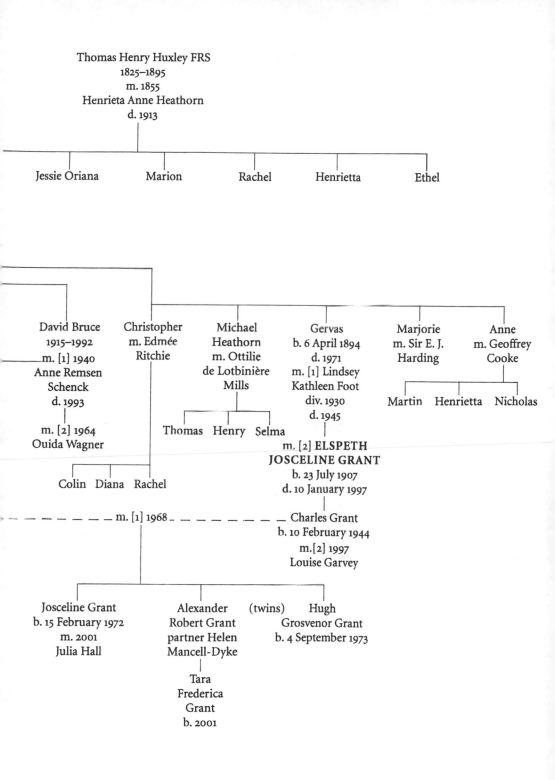

Thomas Henry Huxley FRS
1825–1895
m. 1855
Henrieta Anne Heathorn
d. 1913

Jessie Oriana   Marion   Rachel   Henrietta   Ethel

David Bruce
1915–1992
m. [1] 1940
Anne Remsen
Schenck
d. 1993

m. [2] 1964
Ouida Wagner

Colin Diana Rachel

Christopher
m. Edmée
Ritchie

Michael
Heathorn
m. Ottilie
de Lotbinière
Mills

Thomas Henry Selma

Gervas
b. 6 April 1894
d. 1971
m. [1] Lindsey
Kathleen Foot
div. 1930
d. 1945

m. [2] ELSPETH
JOSCELINE GRANT
b. 23 July 1907
d. 10 January 1997

Marjorie
m. Sir E. J.
Harding

Anne
m. Geoffrey
Cooke

Martin Henrietta Nicholas

— — — — — — m. [1] 1968 — — — — — — Charles Grant
b. 10 February 1944
m.[2] 1997
Louise Garvey

Josceline Grant
b. 15 February 1972
m. 2001
Julia Hall

Alexander   (twins)   Hugh
Robert Grant   Grosvenor Grant
partner Helen   b. 4 September 1973
Mancell-Dyke

Tara
Frederica
Grant
b. 2001

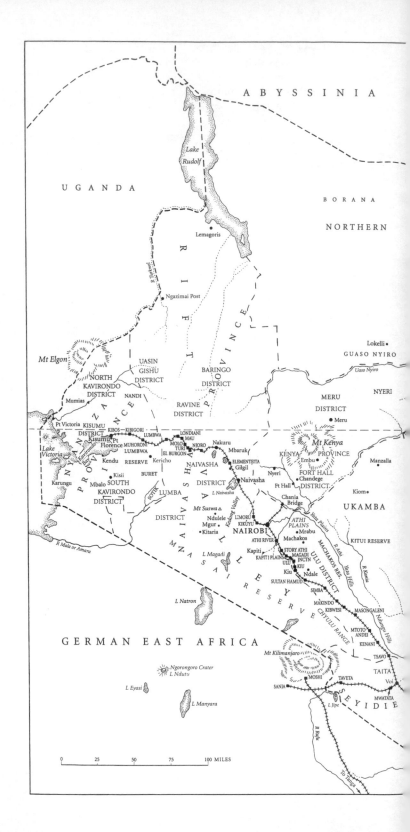

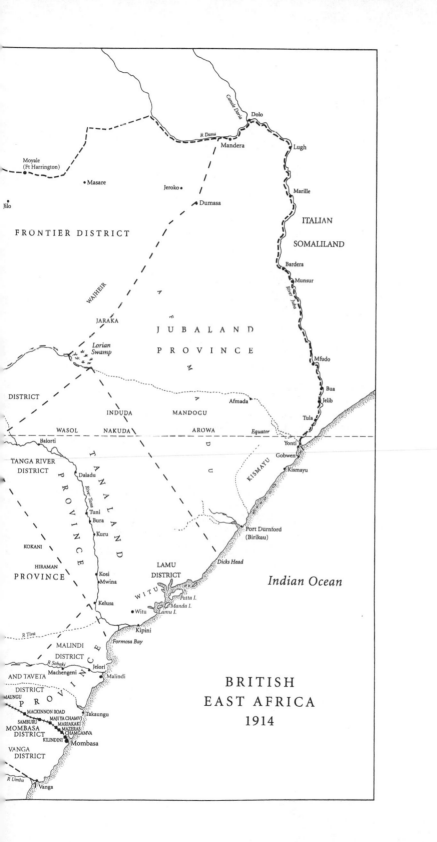

Caniic Daria

Dolo

R Dana

Mandera

Lugh

Moyale
(Ft Harrington)

Masare

Jeroko

Marille

Jilo

Dumasa

ITALIAN

SOMALILAND

FRONTIER DISTRICT

Bardera

WAJHEIR

Munsur

JARAKA

River Juba

J U B A L A N D

Lorian
Swamp

P R O V I N C E

Mfudo

Bua

DISTRICT

INDUDA

MANDOGU

Afmada

Jelib

AROWA

Equator

Tula

WASOL

NAKUDA

DISTRICT

Balorti

Yonti

TANGA RIVER
DISTRICT

Daladu

Gobwen

Kismayu

T
A
N
A
L
A
N
D

KISMAYU

River Tana

P
R
O
V
I
N
C
E

Tuni

Bura

Port Durnford
(Birikau)

Kuru

KOKANI

Dicks Head

Indian Ocean

HIRAMAN

LAMU
DISTRICT

PROVINCE

Kosi

Mwina

W
I
T
U

Patta I.

Manda I.

Kelusa

Lamu I.

Witu

Kipini

R Tiva

Formosa Bay

MALINDI
DISTRICT

R Sabaki

Jelori

AND TAVETA

Machengeni

Malindi

DISTRICT

MAUNGU

P
R
O

BRITISH

MACKINNON ROAD

Takaungu

EAST AFRICA

SAMBURU

MAJI YA CHAMVI

MARIAKAKI

1914

MAZERAS

MOMBASA

CHAMGAMVA

DISTRICT

KILINDINI

Mombasa

VANGA
DISTRICT

R Umba

Vanga

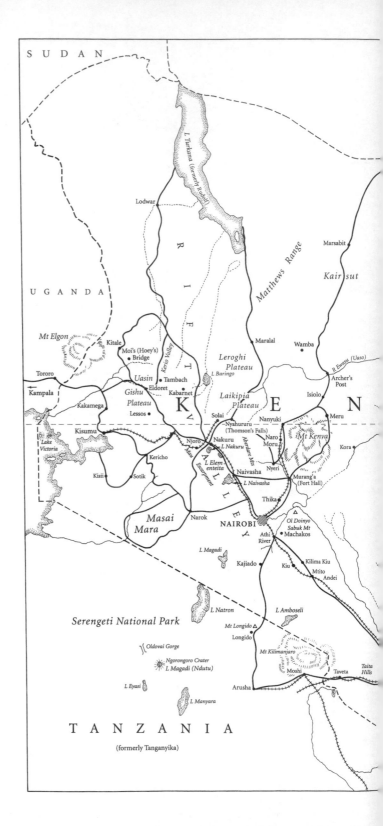

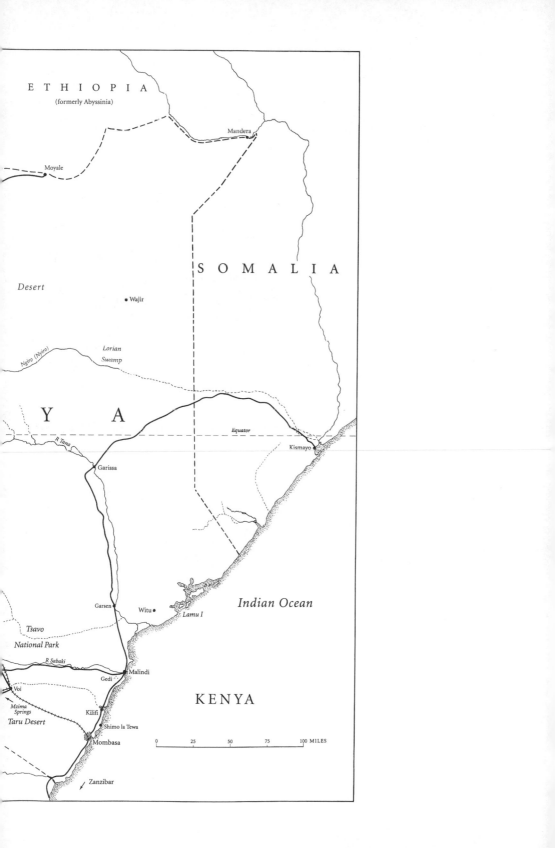

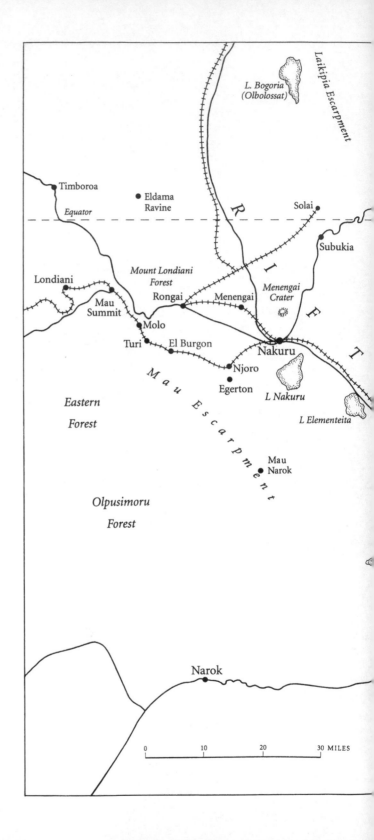

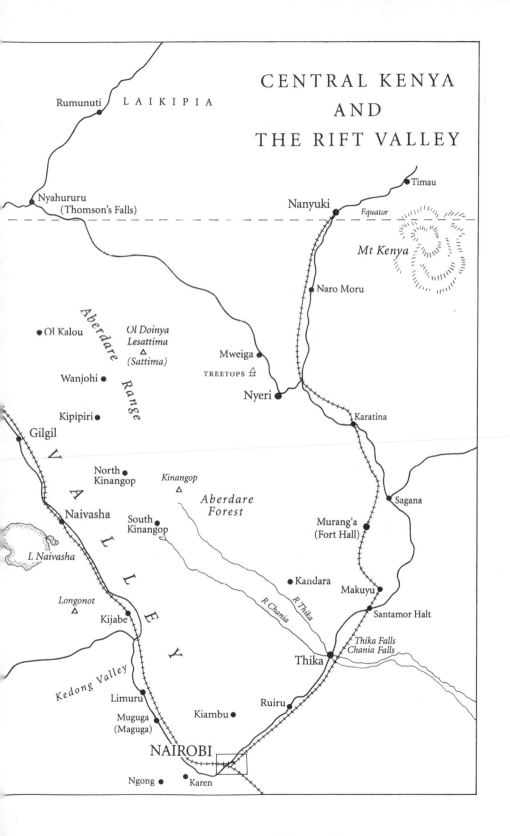

CENTRAL KENYA
AND
THE RIFT VALLEY

Rumunuti

LAIKIPIA

Timau

Nyahururu
(Thomson's Falls)

Nanyuki

Equator

Mt Kenya

Naro Moru

Ol Kalou

Aberdare Range

*Ol Doinya
Lesattima*
△
(Sattima)

Mweiga

TREETOPS ⌂

Wanjohi

Nyeri

Kipipiri

Karatina

Gilgil

VALLEY

North
Kinangop

Kinangop
△

*Aberdare
Forest*

Sagana

Naivasha

South
Kinangop

Murang'a
(Fort Hall)

L Naivasha

Kandara

Makuyu

Longonot
△

Kijabe

R Chania

R Thika

Santamor Halt

*Thika Falls
Chania Falls*

Thika

Kedong Valley

Limuru

Ruiru

Muguga
(Maguga)

Kiambu

NAIROBI

Ngong

Karen

ONE

Off to Africa

In the dying days of 1912 a ship bearing Elspeth Huxley's parents, Jos and Nellie Grant, approached the palm- and baobab-fringed shores of Mombasa on the coast of eastern Africa. The vessel skirted Mombasa island's southern shore to anchor in Kilindini harbour, as yet possessing but a small jetty and a few tin sheds. The ship's gangway was lowered to admit two officials from a launch – a police officer in charge of embarkation and a health officer to enquire about epidemics on the ship.

The Grants awaited their landing passes in the smoking saloon. Then rowing boats took them to a pontoon floating by the shore, from which a ramp of iron steps led up to the corrugated-iron customs shed. They first set foot on the soil of the British East Africa Protectorate – BEA, as it was known – on 28 December 1912. Awaiting them was the representative of Smith Mackenzie, a local firm grown wealthy from the porterage trade to Uganda, far inland. He took them to a sandy road which sloped uphill into the town, past red-roofed bungalows. In the centre of the road lay narrow rails for trolley-cars with canvas roofs – Mombasa's public transport system. They boarded one of these unusual conveyances, powered only by the sweat of Africans who pushed them through the clammy heat along an avenue of shady mango trees. Everywhere grew bright hibiscus flowers.

They reached the Metropole, a dirty, double-storeyed, cement-floored hotel with bedrooms small and poorly furnished. A drink was called for. Propping up the bar was J.D. Hopcraft,* an early settler who immediately tried to sell them land 350 miles away, at Naivasha in the Rift Valley. Nellie, hot and unimpressed, had her spirits further dampened by the luncheon menu, whose principal item was cheap tinned herring.

Elspeth, the Grants' only child, was not with them. Contrary to what she says in her most famous book, *The Flame Trees of Thika* (1959), she did not join her parents until a year later, when they had established themselves on their farm. The book is a work of fiction, though many incidents are based on actual events. As Elspeth herself said, 'How much does one imagine, how much observe? One can no more separate those functions than divide light from air, or wetness from water.'[1] It was not Elspeth, but her publisher, who wanted the book to be subtitled 'Memories of an African Childhood'.

The land to which the Grants had come had been in British hands for only seventeen years. It lay on a cross formed by the Equator and the Great Rift Valley, a four-thousand-mile-long depression in the surface of the continent of Africa. Sweeping savannahs, thick forests and high volcanic mountain peaks gave the land great beauty and texture, but it was burdened with only scanty rainfall which made vast tracts useless to all but nomad, pastoral tribes. In the north the land was too arid for any but the hardiest of human inhabitants. In 1895 the Imperial British East Africa Company, a commercial organisation trying to develop trade in the area, had fallen into financial difficulties. It was rescued by the British government, which declared a protectorate over the region, from the coast inland for six hundred-odd miles. One of Britain's motives was to prevent the Germans spreading northwards from their own declared colony German East Africa (later called Tanganyika).

The only way to transport goods to and from the interior was on the heads and backs of human porters – donkeys and other beasts of burden could not survive the lethal bites of tsetse flies

---

* Hopcraft, who had acquired extensive acres in the Rift Valley, called his farm Loldia and was now trying to sell some of it to newcomers at a profit. There were some who thought he was a rogue.

along the way. The British government therefore decided to support the construction of a railway from Mombasa on the coast to Port Florence (later called Kisumu) in Uganda,* on the shores of Lake Victoria, 550 miles inland, in order to ensure British control over the headwaters of the Nile in Lake Victoria. Britain ruled Egypt, and the Nile was essential for the economy of that country. British control was also designed to assist Christian missionaries already in Uganda and to help suppress the slave trade. Despite persistent attempts by British ships to cut the transportation of slaves from East Africa to Arabia and India, some still got through. 'In Kenya I have listened,' said Elspeth Huxley later, 'to the tale of one old woman who hid in a cave and saw her husband and parents massacred while her three children were taken off as slaves, never to be seen again; and, in Uganda, heard an old man describe how, as a boy, he'd been captured, managed to escape, and made his way back over 700 miles of bush, desert and mountain to rejoin his tribe.'[2]

The construction of the railway began in 1896. Depots and administrative headquarters were established along the route. There was an influx of whites and Indians to build the line, and the inevitable suppression of any African dissent by the power of the gun, a weapon unavailable to East Africa's native inhabitants. The reaction of the Africans to the coming of the whites and Indians was mixed. The Turkana around Lake Baringo were particularly unfriendly to strangers. The Nandi, who stole the shining telegraph wire for 'maridadi', ornament, to be wound around their necks and arms, were roughly subdued by punitive expeditions, and pockets of unrest were put down wherever they arose, such as among the Kikuyu at Dagoretti near Nairobi, where a government caravan was attacked in 1899. The Kikuyu were every bit as good as the Maasai when it came to fighting in daylight, but when it was dark they were much troubled by spirits.

Indians, imported in large numbers to construct the railway,

---

* At that time, unlike today, Uganda was deemed to begin on the westward wall of the Rift Valley.

stayed in BEA upon its completion in 1901 to become skilled artisans and shopkeepers. Scores of relatives joined them from India, and Indian dukas, or small shops, could soon be seen throughout the country. Many whites who had held administrative posts under the Imperial British East Africa Company and during the building of the railway stayed on to rule on behalf of Britain. As regular government expanded, other whites came in ones and twos to explore, hunt and trade.

Once the railway was finished, the easy transport it provided made cash-crop farming possible in the fertile highlands of the interior. Before then, the hostile and waterless Taru desert, lying between the coast and the Athi plains three hundred miles inland, had inhibited such development. The desert could be crossed only in forced marches by men carrying not only their regular forty-pound loads but also their own water. Water is heavy, and the desert claimed scores of lives. Now the train telescoped into one night the eleven days it had taken to traverse the waterless wilderness. But the upkeep of the railway was expensive, as was the administration of a new imperial land. The railway would have to raise money for this from freight, in this case cash crops and livestock, for BEA lacked any mineral resources. African farmers produced enough for their own needs only, so white farmers would have to be encouraged to come and grow the crops and raise the animals. The Grants were part of the trickle of whites from Britain who saw the opportunities ahead.

Thus a future colony was created, not so much by stealth as by reaction to a succession of events, or haphazard pragmatism. Despite resentment and hostility, some Africans adapted to the newcomers and went to work for them. With this labour, a few white farmers could experiment with livestock and crops. Missionaries came and planted coffee. Gradually, over a period of nineteen years before the First World War, there was a slow expansion of direction and control. None the less, some of those who took their orders from Whitehall disliked the very presence of white hunters and farmers and immigrants whose eyes were on the main chance. They thought the land should be ruled for the benefit of the African, not the whites or Indians. Their scruples were overcome early in the twentieth century by a commissioner (the forerunner of the governor) sympathetic to the whites, Sir Charles Eliot, and by the hard fact of economics – Africans could not make the railway pay if they pursued their traditional ways of husbandry or nomadism. And as Elspeth Huxley said later, 'I do not think that you can possibly, in the modern world, seal off a great continent from all intruders as if it were a human game reserve.'[3] There was a tacit acceptance that the region had become a colony when in 1905 the British government moved control of its new acquisition from the Foreign to the Colonial Office.

The administration could not allow whites to come to the country and farm where they wished, however empty the land seemed. The area of Kenya was about 213,822 square miles, or 137 million acres, more than twice that of Great Britain, but far from all of it was suitable for farming. Rainfall varied in different areas from only a few inches a year to more than seventy, and elevations from sea level to 17,000 feet. Below the wet highlands were brown and open savannahs. And more than half the country's area, lying to the north of the highlands, was waterless volcanic rock, desert or semi-desert, where nomads lived, drawing water from scarce wells in buckets fashioned from giraffe hide. The country was slashed in two by the gigantic wound of the Rift Valley, on the floor of which the Maasai lived. The noblest of the administrators wanted to keep African tribes in areas where they were already, but what they did not know was that numbers had been decimated in the 1890s by the triple scourges of rinderpest, smallpox and famine. And the fact that pastoralist Africans moved their herds, while agricultural Africans practised shifting cultivation, often misled the British into thinking land was empty.

A Land Registry was established to oversee the disposition of land to whites – 'alienated land', as it was termed. The rest was to become forest reserve and native reserves in which only members of certain tribes could live. By 1912, the year the Grants arrived, there were 3,175 whites in BEA and 11,886 Indians. But by 1921 numbers had risen to whites 9,651, Indians 22,822, Arabs 10,102,

Goans 2,431, and Africans 2,758,088. In that year native reserves amounted to about 31,250 square miles (twenty million acres, or one-eighth of the area of the country), while forest reserves covered two million acres. The land alienated to whites was 11,859 square miles, or 7,589,760 acres. These were farmed by 1,893 whites, excluding wives and families. Farms varied hugely in size, from vast acreages roamed over by sheep and cattle to smaller agricultural units. African losses from land alienation were severe in southern Kiambu and north-west Nyeri. Altogether about 11,000 Kikuyu lost their land to white settlers in southern Kiambu, but their losses were not nearly as great as those of the Maasai and the Nandi peoples: the Maasai reserve was a tenth of the area the tribe had occupied before 1893.

At Nyali, near Mombasa on the coast, the firm of Smith Mackenzie had acquired land and planted sisal, used for making rope. One of the major shareholders in this enterprise was George Mildmay, a banker, whose wife Grace had been a friend of Nellie Grant in England. It was this acquaintance which had influenced Nellie and Jos to seek their fortune in BEA. Neither of them had farmed before, but they had set sail for BEA with funds to purchase land, armed with introductions from Grace Mildmay.

After lunching at the Metropole, the Grants were visited by Kenneth Rodwell, manager of the sisal estate. He offered to put them up in a cottage on the north mainland, at Nyali. The next day they found their way through narrow streets to the slave steps* in the old harbour, a haven used by Arab dhows but much too shallow to take the larger ships from Europe. The Grants were rowed across the narrow strait between Mombasa island and the northern mainland, where a waiting rickshaw took them through Nyali, with its monotonous acres of olive green and spiky sisal, to a tiny wood-and-iron house full of hornets' nests. It was unbearably hot inside, with the air only quietly disturbed by a hand-operated punkah. Nellie did not like the heat or the insect life – centipedes and giant milli-

---

* These were the steps from which in former days Mombasa's principal export, slaves, embarked on Arab dhows for the sea journey northwards. They were still known as the slave steps in the 1950s.

pedes lay underfoot, while nightly torment was inflicted by ubiquitous, malarial mosquitoes. The cure for malaria was believed to be
five grains of quinine for a week, then ten, then fifteen, then twenty,
and finally twenty-five. By then you should either be cured, or dead
of blackwater fever. This blackening of the urine was possibly a
side-effect of so much medication, as was deafness.* There was
nothing for it but to make the best of things. Rodwell took the
Grants to Mombasa Club, where they dined on the open terrace
verandah cooled by sea breezes. A three-quarter moon lit up date and
coconut palms above the phosphorescent sea. 'Ever eager to extract
from every moment its last drop of interest or pleasure',[4] Nellie
bathed in the sea by day and began to enjoy this coral paradise.

The time came to venture to the interior to seek out farming
land. Nellie selected two personal servants to go up country with
her, one of them, Abdullah, an English-speaking Swahili of Arab
appearance who sported a fearsome knife under his long white
kanzu, the robe worn by the Swahili and Arab people of the coast
and adopted as servants' livery. The knife was apt to clatter to the
floor and startle Nellie. The Grants travelled on the railway overnight, 327 miles to Nairobi, the capital of BEA since 1907, when the
administration was moved from Mombasa. There they were met
by Ali Khan, the Afghan owner of the only livery stable in the town,
slapping his boots with a huge whip to get the newcomers' attention.
He whisked them to the Norfolk Hotel in a mongrel, horse-drawn
vehicle, along Government Road (now Moi Avenue) past rows of
run-down dukas and the one and only solid British store, put up
by Sammy Jacobs, a follower of the Jewish faith and as such not
allowed in local clubs and hostelries. The Norfolk, opened on
Christmas Day 1904, was a long, low, one-storeyed building facing
the road, with two bedroom wings behind the bars and dining
room. In front of it there was a row of hitching posts. No Indians
or Africans, apart from staff, could enter the hotel. From eleven in
the morning the bar was crowded, as it was the general meeting

---

* When synthetic anti-malarials were introduced after the Second World War, blackwater
fever virtually disappeared, which may indicate that it was partly caused by the injudicious
use of quinine.

place of all Nairobi's whites, apart from the Jews. New arrivals were scrutinised as potential buyers of land, and a watch was kept on the post office flagpole. A blue flag meant that a ship had left Aden for Mombasa bearing mail, a red flag that overseas mail had been received, and a white flag, or a white arc lamp after dark, that mail was ready for distribution.

Elspeth was not to join her parents for another year. Her mother, Eleanor Lilian Grosvenor ('Nellie'), was a member of the Grosvenor family, marquesses and later dukes of Westminster. Born in 1885, Nellie was the sixth and youngest child of Lord Richard de Aquila Grosvenor, younger brother of the first Duke of Westminster and son of the second Marquess of Westminster. Her mother, his second wife, was Eleanor Frances Beatrice Hamilton, daughter of Robert Hamilton Stubber, JP and deputy lieutenant of Moyne, in the north of Ireland. Lord Richard was Liberal Member of Parliament for Flintshire for twenty-five years (1861–86). He was called 'Dick the Devil' by Princess Alexandra while he was vice-chamberlain of the royal household (1872–74), because of his wild youth among the red Indians and his exploits in Salt Lake City and China. He held the office of Chief Whip under Gladstone from 1880 to 1885, but his contrary views on the major political question of the day, Home Rule for Ireland, estranged him from the Prime Minister and prompted the demise of his political career. Resigning from Parliament with a peerage (the Barony of Stalbridge), he thenceforth zealously applied himself to the concerns of the London and North Western Railway, of which he was chairman. His family was accorded superb treatment and a private carriage whenever they undertook a train journey. Nellie even launched two of the company's ships on the Clyde, for which she was presented with a diamond brooch. Oddly for a transport chairman, Dick the Devil would not travel at more than fifty miles an hour, a problem the railway company surmounted by doctoring all speedometers he might encounter to show no more than that.

Nellie's siblings were Elsie (from Lord Richard's first wife, who died giving birth), the twins Hugh and Blanche, Gilbert ('Gillie'), and Richard Eustace, known as Ray or Chucks. From 1891 they all lived at Motcombe, a manor house in Dorset inherited by their father. Their time was spent in upper-class activities typical of the time. Horses and foxhunting, of course, loomed large in their routine. But in 1905 Lord Stalbridge suffered a severe setback to his finances, and Motcombe was abandoned for a small house in London, 22 Sussex Square. By then Nellie was engaged to be married. In Dorset she had met and fallen in love with a handsome Scot, Major Josceline Charles Henry Grant, whose birth on 28 July 1874 made him eleven years her senior.

Slim, sandy-haired, handsome and diffident, 'Jos', as he was known to his friends, was charming, easy-going and good-mannered, but he had a lazy and impractical streak. He hailed from the glens of Inverness – his section of the Grant family lived in Glen Shewglie, which branched off Glen Urquhart. His family home was Bearnoch, opposite Shewglie House near the steel-blue Loch Ness, where earlier Grants had lived. It was a place of crevassed hills crossed by cloud shadows, of soaring eagles, deerstalking and the smell of bog myrtle. His grandfather Sir Charles Grant had been Governor of Bombay, while his father, also Sir Charles, rose in the Indian Civil Service to become Foreign Secretary of the Indian government. Josceline's mother, Elizabeth Ellen Baillie, died in 1885, when he was eleven. She was the daughter of Henry Baillie, of Redcastle, Inverness-shire. On his father's death in 1903 he was left £50,000, as were each of his brothers.

As a soldier in the 3rd Battalion of the Royal Scots Regiment Josceline Grant fought in the Boer War, and stayed on in South Africa afterwards. He invested most of his inheritance in a putative diamond mine in neighbouring Portuguese East Africa, in partnership with an Irish peer, Lord ffrench. Following his engagement to Nellie he had to go back to the mine, but he and ffrench so mishandled affairs that he ended up being owed a great deal of money by his partner, none of which he ever saw again. If Nellie is to be believed, the mine only ever produced three diamonds, which were set into her engagement ring.

On his return to England Jos married Nellie in London on 26 July 1906. Of medium height, with fine, straight, brown hair, Nellie had buck teeth which prevented her from being beautiful, but the liveliness of her face and spirit were most attractive. She was energetic while her husband was dreamy, proficient while he was impractical to the point of incompetence. While Jos 'was not at all observant, as a rule, about his immediate surroundings, generally having his mind on distant, greater matters, always much more promising and congenial than those closer at hand',[5] Nellie saw to the heart of the matter and devised a way of coping with adversity. She was the possessor of extreme optimism, believing that everything would be all right next time, if not this. She was never downcast, keeping an ideal always in mind, though her achievements were invariably below it.

Having lost so much money in the 'diamond' mine, Jos took a job of sorts in the City while he and his bride shared a flat in Wellington Court, Knightsbridge, with his younger brother Robin,* an officer in the Rifle Brigade. Nellie almost immediately became pregnant. The shared flat was now too crowded, and a friend of Nellie's, Trudie Denman, offered the couple an old farmhouse on her estate, Balcombe at Haywards Heath, Sussex, at a minimal rent. The early summer of 1907 was spent in a house at Bagshot, Surrey, belonging to Victoria Grant, Jos's aunt, and they also stayed with Jos's stepmother at Sedgehill, Dorset. Every year they visited his mother at Redcastle near Inverness – 'so Scottish and so cold!' said Nellie.

Elspeth, the Grants' only child, was born at 22 Sussex Square, her grandparents' home, on 23 July 1907. 'An odd thing was,' Nellie remembered, 'a few days before Elspeth's birth I caught my fingers in a sash window and distinct blue semicircles appeared on my fingernails and also on those of my unborn child.'[6] While lying in she insisted on having her Pekinese dog on her bed all the time. A monthly nurse was employed to look after Elspeth. Nellie tried to

---

* Robert Francis Sydney Grant, born in 1878, who married Vera Campbell. Jos and Robin also had a half-brother, Allastair Edward George Grant, born in 1892 of Charles Grant's second marriage (1890), to Lady Florence Harris.

feed her daughter herself, but there was strident opposition from both the nurse and Elspeth. Six months after the birth Nellie's mother, Eleanor Hamilton-Stubber, paid a visit to Ireland to see some relatives and there she had a stroke. Nellie and Jos dashed across to Ireland, leaving Elspeth in London. They brought Eleanor back to the Sussex Square house, to be greeted by the corpse of Nellie's Pekinese, which had been run over by a bus. Jos and Nellie stayed with Eleanor until she died four years later, in 1911, from which time onward Dick the Devil slept with her deathmask by his bedside.

Jos now began to reveal the impracticality of his nature. He was ever a fabricator of improbable though infallible (to him) get-rich-quick projects, yet he lacked the organisation and application to make his ideas pay. Now he and a friend invented a car. Motor manufacture was not as crowded a field as it was soon to become, but Jos had no background in engineering, in establishing a sound business or in marketing. Inevitably the car failed, or, rather, never even accelerated away from the starting post. By now Jos had run through almost all his £50,000 inheritance.

His wife was a more successful entrepreneur, and she and Trudie Denman soon set up a thriving business. Trudie was the daughter of Weetman Pearson, an engineering and oil tycoon who became Viscount Cowdray; her husband, the third Baron Denman, became Governor-General of Australia. To start with, Nellie and Trudie bought sixteen Welsh ponies for a total of £50, cleaned them up and broke them in at Balcombe, Trudie's country house. Elspeth was put to practical use: strapped into a child's riding pannier, she was lifted on to the ponies' backs. According to her mother, she yelped with delight as the animals cavorted about on a lunging rein until they were finally still and tamed. The ponies were then sold for about £20 each, making a total of roughly £320 and a handsome profit for the enterprising ladies. The project came to an end when the Denmans went to Australia.

Like all the children of her class, Elspeth was cared for by a nanny. The monthly nurse employed after the birth handed her over to Nanny Newport, for whom Elspeth retained an abiding affection, visiting her well into her old age. Nanny Newport was experienced in child care, and as such was paid £50 a year. Utterly devoted to Elspeth, she never wanted a holiday or even a Sunday afternoon off, though she did go once a year to her own home in Cirencester. Even then, Elspeth accompanied her. She kept Elspeth on the bottle till she was nearly four, and daily wheeled her in her pram to Hyde Park or the adjoining Kensington Gardens. The only things she would not do were carry a tray or wash clothes. She had a second housemaid to wait upon her, and all Elspeth's clothes were sent out to a laundry. The laundry bills, at over a pound a week, exceeded Nanny Newport's salary.

Oblivious of past mistakes, Jos Grant planned to make their fortune in Africa once Nellie's mother died. The idea simmered for months. Initially they intended to go to Angola on the west coast, but it was difficult to establish contacts there. Rhodesia was also a possibility. But when Nellie's friends in Somerset, George and Grace Mildmay, promised to give the Grants introductions should they choose BEA, it was this that decided them. Moreover, a book had appeared in 1909 extolling the charms of this new addition to the British Empire – Somerset Playne's *East Africa (British), its History, People, Commerce, Industries and Resources*, edited by F. Holderness Gale. It portrayed the profits to be made from coffee and sisal plantations, cattle and sheep farming, retail and manufacturing.

Characteristically ignoring possible impediments and austerities, Jos began to think seriously about emigration. Then Nellie's father Dick the Devil died in March 1912, freeing £5,000 left to her in trust by a godmother. Somehow Jos salvaged £5,000 from his motor car fiasco, which brought in £150 a year. With this and Nellie's £5,000 to be used as capital, the Grants reckoned they could buy farmland in East Africa.

Nellie began to make what she imagined was thorough personal provision for her new life. In the summer of 1912, while Jos was doing some special service training as a reserve officer in the Royal Scots, she took Nanny Newport and Elspeth to a farmhouse near Reading. There she undertook a course in poultry-keeping, which was very hard work. She learned carpentry, how to build poultry houses and how to kill cockerels. While Nellie fitted herself for life in the colonies, nanny and child 'were happy as the day was long'.[7] Later Nellie's Aunt Ockie (Lady Octavia Shaw-Stewart), who lived alone with a phalanx of seventeen servants at Fonthill in Wiltshire, had her to stay to learn the rules of housekeeping and cooking. Vast meals were served at which Ockie merely pecked. Experiencing life in Fonthill's maze of corridors, still-rooms, huge kitchen, laundry-room, dairy and pantries was a strange preparation for the grass hut which became Nellie's first home in East Africa, as was her careful observation of three laundrymaids with gopher irons doing the frills and ruffs.

Jos and Nellie left England in the winter of 1912. They took a train to Naples to save time and avoid the stormy Bay of Biscay, and embarked on the SS *Burgomeister*, a German ship of the Deutsche Ost-Afrika Linie (or Dirty Old Accident Line, as it was known in BEA) bound for the Suez Canal and Mombasa. They were the only prospective settlers aboard. Few among their fellow passengers were English, merely one or two officials, including Philip Mitchell, later to become Governor of Kenya, and two couples going on safari. Nellie busied herself trying to learn Swahili on the boat-deck in the moonlight with a young German lieutenant. Her primer had two notable sentences: 'The drunken Europeans have killed the cook', and 'The idle slaves are scratching themselves'. She also claimed that her book began with the words 'God is good; God is great; we must love God', whereas the German one began 'The Kaiser is good; the Kaiser is great; we must love the Kaiser'.[8]

After three weeks the Grants arrived in the 'land of great beauty, beguilement, harshness and infinite variety' which was to become their new home.[9] They had to adjust to a cruelly hot climate and an utterly unfamiliar African culture. They also had to develop the mental stamina required of those who leave family and friends, maybe for ever. They had brought with them saddlery, four items of furniture (a French copy of a Chippendale dressing-table, a sofa and two armchairs), a cookery book by Escoffier, knives and forks, two mattresses from Heal's and a crate containing one cockerel and five hens of the Speckled Sussex breed. They also took a Crossley car. Thus eccentrically equipped, they made their way to Nairobi and the Norfolk Hotel.

Elspeth was left behind in London, in the care of Daisy Learmonth (Balfour), one of Nellie's friends. This was a wise decision, for a tent in the African bush was no place for a child. With blue ribbons in her hair Elspeth started nursery school. When the time had come to replace the nanny with a governess, Nellie had found Nanny Newport another position. But her new employer died in childbirth, a second blow for the nanny, whose young man had returned from Canada and married her sister instead. Upon hearing of it Nellie sent a cable asking her to come out to Kenya to care for the children of some neighbours, Frank and Laurie Allsopp. The intrepid Nanny Newport donned her sequinned toque hat, packed her bags and came immediately. She was happy at the Allsopps', making friends with other nannies and imperturbably exchanging Hyde Park for Darkest Africa.

The Nairobi that greeted the Grants was an accident of a town, three hundred miles from Mombasa. The railway had crept in 1899 from the grasslands of the Athi plains to face huge topographical problems. Ahead was thick forest in land which rose steadily until it reached the edge of the Rift Valley and a sheer escarpment plunging three thousand feet. The engineers and workers had to pause and establish equipment depots, marshalling yards and workshops for the hard grind before them. Finding an uninhabited patch by a river that would give them a reliable source of water, they pitched their rows of tents. The Maasai called the place Nairobi, meaning 'cold stream'. Railway buildings went up, tents were replaced by wood-and-tin shacks, a few merchants arrived to provision the workers, and it was not long before Nairobi had one street, then two, then six, all wide enough to turn a span of sixteen oxen (the city still has its generously wide streets). Fast-growing blue gums were planted for shade.

The place became so substantial that the government moved its headquarters from Mombasa to the hill above Nairobi. A Government House was built, piped water was arranged, and electric light finally appeared in 1908. Nairobi was still a squalid place when the Grants arrived, with no piped sewage disposal (instead, night-soil carts drawn by long-horned Ankole cattle from Uganda, collected waste from bucket-latrines) and unmetalled roads, dusty in dry seasons and a quagmire in wet. People got about by rickshaw. Indians living in the insanitary bazaar area vastly outnumbered white and African inhabitants, and there were frequent outbreaks of pneumonic and bubonic plague. Social life was strictly segregated into white (bar Jewish people), Indian and African.

After several disputes with the central government in London, the administration in BEA distributed to immigrant whites large blocks of land of up to ten thousand acres each, provided that a house was built there and a track cut. By 1912–13 some of the early settlers were selling off parts of their blocks for £3 or £4 an acre. One such land speculator was James Elkington, in partnership with Harry Penton, whose father owned most of Pentonville in London. Elkington, who had arrived in BEA in 1905, had been given ten thousand acres at Chania Bridge (later called Thika), thirty miles north of Nairobi, by a man called Reggie Wyndham in gratitude to Elkington's wife for curing his poisoned foot. At Chania Bridge Penton started a small bar and hotel called Blue Posts, named after a London pub, while Elkington put in a hundred acres of coffee.

When the Grants arrived at the Norfolk Elkington was in the bar. He and Jos immediately recognised each other as former schoolmates from the same house at Eton, and they struck up a conversation. A few hours later there appeared on the scene Cecil Dashwood, a coffee planter from Kiambu (near Nairobi), to whom the Grants had a letter of introduction. He asked them to stay, and installed them at Kiambu. A few days later, Elkington, still hoping to sell them land at Chania Bridge, invited the Grants to stay at his estate, Masara, where the stables were better-built than the living quarters. They were accommodated in a roomy tent on a shady lawn beside the wide-verandahed house.

Elkington's Masara estate boasted a black-maned pet lion called Paddy, and a pack of sixty foxhounds for Sunday meets acquired from a game ranger who had brought them from India. One of the kennel boys was named Njombo; for five rupees a month he cleaned the kennels and tended the water troughs. He was to become the Grants' headman at Chania Bridge, and would feature largely in Elspeth Huxley's book *The Flame Trees of Thika*. On Sundays Elkington wore a Savile Row scarlet coat and leathers for the hunts, which scrambled at little more than a trot over broken ground full of pig holes in pursuit of jackal or small buck, mainly steinbuck and duiker. It was a scene that made the Grants feel at home.

Dashwood volunteered to vet the land at Chania Bridge, between the Thika and Chania rivers, which Elkington had offered to sell the Grants. The highly fertile hills and valleys between Nairobi and Chania Bridge were inhabited by the Kikuyu people. The rich, flowerpot-red soil was well watered by a spider's web of streams flowing from the Aberdare mountains on the edge of the Rift Valley to the north-west. In every valley flowed a river, the Chania and Thika being among the largest. In dry seasons the deep soil was liable to bake hard and crack, but it was easily worked after rain. Waterbuck, bushbuck, steinbuck, dik dik, jackal and hyena abounded, and the nights rang with the whistling of crickets and the eerie laughter of hyenas. Lions were common, sleeping beneath bushes by day, but emerging at night to roar and hunt, as any traveller delayed on the road to Chania Bridge knew only too well.

The Kikuyu occupied an area of roughly one hundred miles by fifty. In the 1890s they had suffered a famine which killed large numbers of them, but they were recovering rapidly when foreigners began to settle on land said by whites to be empty, though considered by the Kikuyu to belong to them. They were agriculturalists who grew maize, yams, bananas, millet and beans, and kept cattle, sheep and goats for marriage settlements, ceremonial purposes and as an indication of status and wealth. As a society they were held together by kinship and age-grades, which marked successive stages of life – for example, the warrior and elder grades. They lived not in villages but in individual homesteads. It was a decentralised and largely egalitarian society, without kings or chiefs. Important decisions were taken by the eldest males in a kin group, or by elders in a kiama (council). A few heads of large lineages rose to prominence – they were called the muthamaki. There was a pronounced streak of individualism in Kikuyu society which allowed its members to embrace new ideas and experiment with new skills. It was this feature that made the Kikuyu attractive to the British, both as workers and as individuals.

When the British came, various local Kikuyu rivalries assisted the newcomers' endeavour to gain control. Those prepared to help the British were created chiefs, an entirely new institution for the Kikuyu. These chiefs in turn appointed their cronies in other districts, and the British also installed as chiefs influential local notables. The British ruled by Provincial (senior) and District (junior) Commissioners, subordinate to whom were the chiefs, who had to maintain local order, oversee the collection of taxes and fines and provide labour for road-building and for white farms. Many chiefs became large landholders and the possessors of considerable wealth in return for raising labour for the whites. While a novel political system was being imposed on the Kikuyu, missionaries were at the same time threatening their traditions by introducing Christianity. The heavy demand for labour from white farmers enabled Kikuyu workers to observe an alien culture at close quarters.

Unsurprisingly, Dashwood's report on the land at Chania Bridge proved favourable, and Jos and Nellie escaped from Jim Elkington's drinking and the pet lion's nocturnal roars that interrupted their sleep, to stay at Blue Posts. The journey from Nairobi to Chania Bridge was undertaken in the Crossley car they had brought from England. It took three hours to do the thirty-two miles over a 'road' deeply pitted with wheel and wagon marks and enormous holes. Once installed at Blue Posts, it was not long before they met their neighbours. Among them were the droll Roy Whittet (the manager of Charles Taylor and Eric Gooch's land,* who could out-gossip anyone) and Alan Cuninghame, who had bought land

---

* Both Taylor and Gooch had married Gaiety Girls, so had had to resign their commissions in the British army. Taylor divorced his Gaiety Girl in 1926 and married Kit Sanderson, a great Kenya character who lived to the age of a hundred.

from Elkington and begun to plant coffee. On the other side of the river lived Arthur Fawcus, who subsequently married an illegitimate daughter of Edward VII. Nellie disliked him, and later hurled insults across the water. Apart from Fawcus, the neighbours were all congenial – except for one Lionel Bury, who was going mad, though Jos and Nellie did not know this. He used to lurk outside the huts and eavesdrop, then accuse the Grants of abusing him in conversation when they had never even mentioned his name. One day he rode to Nairobi with Nellie, trotting beside her on a white mule and claiming he had been a religion to seven women. 'Boy, was I rude!' remembered Nellie.[10] Bury returned to England when his illness worsened in 1914. It was among these people that Elspeth grew from child- to adulthood. She affectionately brought aspects of their personalities to life again in the fictitious inhabitants of her book *The Flame Trees of Thika*.

The Grants were greatly encouraged by the general enthusiasm of the Thika farmers. They agreed to buy from Elkington, for £4 an acre, five hundred acres of land about three miles from the Kikuyu reserve, on a ridge leading down to the river. Thus £2,500 of the £5,000 they had brought to Africa disappeared at once, as Elkington insisted on cash down. But the manager of the Nairobi branch of the National Bank of India, Mr Playfair, was generous with his loans, and the Grants embarked on a system of finance which would sustain them over the next fifteen years. At its peak, their overdraft was £10,000. They called their farm Kitimuru, after the local stream which ran through it.

They intended to plant coffee, copying the methods of neighbours who had planted it two years before. Coffee had been introduced to BEA in 1893 by missionaries who imported the arabica seed from Aden. The first crop of coffee beans was gathered by the Church of Scotland mission at Kibwezi, 150 miles south-east of Nairobi. At the turn of the century it was also planted at St Austin's Catholic mission in Nairobi and St Augustine's Church of Scotland mission in Kikuyuland. The early white farmers obtained their seed from both these missions, and thus grew coffee of predominantly Arabica plant. By the time the Grants arrived, about nine thousand acres

had been planted, almost all of them in Kikuyu country which, at
an altitude varying from five thousand to seven thousand feet, was
ideal for the crop. The coffee bushes, four to five feet high, ran
through the ruddy soil in straight, glossy, dark green lines. They
had white, waxy flowers which smelled of orange blossom and
developed brilliant crimson berries, or cherries, as they were known.
A good yield was one-third of a ton per acre.

Back with Cecil Dashwood at Kiambu, Jos and Nellie were
inclined to have a look at Uganda before they settled down at
Chania Bridge. There was a mild boom there, and while coffee
bushes in Kenya took four years to bear their first berries, in Uganda
they produced them two years earlier. Putting their car on the train,
the Grants made for Jinja, via Kisumu on Lake Victoria.

In Kampala they met the famous Michael Moses, an Armenian
Jew who persuaded Nellie to buy some shares in his company, a
cocoa-growing concern. At first it did well, but then disease hit the
crop and the yearly accounts sent to Nellie told her the true, dismal
story. As the plants failed, so malaria took its toll of the planters.
Nellie's accounts invariably started with: 'To manager's funeral
expenses, 6 shillings', as one hapless manager followed another into
the white man's grave.[11] However, the Grants did have one triumph.
They bought an excellent business plot in Kampala. To fulfil the
conditions they built a house on it, let it as offices at a decent rent
and subsequently sold it for £700, making a handsome profit. But
they found Uganda's heat too moist and unpleasant – even the
creosoted telegraph poles sprouted in this luxuriant land. A depressing visit to a dairy farm whose living-quarter floors rustled with
millions of white ants confirmed them in their reluctance to settle
in Uganda. Not long afterwards the couple who wanted to sell it
to them died of blackwater fever.

In March 1913 they returned to Nairobi, sharing a seat on the
train's cowcatcher with the Colonial Secretary Alfred Lyttelton, in
danger of being set alight by sparks from the wood-burning engine.
Lyttelton halted the train whenever he wished to enjoy a spectacular
view or examine a species of wild animal, so it was a slow journey
through the extraordinary scenery of north-west Kenya and the Rift

Valley. The beauty of the land confirmed them in the view that they had been right to come to BEA.

Blue Posts became their headquarters. The hotel had a rough bar, dining room and sitting room, and a few round, grass-thatched, mud-and-wattle rondavels as bedrooms. Built at the confluence of the Chania and Thika rivers, its triangular grounds stretched to the nearby Chania Falls thundering over a chasm into a foaming basin beneath, curtained by lush ferns and creepers. A post office and an Indian duka completed the tiny settlement known as Chania Bridge, at an altitude of five thousand feet. For £50 the Grants bought a light wagon known as a Scotch cart and four oxen, which transported to Blue Posts the goods they had brought from England, temporarily housed in Nairobi by the safari outfitters Newland & Tarlton. For £75 each Nellie bought two mares from Jim Elkington – a white, imported East Indian called White Lady and an Arab, Wee Woman. Elkington also lent them an old Abyssinian pony, scarred on its flank from being gored by a lion which had killed and eaten its rider.

Gradually a track was cut to the Grants' site. On 1 April 1913 the great day of the move came. Jos and Nellie settled the Blue Posts bill and left 'in style, waggon piled high – on top was the Garden House [lavatory] seat, fashioned by a fundi [Indian craftsman] at the hotel, and on this a small monkey I'd been given rode'.[12] Despite Elspeth's account in The Flame Trees of Thika, the journey did not begin in Nairobi, but at Blue Posts. On reaching their land five miles from Chania Bridge, the Grants found a suitable site for their tent and pitched it in grass five feet high. Their first weeks were spent organising a water supply from the chocolate-brown river (the water was boiled for drinking), putting up grass huts for both the labour lines and themselves, and overseeing the employment of an architect and builders for the stone house they intended to construct. The Crossley was sold to their builder, Mr Wright, for £600, to be deducted from the cost of the house. Skinny, clean-shaven and voluble, Wright was missing his left hand, but had no artificial substitute or hook. A reckless driver, he could not use the car's handbrake, failed to heed Jos's advice about the defective footbrake, and had several accidents. The Grants replaced the Crossley with a four-wheeled light buggy, mules and harness, for the trips to Chania Bridge for mail and the longer journey to Nairobi for supplies.

The temporary grass structure they lived in while the stone house went up was built in one block, with two bedrooms twelve feet by ten feet, a small bathroom between them and a sitting room of fourteen feet by ten feet, which later became Elspeth's schoolroom. The square outside walls were of papyrus lined with local grass. There was a steep pitched roof of Ithanga or swamp grass, real wooden doors and windows painted green, and a stone-paved verandah. Though primitive, the dwelling had cement floors, unusual in those days and a welcome barrier against fleas and white ants. The kitchen was a grass shed, the garden store and stables were of cut stone, and the African employees' round huts and other stores were of the traditional mud and rubble. The horses occupied grander quarters than did their human owners.

That was soon to change. Tate Smith, the architect of the Muthaiga Club* in Nairobi, was commissioned by Jos and Nellie to design their stone house. The house, a pleasant building with Dutch gables, still stands today, little changed. The Grants chose the new firm of Wright, Wingate & Wells as builders. Wright talked business with them on the steps of the National Bank of India in Nairobi, saying, 'I have the Bank of India behind me.'

He began building on 13 May 1913, but things did not go smoothly. Vast quantities of lime and two hundred tons of sand began to arrive from the Athi river twenty-three miles away, for Wright scorned the local practice of filling the inside interstices of the walls with mud. Fifty Indian stonemasons and a gang of Africans also appeared. Wright never kept a tally of the footage cut or proper paysheets, and disputed his Indian employees' claims for wages, saying they lied like a cheap watch. He got into financial difficulties, bolted to Uganda and was never heard of again. Tate Smith found

---

* Muthaiga is the Kikuyu word for the greenheart tree bark, from which the Kikuyu made medicines and arrow poisons.

the Grants another contractor, and he and the fundis finished the house a year after it was begun.

BEA was by now attracting British and American tourists who came on safari to hunt big game, an activity also much indulged in by the local whites. What roads there were were so impassable that safaris always went by foot or horse. Jos and Nellie's first safari was to the Athi plains east of Nairobi to shoot a lion, at the invitation of the game warden, A. Blaney Percival, and the woman he was in love with, Dolly Miles, the sister of Tich Miles, an early settler whose courage belied his tiny size.* Dolly was to be a lifelong friend and benefactor of Nellie's, though her increasing eccentricity as she aged was to try Nellie sorely. Jos and Nellie rode mules to Percival's camp at Athi River, Jos swaying with fever. Percival kept pursuing Dolly and getting drunk. When Dolly shot a lion, Percival said 'The dear girl's eyes were shining like stars,' the sort of romantic talk Nellie abhorred. He later followed Dolly to Mombasa when she went to catch her ship back to England, but took so much Dutch courage to summon up the boldness to propose that he fell off the gangway, thus putting an end to the romance. 'Nellie disapproved of romantics,' said Elspeth later, 'but of course was one herself, though she concealed it like a guilty secret. It is always our own qualities that most appal us when we find them in others.'[13]

A lion eluded Jos and Nellie, and they returned to their farm. Their first priority was to plant shade trees around Kitimuru's living area and to break up and prepare the ground for planting coffee seedlings. They put in blue gums, the most popular and fastest-growing of the shade trees, and an avenue of flame trees, though the latter were put too close together and had to be uprooted and replaced by others spaced more widely. A vegetable patch and coffee nursery were started on a spit of land jutting out into the river, two hundred feet below the farm. Beds were made in the rich red soil, coffee seeds were dibbed in and flat grass covers built above

---

* A.T. Miles, who came to BEA in August 1909 at the age of twenty. He fought bravely in Tanganyika in the First World War, after which he became British Consul in Abyssinia. Always at heart a boy, he died at forty-four in 1934 from the ravages to his health caused by the war.

to shade the tender seedlings. It took six weeks for the little plants to appear. At three months the young seedlings were transplanted and spaced out a little, to remain in situ for eight to eighteen months, until they were big enough to plant out.

Meanwhile more ground was cleared. On average there were seven acacia trees to be uprooted per acre, plus the smaller bushes and the head-high grass. Ploughing proved to be a nightmare because no one knew how to manage the small, hyperactive oxen. Getting them to work together was like trying to herd cats. Eventually the Grants borrowed a driver trained by Boers (Afrikaners), who were famous for their ability to control oxen, and he successfully disciplined the Grants' animals. Then they used as driver a Boer contractor called Becker who had a squalid camp of innumerable relatives at Chania Bridge. Like the other British settlers of the time, Nellie called the Boers 'Dutchmen', and was troubled by their poverty and failure to send their children to school. This was the origin of her later concern about a 'poor white' problem in Kenya.

A ready supply of labour was essential for the stumping, clearing and ploughing. But labour was scarce and difficult to get. It was soon evident that Jos and Nellie would fail to reach their target of clearing a hundred acres a year. Indeed, it was not until mid-1914 that their acreage of planted coffee even reached sixty. One method of recruitment they tried was hanging an oil lantern outside the door at night (as yet electricity had not spread from Nairobi). The Africans, intrigued, would come and ask how to manufacture this permanent light, and then attempts would be made to persuade the members of the captive audience to join the payroll. The Grants also did some recruiting in the neighbouring Kikuyu reserve, in a haphazard sort of way. Nellie sometimes rode into the reserve to recruit, which caused a stir since many Africans had never before seen a horse, let alone a woman riding one. She was once addressed on such a foray as 'Bwana Memsahib' (sir madam), such was the astonishment.

A towering problem was that in Kikuyu society the work of digging and cultivation was done by women, and men did not want to demean themselves by engaging in such activities. Nellie was quite happy to have women workers, who returned to the reserves at night. When the government imposed hut taxes on the Africans, men joined the women workers to earn money, rather than sell their sheep and goats, which were vital for the purchase of brides. Desertion of labour was persistent, since many Africans were unused to working with whites and the notion of labour contracts was foreign to them.

The bait for recruiting was cash, food and rudimentary medical treatment from Nellie for the workers' families. Despite their profound belief in the rituals of African medicine, the labourers adored being doctored by Nellie. Babies were frequently brought to her with appalling burns, having rolled into the fires laid inside all Kikuyu huts. She raged against the Kikuyu habit of putting dying people outside the huts so that they did not perish within, which was considered most unlucky. Neither would the Kikuyu touch dead bodies, which caused many a burial problem. As for household staff, the two Swahilis from Mombasa stayed a short time only, for they found the weather far too cold. Jim Elkington lent Nellie two more Swahilis until she could find servants of her own.

A further bait for labour was the development of the squatter system. While no Africans could own land in white farming areas, they could grow their own crops and keep animals on the farms where they worked, in exchange for labouring for the farmer for 180 days a year. On some farms where all the labour was made up of squatters there would be a double labour force, with a changeover every six months. Nellie and Jos soon acquired several squatters.

Supplies from Nairobi were slow to arrive – the oxen pulling the wagon took a full five days to plod there and back. Matters improved on 1 October 1913 when the Thika 'tramway' from Nairobi was opened, with a great party at Blue Posts. Some years before, the Governor of BEA had applied to London for a railway branch line to be constructed to Chania Bridge. The Colonial Office, with memories of the appalling cost of the Mombasa–Uganda railway, vetoed the proposal. The wily Governor merely reapplied, this time calling the line, which had the same gauge as the railway, a tramway. To this London assented, and the colonists got their branch railway.

Letters, formerly carried to Chania Bridge three times a week by runner, now came by train, as did most provisions.

The Grants' burdens were further alleviated when their neighbour Roy Whittet offered them the use of water from a spring he had discovered on his land. Before her child arrived from England Nellie bought a donkey to fetch this water so that Elspeth would have a pure supply to drink. But she discovered that the water-carrier continued to draw water from the nearby river, spending the extra time he would have required to ride to the spring asleep in the bushes.

Though life was hard, in many ways white farmers had things easy. This was a time when people seldom questioned the power of Britain and her empire. To be British was to be superior. In BEA all heavy work was done by Africans, and housework too. Freed from domestic tasks, Nellie could indulge her penchant for social life. She was alert and witty, with a mind as fast as a cheetah. She became very fond of Captain Jack Kirkwood, whom she had met at Masara, Elkington's estate. A white hunter for the safari outfit Newland & Tarlton, Kirkwood was out of a job in July 1913 and offered to take the Grants on safari round Mount Kenya, the snow-covered, sharp-peaked 17,000-foot mountain which loomed in the distance in the morning mist but was mostly obscured by cloud later in the day. They engaged a temporary manager for the farm, a former railway guard dismissed for leaving the aide-de-camp to the Governor of German East Africa at a station when he went to complain about a delay.

The Grants left for their six-week safari via Meru to the Uaso Nyiro river, which flows throughout the year between the Kenyan and Ethiopian highlands. In the dry season from early January to the end of March its water draws animals from the rocky plains for miles around until it peters out in the Lorian swamp, and they can be seen all along its banks. Unlike the Newland & Tarlton safaris offered to overseas visitors, with their two hundred porters wearing smart blue N&T jerseys, their headmen and gunbearers, the Grants' was an inexpensive affair, with local porters whose most awkward load was a sizeable tin bath. Jack Kirkwood charged them nothing, but they had gunbearers from Newland & Tarlton who insisted on having new boots. To Nellie's chagrin the gunbearers walked the whole safari barefoot, with their boots hung on a piece of string round their necks. The Grants' plan was to shoot an elephant in the Mount Kenya forest above Embu, then get lions round Archer's Post, then trek home. They got no elephant, though Jos did shoot a lion.

On their return from safari they found some forty acres cleared, but an odd creature awaiting them at the farm. He was in khaki clothes, with a long scarf hanging down the back of his neck from his sola topee* and a sun umbrella. He wore blue goggles, three shirts one on top of the other, and a kongoni (hartebeeste) skin over his back. This was the eccentric Anglo-Irish writer Lord Dunsany, who had invited himself to stay on the grounds of having married a cousin of Nellie's called Beatrice Villiers.** In Elspeth Huxley's *The Mottled Lizard* Dunsany is one of the few characters who appears almost as himself, though renamed and provided with some imaginary attributes. He had taken to heart the fear of the sun, so intrinsic a part of settler life and the reason for the thick hats made from two layers of felt, known as 'double terais', worn by women and children (men had topees), and spine pads – red flannel, quilted attachments pinned or buttoned to the back of the dress to protect the spine from the treacherous rays of the sun. Apart from the hats and spine pads, women wore hideous clothing which was far too hot and bulky for the climate. This consisted of ill-fitting gabardine breeches, partly concealed by short, wide, flapping khaki skirts, and a khaki coat and boots. Men's attire was the same, but without the skirts. Needless to say, the wearers suffered sorely from sweating and prickly heat.

*   *   *

---

* The sola is a tall, leguminous swamp plant grown in India, the pith of which was used to make the hats.
** Dunsany became a playwright, poet and international literary celebrity. His work was profoundly influenced by his experiences in the Boer War and visits to Africa, including this one to BEA. The walls of Dunsany Castle in County Meath, Ireland, were adorned with his big-game trophies.

The Grants had spent a year setting up home in Chania Bridge. They talked of bringing their daughter out from England, but no decision was made. This was normal at the time – the children of the British in India spent years at school in Britain without seeing their parents. Then Daisy Learmonth (Balfour), Elspeth's guardian, decided to visit the Grants in BEA while she was accompanying her sister and brother-in-law, the George Lloyds, who were travelling to Africa in December 1913. Daisy took with her the six-year-old Elspeth, the governess Miss Ross Hume and a maid. Nellie does not appear to have welcomed the thought of her daughter's arrival:

> It is settled that Elspeth arrives out here on December 29th, which puts a touch of finality on my ties here ... I'm fairly doubtful about being able to keep Elspeth out here very long; as a country for children I think this has many drawbacks, but I suppose one would give it a year's trial anyway, and the problems of keeping her at home are fairly great ... Oh dear, it is all exceedingly perturbing.[14]

Nellie was apprehensive because many diseases, some of them fatal, were endemic in BEA. Malaria, for which synthetic drugs had not yet been invented, was rife throughout the country and was almost invariably the malignant variety caused by *Plasmodium falciparum* and transmitted by mosquitoes. Plague was frequent and smallpox not uncommon. Yaws was a major problem, as was bilharzia. Relapsing fever, tick typhus, typhoid and paratyphoid were prevalent. There were also plenty of cases of anthrax and tetanus and intestinal diseases such as amoebic and bacillary dysentery. Tropical ulcers, or veld sores, affected everyone.

More grass huts were hastily erected in expectation of the four newcomers, who reached Mombasa by ship on 29 December 1913. They made their way to Mombasa station, a bustling and noisy place, to catch the train to Nairobi. At 5 p.m. the long train with its two engines, stacks of wood fuel and array of first-, second- and third-class carriages waited at a platform considerably shorter than itself. The coaches were of wooden construction, without corridors, and each with four non-communicating compartments. The party entered a first-class compartment with four berths and a self-contained lavatory discharging directly onto the track. The windows were gauzed against mosquitoes and engine sparks. The train crossed Makupa bridge* to the mainland and began its climb, winding upwards and once back upon itself while gaining height. They stopped at Changamwe station where pineapples, finger bananas, fresh coconuts and oranges were offered for sale and there was a magnificent view of the Port Reitz inlet snaking backwards from the sea. At Samburu station there was a stop for tea and the passengers stretched their legs while the engine took on more water.

Two hours after departure, darkness fell with a suddenness Elspeth had not experienced before. At dusk a man walked along the roof of the train, opened a trap over each compartment and lit the carriage oil lamps from above. They were too dim to read by. Now the red sparks cascading from the engine funnel resembled comets in the black night sky. An hour later the train stopped at Voi for passengers to disembark for dinner in the dak, or government bungalow, while their bunks were made up with bedding rolls. After a depressing dinner of tinned food and a long sleep Elspeth awoke to an enchanted scene. The air was cool and faintly misty, and the desert had given way to the vast orange Athi plains teeming with wild animals. Zebra, all kinds of antelope, giraffe, ostrich, wildebeeste and even lion could be seen. The compartment's occupants were covered by a fine red dust which had insinuated itself into every crevice. Breakfast was served and the engine refuelled with wood at Kiu. Then at 9 a.m. the train pulled in to Nairobi station, where Jos and Nellie were among the crowds waiting on the platform.

Jack Pixley put up the whole party at a house in Nairobi he shared with Denys Finch Hatton.** With his slow, crooked smile,

---

* During the Second World War the possibility of enemy action destroying the bridge and cutting the railway link to the mainland would prompt the authorities to replace it with a causeway.
** The house, behind the Norfolk Hotel, had previously belonged to Northrup Macmillan, a wealthy American and benefactor of Nairobi. Pixley was killed in the First World War. Finch Hatton, son of the Earl of Winchelsea, was an Old Etonian and later the lover of Karen Blixen. He died in a plane crash in 1931, and was buried in the Ngong hills, looking over the lands he loved so well.

Finch Hatton was very attractive to women, despite the baldness which he invariably hid with a hat. Farming was not to his taste; he was more of a rover. He dabbled in the safari business, hunting and the ivory trade. He lacked ambition and commitment, but his charm made up for it. The Grants wanted to be in the capital for the grand opening on 31 December of the Muthaiga Club, three miles from the centre of Nairobi. Built of blocks of stone covered with pink pebble-dash, it boasted Doric columns and was intended for settler membership. Settlers and officials were often at odds, which had made the Nairobi Club, built at about the same time and the haunt of the latter, an inconvenient place for farmers and settlers who were not civil servants or businessmen.

At the opening celebrations the King's African Rifles band, the only one in the country, played too loudly in the lounge, and dancing began, although it was not an unalloyed success, due to the paucity of women. Nellie had prevented a sulking Miss Ross Hume from attending because of her duties with Elspeth. The revellers went to bed at 2.30 a.m. but were up at 6.30 to engage in that particularly British importation, a hunt with the Masara hounds. Later in the day Nellie took Elspeth to see a doctor to check her health, because there were no doctors at Chania Bridge.

The Grants (minus Jos, who had returned the previous day) and their party took the train to Chania Bridge at 9 a.m. the next day. There was no one to meet them at the station, for Jos was late with the buggy and ox cart to carry the luggage. At last he arrived, and Nellie and the newcomers clambered into the buggy. As the hill from the station to Kitimuru was very steep, Nellie always took it at a gallop after crossing the little bridge at the bottom. This time the traces of the two leading ponies broke, they raced away, and the other two jibbed. When they finally arrived at Kitimuru the now nervous Daisy Learmonth found that her hut was worryingly distant from the others, so that at night she had to pick her way with a paraffin lamp through logs and litter. Altogether it was not an auspicious start, especially as the household staff was depleted by Tom, a houseboy – settlers in BEA always called their staff 'boys' – who was sick in hospital.

Nellie set about getting to know her six-year-old daughter. Elspeth had inherited her father's wide face and forehead, and her mother's features, without the buck teeth. Nellie soon cut off the ringlets which Daisy had made Elspeth wear, and when they went to Nairobi three weeks later for the five-day January races, a prominent feature of the settlers' social calendar, she ordered tropical clothes for her daughter from an Indian tailor – neat dark-blue tunics and shorts. They shopped for polo sticks and other essentials in the morning, went to the races at noon, played tennis in the late afternoon and had dinner at the Norfolk or Stanley hotels or the Muthaiga Club, followed by dancing to the King's African Rifles band. Such was Elspeth's introduction to her new life, in a country where the social behaviour was not so very different from that in England.

At this time there are frequent mentions of 'CK' in Nellie's diary. This was Captain Kirkwood, who had taken them on safari the previous year and of whom she was growing very fond. Many years later, having retrieved her 1914 diary from Kitimuru where she had left it, Nellie sent it to Elspeth with the comment: 'I was intrigued I must say to find my boyfriend referred to as CK when his name was Jack, but this was for "Captain Kirkwood" would you believe it.'[15] It is unlikely that there was any impropriety, but the flirtation was evidence of Nellie's dissatisfaction with her marriage, a feeling encouraged by Jos's incompetence. On Monday, 26 January Miss Ross Hume arrived in Nairobi with a bad toothache and put an end to the idyll. Everyone went back to Kitimuru, where they found Leo Lawford, the District Commissioner at Fort Hall (now Murang'a), and his wife camping by the house. Nellie promptly tried out the Lawfords' pony Moyale, and bought it.

The new household embarked upon a routine which was to last for several months. Nellie spent the early mornings making butter, then passed the day supervising the African labourers and socialising at Kitimuru or neighbouring farms. She rode miles with Daisy searching for small game for the pot. Daisy had to be instructed how to ride astride, for she was used to a sidesaddle. Nellie did this 'by taking her to the top of a river bank 200 feet down a very steep slope, and giving Reggie [Daisy's mount] a slap on his backside, which started them off, me shouting "Sit back and leave his head alone" and off they went slipping and sliding and Daisy screaming all the way down'.[16]

The Grants and their guests also began to play polo, which was introduced to the district in 1913 and became a favourite pastime among the settlers. The first games were arranged sixteen miles from Kitimuru at Makuyu estate, a sisal farm run by Lord (Bertie) Cranworth,* his brother-in-law Mervyn Ridley and Alan Tompson. Ridley and his neighbour Randall Swift of Punda Milia farm also had a pack of foxhounds. The young, paying, farm pupils from England employed at Makuyu were very horse- and hunt-minded, so there was ample personnel for polo games and hunts, and Makuyu Club was formed. Then another polo ground was made in a vlei (a shallow depression in the land) at Gethungwini, Charles Taylor's farm next to Kitimuru.

Nellie established her own polo team, for which she and Daisy embroidered badges, naming it the Hatton Gardens team, after a remark by Leo Lawford, who had asked the Kikuyu who the new white farmers were. He was told they were Kichanga (bracelet, for Roy Whittet always had one on his wrist) and Kichuki ('earrings', worn by Nellie until one was knocked out by a polo ball), whereupon he said he must have wandered into Hatton Garden. Africans always gave whites nicknames. Jos Grant was called Kofia Mbaya ('bad hat', after a dirty hat he wore), and another farmer was known as 'stinking meat' on account of his rubicund complexion.

On most weekends everyone rode ponies to Makuyu on Saturday, stayed there for the night and played polo or hunted, or both, on Sundays. On occasional Sundays the Grant household and others rode into the Kikuyu reserve and picnicked under a tree. Then those with guns lined out and walked back through the African shambas (cultivated patches of land) shooting francolin (small game birds which run along the ground) and an occasional guinea-fowl.

---

* Bertram Francis, second Baron Cranworth, commercial entrepreneur, part-owner of the Makuyu estate and later founder of the White Rhino Hotel at Nyeri.

Since the supply of meat presented considerable difficulties, this made a welcome change in the diet. Otherwise the only meat available was native sheep or goat, or antelope shot on the farm, mostly reedbuck, duiker or kongoni.

When Nellie stopped to reflect on her life at this time, she said: 'this is quite the slackest country, as far as mental effort is concerned, that you can imagine. As far as material things go, we are getting on all right, spending our capital rapidly, and thanking our stars that living is cheap, but not worrying one way or the other.'[17] She was copying the form of upper-class life she had had in England, with polo and hunting and tennis – the Grants had built a tennis court on their land – and was a long way from developing her later questioning attitude towards her presence in BEA. Her interest in African culture also lay in the future. Like their fellow settlers, the Grants were in BEA to make a living, by methods far superior in their eyes to those employed by Africans on their shambas. In their minds they were improving the Africans' way of life by offering them wages and an opportunity to see how the British lived. At this moment of British imperialism, the settlers' notions of superiority were at their height, for no doubts had yet surfaced to disturb the 'noble' purpose of civilising other races. As Elspeth said later, 'Europeans rarely questioned their own customs; what they did was right and civilized, what others did was savage and stupid. No doubt all people think like this about their own habits. The Kikuyu probably accounted for most of ours as a form of magic.'[18] Such attitudes and personalities were to influence *The Flame Trees of Thika* and *The Mottled Lizard*.

Elspeth spent most of her time in the company of her governess Miss Ross Hume, though her mother did begin to show some interest in her. The day after they arrived at Thika Nellie put her daughter on the mule Margaret,* and she was soon teaching her

---

* Margaret was given to Nellie by her friend Julian Hargreaves when he was dying of cancer in Nairobi Hospital. He also gave her his saddlery and the 256 carbine which she kept for many years.

to ride on a good-looking bay called Lucifer, a charming Dongolese
Arab on which Elspeth looked like a pea on a drum. As she improved
her technique, Elspeth was permitted to ride the very grand pony
Hafid. It was not long before she could accompany the adults on
the sixteen-mile hack to Makuyu on Saturday afternoons and the
return to Kitimuru on Sunday evenings. Elspeth never seemed tired,
displaying an energy she derived from her mother and would keep
all her life. Occasionally Nellie recorded in her diary: 'Elspeth
naughty, so did not come.'

Elspeth was not, however, allowed to go on safari in February
1914. Such an enterprise was considered too dangerous for a six-
year-old. Nellie, Daisy and a party of friends rode through the
Kikuyu reserve to the town of Nyeri forty miles to the north (Jos
stayed behind to look after the farm). Thence they rode on to stay
with Berkeley Cole at his lovely farm on the Naro Moru river,
where he lived with his Somali mistress.* In later years Elspeth
Huxley was to buy a plot on this land, where she hoped to build
a holiday house. An amusing and free-spirited man, liable at any
moment to break into an aria from *Madam Butterfly*, Cole had the
best Goan cook in the country – although his guests seldom got
dinner before ten or eleven, because there was so much talking and
incense-burning beforehand. Goan cooks were highly prized. On
the coast there were good Swahili cooks, but the only other cooks
at this time were Baganda from Uganda, who quickly mastered
English cooking, the only sort most settlers would eat. A few people
had wood-burning Dover stoves, but the ordinary settler household's kitchen had just the traditional three stones, with a fire in
the centre, on which the Africans produced excellent meals for their
employers.

The safari party stayed in Cole's guest house, a severely quadrilat-
eral cedar hut with four identical square bedrooms, each of which

---

* Berkeley Cole was the son of the fourth Earl of Enniskillen, and brother of Galbraith
Cole. His sister Florence married Lord Delamere, an early BEA settler. Berkeley was a
cattle farmer, the inseparable companion of Tich Miles in many enterprises. He also
partnered Cranworth to establish the White Rhino Hotel at Nyeri. He died in 1925, at
the age of forty-three, and was buried on his farm.

represented the statutory development required for his four huge farms. 'Bertie Cranworth had a pretty wit in those days and wasn't at all pompous and we had very good camps and laughed a lot,' said Nellie, who contributed to the humour with her own extraordinarily quick wit and high spirits. 'She had the knack,' said her daughter, 'of tapping every conversational nail on the head deftly, without effort; even before she had spoken, people often smiled and made up their minds to be amused.'

The party returned via the Rift Valley and Naivasha, with its lovely lake dominated by the noble mountain volcano Longonot, where they entrained for Nairobi and home. Nellie felt the trip had done her good and removed her for a little while from 'the rank materialism in which this country, and I suppose all young countries, abounds. Safari is what is good for one's immortal soul – there is little else out here.'[19]

Nellie continued to give Elspeth riding lessons, telling her always to leave the pony's head alone. On one occasion when she fell off she sat on the ground, bellowing, 'Mummy you told me if I fell off I shouldn't hurt myself and I jolly well have, *so there!*'[20] Nellie had been fond of Nanny Newport but heartily disliked the governess Miss Ross Hume, whom she thought 'absolutely foul'. Always a woman of trenchant opinions about her fellow human beings, and a convinced atheist, she found it hard to be polite to someone who had deep religious convictions and who slobbered over her ginger cat, behaviour which Nellie reckoned killed the poor animal.

Nellie and Daisy escaped from the governess by going on a second safari with their neighbour Charles Taylor, whom Nellie said was 'sweet on' Daisy, and Jack Kirkwood, Nellie's beau. Nellie's diary reveals that she was seeing Kirkwood nearly every day at this time, but unhappily for her he brought a girlfriend along on the safari. They left on 3 March, returning on the twenty-fourth. Making their way across the Aberdare mountains to the high country north of Gilgil, they camped on the shores of Lake Olbolossat in the Rift Valley. Daisy, a great walker, shot a zebra, and was so delighted that she had it skinned. The hide was a great talking-point in her English homes for many years to come. Alas, she had two serious mishaps on this safari. She was bitten on the bottom by a poisonous spider and the wound festered until she had treatment on her return to England, and she bruised her ribs falling into the ashpit between the rails at Nakuru station just as the train was drawing in. She was dragged out in the nick of time, and the party then made for Nairobi to seek medical treatment for her.

The Grants' social life became fuller and more unconstrained following their move on 26 March 1914 into their new stone house. It had two Dutch gables, wooden floors, and a tin roof on which thatch had been laid to reduce the heat of the sun. Never a day went by without Nellie and Daisy lunching or dining at home or abroad with neighbours and friends. On one such visit hyenas ate the leather harness and seats of their buggy while they had their meal. There were frequent trips to Nairobi for shopping and socialising at the Muthaiga Club. One day the pony Hafid slipped while Jos was riding and he fell heavily on his shoulder, with his foot caught in the stirrup. Hafid dragged him along until he was able to free his foot. He suffered a badly torn ankle and an injured collarbone. Nellie was not always sympathetic to physical pain, and assured him that nothing was broken. But Jos had to lie up just at the time when the coffee bushes needed planting out, and supervising the work fell to Nellie.

She marked out parallel lines on the newly turned red ground, beginning the planting on 9 April, a year after the Grants had first pitched their tents in the tall grass among acacia and scrub. In two days she oversaw the planting of ten thousand coffee bushes. Perhaps in celebration but more likely because Miss Ross Hume had gone to Nairobi, Elspeth was allowed to sit up for dinner for the first time. The next day Jos could bear his pain no longer and sought refuge in Nairobi so that he could consult the doctor. His collarbone had indeed been broken, and had set with the ends of the bones overlapping.

Daisy departed for England on 18 April, leaving Elspeth in the charge of Miss Ross Hume and her parents. Until now, apart from her riding lessons, Nellie had paid little attention to her child, as was the custom in upper-class British families. Elspeth pottered about, watching Nellie working hard on the house, farm and garden, putting up curtains, planting more coffee (33,278 bushes were in by 28 April), preparing garden paths, planting delphiniums, carnations, sweet peas, hibiscus, lavender hedges and fancy trees, and making a pergola. The planning and supervision was Nellie's but the actual labouring was done by African employees.

Nellie saw Jack Kirkwood every day while Jos was recuperating from his injury in Nairobi, but there is no direct evidence of a physical affair. She made a plaintive entry in her diary on Friday, 1 May: 'Miss RH seedy, in bed all day, so had Elspeth to look after.'[21] Gradually, however, she was getting to know her daughter better. When she was nearing the end of her life, Nellie expressed regret to Elspeth that theirs had never been a 'cosy' family. It is likely that Jos, with his kindlier manner, formed a closer relationship with Elspeth at this time than did her mother.

The Grants were full of optimism in 1914. They had planted sixty acres of coffee and fifty of lemon trees, the rains were good, and there was still a little capital left. Jos had a new money-spinning idea – essential oils, used for perfumes and for scenting a variety of cosmetics and household cleaners. Despite his lack of any technical knowledge, he imported a still from England and planted vetiva grass and sweet geraniums. The first bottle of oil, drawn on 4 August 1914, was never sent home because of Britain's declaration of war with Germany the following day. As for the coffee, it would bear in 1916, when the farmers at Chania Bridge who had started planting in 1912 hoped to make great profits. The Grants' neighbour Alan Tompson had the idea of chartering an entire ship, to be called the *Punda Makuyu* (Makuyu Donkey) to take everyone to England on leave after the first coffee crop was picked. It would tie up in the Thames until all were ready to return. On the outward voyage the cargo would be coffee and sisal, and on the return trip drink, polo ponies and luxuries.

Elspeth now found a friend who sometimes came to stay – Kina Chandos Pole, daughter of the new manager of Blue Posts. Harry Penton had finally succumbed to delirium tremens, and the hotel had been taken over by another friend of Jim Elkington's. On Kina's birthday Elspeth gave her the skin of a python Nellie had shot, in lieu of a toy, which was not to be had in this remote corner of the world.

This was the world which the six-year-old Elspeth was observing and absorbing. There was hard work tempered with a great deal of frivolity. The white settlers in BEA were the dominant class, and as far as they were concerned Africans were there to be labourers. Although they sometimes found it charming, whites rather despised the Africans' belief in 'witchcraft' and 'magic'. Mission-educated Africans were regarded as 'above themselves' and cocky. This created an undercurrent of tension in African society. Elspeth later described the British as 'steeped in complacency and arrogance . . . It is hard to credit what a good opinion we had of ourselves in those days. There was the Empire, and there were we at the heart and centre of the world. No one questioned our position. Everyone else was a barbarian, more or less.'[22] She was soon to have her singular and curious world turned upside down. The First World War was looming.

TWO

The First World War and its Aftermath

The BEA colonists were full of optimism in 1913–14. The country seemed capable of offering them a good income and a privileged way of life. The only drawbacks were its detrimental effect on health and doubts about whether it was suitable for children. As compensation, there was a cohesion stemming from the shared class and educational background of most of the settlers, which enabled people in an alien country to feel at home among their own traditions and allowed the development of familiar upper-class pastimes such as polo and tennis, racing and hunting. The Muthaiga Club even held an Eton dinner for Old Boys. As yet there was no serious opposition from the country's original inhabitants, still reeling from the introduction of an alien culture. All seemed secure and peaceful; but in BEA calamity was never far away.

In May 1914 Jos fell ill with fever – probably malaria. Despite his athletic physique he was not as strong as Nellie, who was now obliged to take over the supervision of all the farm work from him. While waiting for the coffee to bear, she made a little money by landing a contract to supply Blue Posts with vegetables. She also helped their neighbour Roy Whittet ('Kichanga') pick his first coffee crop, a special occasion for Chania Bridge, furnishing farmers whose bushes had yet to crop with ample hope for the future.

Nellie worked and played hard. Her restless intelligence forced her always to be doing something, always to have her hands occupied –

stillness was strange to her. Even when the day's work was done and darkness at seven forced her inside, she knitted by lamplight, sewed cushions and curtains, covered chairs and the sofa. By day she found time to give riding lessons to Elspeth. A typical entry in her diary is: 'Took Elspeth out riding and over jumps. She fell off three times.'[1] Poor Elspeth. Nellie had an open lack of sympathy for other people's pain, and was dismissive of her own. She even made light of her veld sores, that ubiquitous scourge when a small scratch would fester and form a deep ulcer which took months to heal.

Yet the sufferings of domestic animals were altogether a different matter, and she took considerable care to avoid them. In this region horses suffered from what, for want of a better designation, was called horse sickness. There was no cure, but Nellie reckoned that if she could reduce the animals' temperatures they might have a chance of survival. She organised rotas for the treatment of ailing horses, keeping their flanks drenched with cool water. Sometimes this worked and the horses pulled through. When her mule Margaret became ill, Nellie treated her with quinine, whisky, ginger and hot fomentation, but Margaret was dead within eight hours. Then the pony Dudy died of colic, so the Grants lost yet another animal. Nellie inclined to the sentimental, and grieved. She became deeply attached to ponies, and pet dogs in particular, in a country that was hostile to such alien intruders. She passed on her love of dogs, especially dachshunds, to her daughter. Elspeth also befriended an orphaned duiker, which she called Twinkle. She was vigilant in protecting her pet from leopards, those enemies of dogs (they would even venture on to verandahs to take them), while Nellie so secured her flowerbeds against the duiker with barbed wire that they resembled a fortified camp.

The casualties among their horses meant that the Grants could not participate in the most important events in the social calendar – the January and July races in Nairobi. These were more informal than similar events in Britain, with farmers acting as their own jockeys. All the colonists, whether entering horses or not, flocked to the capital for the biannual event. As the daughter of a baron and granddaughter of a duke, Nellie was welcome to dine or stay at Government House. Elspeth was included in the invitation, and on 23 July 1914, her seventh birthday, she went to stay at Government House with her mother and Miss Ross Hume. As a special treat, she sat up for the formal dinner in the evening. The pleasure was somewhat marred by the arrival next day of Miss E.B. Seccombe, who ran a small school for white children in Nairobi. Nellie had asked to see her for nefarious purposes. Her relationship with Miss Ross Hume had deteriorated and she was considering dismissing her. She would then be faced with the problem of what to do with Elspeth. At the age of seven English boys of the titled classes were sent away to boarding school, so why not Elspeth? The exploratory talks between mother and schoolmistress went encouragingly well.

Almost immediately everyone's attention was distracted by events in Europe. The Grants had the first inkling of war on 30 July, when a friend told Jos that Austria and Serbia had opened hostilities. The next day Nellie was at Chania Bridge post office collecting what she hoped was word of a money-making scheme in Luxembourg in which Jos was interested. The expected cable from his partners was awaiting her. She opened it to read: 'Nothing doing. General European war expected.' The news was difficult to accept, but was confirmed by regular chits sent by African runner by Arthur Fawcus across the river (before radio became widely available, this was the usual method of communicating between farms). The Grants were bombarded with such items as 'Vienna Bourse closed' and 'Troops mobilising'; when Nellie received 'War expected', she scribbled across it 'What war?' and sent it back. 'That shut him up,' she said.[2] On 1 August Nellie confided to her diary: 'War news sounds very bad. Belgrade in flames. Bank of England shut. Hens came − 1 old cock, 4 ditto hens, 8 pullets, 6 cockerels, 1 drake.'[3] The next day Jos cabled his regiment, the Royal Scots, asking if he should return to England. He also approached the officer commanding troops in Nairobi, who cabled back: 'Hold yourself in readiness.' Bordering German East Africa, BEA was in a very vulnerable position should war break out. Its umbilical cord, the railway line, ran within fifty miles of German territory. The King's African Rifles, BEA's sole military force, was mobilised and sent to Voi, the most exposed spot on the Mombasa–Nairobi section of the line.

War was officially declared on 5 August 1914, and all the Germans in BEA were arrested. A khaki-clad Jos and his wife immediately went to the Norfolk Hotel in Nairobi, where settlers from around the country were gathering to discuss whether it would be wise to let Africans see whites shooting whites, and the even more thorny question of whether Africans themselves should be taught to shoot whites. Nellie visited the bank to withdraw all the cash it would give her, lest there should soon be no more, and then returned to the farm. Jos was promptly offered a staff appointment as Commander of the Intelligence Office because he could speak German, and was put in charge of the Railway Troops. A few settlers raised white commandos of their own, such as Bowker's Horse, Arnoldi's Scouts, Ross's Scouts and Wessel's Scouts.

A new body was formed to amalgamate these into the East African Mounted Rifles (the volunteers brought their own rifles – they ranged from elephant guns to light carbines), which included a squadron from each district. The most popular was Monica's Own, colloquially named after one of Governor Sir Henry Belfield's two pretty daughters. It even included a Turk, until the other colonists discovered which side Turkey was on, whereupon he was hastily interned. There was no settled uniform, but most men wore breeches and puttees, bush shirts and felt hats. Belfield himself was an impressive sight at inspections, with his gentleman's boater and eyeglass, in contrast to his ADC, who trotted beside him in cloth cap and shorts.

Jos's post required him to travel up and down the railway line between Nairobi and Mombasa, gathering information about possible German sabotage. In September he joined the 4th Battalion of the King's African Rifles as a subaltern and was sent to the frontier post of Taveta, where he participated in several skirmishes with German troops. The Germans managed to capture Taveta and dashed across the border at Kajiado. They then attacked British bomas (farm and government enclosures) and tried to blow up the railway line at Voi.

Meanwhile Nellie arranged for Kichanga, who had recently suffered from tuberculosis and was not passed fit for service, to come and live on the Grant farm, so as to economise on household expenses. The neighbouring farmers formed the Thika troop, drilled at Makuyu, and were seen off to war by Nellie and Elspeth from Chania Bridge station on 1 September. Now Nellie, Kichanga and the Cuninghames were the only whites left in the area, apart from Elspeth and Miss Ross Hume. Nellie and Kichanga volunteered to oversee the other farms while their owners were away, and for this purpose Mervyn Ridley lent Nellie his two-seater Mitchell car. This vehicle made journeys to Nairobi easy, and Nellie kept up with the war news by lunching at the Norfolk with her friend Denys Finch Hatton and others.

As casualty lists began to be printed in local papers, Nellie recorded in her diary the deaths of many pioneer friends. Her mules and ponies were commandeered for the soldiers, but when her Scotch cart and oxen were likewise taken she pleaded for their return because she could not manage the farm work without them; eventually she got them back. Sixty-six years later a soldier who had ridden the Grants' pony Nyeusi, small and dark and named for the Swahili word 'black', recalled in a letter to Elspeth how the animal saved his life: 'Nyeusi soon got into his steady one-speed canter and when the sun had been up for half an hour I realised that the old pony was increasing his speed and all my advice to him to go easy . . . went unheeded and I began to worry as he was showing signs of distress, then I saw out of the side of my sight a movement and at last I realised we were being run down by a pack of wild dogs hunting.'[4] Pony and rider escaped, but only the rider survived the war.

Jos made a momentous decision – to go to Britain to rejoin the Royal Scots. He left Nairobi station on 17 December 1914 on the train to Mombasa, waved off by Nellie and a host of friends, 'wide-shouldered and strongly built, his sandy hair cut very short, a small moustache, a wide-boned good-humoured face crinkled by a huge grin, and blue eyes twinkling with pleasure'.[5]

Nellie now felt she ought to undertake some active war work.

Jack Pixley and Denys Finch Hatton's house in Nairobi, where the Grants often stayed, had been converted into a convalescent home for the military, and she offered to provide it with vegetables and go there twice a week to do odd jobs. Her first assignment was to mend a huge pile of linen. Her enthusiasm was somewhat diminished when she was interrupted by a petty officer from HMS *Fox* who said he could do it much better, and did. After a few months the convalescent home died a natural death.

Under the stress of war, Nellie's relationship with Miss Ross Hume, always precarious, finally broke down. Miss Seccombe came to stay at Kitimuru for a couple of days, possibly to assess Elspeth for her school. But a stroke of good fortune intervened for the child. An invitation arrived from John and Gertrude Hill-Williams of Molo for Elspeth and her governess to come to live on their farm Marindas, situated in the Mau highlands on the western side of the Rift Valley. Mrs Hill-Williams would thereby obtain a free governess for her own two children, Hilda and Kathleen ('Tuppence'), who was the same age as Elspeth. Nellie leapt at the chance and waved a relieved goodbye to her child and governess at Nairobi station on 26 November. On arrival at Molo station Miss Ross Hume, who had failed utterly to adjust to the exigencies of life in Africa, made a monumental fuss about having to go the eleven miles from the station to Marindas in an ox wagon. Nellie's contentment at her release from the governess's presence was crushed a week later on receipt of a cable informing her that Mrs Hill-Williams was glad to keep Elspeth, but that she was returning Miss Ross Hume immediately. 'It was *frightful* being alone with her, but I soon pushed her off to Nairobi and she got a job of sorts and troubled me no more,' said Nellie.[6]

In *The Flame Trees of Thika* Elspeth fictionalised her time at Molo. She names the family she went to stay with the Crawfurds, and invents many incidents. Her description of the location is, however, accurate:

> At Molo everything was much bigger than at Thika – hills, trees, distances, even sky and clouds. The trees were black and

clumped, the grass naked and tufty, and bent over on one side, and you felt as if you had reached the very top of the world. The air was sharp and clean as iced lemon juice, and a wind blew, and spikes of pink and bronze wild gladioli grew among the buff sedgy grass.[7]

In the book Elspeth creates the character Ian Crawfurd, younger brother of the husband of the couple with whom she was staying, whose death in the war is so moving. She was an observant child, and much of Ian had been embodied in the carefree Captain Jack Kirkwood, Nellie's beau.

Elspeth's stay at Molo with children of her own age was infinitely preferable to being looked after alone by Miss Ross Hume. Marindas was a busy dairy farm, producing two hundred pounds of butter a week, and there was much of interest there for children. The small Dorobo people of the forest came out to barter for maize meal, gourds of wild honey and the beautiful black-and-white skins of the colobus monkey. With them came their barkless dogs, communicating in whines, foxy-faced and red with white paws and a tip to their tails curling back over their spines. Below the farm garden was a pool where the children sought tadpoles. There were scores of wild dogs around, animals more feared than lions by the African workers. Tuppence Hill-Williams describes how they went to C.B. Clutterbuck's farm nearby to have their ponies served because Clut, as he was called, a breeder of racehorses, had the only available stallion in the area – he had ninety horses in his stables and once entered thirteen races on one day, of which he won eleven. There the girls groomed horses with Clut's daughter Beryl, a few years older than Elspeth. Later – as Beryl Markham – she became the author of the renowned *West With the Night*, the story of her African childhood (she was a noted aviator and the first person to fly from England to America). Elspeth revisited this scene of her childhood in 1983, to find the stables all awry, the boxes still with their old latches and dust floors, and the rafters which had seemed so lofty to a child now leaning sideways and askew. The little girls also watched the adults hunt over wire fences, invisible and treacherous for the horses to jump. They heard lions at night attacking the cattle, and sat up in tree machans (hides) over bait left for lions, which they attempted to shoot. One day Elspeth, called in to lunch by Mrs Hill-Williams, arrived completely covered in dust. She explained she had been a chicken having a dust bath.

Elspeth's idyllic six months at Molo came to an end when her mother arrived to collect her in May 1915. Nellie was facing mounting troubles. She was worried about the seven-year-old Elspeth's education, her finances were straitened, labour was hard to get, and the work on Kitimuru and the other farms she was caretaking was getting her down. However, Mervyn Ridley had given her an excellent Maasai overseer, Sammy. 'Sammy was a terrific help on the farm,' said Nellie, 'and very sweet. His morals were peculiar – he had a Christian wife from Zanzibar, but peopled the Kikuyu reserve very efficiently. He always collected Masai around the place and gradually I collected a 100% Masai household. I had a Baganda cook but one day riding back from Thika an enormous Masai rose from the grass and said he wanted to be my cook. I said I had one, he said he knew he was leaving (I didn't). I said, "Can you cook?". He replied, "I have looked after 700 goats for two years." So I took him on.'[8]

It was rare for whites to have Maasai domestic staff, but labour of any sort was scarce because so many Kikuyu from the region had been called up for the Carrier Corps,* to convey supplies for British troops now that the soldiers' mounts had perished from tsetse-fly bites and horse sickness. The Maasai had refused to be recruited, thinking it beneath their dignity and failing to understand why one group of white people should wish to shoot at another, apparently indistinguishable, group. They were therefore able to fill labour gaps left by the Kikuyu.

As Nellie and Elspeth rode from Marindas to Molo station, Elspeth looked tiny, with her legs stretched out sideways on the back of a vast South African mare whose foal was trotting behind. For

---

* The Nairobi suburb of Kariokor derives its name from the settlement of these valiant men after the war.

a while mother and child stayed on the farm at Chania Bridge. Elspeth was allowed to ride the pony Moyale by herself, provided she was followed by a Maasai on a bicycle. She would gallop off, the Maasai pedalling wildly behind her, his kanzu tucked up around his waist, revealing all. One day Nellie drove into Nairobi to get £50 in rupees from the bank to pay her labour. On her return to the farm she was distracted by a 'shauri' (the universal word for any sort of bother), and the bag of money went missing. It was beginning to get dark, and Nellie summoned all the labourers and told them that unless she got the bag back she would set light to every hut on the farm. This highly illegal threat produced the desired result – before half an hour was up a sheepish African arrived with the bag, saying he had found it under a sitting turkey. 'Oh, the naughty bird!' said Nellie. The incident is recounted in *The Flame Trees of Thika*, but Elspeth makes the threat issue from Jos.

Soon Nellie sent Elspeth to board at Miss Seccombe's school in Nairobi. There is no record of what the child thought of yet another disruption in her life. Seven is a difficult age at which to part from one's mother, but Elspeth was nothing if not used to doing so. Nellie struggled on with her farming, hearing increasingly depressing news from Europe. Eventually her finances got so bad that, 'eager always to ameliorate rather than to repine',[9] she contemplated returning to England. She was also worried about Jos and her three brothers, all of them in khaki. Once she had made the decision to go she learned that there were no vacant berths on the scarce ships. Then one day in June she got a wire to say that an insane woman who had been intended to go home in a French boat with her keeper had grown too mad to go, and she could have the two berths. The ship was leaving in two days. She dashed into Nairobi to arrange finance and tell Miss Seccombe, then drove back to Chania Bridge so fast that the car shed both second gear and reverse.

Nellie packed and arranged matters for the farm employees well into the night. Kichanga would continue to live at Kitimuru, and Alan Cuninghame said he would keep an eye on the farm, which

Sammy was to oversee. Nellie's personal servant, the Maasai Andrew, tried hard to get her to take him with her to England. When she told him he would hate it and there would be nowhere for him to sleep, he asked, 'Are there not kitchens in England?'* Nellie had a mental picture of a Maasai occupying the kitchen at Cherry Orchard, her sister's traditional upper-class house near Shaftesbury, for which she was bound. She said no. Andrew picked up a clod of earth and dashed it to the ground, saying, 'That is how you treat me because I am black.' After this dramatic gesture he went back to Maasailand, where some months later he was killed by a lion while protecting his sheep.

The next day the car would not start. Nellie leapt on a pony of Kichanga's and galloped all the way to Chania Bridge station. She was just in time to catch the train. But there were locusts on the line and the train repeatedly failed to get up hills – it had seven shots at Ndurugu hill. Nellie was frantic, but she got to Nairobi station half an hour before the Mombasa train left. There was Miss Seccombe waiting with Elspeth on the platform. Mother and child bundled into the Mombasa train, which was held up for twenty-four hours at Voi because the Germans had blown up the line. Eventually arriving at the port of Mombasa, Nellie was convinced they had missed the boat, only to discover that it had been delayed for five days. They spent the time waiting in the dreaded Metropole Hotel, which Nellie described as 'stinking'. At length they embarked on a slow French cargo ship, formerly on the China route, and sailed to Djibouti in the Red Sea, where they were forced to disembark because bubonic plague had broken out on board. The Red Sea is one of the hottest places on earth, and Elspeth suffered miserably from prickly heat as they waited ashore for six days. The ship then continued to Marseilles, where they caught a train across war-ravaged France. The little luggage they had with them got lost, and it was a bedraggled pair who eventually knocked at the door of Trudie Denman's London mansion at 4 Buckingham Gate.

---

* Karen Blixen was asked a similar question by her servant when she was returning to Denmark – see *Out of Africa*.

Once they had negotiated a disapproving butler, Nellie's former partner in the Welsh pony enterprise welcomed them with open arms.

Trudie was the moving spirit in the organisation 'Smokes for Wounded Soldiers and Sailors', or SSS. Since she used the ballroom at Buckingham Gate as a packing depot, the house was crowded with cigarettes and packers. Nellie found a day school for Elspeth in London and gleefully joined the fray. Her zest for life spurred Trudie into starting another joint enterprise. Since Nellie had had some experience with poultry, she and Trudie conceived the idea of encouraging all British households to keep hens. While providing food and thus cutting imports, this would also make use of household scraps. The pair took an office in Pimlico, persuaded a friend to design a backyard henhouse, and undertook the business of advertising and persuading the public to follow their lead. They answered thousands of queries, even from professional poultry-keepers.

Meanwhile Jos was fighting in France. On Guy Fawkes Day 1915 he was wounded in the chest by a hand-grenade which exploded accidentally. He was repatriated, and declared unfit to return to active service. His brother Robin, a staff officer in the Rifle Brigade, tried to get him a job, and as a good linguist he was almost sent to Bucharest, but his knowledge of Spanish caused him to be despatched instead to neutral Madrid, as military attaché – 'he was not a spy, he was the respectable military attaché,' said Nellie[10] (the unrespectable attaché in Madrid was the writer Compton Mackenzie).

In February 1916 Nellie and Jos moved to a flat in Madrid with a cook and a footman, leaving Elspeth in England. Nellie worked for the Red Cross in Spain, making pyjamas for wounded Allied soldiers. One of her letters from Elspeth described a Zeppelin raid on London: 'Darling Mum, I very much enjoyed the last Zeppelin raid, I slept in the butler's bed.' Nellie stayed only three months before returning to England. Jos, looking for the affection Nellie could not give him, then embarked on a love affair with Phoebe Baring, the wife of the naval attaché in Madrid. Nellie was told of the affair, and her relationship with Jos was never the same again. For many years thereafter Jos kept a yellowing photograph of Phoebe in a little silver frame on his dressing-table, until Elspeth's pet genet smashed it.

Nellie had been irritated for some time by what she saw as Jos's faults. Dreaminess, charming in a suitor, was less so in a husband. Nellie and Jos were fundamentally incompatible. Resolutely realistic, quick-thinking, witty, sociable and confident, Nellie found her husband, ever the gentleman, ponderous and boring. Unlike Jos, Nellie could draw humour from the most quotidian events. She was also exasperated by his propensity to declare 'I'll fit in with whatever you say,' which passed the buck to her while appearing to be considerate of her wishes, and was in reality an indication that he could not make up his mind. This good-looking and charming man, with the bearing of a soldier, was, however, very attractive to women, and on this occasion looked elsewhere for love.

Nellie's youngest brother Chucks was killed in France in September 1915, and Jos's younger brother Robin was wounded in the spine and paralysed for life. Once again Nellie joined her friend Trudie Denman, this time in the Women's Land Army, which Trudie had formed to provide the nation with women to work the land while the men were away at war. Nellie's job was to be travelling inspector for Hampshire, Dorset, Surrey and the Isle of Wight, finding billets for Land Army girls and looking after their welfare. She rode around the counties on a second-hand motorcycle, or with Trudie in a car, stopping to hold recruitment rallies in towns and villages. They attracted attention by using a vehemently raucous football rattle, which soon drew the crowds. Nellie thoroughly enjoyed herself.

In the very cold winter of 1916–17 Nellie and Elspeth found a home in Aunt Victoria Grant's house at Pitchford, near Shrewsbury. The water froze in the basins of the bedrooms and Elspeth began to ail; indeed, she had to have her tonsils out in Shrewsbury in January 1917. As she was now nine, Nellie decided to send her to boarding school; she chose Belstead School, at Aldeburgh in Suffolk. Elspeth described her time there:

After the freedom of Africa, and the haphazard attitude towards lessons at Thika, any English school would have seemed a prison at the best of times; in wartime, with increasing shortages of everything, especially the sources of warmth, to be deposited on the coast of East Anglia was like hell itself. Winters cannot have lasted all the year round, although in retrospect they seem to have; my chief memories are of cold, chilblains and at times hunger, since rationing in that war was sketchy, and the school's housekeeping inefficient. I remember, in desperation, eating my toothpaste; the flavour was nice but the actual paste not at all sustaining; I have sometimes wondered since, without ever finding out, what toothpaste is made of.

There were, of course, lighter moments. These included watching a Zeppelin crash in flames near Felixstowe; no doubt the crew were burnt to death but it did not occur to any of us to feel distressed about this, since they were German. A day or two later we were taken to see the wreckage, and picked up little bits of Zeppelin as mementoes. Several of us had these made into brooches. Gruesome as this may seem now, it was, like Nellie's blood-sports, quite in order at the time. Otherwise the war did not impinge upon us directly, but somehow it was always there. Mines were washed up on the windswept shingle beach where we were made, reluctantly, to go for walks, or even more reluctantly to bathe in an icy North Sea during the summer term. Among the dunes were disused, sandbagged trenches which we could briefly explore, peopling them with khaki soldiers in tin hats and puttees waiting to go to their deaths over the top.

Men in the blue uniforms and red ties of the wounded were seen in the street of the little town along which we marched on Sundays to the grey church. Brothers would come sometimes to see their sisters, clad in their clean and tidy uniforms, neatly pressed, with polished buttons and Sam Browne belts. There were uneasy moments when a pupil would vanish for a few days looking pale and weepy, and we knew that the name of her brother, or possibly father, had been added to the casualty lists. In due course the girl resumed her place and there were no comments; a stone had been dropped into a pool, the ripples died away and all was as before; but somehow, without consciously thinking about it, we knew another stone lay, its journey over, at the bottom of the pool.[11]

Elspeth had grasped the indifference of war, the bullet's ability to kill the poet and the ploughboy alike. In war nothing is permanent, nothing lasts.

During the school holidays she was sent to stay with Aunt Blanche, Nellie's sister, on her farm Cherry Orchard, near Shaftesbury. There she had three girl cousins to amuse her, two older and one younger than herself. It was not a happy household, for Aunt Blanche was subject to fits of depression, which could strike at any time and last for days. Elspeth and her cousins would time Blanche's depressions: the record was a day short of three weeks. They tried to ignore them, 'but it was like trying to ignore a bad smell in the room, even a corpse'.[12] A farmhouse full of snappy fox terriers, the smell of boiling tripe and a gloomy Aunt Blanche could not have been an ideal place for a young girl, but many years later Elspeth transformed the experience into one of her wittiest books, *Love Among the Daughters* (1968), in which Blanche became Aunt Madge and Cherry Orchard Nathan's Orchard. She described the return of Aunt Madge from an evening walk: there would be dogs yapping and jumping with muddy feet on to sofas covered by blankets harbouring fleas which were not supposed to bite human beings, and Aunt Madge claiming that it was all clean dirt.

When the war eventually came to an end in August 1918, Nellie and Jos, now reunited (there was at this stage no question of them separating), wanted to return to BEA and Kitimuru. It was impossible to obtain passages immediately, so Jos occupied his time on the waiting list by taking a senior officers' course at Aldershot, while Nellie enrolled in a one-year course in agriculture for ex-servicemen and women in Cambridge. Nellie, Jos and Elspeth spent the Christmas of 1918 in Brighton with the paralysed Robin and his wife Vera.

Nellie devoted the entire visit to telephoning the War Office and trying to get a passage for Jos; finally she succeeded.

Nellie finished her course in Cambridge and Elspeth returned to school in Aldeburgh, where she found the going very hard. She had the colonial child's characteristic ignorance of British topography: 'Half the time I had no idea what people were talking about, and what the place names signified. I had to feel my way like someone traversing a minefield. It was all right with big centres like Manchester, Liverpool and Glasgow, made familiar by schoolroom maps . . . but when people talked of Wincanton, Barnstaple and Saxmundham, I did not know if these were neighbouring villages or Scottish castles or important towns; and whether you could get there on a bicycle or needed two days in a train.'[13]

The only way Nellie could return to BEA when she finished her course was by boarding a ship to South Africa. Before she left she had, with infinite trouble and largely due to the help of the Master of Gonville and Caius College in Cambridge, put her name down for a soldier-settler scheme allocating land to ex-servicemen in BEA, and had drawn a plot on the lower slopes of Mount Kenya at the extreme edge of the White Highlands near Meru. It was this scheme, and a similar one after the Second World War, that was instrumental in encouraging white settlers to believe that the British government intended BEA (renamed Kenya in 1920) to be a British colony in which it was safe to invest.

Having received a last-minute cable from Jos – 'Please bring me shaving brush and windmill' – and carrying fifty pounds of flax seed, which she later sold at a profit, Nellie embarked alone on a tiny, overcrowded vessel, with the comparative luxury of at least a cabin of her own. It was a dreary voyage, twenty-eight days non-stop to Cape Town, enlivened only by the growing fury of a Mr Onions and a Mr Pickles, obliged to stand next to each other in the daily boat drill, organised alphabetically. The ship stayed in Cape Town only half a day, then proceeded on its storm-tossed way to Durban. That was as far as the passengers could go, and those bound for BEA stayed in hotels until a boat to Mombasa should happen along. 'The bosomy Afrikander [sic] ladies perpetually eating ice creams seemed to get ever fatter,' said Nellie, 'the rickshaw pullers, befeathered Zulus, ever more bogus.'[14] After a week a ship bound for Mombasa arrived, and Nellie was back at Kitimuru early in December 1919.

She was pleasantly surprised by what she found. Jos's letters had described 'woe, frustration, near bankruptcy', but Sammy, the Maasai headman, had been loyal and reliable while they were away: 'If it hadn't been for Sammy I don't think we'd have had *anything* left on our return. He was a great servant, marvellous at working labour.'[15] Alan Cuninghame, who had been left in charge, had not been very practical or energetic. The coffee crop was full of weeds, but redeemable. The problem was finding labour to do the work. The Kikuyu people had had a high casualty rate in the war, forced as members of the Carrier Corps to supply the troops further and further afield as they chased the German General Von Lettow Vorbeck southwards through Tanganyika into Nyasaland. It is said that one-tenth of the Kikuyu perished in the war. Immediately afterwards their numbers were further reduced when Spanish influenza hit BEA and the 1918 rains failed, causing famine. The Kikuyu that were left seemed reluctant to work for wages. They soon found, however, that this unwillingness prevented them from paying the hut tax, one of the ways by which the government raised revenue.

Before the First World War provincial administrators had been given contradictory instructions about encouraging native labour for white farmers, especially through the medium of African chiefs appointed by the government. In 1919 the new Governor, Sir Edward Northey, issued a circular asking officials, including chiefs and headmen, to help in producing labour. He did not mention compulsion, but in effect compulsion would be employed. Missionaries in Kenya complained, and there was a debate in Parliament. Winston Churchill, Secretary of State for the Colonies, sent a letter to Northey stating that officials, beyond giving Africans information about where labour was required, were 'to take no part in recruiting labour for private employment'. BEA officials, pressurised on all sides by settlers angry about this restriction, found themselves in a quandary. The Grants and their neighbours were used to a system of indenting the District Commissioner of Fort Hall for labour and being immediately supplied it through the medium of local chiefs, who had a variety of ways of getting their young men to work for whites, and who often enriched themselves in the process. Heeding Churchill's instruction, the new DC, A. Feild Jones, refused to entertain their request. This drove Jos and his fellow farmers to complain to the Governor, and to try to bring the Provincial Commissioner at Nyeri into disrepute with the Secretary of State for the Colonies.

At this point the Grants faced another crisis: Elspeth was expelled from Belstead School for running a betting syndicate on horses, and was banished to the school sanatorium to await a passage to BEA. Nellie hastily asked the headmistress to find a governess to accompany her daughter to Africa and teach her at Kitimuru. A Miss Holt was engaged, and in 1920 the pair arrived in Thika (as Chania Bridge was renamed that year), the governess's baggage, according to Nellie, consisting mostly of six pairs of double sheets. The headmistress's choice was catastrophic. Miss Holt was prone to wander around the houses of the bachelor neighbours at night, which terrified them. To alleviate the stress Nellie arranged to share her with Leo Lawford's family – on alternate weeks Miss Holt would go to the Lawfords to teach their daughter Marjorie. This arrangement lasted precisely two weeks. The Lawfords could not endure Miss Holt, who insisted on joining Leo at his breakfast at 5.30 a.m., clad in a nightdress with greasy locks streaming. The end came when Jos caught the governess reading a pornographic novel to her charge. A first-class fare was grubbed together and she was bundled back to England by ship, her double sheets unused. Aspects of Miss Holt would surface as Miss Cooper, who 'tramped through life with heavy boots and no humour' in Elspeth's book *The Mottled Lizard* (p.200).

What was to be done about the thirteen-year-old Elspeth's education? Nellie and Jos decided to teach her themselves, enlisting Hugo Lambert on the next-door farm to instruct her in mathematics and Latin. Lambert's lessons were more concerned with discussing details of the 1920 equivalent of the football pools, and Jos was too gentle a teacher to instil any French into his daughter. Nellie was the only one who took Elspeth in hand. Her own education had been at the hands of governesses, except for two and a half years at Cheltenham Ladies' College, which she left with excellent results.* She could easily have entered one of the women's colleges at Oxford or Cambridge, and indeed wanted to, but her parents insisted she return home to 'come out' in the next London season. As an exceptionally clever woman, Nellie did a splendid job of teaching Elspeth, despite her lament that 'education and farming and social life all got muddled up together for the next four years'.[16]

A room in Kitimuru's original grass house was used as a schoolroom, specific hours were set aside for schoolwork and any books to hand were employed as teaching materials. The Grants had J.C. Stobart's *The Glory that was Greece* and, from 1922, H.G. Wells's *A Short History of the World*, and Nellie also shared with Elspeth her own current enthusiasms. She was a wide reader herself, when she could acquire books in that remote part of the world, and relatives helped by sending packages of novels, or manuals of instruction for her new notions. Nellie made learning fun, and encouraged the development of a mind as enquiring as her own. Elspeth liked writing historical plays and drawing maps of imaginary countries best. She co-operated in needlework lessons, provided her mother let her cut the thread with the enormous scissors used to trim the ponies' tails. 'It was a strange time,' said Elspeth, 'looking back, with the war over, and people who hadn't expected to live finding themselves alive and with the world their oyster, in the extraordinary surroundings of a Kenya which was still wild and full of animals and uncertainty and beauty and the unexpected just around the corner, or actually there.'[17] In later years she said: 'I don't think I was repressed in childhood, but I had a dynamic, witty and laughter-loving mother who sparkled in company, with the unintended result that I knew myself to be by contrast a boring grub instead of a resplendent dragon-fly. Perhaps I still am, but whereas in my youth

---

* She took the Oxford Delegacy of Local Examinations exam, coming fifty-fourth in the country, and first in English History, third in Shakespeare, ninth in French, thirteenth in German, nineteenth in English, and obtaining a distinction in harmony for Music.

I minded terribly, now I don't mind at all.'[18] Her own view of herself may have been unnecessarily harsh: Charles Taylor, who knew her well at the time, regarded her as self-sufficient and fun to be with.

The war had changed BEA, which suffered much in the conflict. Because the country was allowed but a small shipping quota, the export of flax, a crop which showed great potential, had been curtailed. BEA's other products, such as sisal and wool, were also adversely affected. But the most serious blow had fallen in 1917 when Britain listed coffee as a luxury inessential in time of war, and prohibited its import.

After the war, as if to mark that things were now different, London changed the name of BEA to Kenya. On 11 June 1920 an order-in-council was signed upgrading the territory to a colony, meaning that it could now raise sorely-needed funds under the Colonial Stock Act. There has been much debate about the origin of the name Kenya, which formerly applied only to a mountain and the administrative region around it. The colonists had called the white-peaked mountain Kenya because that was the name given it by the Wakamba, in whose language the word 'kegnia' signified the white plume in the tail of a male ostrich. The Kikuyu call it 'Kirinyaga' (literally, 'it is glorious'), and it is also possible that 'Kenya' is a corruption of this. Sir Halford Mackinder, the first person to climb the mountain, in 1899, thought 'Kenya' was a corruption of the Maasai name for 'mists'. The colonists pronounced Kenya with a short 'e', but this pronunciation upset the Royal Geographical Society, and a circular was issued forbidding members of the administration from calling it aught but 'Keenya', with a long 'e'. So it remained until independence in 1963, whereupon the Africans reverted to the short 'e'.

Kenya's settlers interpreted the change to colony status as an invitation to advance themselves further politically. In 1907, in response to demands from the increasing number of white settlers, who had formed a Colonists' Association to promote their interests, a BEA Legislative Council had been created, with a majority of officials and a minority of nominated settlers. The power of the white settler community was enhanced by the presence among them of many members of noble families, such as Lord Delamere, Lord Francis Scott and the brothers Galbraith and Berkeley Cole, sons of the Earl of Enniskillen. These people did not hesitate to wield their influence with friends and families in Britain to press their point of view. Lord Delamere encouraged the scattered white farmers who had formed various district associations to join together in a Convention of Associations in 1911. This body behaved as an unelected legislature, debating bills brought before the Legislative Council.

In 1919 white settlers obtained the right to be elected to the Legislative Council in eleven single-member constituencies, with white adult franchise on a residential qualification, and settler opinion became even more influential (it is interesting that women got the vote in BEA earlier than they did in the mother country). By the time Kenya became a colony in 1920, therefore, the white settlers had already achieved both the right to elective representation on the Legislative Council (though it still contained a majority of officials) and admission to the Executive Council. No other racial group had these privileges – the Indians had two nominated representatives only, and the Africans no representation at all. This discrimination caused great agitation among the Indians, who were mainly clerks, mechanics, shop assistants, small traders and labourers, though they also included professionals and merchants of high standing. They immediately claimed equal rights with the whites, and a common franchise. The Colonial Office drafted a set of proposals which would give the Indians substantial concessions, including a common electoral roll, with property and educational qualifications. The whites protested vigorously, fearing they were in danger of being overwhelmed by Indians, whom they also considered a bad influence on the Africans. Indians vastly outnumbered whites (in 1921 there were 9,600 whites but over 23,000 Indians), and theoretically might control policy if given the vote. Eventually the British government organised a compromise – five Indian members were to be elected to the Legislative Council on a communal roll, while Europeans kept their eleven elected members – and matters settled down for a while, although some whites wanted to press for self-government.

The other burning question of the day was the revaluation of the rupee, an Indian currency adopted by BEA in its early days. It was a legacy of the past, when the east African coast had close trading links with India. Rupees had then been valued at one shilling and fourpence in English money, but recently their value had risen to two shillings and fourpence. The Governor of Kenya, Sir Edward Northey, demanded that the old value of the rupee be restored. This was fiercely opposed by the banking interest and those on fixed salaries, such as government officials. A new rupee (known as a florin) was introduced in February 1920, its value fixed at two shillings. The appearance of the florin raised farmers' overdrafts by 50 per cent overnight. People who had gone to bed owing the bank £2,000 woke up owing £3,000. It was a crippling burden for the Grants and their neighbours, plunging them into a spiral of debt. The settlers had to reduce costs or fail, so they lowered the wages of African labour by 33 per cent.

It was problems such as these which persuaded Jos Grant to enter politics, and in 1921 he stood as a candidate for the Legislative Council for Ukamba province. His manifesto began by stating that the enhanced value of the rupee, the difficulty of communications and the shortage of labour had brought the country to a critical stage. In his opinion it had been allowed to drift into a state which would bring about the ruin of a large proportion of the settlers if nothing was done. Hurrying over the currency question, which he considered a matter for experts, he considered the labour problem in language which would be condemned today but at that time was typical:

> The native . . . no longer obliged to fight to preserve himself from annihilation, or capture and slavery, is already losing what qualities of courage and endurance that he may have possessed, while disease is taking a heavy toll from a race relapsing into sloth and vice.[19]

He suggested a Labour Bureau be established immediately to compel all adult, able-bodied Africans to work for whites for six months of the year. Furthermore, the mission schools should provide Africans with technical education rather than give refuge to those who wished to avoid work. As for the Indian question, he wanted all Indian staff on the railways replaced by whites. While admitting that Indian traders were of great value, 'an unrestricted influx of low-class Indians . . . who corrupt the native and spread disease, is to be deprecated by all'.[20]

To his grievous disappointment, Jos was informed that because of his absence during the war he was five days short of the two years' residence required for Legislative Council candidates, and Sir Northrup McMillan won the seat.* However, McMillan left Kenya for a visit to the USA and invited Jos to stand in for him, offering him his luxurious American car while he was away. Jos agreed and served on the committee established to investigate Kenya's currency, at which it was proposed that rupees be changed to shillings and cents. This was a matter about which the fourteen-year-old Elspeth was much concerned in a letter to her Uncle Robin, the earliest surviving example of her writing: 'There is a tremendous comotion [sic] about the currency question . . . My illustrious Pa was asked to serve on the Committee, and as it was going on in Race-week [which required residence in Nairobi], of course he accepted.'[21] She enclosed a caricature of her father sitting on the rupee, with a poem about the currency question on the back. A fortnight later Elspeth reported to Robin that Jos had taken over the secretaryship of the Thika District Association, into which he was putting a lot of heavy work with the typewriter. She too had been conscripted: 'I am hired by the TDA,' she said proudly, 'when there are lots of circulars etc

---

* Sir William Northrup McMillan, a wealthy American of Canadian parentage, lived at Juja farm on Ol Donyo Sabuk mountain, near Thika. Of considerable girth (he weighed about twenty-two stone), he lived in Kenya until his death in 1925. He and his wife were great benefactors, one of their gifts being the McMillan Library in Nairobi. He received a British knighthood in 1918. He wished to be buried at the top of Ol Donyo Sabuk, but such was the strain on his pallbearers that they failed to attain the summit and buried him as far up as they could go.

at the rate of 25 cents (6d) an hour! Daddy is rapidly becoming a Kenya celebraty [sic].'[22]

Following his work on the Currency Committee, Jos was appointed to sit on a commission to inquire into the conditions of labour. In 1920 two changes had been introduced – it was decreed that all adult African males had to carry a kipande, a fingerprinted card used by employers to sign people on and off work; at the same time there was a doubling of the hut- and poll-tax the Africans had to pay. These measures caused Africans to begin to stir politically, encouraged by the Indians, who hoped for a strong united front against the whites. Lord Delamere, leader of the unofficial members of the Legislative Council, went to London to see Winston Churchill, the Colonial Secretary, but the British government rejected his demands for the segregation of Indians in townships and for restrictions on Indian immigration, although the practice of reserving land in the highland areas for Europeans was maintained.

Elspeth found it 'most thrilling' that Jos travelled round the country in 'a rich Ford' in execution of his duties. She reported that the commission was trying to get every white man in the country to reduce African wages: 'The Polatics [sic] are *most* involved and quite above me . . . Daddy is a leading light.'[23] During 1921 Jos regularly attended the Legislative Council. Elspeth reported that he made only a few speeches, for 'he spends most of his time making up poems. He belongs to the "Reform Party", the East African "Anti-Waste League", and spends all his time cutting down the Officials' salaries.'[24] In fact, Jos was far too mild a man to be an effective politician, and after McMillan returned we hear no more of his political ambitions.

Elspeth's introduction to politics had moments of high drama, which must have put into the shade the tamer politics she experienced in England in later years. There was a meeting at Thika on 2 February 1923, at which the white farmers took an oath in a secret session to rebel against the British government if it acceded to Indian demands. This was followed by a requisitioning of arms and the listing of individual abilities. The pattern was repeated throughout the country. After the British government retreated matters settled down for a while, although some whites wanted to press for self-government.

Meanwhile, Jos was forced to concentrate on his coffee farm, for the Grant finances were deteriorating. The whole family went to inspect the land on Mount Kenya which Nellie had drawn in the soldier-settler scheme, but it proved to be useless – it was on the Maraina river, in high, bleak country, suitable only for sheep. Nellie devised another scheme to make ends meet. The local medical committee, of which she was a member, had imported a doctor to Thika so people would not have to go to Nairobi for medical treatment. When he arrived, nothing was ready, and he threatened to leave. Nellie offered to rent their stone house as a nursing home until the doctor's premises were built. The family would return to the grass home they had originally occupied. This money-spinning idea was rejected by the locals, to Elspeth's delight. She recoiled from the thought of hearing 'the chuckles of surgeons and screams of patients', and reckoned it would be 'perfectly beastly living in three small rooms with a tin bath etc. after this topping house. Especially as the roof leaks hopelessly.'[25]

A far from reluctant correspondent, Elspeth reported despondently to her relatives in England that something went wrong nearly every day with the new coffee-drying machinery her parents had installed. The belt came off, the shafting twisted, the huller collapsed, and the coffee came out as a solid, black, burnt cake rather than cleaned beans. Then the engine's bearings seized and the ignition valve collapsed. Jos and Nellie took it in turns to stay with the machine day and night to nurse it along. The colossal wage and paraffin bill during coffee-picking left them with less cash than ever. By the end of 1922 their overdraft stood at £10,000, despite the farm producing twenty-seven tons of coffee that year. The price it fetched in London was £101 a ton, too little to be of great assistance. To add to their misery, bushfires drove rats into the house, there was the worst epidemic of horse sickness since 1910, and in 1922 Thika suffered a severe outbreak of plague. The Grants were not alone in their financial predicament – at that time few white farmers in

Kenya could make ends meet, presenting a problem to the Governor who had to balance his budget despite the absence as yet of income tax.

It was a lonely life for a teenager on the farm, and Elspeth busied herself with conjuring tricks. Her father had bought her a set of tricks in 1920, and for Christmas 1921 her Aunt Vera sent her a further supply. Thanking her, Elspeth said, 'I am preparing a sort of repetoire [sic] with patter, but of course one dosen't [sic] really have much chance of performing out here.'[26] She subscribed to the *Magicians' Monthly*, and began to invent tricks – 'it amuses me awfully, thinking tricks out'.[27] With an eye to earning money she asked Aunt Vera in London to take her ideas to the magic shop Coldstone's and to Gamage's toy shop. Vera did as she was bid, but both establishments turned down the tricks. Elspeth also became a bridesmaid for the first time, at the marriage at Makuyu church on 18 June 1923 of Roger Money, a coffee farmer, to Charlotte (Carlo) Plowden.

Spirits were raised by a Christmas party at Makuyu given by Mervyn Ridley. Mud huts were specially constructed for his numerous guests. Everyone ate communally and indulged in motley sports. Unfortunately it rained all the time, giving rise to Jos's remark on waking after a heavy night of drinking, 'The only dry thing in the camp is my mouth.' Before the war crème de menthe had been the settlers' tipple, but the Grants and their friends had not over-indulged in alcohol. After the war Nellie confessed they all became 'very alcoholic'. She found a new friend at the Makuyu Christmas party – the ebulliently witty Jacqueline ('Cockie') Birkbeck. The sister of Ulick Alexander, the Prince of Wales's equerry in the royal household, she had married Ben Birkbeck and come to Kenya on the soldier-settler scheme. Her schoolgirl complexion, girlish face, appealing brown eyes and air of innocence misled the listener into believing her wildest stories. She and Nellie, being much alike in vivacity and sense of humour, soon homed in on each other. Cockie was a great gambler at cards, and played with Nellie into the small hours, singing a refrain throughout the evening: 'You don't know Nellie as I do, Said the naughty little bird in Nellie's hat.' A chaplain, present at the party, perhaps wisely prevailed on the guests to attend church during breaks in the amusements.

To give Elspeth a change, Nellie arranged for her to spend three weeks in August–September 1922 with friends at Nyeri, where she spent a night perched in a tree waiting for lions. The lions watched from afar while the marksmen made preparations, then walked off disdainfully. This was disappointing for the bloodthirsty Elspeth, anxious to bag her first lion. She was at the height of her shooting period – it was not until later that she developed her passionate sympathy for animals and condemnation of big-game hunting. She had a .22 rifle with which she shot reedbuck and doves around the farm until her parents gave her a 16-bore double-barrelled shotgun. On one occasion the Grants' cook made a pie with eight doves Elspeth had shot.

The question of her education was still pressing. In despair, Nellie wrote to Vera: 'Perhaps my views wouldn't be so jaundiced if her damned arithmetic book had answers, and if she could put two words of French together, which she can't.'[28] Apparently there had been several crises, almost entirely over French:

> She is better at some things than I am, and much worse at others, so she gets smacked indiscriminately in either case. But French is too awful. She appears still to wish to go to Newnham [a women's college at Cambridge University] in 1925. I have written to Blanchie Holford [Nellie's sister], and asked her to interview the school dame at Sherborne School, and to let me know the figures, and also if they could, or would, take Elspeth next Summer term. By the time we get her answer we shall know if we can scrape enough for Elspeth's passage home, and also afford to pay her schooling. Neither is likely to be the case.

Asking Vera to have Elspeth for one or two holidays, Nellie told her that her daughter was sixteen, which was not as bad as six, appreciated all their jokes, disappeared by the hour to her own jobs, and was not inclined to argue. Nellie's suggestion prompted relatives in Britain to discuss the matter. Uncle Eddie, Jos's half-brother by his father's second wife, nobly volunteered to help with Elspeth's education, but at this stage Nellie felt she could not accept the offer.

The lemon trees planted at Kitimuru before the war had to be pulled out when a promised citrus-juice factory failed to come to Nairobi, and Nellie had sold the essential oils still when Jos went off to war. In dire financial straits, and in complete contrast to her pre-war optimism, Nellie was actively thinking of selling Kitimuru to a friend of Uncle Eddie's, Sir Charles Markham,* who was in Nairobi trying to arrange a safari, and who wanted land in Kenya. Nellie was not impressed with Markham, whom she decided was 'a hopeless cub', too busy abusing the country and calling the settlers 'a disloyal set of swine'.[29] What Markham was referring to was a plan concocted by the more hot-headed of the white settlers to take control of the railway and telegraphic communications and to kidnap Kenya's Governor and senior officials, keeping them in a remote farm until the colonists' political demands were met. Nellie was worried – 'everyone is so busy doing the Die-Hard act over the horrid Hindi question that it is difficult to make any plans'.[30]

Nellie had lost interest in Kitimuru, and wanted to leave Thika and abandon loss-making coffee farming. The opportunity to do so soon arose, during a visit to Lord Francis Scott's house, Deloraine, built at Rongai on the top of the western wall of the Rift Valley when the Scotts went to BEA at the end of the First World War. Lord Francis, the sixth son of the sixth Duke of Buccleuch, and his wife had stayed at Kitimuru in December 1921, when as visiting polo players competing for the McMillan Cup being staged at Makuyu they had been billeted on the Grants. Despite her own aristocratic ancestry, Elspeth poked fun at the visitors. She told her aunt in England that they arrived in the Governor's Cadillac, spent most of their time in bed, brought a brace of maids who even pulled out the plug of their bath, and Lady Scott's sister Lady

---

* The brother of Mansfield Markham, the husband of Beryl Clutterbuck.

Cromer thought the sound of the African employees spitting under her bedroom window was so much nicer than the Cockney voices she heard at home. In July 1922 Nellie paid the Scotts a return visit, and found Deloraine 'a comfy, delicious spot'. Eileen Scott, Lord Francis's wife, had many affectations – one day her daughter Pam told Nellie that every night she prayed, 'Please God don't make me a lady, make me like Mrs Grant.'

At the foot of Londiani hill, Deloraine was, unusually for Kenya, a two-storeyed house with sizeable rooms, each with a large fireplace, polished wooden floors, and furniture of black and gold. Round the walls books were shelved, each room having a different theme, like Africana, or history, or light novels. The house was set in acokanthera and olive forest, dark and silent, where orchids grew. Its enormous garden was filled with flowers – oleander, frangipani, yellow iris, geraniums – and blue salvia carpeted the terraces. Lord Francis had been aide-de-camp to the Viceroy of India, the Earl of Minto, and had married Minto's daughter Eileen. He was the Legislative Council member for the Rift Valley and after Lord Delamere's death became leader of the white elected members of the Legislative Council from 1931 to 1948. In the First World War a shot through the sciatic nerve left him with no feeling in one leg, which was amputated in 1935. An irascible and outspoken man, he was impatient and often intolerant, and wanted Africans to abandon their own culture and become as Europeans. He died in 1952, thus avoiding the African rebellion which would have appalled him.

Nellie loved the area near Deloraine. She and Jos had been drifting apart for some years, and their relationship was put under further strain by the war and post-war austerity. Contemptuous of her husband's inefficiency, Nellie reckoned it would be better to strike out on her own, running a farm in the way she thought best and not having to consider Jos. At Njoro, near Deloraine, the farmers Trevor Sheen and Algy Cartwright took advantage of her interest and devised a plan to offer her 1,002 acres Cartwright owned nearby. Sheen, always the ebullient Irishman, told her: 'You can't describe yourself as broke unless you can't pay the interest of your fourth mortgage.' He had previously been the 'strong man' in a circus, lifting cardboard weights, and had arrived in BEA in 1896 with £5 and some opium seeds, enough to buy a camel and run a small caravan trade into Uganda for the railway. Algy Cartwright was an unpleasant man who was later convicted of stealing stamps. The magistrate remarked that the accused had had to put gum on them, whereupon Algy said Kenyan stamps were of such poor quality that you had to put gum on them anyway. He showed Nellie over the land, which possessed a small house built to conform with government regulations. 'How I did fall for this farm after the dreariness of Thika!' said Nellie, much preferring it to the area round Kitimuru, with its depressing planters' atmosphere.[31] She wrote to her old friend Trudie Denman, encouraging her to invest some money in the land, which was going for a song at £5 per acre. Trudie immediately bought a thousand acres and gave it to Nellie. It was a magnificent gift. For the moment, however, Nellie had to return to Thika to continue teaching Elspeth, who cannot have been unaware of the tension between her parents.

The following year, in March 1923, Nellie took her husband and daughter to see her new land at Njoro. They rode from Thika across the Aberdare mountains to stay with the Scotts at Rongai. Mounted on the pony Mzee, Elspeth was in acute discomfort all the way from boils on her behind. On the first night they camped at the edge of the Kinangop forest. The following day they had difficulty avoiding a herd of elephants, then rode through the bamboo, crackling like rifle shots beneath the ponies' feet, higher up the Aberdares until they crossed the ridge at nine thousand feet and came upon Njabini on the Kinangop plateau on the Rift Valley's eastern wall, the farm of Ernest ('Skipper') Fey,* an ex-sea captain who had arrived in 1906 and could not refuse them a roof. In the morning they descended two thousand feet into the valley, spending the night in the hotel at Naivasha beside the papyrus-fringed lake ('very primitive', said Nellie).

They then proceeded to Soysambu, Lord Delamere's farm on the

---

* The Feys became the Duncans in *The Mottled Lizard*, where their nautical house is described on pp.214–15.

Rift Valley floor, where they were put up by his manager Bobby Roberts, who was later killed trying to rescue a woman from a grass fire.* After a night there they rode past scores of wild animals up the Mau escarpment above Nakuru to Trevor Sheen's farm. Such rides gave Elspeth a true perspective of the vastness of Africa, and she was entranced: 'Like Nellie, I loved Njoro from the first. There was a freshness in the air, an exhilarating sparkle in the sunlight. To wake each morning to regard that great, spreading view across the Rift, with the turquoise gleam of Lake Nakuru far below . . .'[32] Trevor Sheen, the coiner of the description of Njoro as 'days of toil and nights of gladness', displayed the hospitality learned from the Africans that was such a feature of early Kenya – you merely turned up and were given meals and a bed – and put the Grants up before they returned to Thika for the resumption of Elspeth's lessons.

Elspeth was very conscious of her parents' marital strains and the family's worsening financial straits. Clothes were not a problem because Aunt Vera gave her frocks for Christmas and Trudie Denman sent her daughter Judy's hand-me-downs, which came in 'very useful to the poor and humble who have too large an overdraft to afford decent clothes or be proud!'[33] But Elspeth needed money for her magic tricks and photography – after she won a Panaram camera at a gymkhana her parents gave her an enlarger for Christmas, and for many years she developed and printed her own photos.

Elspeth decided she must earn some money. She knew Kenya's Governor, Sir Edward Northey,** and his wife, a genial South African who lacked the pomposity of many governors' wives, fairly well, because they had a daughter of about her age who invited her to stay in Government House, then a small two-storeyed villa in stockbroker mock-Tudor. Northey had a zoo in the garden and the

---

* The story of the fire appears, with many embellishments, in *The Mottled Lizard*, pp.316–17. See also below, p.160.
** In *The Mottled Lizard* (p.92) Elspeth describes Northey as 'a small, dapper, fierce and monocled General who, in the war, had taken a leading part in the local campaign. His fierceness was a shell; he was a man of kindness and goodwill, anxious to do his full duty but handicapped by a lack of experience in politics and bureaucracy.'

two girls used to ride about on zebras. Diners at Government House maintained a stoical silence as cheetahs beneath the table tore their trousers and stockings. The zoo animals attracted lions at night, and when one was found in the Chief Secretary's sitting room it was felt things had gone too far and the zoo was terminated.

The president and secretary of the Makuyu Hunt thought the Governor's participation in one of their chases ought to be noted by the local paper, and requested Nellie to write about it. Too busy, she casually asked Elspeth to do it for her, intending to correct the copy and send it in. Elspeth's effort was so competent that all Nellie did was amend the spelling before it was despatched, under the name 'Bamboo', to the *East African Standard*. The editor approved Elspeth's piece, and she was thrilled to see her first work in print on 10 December 1921. She described collecting the newspaper from the Thika post office and seeing her own words on the page: 'The world changed immediately; the sun was generous but not unkind, the flies bearable, the postmaster's numerous children squatting on the bare wooden steps of his tin bungalow appealing rather than squalid, the black clouds that had gathered over the Aberdares magnificent and awe-inspiring rather than an indication that I should get soaked on the way home.'[34] She told Aunt Vera: '. . . The budding genius, me. My career is decided. I shall undoubtedly become a reporter.'[35]

And become a reporter she did. When Elspeth saw there was no newspaper presence at the McMillan Polo Cup competition at Makuyu in January 1922, she wrote a description of the activities and sent it in under the same pseudonym. Again it was accepted. She suggested to the paper's editor that he take further polo and hunting reports, and he agreed. Over the next two years her articles appeared in the *East African Standard*, the *Kenya Observer* and the *Kenya Sunday Times and Sporting News*. When there was no polo to describe she wrote articles based on information gleaned from *Polo Monthly*, to which she hoped no readers subscribed, until her editor told her to confine herself to reporting matches. She advised her readers how to build a riding school, told them that 'there is no finer game in the world [than polo] from the spectators' point of view', and indulged in some moralising – 'Is not a man who plays for the sake of the game in puttees, because he cannot afford boots, of more value than the man who plays to show off his breeches and shining boots to admiring ladies to the music of the band?'[36] She even broke into verse, though it was probably copied from *Polo Monthly*, when providing hints for the budding polo-player:

> If you follow these suggestions you will soon improve
>   your game
> And you'll find the doorway open to proficiency
>   and fame.[37]

She also provided photographs, quibbling with the editor over the fee. She received ten shillings per article (she misremembers and says five shillings in *The Mottled Lizard*) and fifteen shillings for three photos.

Elspeth had ambitions to break into journalism beyond East Africa. In a book into which she glued her printed articles and noted beneath them her payments, there are three articles from the English magazine *The Field*, signed 'L.S.' but written by her. The first, in the issue of 1 April 1922, entitled 'Hunting in Kenya', informed readers that the hunting months in Kenya were November, December, part of March and April, May and part of June, when the rains had recently ceased but the ground was not yet too dry. The quarry was jackal or small buck, such as steinbuck and duiker. The second article told the reader that polo in Kenya had gone ahead with remarkable rapidity since the war, on mounts which were farm hacks during the week. *The Field* printed a third article, with Elspeth's photographs, on 12 April 1923. She teased the readers of the *Kenya Sunday Times and Sporting News* on 5 November 1922 by drawing their attention to the second piece in *The Field* and saying it would be interesting to know the identity of its author.

Journalism was excellent writing practice, and when in 1923 Elspeth entered a competition run by the Council of the Royal Colonial Institute in London for the best essay by a pupil in schools of the British Empire, she won the Class A prize. The subject was

'Improved Communications as a Factor of Imperial History', and the *East African Standard*, which printed Elspeth's entry, commented on its 'surprising maturity of judgement and felicity of language'. In her essay Elspeth wrote: 'The future history of the Empire depends largely on the strengthening of the ties of inter-Imperial affection, since the British Empire is held together not by the sword, but by the intangible bond of sentiment. Improved communications greatly increase sympathy between homeland and dominions.'

In 1923 she branched out into the *East African Observer*, describing the early history of polo in England and including among her subjects society, weather and politics. She noted the splitting into two of the Thika District Association, described a wedding at Makuyu (at which she was bridesmaid), gave instructions on the training of ponies – including points to remember when buying them – and commented on cricket and rugby. This must have required a considerable amount of work, since the articles appeared weekly or even more frequently, and few could have suspected that these highly competent compositions were not written by an adult. The almost exclusive company of adults and the absence of teenage companions had given Elspeth a maturity beyond her years.

For Elspeth's sixteenth birthday in July 1923 she was treated to a safari down the Tana river with her mother and Jock Heron-Maxwell, a white hunter. There is a particular power about the Kenyan safari that Elspeth experienced at the time and described later:

> To depart on a safari is not only a physical act, it is also a gesture. You leave behind the worries, the strains, the irritations of life among people under pressure, and enter the world of creatures who are pressed into no moulds, but have only to be themselves; bonds loosen, anxiety fades, the mind closes against the world you left behind like a folding sea anemone. Enjoyment of the moment, the true delight in living, in life as it is and not as others in the past have made it, all this returns.[38]

Two buffaloes were bagged, but no lions, despite the party sitting up all night in a machan with a kill tied below.

Jock Heron-Maxwell features as Alan Beattie, the safari leader with whom Elspeth falls in love, in her semi-autobiographical *The Mottled Lizard*. The adolescent yearning is treated with such tenderness and compassion in the book that it is likely that Elspeth was writing from memory and had actually been in love with Heron-Maxwell. In the book Beattie dies of blackwater fever and is consigned to a nameless grave in the bush just before Elspeth leaves Kenya, whereas in actuality Jock Heron-Maxwell's death was slightly different. He was intending to take a guest of the Ridley family out on safari, but sent a note saying he was ill and asking for help from the Ridleys. The note lay unopened on the mantelpiece for two days. Meanwhile Jock's malaria turned into the dreaded blackwater fever. He asked some Africans to carry him to the Ridleys' farm at Makuyu on a stretcher. But sufferers from blackwater fever frequently fail to survive if they are moved, and he died soon after he arrived. Feeling utter remorse, the Ridleys buried him beneath a large slab of grey marble under a tree in the cemetery at Fort Hall. The Alan Beattie of *The Mottled Lizard* also has many characteristics of the hunter Roy Leny, another friend of the Grants, who died in 1949 from gas gangrene caused by a buffalo gore.

Nellie now began to find that teaching her daughter was beyond her. Elspeth needed Latin if she were to realise her ambition to go to Cambridge, and this Nellie could not provide. Nellie also wanted to go to live on her Njoro farm, leaving Jos to sell Kitimuru as best he could. At the beginning of 1924 Elspeth was sent to Nairobi High School to acquire Latin and prepare herself for university. A co-educational school, it was housed on the Hill (the name by which the land that rose to the south-west of Nairobi township was known) in corrugated-iron huts condemned some time before as government offices for being too hot, stuffy and termite-eaten. There was only one other girl in the top class, and the teaching was spasmodic, with some of the teachers always on leave, and the headmaster courting the matron and often away. Because the boarding houses were unhygienic (or full, as she claims in *The Mottled Lizard*), Elspeth was lodged with a kind Boer couple, the Cloetes, who lived beside the polo ground near the school.

She spent the weekends at Thika with Jos after Nellie departed to Njoro. One weekend, after playing tennis at a friend's house at Ngong, she visited Karen Blixen, later the author of *Out of Africa*, a poetic distillation of her experiences at her coffee farm near the Ngong hills, twelve miles from Nairobi. Elspeth found her 'a fascinating, small, dark woman with a beaky nose and make-up all awry, full of magnetism and restless energy, like a benign witch'.[39] Nellie did not like Karen, whom she felt was a monumental snob with an obsessive hatred of the middle classes, and looked down on her fellow colonists. Karen had arrived from Denmark in 1913 to join her husband, Baron Bror von Blixen, a merry, happy-go-lucky man, and filled her house with lovely Scandinavian furniture and silver.

Kit Taylor, whose husband Charles was helping Karen with her coffee planting, described one of her elegant, candle-lit dinners in her dark cavern of a dining room. Karen illustrated how differently whites and Africans saw things by recounting what had happened to a friend driving along the road from Nairobi to Ngong. Her friend had come across an overturned lorry and several people lying injured in the road. She asked the driver where he had come from and how many had been in the lorry. He said, 'Arusha, and six people were in the lorry.' As there were only four people to be seen, the friend said they must push the lorry over to get at the others, and with much difficulty this was done. When no one was found beneath the vehicle, the friend was cross and said, 'But you said there were six people in the lorry.' 'There were,' said the driver, 'but two got off at Kajiado.'[40]

Denys Finch Hatton, Karen's lover, came into the dining room and sat at the table at which Karen was presiding with her huge dark eyes and white face. In a polite and somewhat bored fashion he talked about what he had seen on safari. Kit Taylor said it always surprised her when people talked of how many gazelles they had seen, because when she first lived in Nairobi it would have been like saying how many native goats were visible. At that remark Finch Hatton lost his air of boredom, smiled at Kit and began to talk to her. He told her of an orange baboon he had seen on the northern frontier, an albino which was treated as a king by the other baboons.

Karen hoped to marry Denys, but he was never one to commit himself to anything, and was believed to be in love with his sister-in-law. Beryl Markham liked to make out that he left Karen for her, but he was also attracted by Rose Cartwright and other women. He was rather a selfish man who dropped Karen when she became too possessive. After his death in a plane crash she immortalised him in *Out of Africa*.

Karen was defeated by the slump of the late 1920s and sold her six thousand acres for less than £1 an acre. She was later condemned by her husband's friends, including the Grants, for suggesting to a biographer, erroneously in their view, that she had acquired syphilis from her husband. Bror did not pass syphilis on to any other of his partners, including his subsequent wife Cockie (who divorced Ben Birkbeck). Elspeth and others thought she had either inherited the disease, from which her father suffered, or had caught it during student days in Paris or from her servant Farah. Elspeth maintained that Bror was very badly treated by Karen, who turned him off the farm with nowhere to go and not a penny. He had put all his own money into the farm and lost the lot. It was true, she conceded, that Bror was a hopeless manager, not a coffee farmer by nature, and very extravagant, but so was Karen. After Bror was excluded from his farm he made a living from the safari business. Never having shown any signs of syphilis, he died in a car accident in Sweden in 1946, in robust health.

So far Elspeth had had an unconventional upbringing, and a severely and regularly disrupted life. There were times when she was almost treated as a parcel, being passed from hand to hand. Yet she was able to imbibe the influence of a clever, funny and ambitious mother, as she herself would become. Nellie hated to be defeated – she invariably played polo and other games to win – and Elspeth was similarly tenacious and unsettled. She found it difficult to relax, always having to be at her work of writing or doing something else productive. Her childhood was dogged by her parents' money worries, which Nellie never kept a secret. This was the origin of Elspeth's later anxiety over money and her determination to continue writing until the week before she died. This apprehension was responsible for her extraordinary output of journalism and books – usually at least one of the latter every year. As she said to her friend Margery Perham many years later, she continued to write not because of poverty caused by 'drink or gambling, which you perhaps attribute to me, but because I can't stop needing the money. I wish to heaven I could, but have no pension or other sort of income and, as you know, it becomes increasingly difficult to live on a fixed income.'[41]

Elspeth had anything but a tranquil childhood, and was going through experiences that were for ever remarkable. She was becoming absorbed by the African people, who had adapted themselves so skilfully to life in a continent hostile to man. Unlike many an immigrant adult, having grown up among Africans she understood their ways of thought:

> I began to perceive that a third way lay beyond, inside and intermingled with the two worlds I already knew of, those of ourselves and of the Kikuyu: a world of snakes and rainbows, of ghosts and spirits, of monsters and charms, a world that had its own laws and for the most part led its own life, but now and again, like a rock jutting up through the earth and vegetation, protruded into ours, and was there all the time under the surface. It was a world in which I was a foreigner, but the Kikuyu were at home.[42]

After her wartime experiences in England she was also very aware of the magnetism of Kenya, and of the highlands in particular, the pull that was exerted by the magnificent climate and countryside, which remained for ever

> in the memory of those who have left it, flashing back on to the mind so vividly that the nostrils seem to sense the sweet smell of a vlei after the rains or the tingling of red dust from

untarred roads, the ear to catch the melancholy hoot of a rain-bird or the strangely moving rhythmic chant from the throats of distant Africans.

It is a land where the individual counts for more than in Europe because he is not elbowed out by his fellows; a place of opportunity and of disappointments, where years of work may be wrecked by sudden calamities and where fortunes are easier to lose than to make. Perhaps its attraction lies in the downs swept clean by wind, a depth of tone in the blues and purples of far-off hills not found in sunless northern countries where the air is denser than it is among mountains.

It is a country that always holds the unexpected in store, that rouses high hopes and seldom satisfies them, and yet charms the bitterness out of disappointment. Its scenes live partly in the challenge that it throws down – the challenge of all new countries – to master its resources: or perhaps it lies in the pleasantness of life in constant sunshine and on a fertile soil. Whatever the secret of this charm, it draws back to the country men and women who have left and inspires many of those who have adopted Kenya as their home with an almost passionate concern for its future.[43]

THREE

Njoro, Reading
and the United States

Elspeth felt the move from Thika to Njoro so acutely that the pain remained with her for years. She attempted to exorcise it by writing in *The Mottled Lizard*:

> I was heartbroken, and went round saying good-bye to every-thing almost every day, although . . . all the animals would come with us, as well as several of the Kikuyu, most of the furniture and all our personal belongings. But not the twisted erythina on the edge of the vlei where doves always cooed, not the vlei itself with its flighting wildfowl, not the pool below the waterfall where pythons lived, not the sweet-scented orange-trees beside the coffee nursery, not the bluff across the river where reedbuck lay concealed, not the grenadilla creeper over the lizard-sheltering wall, not the hillside shambas where guinea-fowl cried after tea, not the bright flame-tree avenue, nor the old grass house whose walls rustled with white ants, not the house itself with its veranda looking towards the snow-topped early-morning mountain, and its comfortable, untidy sitting-room with Tilly's hand loom in one corner where she struggled with fluffy angora wool, and a worn lion skin by the fireplace, the walls hung with water-colours of scenes in India painted by my grandmother which had come out by mistake in a crate labelled Kitchen Utensils.[1]

Nellie's new home at Njoro was the little wood-and-iron bungalow Algy Cartwright had built. In the Mau hills on the west side
of the Rift Valley, Nellie's thousand acres of mixed farming land,
as yet uncleared, lay at a bracing 7,800 feet. Leaving Jos behind at
Kitimuru, she travelled to Njoro by train to set up her household,
taking with her camping equipment, her three beloved dachshunds,
Bluebell, Foxglove and Hollyhock, and her Siamese cats. She asked
the syces* to ride there beforehand with their ponies, so that she
would have transport immediately on arrival. She also asked Tom
Petrie, her nearest neighbour at Njoro, to have an ox-cart waiting
to meet her at Njoro station, to take her belongings to the new
farm. To her amazement and delight, she found awaiting her at the
station not only the ox-cart but also Njombo, who had worked at
Kitimuru for years, and five other farmworkers from Thika. Without
saying a word, they had walked all the way to Njoro over the
Aberdare mountains so as to be on the spot to ask for shambas
(small plots of land) on the new farm. She therefore had a ready-
made, miniature labour force.

Njombo wa Kamau was first spotted by Nellie on Jim Elkington's
farm in 1912. A boy then, he had now grown to manhood. He hailed
from Gethumbwini, near Thika, from where at a time of famine
his mother went to Ukamba to get food and never returned. Then
his father died, and his brother, and his twin brother, and his sister.
There was no food and no one to look after the remaining children.
Njombo, aged about twelve, left his two small siblings with an uncle
and went to Nairobi to work digging stone from a quarry for
roadmaking. A Boer taught him how to drive oxen, and he then
took a variety of jobs on farms, ending up in Kiambu, where Nellie
saw him at Elkington's place. A boy of enquiring mind, for a term
he attended the African Mission School at Kabete, whence he went
to a Roman Catholic school. Back making roads again, he was told
he had syphilis, but he ran away from hospital and went to work
for a farmer called Henderson at Thika. All the while he attempted
to avenge the death of his father, whom he believed had been

---

* A syce, or sais, was a man wholly responsible for a horse or pony.

poisoned. For his efforts, he was rejected by his clan. Nellie took him on at Kitimuru.

When he heard she was moving to Njoro, he realised he might be able to get land on her farm, so went ahead on foot to be ready on the station platform when she arrived. Nellie offered him and the five others shambas and posho (maize meal flour) if they worked alternate weeks for her. Njombo was made neapara, or headman. At first he had no house, only a wooden shelter, but when he had built a hut he fetched his wife and three children from Thika. He raised good crops and bought goats, with which he was able to buy another wife, Kibuba's daughter. His son Mbugwa also worked for Nellie for decades. Njombo features largely in both *The Flame Trees of Thika* and *The Mottled Lizard*, most notably in the former when a spell is cast upon him. Elspeth said of him: 'Njombo the smiling, the robust, the gay, with his dashing air, his laughter, his lively and intelligent expression and his gift of rhetoric. He was a sort of Irishman among the Kikuyu, an actor to his fingertips with all the world for his stage.'[2]

Nellie and the dogs walked the five miles to the farm alongside the ox-cart loaded with her belongings. Half a mile from the station ran the Njoro river, and as they forded it the ox-cart slipped backwards down the steep bank and capsized in the fortunately shallow water. First to be rescued were the Siamese cats, and second the bottles of alcohol. When Nellie arrived on her farm she found the farmhouse largely occupied by stacks of maize grown by illegal squatters. One room was, however, empty. It had no doors or glass in the windows, no floorboards, and only the beginnings of a chimney. It was extremely cold. A few days later Nellie, on her hands and knees measuring the room for floorboards, slipped a disc in her spine. Unable to rise from the floor, she managed at length to manoeuvre herself into a chair to await rescue by the Africans the next morning. When they arrived she was lifted on to a pony and led three miles through the forest track to the Lindstroms' farm. There she made the acquaintance of Ingrid Lindstrom, who restored her mobility with a good massage and who was to be her closest friend for decades. Ingrid and her husband Gillis –

always called 'Fish' on account of his protruding eyes; his Swahili name was 'Bwana Samaki' (fish) – and their four small children had arrived in 1920 from Sweden, as friends of Bror Blixen. Ingrid was to feature in Karen Blixen's *Out of Africa*, in a portrait unrecognisable to herself and others, for the author, as was her habit, projected her into an archetype, a symbolic human being.

Nellie started to make the house habitable. She engaged Indian fundis and pretended that the free timber-cutting rights in the Mau forest, given to Cartwright for seven years with his 999-year lease in 1912, actually dated from 1920. Apart from what she had to pay the fundis, the farmhouse cost her nothing to build. She hung unsuitably heavy red velvet curtains in the small sitting room, crowded with far too much furniture – a sofa covered in dog hair, a writing table obscured by silver vases and a bottle of cattle-drench, a brass-studded Zanzibar chest holding tools for the garden and dress-making patterns, 'an old sewing-machine in a corner and the Goya [a neo-Goya painting had been bought by Jos] over the fireplace and a patch from last year's rain on the ceiling'.[3] She arranged for a cart with two oxen to get water from the river. It arrived very muddy, so she installed a ram (an automatic water-raising machine) and eight hundred yards of piping that worked very well. The household staff, never having seen water emerge from a tap before, thought it flowed for ever like a river; they did not understand that taps had to be turned off. A twenty-foot pit was dug for the lavatory, or garden house as it was called. The farmhouse itself, which at first consisted of only a sitting room and bedroom, both 14 × 14 feet, an open verandah and another, narrow bedroom of 14 × 9 feet, was enlarged by two bathrooms, and the verandah enclosed to make a pantry, dining room and another bedroom (10 × 10 feet). Elspeth was given her own bathroom and bedroom, with walls of heavy cedar offcuts, interior mud plaster, and hard wooden floors, also of cedar, which was unpalatable to white ants.

Nellie called the farm Gikammeh, from the Kikuyu word for the hyraxes which screamed through the night in the trees of the forest behind. Elspeth spent her school holidays at the farm, and fell in love with it. It had a wonderful view across the Rift Valley to the

Aberdare mountains, rising to ten thousand feet with their three peaks of Satima, Kipipiri and Kinangop. Nakuru and its lake shining in the sunlight lay 1,500 feet below.

Nellie, ever energetic and enthusiastic, had to start farming again entirely from scratch. The land was cleared, with laborious digging and hauling of the stumps which were all that was left of the farm's trees, felled by the illegal squatters. Fifty Kisii men from Kericho started the work but became homesick after a few days and disappeared into the blue. An unusually pro-settler District Commissioner at Nakuru found them and had them sent back. Nellie docked them their pay for a month, a punishment persuasive enough to encourage them to complete their three-month contract. Nellie's treatment of Africans was typical of the time. She only mentions losing her temper and striking an employee on one occasion, when the man said he would not be given orders by a woman. She was deeply ashamed of what she had done. Many of her employees were devoted to her, and stayed for years. She, in her turn, developed a real bond with some of them, particularly Njombo and his son Mbugwa.

Meanwhile Jos was back at Kitimuru trying to sell the farm. Sir Charles Markham had faded out as a prospective buyer, but someone else was interested – Guy Repton and his Russian wife Doushka.* The Reptons were on the fringes of the Happy Valley crowd, a group with ample private funds and no pecuniary occupation, some of whom lived in the Wanjohi valley in the Aberdares and tended to squander their talents on drink and drugs. Jos negotiated the sale of Kitimuru with the Reptons as a fifty-fifty partnership, but ultimately Guy and his wife took over the entire farm for £10,000. This cleared the Grants' £10,000 overdraft with the bank, and left them to begin again with nothing in the kitty. Had Trudie Denman not provided Nellie with the farm at Njoro, they

---

* In *The Mottled Lizard* (p.245) Elspeth said of Doushka: 'She was beautiful and Russian and smoked long, black cigarettes embellished with a monogram, and stayed in bed until lunchtime, when she emerged in a Turkish sort of attire made of black velvet, with jade ear-rings and the most delectable scent.' Guy once challenged a man to a duel for using her bathwater.

would have had to return to England to rely on the generosity of relatives.

Elspeth's ambition to go to Cambridge was dashed when she fell at the hurdle of Latin. Reading College (raised to university status the following year, 1925) offered a course in agriculture which required no Latin. Elspeth applied, and was accepted. Although Elspeth would be best known for her writings on Africa, as a young woman she was excessively impatient to get away. The world beckoned, she answered the call, and she never returned to live permanently in the continent of her childhood. But Africa had cast its spell on her, and would tug her back for almost annual extended visits. She keenly watched the unfolding drama as Britain's African empire disintegrated. Mindful of her mother's experience, she lyrically reminded her readers of the trials the colonists had faced, the human and financial investment they had made, their sorrows and triumphs, hopes and failures. In later life, she looked back on her parting from Kenya:

> To part is to die a little, and things that die are gone for good. But I would be coming back; and as the train steamed out and everybody waved and Tilly and Robin [her fictitious names for her parents], standing side by side, grew small and vanished, I remembered the Swahili proverb: he who has tasted honey will return to the honeypot.[4]

In September 1924 Elspeth was entrusted to the care of Cockie Birkbeck, and they embarked at Mombasa on a small and slow Dutch ship for England, sharing a cabin in the cramped vessel. The portly and jovial captain treated them to Van der Humm liqueurs every night. Cockie and her husband Ben had been taken on safari by Bror Blixen soon after their arrival in Kenya in 1920. The flirtatious Bror, six feet tall and not particularly good-looking but with a smile that charmed the ladies, got up to his usual trick of seducing the wives of his clients. This time, though, the affair continued once the safari was over. Karen Blixen got to hear about it and divorced

Bror, leaving him free to marry Cockie, which he would finally do in 1928.

Elspeth arrived in an England

> which was always called Home in those days, but it was not. It was a foreign land whose people spoke our language; little else was the same. To begin with, everything was tiny, almost miniature . . . The train glided away with nothing but a gentle hoot and the flicker of an emerald flag, instead of a great deal of shouting, waving, last-minute boarding and leaping clear, a pandemonium of wails, clanks and hootings, as if a pirate vessel were being boarded in mid-ocean. The quiet English train then passed decorously between rows of tidy, symmetrical, identical and, again, very small houses, their gardens trim and paintwork clean, and women to be seen scrubbing steps. There was an indefinably alien look, perhaps because of the monotony and packed-togetherness. You proceeded into a checkerboard of little paddocks, each one separate, and each one incredibly green.[5]

Elspeth described her two years at Reading University in *Love Among the Daughters*, but the book can be trusted as little as *The Flame Trees of Thika* and *The Mottled Lizard*, although these works were described by her publisher as autobiographical. What Elspeth did was to portray locations accurately, but conceal the truth about events and people who were still alive. She would often transfer a remembered incident to a different time, and always amalgamated or distorted characters so that there was no danger of libel. Her university vacations she spent with Aunt Blanche, her mother's sister, or with Aunt Vera, the widow of the paralysed Robin, her father's brother who died in 1927.

Reading University was situated near the Royal Berkshire Hospital, which Elspeth thought a more suitable building for a university than the real establishment, whose narrow wooden porch led to a lobby and two offices less imposing than the booking hall of a country railway station. She lived in a tall, early Edwardian house with a landlady and about fifteen other students, each with their own bedsit. There was a small communal sitting room with balcony, upright piano, threadbare carpet and a grate that smoked, and a narrow dining room smelling always of cabbage. No visitors could be brought in after 7 p.m. and students had to be in by ten at night, though twice a week they could sign out till midnight. Those who knew they would be unlawfully late arranged with friends to unbolt the door secretly.

Men vastly outnumbered women at the university, particularly in Elspeth's chosen field of study, agriculture, which had only one other woman student in her year. Like the men, the women called each other by their surnames. At the time Elspeth said she was disappointed with Reading – wisdom, learning and scholarship seemed even more remote than they had been in Africa. Lectures and 'practicals' in laboratories were compulsory. She had to study botany, zoology, entomology, bacteriology, agricultural history and economics, together with elementary accountancy, farm management and law. She was instructed on how to mark a field for ploughing, 'to distinguish Yorkshire fog from cocksfoot and sainfoin from broad red clover, to master the show points of bulls, cows, pigs and fat bullocks, and to calculate the areas of fields'.[6]

The work was not beyond her, and left time for social life. Elspeth does not appear to have suffered from shyness. Confident and mature for her age, she went to student dances, punted on the Thames and discussed with other girls their mutual terror of 'starting babies' in this pre-contraceptive-pill age. She had her first tentative sexual experience: 'I was not in the least in love with him, but he had experience and clever hands and, being unprepared for this, did not proceed to its ultimate conclusion, though he got as near to it as safety permitted.'[7]

At Reading Elspeth was financed by Uncle Eddie Grant, her father's half-brother, whose second wife Bridget (Evelyn Waugh's sister-in-law) became a good friend of hers. To supplement the funds he provided Elspeth tried writing short stories and reportage, but she failed to get any takers for her work, and remained very short of money during her two years at Reading. In 1926 she emerged with her diploma, on condition that she completed her fieldwork. The university's archives are silent as to whether she fulfilled this obligation.

As yet Elspeth had no desire to return to East Africa. Aunt Blanche, Nellie's sister, presented her with a wonderful opportunity by offering to pay for her to spend a year at Cornell University in the United States. Nellie protested at this generosity and somehow scraped together £125 which she sent to England, only to have Blanche return the money. Elspeth longed to go to America, which she saw as 'a magnet, a lodestar, a beacon', and in 1927 she embarked on a crowded ship, the *Minnesota*, for New York. On board she met Mrs Culin, wife of the head of Chinese and Japanese Art at the Brooklyn Museum, who was returning from a summer spent painting in the south of France. On arrival at New York Mrs Culin invited Elspeth to spend a night at her apartment in Brooklyn, which considerably eased her introduction to a strange country. 'I was quite unprepared for the beauties of New York,' said Elspeth. 'Approached from the sea, it had all those qualities of fable and illusion I had previously imagined it to have. Towers, spires, gleaming pillars pierced a pinkish mist to stab a tender sky.'[8]

Cornell University is in Ithaca, New York State, on a lovely site overlooking the forty-mile-long Lake Cayuga, replete with Indian legends. Ithaca was then a little town, of only 16,000 inhabitants, and initially it bored Elspeth, who realised she had been spoilt at Reading, within forty minutes of London; no longer could she run up to the metropolis to see a show whenever she desired. The first two days at Cornell she spent in queues trying to unravel the red tape of registering as a student, of whom there were five thousand in all. She was put into a good-sized but bare room in Risley Hall (a letter was swiftly despatched to Aunt Vera requesting the centre pages of *Tatler*s for wall decoration), a grand residential hall for female students modelled on Hampton Court, with a dining room exactly copied from Christ Church hall at Oxford. Having started to smoke at Reading, Elspeth was dismayed to find smoking prohibited in Risley Hall, and there were other petty restrictions, such as only being allowed to play the gramophone at certain hours. But at least, unlike at Reading, she could be out till midnight any night, and 1.30 a.m. twice a week. In fact, at Cornell there was almost complete personal freedom, with discipline in the hands of the students rather than the university authorities.

It was quite the opposite with the teaching methods, which Elspeth found extraordinary, and utterly different from her experience at Reading. For her, it was like being back at school. Whereas at Reading the attitude had been: here is knowledge, take it or leave it, at Cornell there was spoonfeeding. Elspeth thought the students were given much too much work, with endless reports and assignments to complete and quizzes to prepare for. The teachers were not interested in the students' opinions, merely in getting them to absorb scores of facts: 'Ours not to reason why, ours to absorb a mass of facts and regurgitate them correctly.'[9] Elspeth regarded it as complete intellectual bondage, and lamented that she would never have such fun again as in her final year at Reading.

She chose five courses, on animal nutrition, crop production, news writing, marketing and rural sociology; among those she rejected were lawnmaking, greenkeeping and poultry-house design. Elspeth described her impressions of Cornell to her former student colleagues at Reading in *Tamesis*, the University of Reading magazine. The campus was so huge, she said, that it required an aeroplane to get around. The Poultry Husbandry building was 'decorated tastefully with photographs of beauty competition winners in the hen world', while the Animal Pathology building 'put up an offensive calculated to keep off any but the most hardened veterinarians and those suffering from chronic colds'.[10]

There were, however, compensations. The academic staff lacked the aloofness and indifference of those at Reading, particularly the Professor of Journalism, Bristow Adams, with whom Elspeth became friendly. He was most encouraging of the pieces she contributed to the campus newspaper, the *Cornell Daily Sun*, which she studied carefully to see what other students were doing. She would find out the names of their home towns and local newspapers, and send them reports along 'home-town-boy-or-girl-makes-good' lines. Her efforts were almost invariably printed, though she received no payment. It was excellent training for a putative journalist. Constantly keeping her eye open for news, she came to the conclusion that the essence of news is what people do.

Social life for co-eds, as the girl students were called, revolved around 'natural intercourse' (conversation) and having as many boyfriends as possible, whereas at Reading the custom was to have only one at a time. Elspeth boasted of having 125 dates in one term. Slim and of medium height, she could not have been described as pretty, her face and nose being rather too wide, and her fine brown hair rather too unruly, but the vivacity of her features was alluring. Unlike at Reading, it was not so much pregnancy that was dreaded as disease. There were notices everywhere about the dangers of syphilis and gonorrhoea, and addresses for treatment and check-ups. 'I was not,' said Elspeth, 'promiscuous by nature and was nervous about pregnancy and disease . . . the "full rights of love" were not as a rule accorded unless you wore a boy's fraternity pin, or demanded unless this had been given; the pin was the pledge.'[11] Love-making between girls was, however, quite popular, although Elspeth does not tell us whether she indulged in it.

There were 'necking parties' in the woods, night picnics, trips to nearby Niagara Falls, and football matches with cheerleaders and a coach paid more than the University President himself. Though it was the era of Prohibition, bootleg alcohol was easy to obtain. Much of the social life revolved around that very American female institution, the sorority, of which Cornell had twelve. Sororities had ideals, rituals and insignia, and like Freemasons, members were expected to favour sisters for the rest of their lives. At first Elspeth was undecided about joining one, largely because of the cost, but she soon accepted that life would be duller without membership. After attending a series of deadly introduction parties she was chosen by, and accepted, Alpha Omicron Pi, which required of her only that she attend supper in its house on Sunday evenings. There they sang the song:

> When the sun fades far away
> In the crimson of the west,
> And the voices of the day
> Murmur low and sink to rest;

Music with the twilight falls
O'er the dreaming lake and dell;
'Tis an echo from the walls
Of our own, our fair Cornell.

Elspeth came to the conclusion that 'Americans were not just rather comic English people who had developed, with their accent, a number of peculiar ways, but were real foreigners, like Turks or Germans'.[12] She had at least one criticism of America: she disliked the regimentation of life there, the sweet politeness that obscured callousness, and she longed for 'the unofficial English rose' of Rupert Brooke's hedgerows, a metaphor for a particularly English casualness.

At Cornell Elspeth was extremely short of money. The American girls had short-sleeved silk dresses to wear at supper, but she had none. However, working to support yourself through university was widely accepted, and many of the girls had jobs on the campus. Elspeth joined them, waitressing for $3.50 an hour. While everyone else went away for Thanksgiving she stayed at the barracks-like and deserted campus to conserve funds. Christmas did not find her alone, though, because she had two invitations to New York – from Mrs Culin, her shipboard companion, and from a fellow student. She spent Christmas day with the Culins, where she opened a parcel of clothes and a fat cheque from Aunt Vera. She saw three plays and ran amok in the shops. Aunt Vera was informed that the electric signs on Broadway had got Piccadilly completely knocked sideways. From the Culins Elspeth went to the Munsens in Yonkers, returning to Cornell on the midnight train on 31 December 1927.

Thoughts of what she would do when she finished her course now intruded into Elspeth's studies. She wondered whether she should go to the southern United States in June, for it would be 'folly to let slide the opportunity for getting first hand knowledge of tobacco'[13] now that her father had begun to farm the crop. She told Vera that her mother and father were practically penniless, and that the future filled her with gloom. Kenya, she said, sounded unbearable. If she returned she would be completely isolated from

87

friends, people, ideas, books, amusements and everything that made life worth living. It was a typical complaint of youth, but in this case undeniably true.

While Elspeth was away Jos had bought land in Tanganyika, the former German territory handed to the British by the Treaty of Versailles at the conclusion of the First World War. He was encouraged by the rumour that a railway was proposed near his land. With no money of his own, he had borrowed from his brother Robin and gone into partnership with another man, who, as usual in Jos's undertakings, failed to come up with the cash. Jos was living rough on the land, which he called Saa Mbusi (the time of the goat), in a hut with a leaky roof and no doors and windows. He had one camp bed and chairs knocked up from petrol boxes.* Nellie went with a party of friends, including Cockie, to see Saa Mbusi in 1927, but was dismayed by the number of Germans settling in Tanganyika. She wrote to Lord Delamere, the Kenya white settlers' leader, about that pressing problem, drawing his attention to the importance of establishing British numerical supremacy over the Germans.

Jos decided to plant tobacco, though knowing nothing about it chose Turkish, the wrong sort for the climate. It was utterly destroyed by frost. The rumoured railway never came, and he felt completely cut off from the outside world, reluctant as he was to participate in the local distraction – getting drunk at a pub in Iringa, the nearest settlement. He hoped that profits from tobacco would enable Nellie or himself to go to England to meet Elspeth on her return from Cornell, though he admitted to his sister-in-law Vera that 'she does not seem at all anxious ever to return to Kenya or here [southern Tanganyika], which rather complicates matters. It is a bit worrying as she seems mad on London and "the flickers" [cinema] etc. I fear she'll loathe this country and be unhappy here. It's all very difficult.'[14]

---

* Petrol came in tin 'debes', or four-gallon cans, and two of these were packed in a small wooden crate. The crates were made into furniture by the early settlers.

After her trip to see the Tanganyika land, Nellie returned to Kenya to prosecute plans of her own. The marriage was all but dead, though there was never a divorce. Nellie found it difficult to live in the same house as Jos, but she never refused him a home when his various plans went inevitably awry, although she complained bitterly about him in letters to her daughter. Nellie's treatment of Elspeth as an adult, which she had only recently become, suggests that hostile murmurings had almost certainly occurred while Elspeth was a teenager. Elspeth never responded to Nellie's criticism of Jos, of whom she was really rather fond, while understanding his faults. She confided, however, to Aunt Vera, that if she were to join her father in Tanganyika

> the only neighbours within hundreds of miles [would be] Germans who know no English and hate us. If one was desparately [sic] keen on the job it would be worth it. I can no longer pretend that I am. I took up agriculture in a burst of enthusiasm when I was seventeen . . . but the more I learnt about it the more discouraged I have become, and all the time the only reason I ever learnt enough to pass anything was because the purely theoretical parts interested me . . . Heaven knows what I would do when I am landed in that God-forsaken country . . . thoroughly insulated from every idea by the ocean and equatorial apathy. My parents are wearing themselves into mental and physical wrecks when they ought to be enjoying themselves and living in comfort – and they have done absolutely everything for me. If it wasn't for that I would try to get a job over here in Journalism.[15]

Elspeth was not only disinclined to go to Tanganyika – Kenya too seemed unattractive. Her mother had let her Njoro farm to another settler, Gerald Annesley, and his wife, and was living in straitened circumstances ten miles away in a hastily erected house of mud and wattle with a grass roof. Lord Delamere had built a fourteen-mile pipeline and sold off blocks of land alongside it. Nellie had managed to lease ten acres for three years and was raising pigs there, hence her name for her dwelling, 'Piggery Nook'. One night she was called up the hill to Gikammeh to help deliver Mrs

Annesley's baby, but it was born dead. She described burying 'the heir to all the Annesleys and the beautiful Castlewilliam in a petrol box under an olive tree on the edge of the forest'.[16]

The ever-resourceful Nellie, with her imported middle white pigs feeling the sun too much, joined together with a Mr Maxwell and Reginald Pelham Burn to form the MPG Syndicate, which took on contract ploughing for the owners of the pipeline farms, now clamouring for someone to break and harrow their land for them. The syndicate built up its business to plough seven thousand acres a year on contract. Then Maxwell died, tractors were arriving on the scene, and the partnership was wound up. On the cessation of the Piggery Nook lease in the late 1920s, Nellie returned to Gikammeh. She had lost her three faithful canine companions. Foxglove disappeared out hunting at Saa Mbusi in 1927, Bluebell was taken by a leopard in 1928, and Hollyhock was killed by Africans hunting at Piggery Nook. To add to her woes, she suffered constantly from veld sores, frequently having her hands in bandages for weeks at a time. It was a hard life indeed, and Elspeth was loath to return to it.

Nellie was delighted to have instead three visitors from England – Aunt Vera, who had done so much for Elspeth, and her benefactor Trudie Denman with her daughter Judy, who arrived at the end of 1930 to find

> a blaze of colour – hollyhocks, carnations, every kind of lily, and hiding behind them a series of little houses made of mud covered with white plaster and a tin roof. And this was Nellie's house. It doesn't look very grand from the outside, but inside it is lovely. All small rooms but lovely comfy chairs and beds and a bathroom for me next my bedroom and 3 others as well![17]

After the visitors from England arrived, Nellie was called on by the writer Evelyn Waugh, who was spending a few days with Raymond de Trafford, one of the Happy Valley set, in January 1931. In his diary Waugh describes dinner and a picnic with the Grants, Denmans, and Mr and Mrs Oliver Baring, 'a nasty couple'.[18] Mrs

Baring was Phoebe, Jos's amour in Madrid during the First World War, now staying at the Grants' house with her husband. Trudie Denman did not like the Barings either, and complained that their peace had been interrupted by Oliver, who 'looks unwholesome and talks clever and makes lewd and familiar remarks'.[19] Waugh rang up Nellie next morning to complain that there was no food at de Trafford's house, so Nellie sent a car for him and they all spent the day picnicking on the Molo river. Nellie also arranged a trip from Kisumu to Uganda with Waugh, Trudie and Judy. They visited Jinja and Entebbe, then dropped Waugh – whom they now called 'Mr Wuff' – in Kampala: 'it seemed a sad spot to leave him for five days until he could get a boat and find his way to Liberia to study the only native republic.'[20] Waugh recorded his travels in *Remote People* (1931), and his high-spirited and triumphantly funny novel *Black Mischief* (1932) was another result of his African journey.

Elspeth returned to England in 1928, at the end of her course at Cornell, as her student's visa had expired. Her plan was to work for a while, then return to the United States under the quota system. She much preferred the USA, she said, because England's class system appalled her, and 'America shone like a kind of morning star, symbolising opportunity, equality, progress, action, youth – escape from a stuffy, hidebound, convention-ridden England where no one had a chance who wasn't old, bowler-hatted and effete.'[21] Sprung from the nobility herself, she had only contempt for most of their doings, though she reckoned it was salutary to visit them occasionally to remind oneself of their truly undemocratic nature. America, in contrast, took people at their own merits.

Elspeth had arranged a job for herself which combined both her skills, journalism and agriculture. Professor George Stapledon, who ran a plant-breeding station at Aberystwyth, wanted to revivify the Welsh mountains and valleys, restoring them to fertility. He employed Elspeth to help him do this. A Devon man with a mop of ginger hair and the weatherbeaten face of a countryman combined with the nervous energy of a scientist, he and his Australian colleague Frank McDougall ('Mac') made Elspeth feel she would be running away if she returned to the USA.

She was torn. She may have had a young man awaiting her in New York, tall and thin and dark and struggling to be an artist in Greenwich Village – at least, that is what she claimed in *Love Among the Daughters*. She was staying with relatives when, a week before her boat was due to sail, the twenty-two-year-old Elspeth received a letter from Mac, a great wire-puller, suggesting she go to London for an interview with a new, semi-independent government organisation which needed a junior press officer to write about its research in a popular way. Elspeth later claimed that her return to America was prevented by a tightening of the quota regulations resulting from the huge unemployment following the Wall Street Crash of 1929. Whatever the truth, she went to London and was interviewed by a young, enthusiastic, tall, ginger-haired man – Gervas Huxley, cousin of the writer Aldous and the biologist Julian. She was offered the job, at £5 a week, very good pay in those days. Living in a room in Ebury Street, near Victoria station, she walked to work in Queen Anne's Gate to save bus fares, allowed herself sixpence for coffee and a bun at lunchtime, cadged most of her dinners, and saved enough for a down-payment on a second-hand Austin 7 car with a racing body, which took her eighteen months to pay off.

The organisation she had joined was the Empire Marketing Board, established in 1926 to promote the products of Commonwealth countries. It was essentially a marketing operation, and pioneered the entry by government into the publicity field. Gervas Huxley was head of its Publicity Committee, and worked closely with Elspeth in her role as assistant press officer. Elspeth was an immediate success, revealing a flair for making articles on scientific research comprehensible and readable for the layman. She described herself at this time as having hooded eyes, a wide nose and mouth, and a strong jaw beneath the ears. Gervas Huxley, thirteen years older than her, began to take her out in the evenings to restaurants in Soho. He had married Lindsey Foot in 1919, but the marriage had been a failure, and Lindsey was having an affair with Walter

Elliott, one of the members of the Empire Marketing Board. Gervas found Elspeth's intelligence and gaiety and what he considered her good looks most attractive, and he soon procured a divorce by the usual method of the time – hiring a woman to be found in bed with him by the chambermaid of a hotel.

Gervas was born at 2 Queensborough Terrace, Bayswater, London, on 6 April 1894 into a well-to-do upper-middle-class family. His father Henry Huxley, a general practitioner, was the younger surviving son of the great Victorian socialist and humanist Thomas Henry Huxley. His mother, Sophy Wylde Stobart, the daughter of a colliery owner with large interests in iron, steel, docks and shipping, had been a nurse at St Bartholomew's Hospital. When Gervas was nine he was sent to preparatory school at Hillside, Farncombe, near Guildford, where he encountered bullying but found his cousin Aldous a staunch ally. They became firm and lifelong friends. From prep school he went to Rugby public school, which encouraged his natural tendency to conform with the accepted conventions of his time and class. Both he and Aldous, who had been to Eton, went on to Balliol College, Oxford, but the outbreak of the First World War interrupted Gervas's studies. In August 1914 he was commissioned as a second lieutenant in the Special Reserve of Officers in the East Yorkshire Regiment. Miraculously, he survived months in the trenches of the front line and the battle of Passchendaele, to be demobilised on 1 April 1919. Unwilling after his dreadful experience of war to return to undergraduate life, he abandoned his degree. Instead, he joined the firm of ship-owners and bankers Alfred Booth & Co., got married, and lived in Liverpool, then London, then Abingdon near Oxford, where he built a house, Greenheys, and made a garden, his favourite leisure occupation.

In 1926 Stephen Tallents, the head of the new Empire Marketing Board, invited Gervas to join it. The EMB funded scientific research aimed at boosting the quality of Empire produce, and Elspeth's job was mainly to publicise this research. To this end she visited several research centres in Britain, such as those dealing with cold storage in Cambridge, pasture research at Aberystwyth under Stapledon, stored produce research in Slough, fruit tree research at East Malling, near Maidstone, and veterinary research in Kent: 'It sounds very dreary but in fact was not, because a lot of new ideas were being developed and many of the scientific people were young and enthusiastic and improvising because chronically short of funds.'[22]

Soon after Elspeth joined the EMB, a general election brought the Labour Party to power, and the Board's fortunes began to fade. It limped along for a time with a reduced budget, but finally came to an end in 1932. Elspeth had found her work invaluable training in journalism of the respectable kind, and of writing in general. One of her colleagues in the press department, the journalist Patrick Ryan, had taught her a great deal.

While she was at the EMB Elspeth wrote articles for British and Empire newspapers, among them *The Times*, *Manchester Guardian*, *Tit Bits*, *Cape Argus*, *West Australian*, *East African Standard*, *Melbourne Herald*, *Trinidad Guardian* and *Ceylon Observer*, on numerous subjects, including the sociable apple, war on the tsetse fly, warble fly, pedigree grasses, fruit tree behaviour, helping Empire cotton to grow straight and new metals for new industries. She also composed many pamphlets issued by the EMB. The placing of her EMB articles gave her an entrée into the British newspaper world, and she found homes for several pieces not inspired by the EMB. The most substantial of these was a series which ran weekly from May to June 1930 in the young persons' section of the *Daily Mail*, entitled 'Strange Tasks for the Scientist'.

On 31 December 1931 Gervas and Elspeth were married in the Kensington Register Office with four witnesses, including Gervas's father Henry and Nellie's great friend Trudie Denman. Elspeth's parents were not there, but Gervas had met them shortly before when they visited England. At the time of the marriage they were on safari at Lake Baringo in Kenya with Cockie and Bror Blixen. Gervas thought Jos 'a man of much charm but singular incompetence in business affairs', while he appreciated Nellie as a tremendous personality and the dominant partner in the marriage.[23]

With his slight, aristocratic stoop, Gervas was outwardly unemotional, the sort of person who would never dream of showing his wife any affection in public. The newlyweds spent their honeymoon in Cornwall and then returned to work. The Civil Service rule was that either Gervas or Elspeth would have to resign from the EMB, because a married couple could not be employed in the same department. Stephen Tallents got the rule waived for six months, but in any case the EMB was soon to be abolished. After the couple had a summer holiday on the Riviera with Aldous Huxley and his wife Maria, Gervas quickly found himself another job, as Chief Commissioner for the Ceylon Tea Board from 1 January 1933. This soon mutated into the International Tea Board representing Ceylon, India and the Dutch East Indies, with Gervas as its chief executive. His job was to market tea worldwide.

At the end of June 1932 Elspeth left the EMB and devoted herself to a new project. Hugh Cholmondeley, third Baron Delamere, the pioneer farmer in Kenya, died in 1931 and his widow Gwladys (always known as Glady) agreed to Elspeth's request to write his biography. As a child Elspeth had known Delamere, 'with hair flowing almost to his shoulders, a huge sun helmet which gave him the look of a mushroom, and a dirty old cardigan',[24] and she was glad to undertake the job, particularly as much of the research would have to be done in Kenya. Her youthful reluctance to return to the land of her childhood had vanished now that she was married and had a secure base in England. Gervas had to visit Ceylon for his work, and the pair travelled together to Marseilles by train on 19 January 1933 after a farewell lunch given by Malcolm MacDonald, Prime Minister Ramsay MacDonald's son and many years later the last Governor of Kenya, who was then in the Dominions Office. From a snowbound Marseilles they boarded separate ships, one sailing for Ceylon and the other for Mombasa. Elspeth left on the SS *Malda* on the twenty-second, to endure a rough and chilly journey to Port Said which made her seasick. Cheering herself with the purchase of a panama hat, she sailed into the Red Sea and lost her old-fashioned double terai hat overboard at Port Sudan. She never wore a double terai or topee again. The *Malda* reached Mombasa on 13 February, and Nellie was waiting on the quayside.

Elspeth stepped ashore to a Kenya somewhat different from the one she had left eight years before. Farming had not prospered in the late 1920s. The world slump did not help, but the true culprits had been the twin scourge of locusts and drought. Swarms of locusts had come from the north in lethal copper-coloured clouds accompanied by a peculiar sibilant humming sound, and settled on crops. When they lifted off again not a bush was green, not a blade of wheat or leaf of maize still stood. The land was stripped bare of vegetation as the locusts proceeded on their dark and lethal way. And then the rains failed. Petrol became prohibitively expensive, so some settlers converted their vehicles to run on strange concoctions, while others hitched oxen to their cars.

Nellie and Elspeth did not go straight to Njoro, but enjoyed three days on a trip up the coast to Gedi, an ancient ruined town, and to Malindi, where a break in the reef skirting the East African shore allows surfing on the rolling waves. They took the train to Nairobi on the seventeenth. It was a new style of train. Gone were the corridor-less carriages, the halts for food at dak bungalows, the dim oil-lamps lighting the compartments after dark. Eucalyptus logs for engine fuel spat no more. New Garrett engines ran on coal, and there was a dining car and comfortable bunks.

Glady Delamere met Elspeth at Nairobi station and took her to her house, Loresho, six miles outside town. They drove through a Nairobi with several new buildings but still essentially the same. Owing to the work of a Nairobi Beautification Committee formed in 1929, the town had improved in appearance. Evelyn Waugh described its architecture as surprisingly good, though rendered insignificant by the great breadth of the streets. The Norfolk Hotel looked much as it had done before, though the hitching posts at the front had gone. There was a new hotel, Torr's, on Sixth Avenue, which had usurped some of the Norfolk's functions, particularly 11 a.m. drinks. It had a cage in the lobby in which guests put their animal as they entered, be it pet cheetah or dog. The blue gums still lined Government Road, dropping parchment-like leaves to crunch underfoot. There remained gaps between buildings, encouraging dust. The rickshaws had gone and everywhere cars could be seen. They looked as if they had been constructed in a Heath-Robinson factory, for all their bodies were different. This arose from the local habit of buying only the chassis and building on to it a wood, canvas and chicken-wire superstructure to suit your own needs. The backs of the vehicles were crammed with Africans, prudently given lifts by white settlers so they could push them out of ruts and quagmires and sandy dust. Jos Grant called them 'pushengers'.

Loresho, the Delameres' house, was built round a lawn quadrangle beside a huge, wild fig tree sacred to the Kikuyu people. At the front of the house was a deep verandah which rendered the rooms inside dark though not gloomy. In the drawing room were two deep golden sofas. The scent in the room by day was of gardenias and Chanel No. 5, Glady's perfume, and by night of cigars when Delamere (always called 'D') was alive, and now of candles and paraffin lamps. Guests stayed in rooms around the courtyard, while Glady had her own little cottage away from the house. She and D had disliked sharing a room – at the Outspan Hotel in Nyeri D had been forced to sleep in the bath when a double room was the only one available. Separated from the main house by a hedge was the nursery cottage inhabited by Glady's three children by Sir Charles Markham, her first husband. There were Somali servants with long white kanzus and red cummerbunds, and a Nandi chauffeur to drive Glady's car. A frequent visitor, with his scarlet Somali shawl flung carelessly round his shoulders, was the debonair Caswell (always called 'Boy') Long, the manager of D's farm Soysambu in the Rift Valley until 1927, when the pair fell out over Boy's marriage, which D resented.* The Prince of Wales had once been to stay, but his licentious and erratic behaviour made him an unpopular visitor.

---

* Elspeth described him thus: 'Boy Long, whose handsome looks and gaudy shirts and broad-brimmed hats dazzled eyes and broke numerous hearts' (*Forks and Hope*, 1964, p.78). Long had arrived in Kenya as tutor to Delamere's son Tom. When Tom went to school in England, Long remained in Kenya as Delamere's untiring and devoted farm manager, becoming an expert on cattle and sheep.

When Eric Dutton, the Governor's aide, innocently wrote a memo, 'It is confidently expected that owing to the arrival of His Royal Highness the population of Mombasa will be considerably increased,' he was nearer the truth than he knew.

Glady, whom D married in 1928, was small and brown-eyed and high-complexioned, with dark hair and a startlingly white skin. She laughed and cried a lot and spoke in a deep voice, expressing her strong personality in frequent argument. Vivacious and high-spirited, she could be outrageously frank. Her daughter Rose summed her up with the words: 'She was not even-tempered and her tongue when provoked could be extremely sharp but that was rare. She lit up a room as she walked in and everyone present immediately responded to her warmth and tremendous personality. She came across as someone quite special . . . She threw herself into public life with zest and enjoyment. She was not in the least bit domesticated . . . her council work was her top priority.'[25] Later she was three times mayor of Nairobi, driving herself by hard work to an early grave. She had tick typhus at the end of 1942, which can put a strain on the heart, but continued working despite medical warnings and had a severe stroke, dying at the age of forty-four.

Many men admired Glady, but her new love after D's death was Alistair Gibb, who would turn up in a small Morris car and delight her children by driving it round the nursery verandah. On the outbreak of the Second World War she wrote in her visitors' book: 'Alistair went to England to rejoin. Finis?'[26] Glady gave and went to suppers in pyjamas and dressing-gown, the style in vogue in Kenya at the time but much frowned upon by the Governor Sir Edward Grigg:

> [The King] had heard that men who, as he said, 'ought to have known better', had taken to the habit of dining in pyjamas and he hoped I would never allow this to be done in my presence. He was quite correctly informed, as I found when I began to visit prominent settlers in their houses up country . . . The men dined in dressing gowns of figured silk covering pyjamas in which they afterwards went to bed. I do not know how this habit came into being, and it caused me a great deal

of embarrassment, since it is not easy even for Governors to lay down the law in other people's houses ... I managed, however, to carry out the King's orders without a breach, though protests were often thick about the ears of my staff.[27]

Elspeth left Glady in order to do the research for two articles for which *The Times* had contracted her (they appeared on 21 and 22 March 1933) on the current Kakamega gold rush. In 1931 alluvial gold had been found in the Kakamega area, north of the Kavirondo Gulf, by L.A. Johnson, an American who had participated in the Klondike gold rush. As news of the finds spread, farmers and businessmen hurried to the area, to escape the worldwide depression from which they were suffering. Gold-bearing reefs were found from 1933, and by 1934 there were some six hundred whites living at the goldfield. Elspeth went to the mining camp and interviewed Johnson, 'who looked every inch the tough prospector, and was as uncommunicative as a mule. "A grunt or two", wrote one of his neighbours, "a great hoik and hefty spit and the word 'Jesus' was L.A.'s usual comment on most subjects." '[28] By 1938 gold was Kenya's second largest export, but after that it petered out. Elspeth indulged in speculation of her own and bought some shares in one of the gold syndicates, Paka Neusi (Black Cat), but she never received a dividend.

Elspeth went to Gikammeh to write the newspaper articles, and Nellie gave over her outside private office to her daughter. She hung up American curtains with twenty new floral hybrids on each, and furnished the room with a writing desk she had found derelict in the nearby Grahams' house and painted a bright blue, and a converted meat safe for a bookcase. Temporarily teetotal since landing in Kenya, Elspeth began work.

She found Gikammeh much changed. It now had six and a half acres of market garden, and acres of pyrethrum (used in making insecticides), peppermint, oat hay, almond trees and edible canna lilies. Nellie had great hopes of her almonds, but the climate was unkind. Because there was no real dormant season, the flowering was haphazard, hail stripped the flowers, and only a few pounds of nuts were cropped. Lying awake one night, Elspeth made some notes vividly evoking Gikammeh:

> Dark shapes – silent – motionless – but each one might move. Fears still latent within us of enemies, human and bestial. Noises: frogs: throaty rattle on one side, higher whistle on the other. What do they celebrate or warn? Why stop and resume? Dogs barking – at what? Fear and protest. Grass soft underfoot and white flowers. Trees sharp against starlit sky. The house in the bush – garden round and one lighted window. Very solitary and brave, a defiant gesture – the sleeping animals, the watchful night. The eyes moving, the rustling grass. Smell of honeysuckle and moonflower. Sharp black shadows and a movement in the paleness between. The frogs like crows caw-ing. The bird cry. No wind. A hush. Possession. Fear. No night for lovers. Mindlessness. Nerves. Indifference. The thorn spreading shape in the sky.[29]

During the day Nellie's lovely flower garden dominated the view. Elspeth walked on the grass, as dry and bristly as an unshaven chin, and wandered among the pentstemons, sweet Williams and phlox, the carnations, nemesias and gazanias. There were roses in a wire cage to deter duikers. Honeysuckle draped the house, obstructing the gutters and entirely blocking one window. Freesias were planted in a raised bed under pepper trees. Below the house was a gully made by natural erosion in whose walls

> the green bee-eaters nested. They flashed by like animated emeralds, with bands of rose on their wings and a creamy white front. Little seed-eaters that we wrongly called humming-birds grew so tame they hopped about round the door; some were blue as turquoises, others a dark-red plum-colour; and sun-birds with their long, curved beaks and quivering wings were always busy among the creepers and the wild scarlet and orange *gloriosa* blooms. Early in the morning anvil-birds (a kind of cuckoo shrike) kept up their bell-like double call and response, high-low, high-low, like a blow on an anvil followed by a lighter sound as the hammer bounced. This was made by two birds, not one: a cock calling and a hen answering, as regular

as the tick of a clock. The rain-bird (a kind of bulbul) rolled his soft notes from his throat like water from a bottle, in a sad falling cadence that quickened as it fell; doves cooed as they had at Thika; flights of green parrots whirred by, coming from the forest.[30]

As soon as her Kakamega articles were posted Elspeth returned to Loresho to begin work on Delamere's papers, of which there was a meagre assortment bundled together in baskets. There were no journals or diaries. She lived with Glady while consulting them, and took advantage of her proximity to Nairobi to read files in the Secretariat.

On 15 April Gervas arrived by ship from Ceylon to spend a fortnight in Kenya before sailing to South Africa on tea business. Elspeth took him to Njoro to stay on the farm and Cockie arrived with champagne and lobsters for an impromptu party. Gervas fell under Kenya's spell, appreciating the bracing air of the highlands, the sunshine, the vistas of sky, plains and mountains. Nellie offered to make over a portion of Gikammeh land to the couple, and Elspeth was certainly keen on the idea. They chose a pretty area on which to build a house, and Elspeth wrote to her Aunt Vera, a skilled woodcarver who had already provided some panelling for Gikammeh farmhouse:

> If and when we build a house in Kenya we will arrange a wall for it and will engage you for a large fee to do a piece of high-class carving for it as for the Goya. The panelling is standing up marvellously though a good deal of the rest of the house is falling down – we had a heavy rainstorm the other day and the bathroom roof fell in.[31]

Gervas departed for South Africa by ship from Mombasa on 29 April. He was due to fly back to Kenya on 10 June. Elspeth waited for him at Nairobi aerodrome for three days, not unduly worried because in the absence of any news she merely thought the plane was late. Air travel was as yet unreliable and slow, commercial routes having been introduced only in 1932. There had, however, been a serious accident. Gervas's plane had landed at Broken Hill,

Northern Rhodesia, to pick up the Governor of Nyasaland en route for Kenya, and taken off for the next stop, Mpika. Then bushfires obscured the ground, the pilot got lost, the plane ran out of fuel and they had to ditch. The passengers stepped out unhurt, but they were surrounded by thick bush, no one knew even what country they were in, and the emergency food was found to have gone putrid in the heat. Fortunately they located a small stream which provided drinking water, but they could do nothing but wait and hope for rescue – it would have been lethal to wander in search of other human beings. Having a Governor as a fellow passenger proved to be their salvation – a thorough search was being made across the vastnesses of Africa, and after two days and nights they saw a small plane. It landed on a patch of ground they had cleared of bush, and its pilot informed them they were on the Tanganyika–Northern Rhodesia border. The next day they were taken off one by one.

After a fortnight's holiday, Elspeth and Gervas returned to Europe by plane, with the Gikammeh staff waving bath towels as they flew over Njoro. The flight from Nairobi to London took nine days, beginning with a trip on a biplane from Nairobi to Kisumu on the shores of Lake Victoria. A flying boat took them from Kisumu to Khartoum, from where they flew to Cairo. There followed a train journey to Alexandria, where they embarked on a flying boat to Brindisi. After a train journey to Paris (flying over the Alps was regarded as too dangerous), the final leg to Croydon aerodrome involved a struggle against headwinds over the Channel and a race with a fishing boat – the fishing boat won. The journey would have been relaxing had Elspeth not suffered from chronic airsickness which made her miserable. The plane pitched and wallowed as it flew at two thousand feet over the Sudanese desert at about ninety miles an hour. But the route was shorter by fourteen days than the journey by ship, and gave the Huxleys an opportunity to see the ancient Egyptian sculptures when they landed at Aswan.

After seeing the couple off at Nairobi Nellie had returned sadly to the farm, to find that four calves and her expensive prize bull had perished in her absence, and the bull's carcase had been fed to her dogs.

Elspeth's trip to Kenya left her most concerned about her mother and father. Ordinarily, it is the prerogative of the parent to help out the child who has recently married. It is unusual for a newly married daughter to have to assist her parents, but Elspeth realised this was necessary, and did what she could. She bought them a Ford V8, since their own car, provided by Aunt Vera, was so decrepit as to be almost unusable. But she was not yet in a position to bolster her parents' income, as she did later. Their severe financial difficulties in these lean years had a profound effect on her attitude to money throughout her life. Perhaps leaving Kenya would be the answer to their troubles, suggested Elspeth, but Nellie told her, 'I have no wish whatsoever, *of any kind*, ever to live anywhere except here.'[32]

Nellie had visited England only once since Elspeth left for university, and did not like what she saw. She no longer appreciated upper-class life, of which she had always been scornful and which had changed a great deal since the First World War. She now found it empty and lacking in interest. Gone were the large complements of servants and the notion of a ruling class. The upper classes were beginning to contemplate other ways to survive, such as opening their houses to tourists, or selling them to schools and institutions. Of course Nellie had no house of her own in England, so the decision to stay in East Africa was not difficult. Jos had previously failed to make a go of life in the City, and she herself had few marketable skills to offer. Never a snob, she relished the challenge of making a living from scratch in East Africa, as she had had to do twice. There would be no income in Britain, so to stay where she was seemed prudent and natural.

As for Jos, after the failure of Saa Mbusi, his Tanganyika tobacco farm, he embarked on a new enterprise. Since he was having trouble with his heart at the high altitude of Njoro, he planned to set up a business in Mombasa, at sea level. Elspeth said of him: '[He] cover[ed] scraps of paper with detailed, complicated calculations which invariably proved, beyond all question, the brilliant success of any plan he was hatching.'[33] At the foot of these notes he wrote, 'Therefore, small sums do not matter.' This attitude was to be his downfall.

It was the habit of most Kenya settlers to take an annual holiday at the coast, where they could swim in the warm Indian Ocean and relax on the hot, white coral sands. Jos envisaged creating a simple holiday camp where up-country people could stay from May to October. He acquired land on Mombasa's southern mainland at Flora Point (Ras Kigaangoni) opposite Kilindini harbour, and began to build. The long-suffering Vera, his brother Robin's wife, provided the capital of £600, which she was assured was secured by a mortgage deed on the land and the buildings. On her visit to the Grants at Njoro in 1929 she had seen their financial situation and bought them a Ford car (whose bonnet Nellie painted crimson lake), and she should have known better than to trust her brother-in-law. Apart from Vera's money, Jos put up £400 from another relative, £200 out of income and a further £120. He went into partnership with a man called Fuchs whose company he could not endure, not an auspicious basis on which to build a partnership.

Jos would have done better to buy land on the north mainland, because in 1931 the 1,300-foot-long, fourteen-span, floating Nyali bridge had been opened, joining the island to the mainland. His holiday camp, called the Azania, was difficult to reach by ferry from Mombasa. The place Jos had chosen was singularly inappropriate, with shark-infested waters at high tide and sticky mudflats at low. He made a further error by providing sewage arrangements which contravened Mombasa's regulations and had to be redone. Fuchs, getting the better of Jos, who retired from the fray, died at the Azania early in November 1935, leaving the holiday camp to his wife. It was taken over by the Royal Navy in the Second World War and never used as a hotel again. Needless to say, Jos lost all his money.

Nellie was furious with Jos, insisting that he pay her rent for staying idly at Njoro. As he had no money to contribute to household expenses, their relationship deteriorated further. Perhaps inspired by his daughter's success with writing, Jos tried his hand at short stories. One of them won a competition in the local paper, but he failed to place any others. They were miserable efforts, and Nellie knew he would never make any money from them – one which he gave her to read was so sloppily done that he had changed the name of the hero halfway through without noticing. He was wont to read his stories aloud to neighbours, which failed to endear him to them. Nellie got a £700 overdraft from the bank by saying that if they insisted on repayment Elspeth would take over the mortgage; this would have put her daughter in an impossible position, because she would not want to sell and thereby expel her parents from their home.

Elspeth busied herself with writing the Delamere book as she accompanied Gervas on a working trip to Canada and the United States from October to December 1933. After crossing the Atlantic on the *Duchess of Bedford*, Gervas found her a retreat deep in the Laurentian mountains north of Montreal, where she could write undisturbed, albeit in a temperature of -20 degrees Fahrenheit. Early in December she took the opportunity to look up Bristow Adams, her former Professor of Journalism at Cornell, and celebrate the repeal of the Prohibition laws that month. Christmas was spent on the Atlantic returning home on board the *Olympic*, but Elspeth wasted no time playing shuffleboard on the ship. Much taken by the observation of Emperor Shi Hwang-ti, creator of the Great Wall of China, that 'he who squanders today talking of yesterday's triumph will have nothing to boast of tomorrow', she avoided socialising when she could be writing in her cabin.

Elspeth finished the Delamere biography, which she unwisely called *White Man's Country*. It had emerged at twice the length its publisher Macmillan expected, but recognising its quality, Harold Macmillan, the future Prime Minister and head of the firm, agreed to publish it in two volumes in 1935. Far more than a mere biography, it was rather a history of the early days of colonial Kenya, with D playing the leading role. He was a powerful character with eccentricities enough to delight any biographer. Originally introduced to Africa by big-game-hunting in Somaliland, he travelled southwards with his friend Dr A.E. Atkinson and entered northern BEA in 1896. The beauty and potential of the Rift Valley captured his imagination and he persuaded the Governor, Sir Charles Eliot, to grant him land there. Coming from the landowning class in Britain and the possessor of thousands of acres in BEA, he lived in a mud hut, its floor strewn with Persian rugs, with no mod cons bar a gramophone with a single record, 'All Aboard for Margate'. He brought his wife Florence out to BEA, installing her in another mud hut. In the evenings after dinner, the seat of an American buggy, a cushion on springs, was taken into D's hut and put down next to him on one side of the open fire, and his Maasai herdsmen would troop into the hut. With the headman sitting on the cushion and the rest squatting on their haunches they had long conversations with D in the Maasai language, in which he was fluent, about sheep and other matters of mutual interest. 'There was a terrific smell,' said Powys Cobb, one of D's neighbours.[34] Unsurprisingly, Florence did not participate in this evening entertainment.

D had a beautiful speaking voice and perfect manners, except towards Florence, to whom he was very rude. His view of the civilising mission of the British, and of the African – particularly the Maasai – as a noble savage, never wavered. Politically he favoured white rule, preferably self-rule divorced from meddling central government in London, and he dominated settler politics until his death in 1931. He spent years experimenting with crops and animals in the Rift Valley, built miles of expensive pipeline to irrigate his lands and introduced different breeds of sheep and cattle.

His losses were heavy, and gradually he used up his fortune, until his English estate, Vale Royal in Cheshire, was sold to pay the creditors. Originally an ascetic teetotaller with no interest in women, after the First World War he became a socialite and giver of parties. He died in 1931, and was buried at the spot he had chosen on his farm Soysambu. Many Maasai came to his funeral – the first time Africans had appeared at a white man's graveside – and their fellow tribesmen who could not make it asked the DC to organise a wreath. Whatever the rights and wrongs of Delamere's acquisition of Kenyan land, his persistent experimentation led to the introduction of varieties of crops and animals that were the foundation for a modern economy.

In her research for the book Elspeth did not confine herself to the Delamere papers. In England she interviewed the South African soldier and statesman Jan Smuts, who had led the BEA army in pursuit of the German general Von Lettow Vorbeck in the First World War. Smuts thought the problem of conflict with Africans would solve itself because the white man 'has a germ – the germ of progress – in him and other races [have] not got it'. In his opinion African peoples did not understand this fever, and their desire for education was really a desire for 'white man's magic'. 'Whites are the yeast to leaven Africa,' he concluded.[35] Elspeth also interviewed surviving former Kenya Governors and officials, and tried unsuccessfully to get permission to read despatches in the Colonial Office. Upon being told that these were closed from 1885 onwards, she neatly sidestepped the obstacle by arranging matters with Sir Charles Bowring, formerly Chief Secretary of BEA and afterwards Governor of Nyasaland. She sent him a detailed questionnaire, which he passed on privately to Sir Cecil Bottomley, Assistant Under-Secretary of State in the Colonial Office. Bottomley answered all her questions and returned the document to Bowring.[36]

Elspeth also spent some time in the library of the Colonial Office, which gave her permission to quote D's statements to the Hilton Young Commission, appointed in 1927 to examine the possibility of federating the three British East African territories of Kenya, Uganda and Tanganyika. The library insisted she conceal the source because many witnesses had not wanted their evidence made public. Much of the information for her book came from people she had interviewed in Kenya, including all the settler pioneers. Dr A.E. Atkinson, D's companion on his early travels, was particularly helpful. Atkinson recounted that when he had found it necessary in the early days to shoot two Africans to quell a threatened tribal war he was sent to the only prison which could accommodate whites –

Fort Jesus in Mombasa. He was put on the train and told to make his own way there, and on arrival at Mombasa station the Governor, Sir Charles Eliot, greeted him warmly and asked him to breakfast at Government House. Atkinson explained he was on the way to prison, but Eliot said, 'Never mind, have breakfast with me first and go to jail later.'

Elspeth was not a trained historian, and her treatment of documents and quotations was sometimes positively cavalier. She occasionally extracted pages from Delamere's papers to take away with her, no doubt a temptation before the age of the photocopier, though perhaps Glady had given her permission to do so. She also rarely quoted accurately, not exactly falsifying quotations to suit her argument, but often omitting sections without any indication that this had been done, and amalgamating two documents into one. But she had an extraordinary ability to enliven any narrative and to simplify political manoeuvrings, making them stimulating and comprehensible to her readers. *White Man's Country* gave full rein to her ability to write well, and she displayed in it a remarkable facility with style and vocabulary. Her skill with metaphor and simile was one of her greatest talents. Her prose was poetic and subtly energised by her use of visual imagery.

Elspeth succeeded in the difficult task that faces all biographers – conveying to the reader the essence of the man or woman being written about. She hid neither Delamere's faults nor his eccentricities, while leaving readers with a full understanding of how and why he became the settlers' leader. In the early years of BEA private citizens had no say in the country's laws, which came by decree from London and were enforced by officials. The British government's attitude often caused resentment among the settlers, who were more individualist and self-reliant than most – that was why they had come to BEA. As there was no official procedure for putting settlers' views before the government an unofficial spokesman was necessary, and Delamere was elected by common consent to fill this role.

Delamere considered that BEA officials took shelter from the rough-and-tumble of competition, from the struggle for existence,

behind a safe salary and the prospect of a pension after twenty
years. He therefore saw his role as leader of the opposition to them.
Elspeth detailed all his contests and endeavours, both political and
financial. He sank so much money into BEA that receivers took
possession of his Cheshire estate. The book also offers fascinating
little details, such as Delamere's attempt to breed a hybrid equine
perfectly suited to the country's conditions. He allowed a zebra
stallion to run with donkey mares. The resulting foals were fawn
in body with zebra heads, legs and tails, and a black stripe down
their backbones. Unfortunately they turned out to have vicious
and surly natures, and only one was tamed. Delamere sold it to a
chemist, who for many years drove it around Nairobi pulling a
buggy.

The story of the white colonists' labours and conflicts in early
BEA was close to Elspeth's heart, for she had grown up in the
country while they were taking place. In the early 1930s her sympa-
thies were all with the colonists, and she used the opportunity of
writing D's biography to counter some of the arguments put forward in books and newspapers by Norman Leys and William
McGregor Ross, who were both of the opinion that Africa should
be for the Africans and the sale of land to white farmers was wrong.*
Elspeth's attitude was very much that of Rudyard Kipling, who
scribbled this verse for Sir Robert Coryndon, the Governor of Kenya
from 1922 to 1925, while they were aboard ship together:

> They that dig foundations deep
> Fit for realms to rise upon
> Little honour do they reap
> Of their generation
> Any more than mountains gain
> Stature till we reach the plain.[37]

Upon the publication of *White Man's Country* in May 1935,
McGregor Ross predictably gave it a hostile review in the *New*

---

* Leys was a Government Medical Officer who criticised the Maasai move from Laikipia
and the BEA settlers – see his *Kenya* (1924). McGregor Ross was Director of Public Works
in BEA. He published *Kenya from Within* in 1927.

Statesman. The Times, however, called it 'a remarkable book . . . The main controversies are set out, for all to appraise, not only with understanding and accuracy, but also with humour, perspective, and a keen judgment . . . If Imperial history were always made so readable, it would be better understood.' The *Times Literary Supplement*'s anonymous reviewer wrote (13 June 1935): 'Mrs. Huxley's book is . . . excellent. She has shown great industry in the collection and sifting of material; and while she handles it with that sense of the picturesque which it deserves, she never loses perspective or a sound historical sense. Of dropsical and unbalanced biographies we have nowadays more than enough. This is nothing of the sort. Mrs. Huxley writes with lucidity and restraint, but she makes her story fascinating, and these two volumes, for all their detail, are easy to read. She is, moreover, no hero-worshipper, and she paints Delamere's curious personality, which was at once engaging and aloof, with a sure and vivid touch.'

Elspeth received several letters from colonists thanking her for putting their point of view. Lady Eleanor Cole, the wife of Galbraith Cole, brother of Delamere's first wife Florence, said the book would put new heart into the white colonists. Sir Edward Grigg, Governor of Kenya from 1925 to 1930, said, 'Of course one can always interpret this or that episode a little differently, but I feel you have produced a very fair and balanced account of the colony's many vicissitudes . . . More power to you in wrestling with Norman Leys.'[38] T.J. O'Shea, a garage owner in Eldoret and prominent in Kenyan political affairs, liked the book but felt he had been denied recognition for the vital part he considered he had played on the colonists' delegation to Britain in 1930 when, he said, Delamere was in the first stages of senile decay. If she published a revised edition he begged her to do him the compliment of reading some of his speeches. Cecil Bottomley of the Colonial Office thanked her for saying in her preface that his help was limited by official discretion, 'because it makes it impossible for anyone to regard me as the source of the more startling information which you have put in your book'. He wondered if she was sure about the details of an interview in 1923, because 'there are two of us still here who had a great deal to do with the events of that time, but that particular point is fresh to us'.[39]

Lord Francis Scott, Delamere's successor as leader of the Kenya whites, called the book 'a supreme masterpiece', while Margery Perham, making her name in academia as a thinker about the British Empire, wrote in the *Spectator* that Elspeth had 'surely laid for ever the almost ogre-ish figure of the greedy capitalist growing fat upon the easy loot of a new continent and by the callous exploitation of the natives'. She did, however, add a trenchant criticism of colonialism:

> A general view of Africa today suggests serious doubts as to the soundness of Delamere's view that colonialization is the best agent of civilization. It introduces a deep conflict ... What it gives natives by way of example or material development it takes away in more imponderable, but perhaps more vital elements, tribal pride, individual self-respect, full scope for development and that very sense of responsibility which settlers so earnestly desire for themselves.[40]

As for Glady Delamere herself, Nellie reported that she 'is trotting round culling kudos for herself for having discovered the New Young Writer. Alone she did it. Damn her eyes, when it was *entirely* your initiative.'[41] Nellie also took some of the credit herself: 'I can't understand your remarks about not knowing grammar. Have you entirely forgotten those grammar lessons in the grass hut in the old home?' Today the book still stands as a fine achievement. Elspeth was pleased with its reception, which encouraged her in her tentative plan of trying to make a living from writing.

What she failed to realise, understandably enough in the intellectual climate of the time, was the detrimental effect of white colonialism in Africa. She accepted Delamere's view that colonialism was the best agent of civilisation, ignoring, or perhaps not understanding, that it denied Africans self-respect and tribal pride. In later years she felt she had to justify the title of the book by saying she had meant the words 'White Man's Country' to refer to the climate of the highlands of Kenya. When it was reprinted in 1968, she pointed out in an exculpatory preface the beliefs of the period in which she originally wrote it:

> The land to which Delamere came was, by European standards, wholly primitive. Its scattered peoples, grouped into separate and mutually hostile tribes, were pagan, frequently nomadic, ignorant of the outside world and of such simple devices as the plough, the wheel, the pump, the loom, the coin; they had evolved no alphabet, built no cities, made no roads; their tool was the digging stick, their dress the skin, their weapon the spear ... Europeans were civilised, Africans were not; *ergo*, the European incursion that carried with it Christianity, literacy, the *pax Britannica* and an end to famines and epidemics could be nothing but a boon to Africans. It was as simple as that.[42]

Later still, having lived through Kenya's independence from Britain and personal soul-searching about the legacy of colonialism and, indeed, the very nature of 'civilisation', she wrote:

> The colonialist hyena [is] emerging from the shadows into which the comrades drove him in the bad old imperialist days. Now that western imperialism (though certainly not other forms) has receded into history, the white colonist can be seen not only with his manifest failings, but with virtues it is no longer blasphemous to recognise.[43]

With the development of global communications in the late nineteenth and the twentieth centuries, Africa was bound to encounter the cultures of other peoples not only along its coastline, as formerly, but far inland. The resulting contact inevitably altered Africa profoundly. There was good as well as bad in these developments, as Kenya's first African President, Jomo Kenyatta, recognised when he said goodbye to Arthur Cole, Galbraith Cole's son and Delamere's nephew, on his final departure from Kenya. Now an old man, Kenyatta struggled to his feet to shake Cole's hand and thank him for all that his family had done for the country.

FOUR

Red Strangers
and the Early Crime Novels

The critical success of *White Man's Country* confirmed Elspeth in
her ambition to be a writer. Because it can be done anywhere,
writing is a useful occupation for someone accompanying a
peripatetic spouse. Travel also provides an ideal opportunity
to collect material for books and newspaper articles. In the 1930s,
before the Huxleys settled into a house of their own, they toured
the world widely together, frequently by sea because air travel
was still novel and expensive. Passengers on pre-Second World
War liners lived a life of games and entertainment and dancing
to bands in the evening. There were competitions and ship-
board sports such as shuffleboard, 'horse' racing with wooden
horses pulled along by string wound on to bobbins, deck quoits
and, in warmer climes, swimming in a small deck pool. 'Housey
housey' (bingo) or whist drives were organised for the evenings,
and there was a daily printed news-sheet. Fancy dress was popular,
and ships kept stores of strange clothes for dressing up. Passengers
could guess the distance sailed on the previous day, and those who
guessed the nearest to the correct mileage won prizes. There were
cocktail parties and the much-prized invitation to the captain's
table. It was a closed and cosy world, but Elspeth seldom wanted
to participate in games or competitions. She found sea voyages
tedious, and filled her days by writing on deck or, preferably, in
her cabin to avoid over-friendly fellow-passengers. Meanwhile

Gervas liked to join in with the other passengers, being good at deck games.

A typical sea voyage the Huxleys undertook was to South Africa on the *Carnarvon Castle* in January 1933. For once the Bay of Biscay was as gentle as if oil had been cast upon it. Elspeth thought the passengers a lot of decrepit stuffed owls, very different from those on the east coast run, via the Suez Canal, on which one always met interesting fellow-Kenyans. Edward the Prince of Wales was on board, with his equerry Ulick Alexander, Cockie's brother, but he had a couple of plump females to play with, so was fairly self-contained. Gervas won all the deck-tennis events, and Elspeth, when not writing, concentrated on learning to dive, as an instructor went with the swimming pool. After landing at Cape Town the Huxleys hired a car at Ceylon's expense and drove to East London and Natal and thence to Basutoland, where Gervas tried to teach the Africans to drink more tea. Elspeth found the white South Africans amiable but 'asleep'. From South Africa she caught a boat to Mombasa, while Gervas continued on to Calcutta.

'Tea,' said Elspeth, 'seems to demand great nobility of its servants.' Before the outbreak of the Second World War the Huxleys went at various times to the Dutch East Indies, Belgium, Holland, Scandinavia, South Africa, Ceylon, Australia and Mexico. They had a trip to Tanganyika in 1936 and annual visits to the United States, which they explored from coast to coast. They also tried to visit Kenya every year. In April 1935 Elspeth went to Yugoslavia alone to gather material for newspaper articles.

The years 1933 to 1936 were those in which they travelled most. They returned from a visit to Canada and the United States at the end of 1933, to have only a month at home in London before they set off once more, for South Africa. October 1934 saw them bound for the United States and Canada yet again. On this occasion Gervas ended up in a Montreal hospital with a broken rib after a fall. The following September they embarked again for the USA. While Gervas went to Chicago 'to set up tea rooms for gangsters', Elspeth struck off on her own to do research in the South. The outcome was two articles for *The Times* (16 and 17 April 1935) on 'A New

Deal for Farmers – the American Experiment' and one for the *Geographical Magazine* of July 1935, 'In the New South: An American Experiment', in which she discussed Roosevelt's 'New Deal' politics and their effect on farmers. Roosevelt had created the Tennessee Valley Authority in 1933, to spend $100 million on transfroming an area in the southern states larger than England and Wales. Erosion was tackled, land was treated with fertiliser, and a network of dams was designed to provide water power to electrify homes and generate electricity for new industries. The rugged individualism and poverty of the hillbillies was put an end to, and the standard of living of the southerners rose.

Gervas and Elspeth crossed the United States together before embarking at Los Angeles on the SS *Mariposa* for three weeks in Melbourne, Australia, via Hawaii and Fiji. They travelled on to Java and Ceylon before crossing the Indian Ocean to Mombasa, Elspeth destined for another stay with Nellie at Gikammeh while Gervas continued onwards to South Africa.

Encouraged by the success of her American articles, Elspeth wanted to repeat her travels the following year, when the Huxleys returned to America in September. She set off on her own by car to visit the Adirondacks, Ithaca, Louisville (Kentucky), Ohio, Nashville (Tennessee) and Atlanta (Georgia), at the same time writing the first draft of a crime novel, before meeting up with Gervas for the return voyage in November. This time she concentrated on America's major farming problem – soil erosion and the bare lands of the Dust Bowl in the Prairie states. She foresaw that her beloved Kenya would suffer the same fate if Africans were allowed to keep the huge numbers of cattle required for wealth and status, and her warnings became a dominant theme of her later writings on East Africa. Elspeth was unusual for her time in being a woman unafraid to travel alone to lands unknown to her. She seemed fearless, transgressing with aplomb society's protective strictures about lone women.

The Huxleys' hectic pace and constant travel made it uneconomic for them to have a place of their own, and when they were in London they stayed in Gervas's brother's flat, or rented others (in

Jermyn Street and Clarges Street) for short periods. In London Elspeth embarked on a way of life which sometimes irritated Gervas. She filled their weekends with trips to see people like Aunt Vera in Eastbourne and Trudie Denman at her mansion, Balcombe in Sussex, seeming unwilling to have a quiet weekend at home with her husband. This restless behaviour was a symptom of her prodigious energy, but also hinted at a lack of satisfaction with her domestic lot. She was the driving force in the marriage, as Nellie was in hers, though the exquisitely mannered Gervas was never as easily cowed as Jos. He accompanied her on the weekend jaunts, despite his tiring weekdays in the office.

By January 1935, however, the peripatetic existence was beginning to pall. The Huxleys decided it was time to have a more permanent flat of their own, and rented 112 St Mary Abbot's Court in Kensington. Now the possessor of her own kitchen, Elspeth cursed her mother for not having taught her to cook, which provoked the riposte from Nellie, '*You* insisted on leaving the home before there was time, and got sacked from the seminary before you could do Domestic Science.'[1] The new flat had the advantage of a ground-floor room which would be a suitable study for Elspeth. It came in useful for reading the page proofs of *White Man's Country*.

With a place of her own, Elspeth could now invite Nellie to come to England and stay with her.

Her regular visits to Nellie in Kenya allowed Elspeth to keep in constant touch with the financial rollercoaster of the Grants' affairs. Nellie had persisted with farming at Gikammeh, and having failed to sell her pigs at any price was now attempting to breed angora rabbits for their wool. She also tried to grow pyrethrum, used for making insecticide, and was one of the first farmers to experiment with it successfully. Pyrethrum was a labour-intensive crop, and Nellie persuaded her squatters' wives to do the work of picking the flowerheads. She undertook several voluntary activities, becoming a flower-show judge, which took her to various parts of the country. When not judging flowers she was mightily successful herself at exhibiting them, and walked away with many prizes. She sought seeds from all corners of the world, and Elspeth's journeys to America were opportunities for Nellie to beg her to buy American geranium and fuchsia seeds. Until Nellie died, a fair proportion of Elspeth's time was spent finding obscure seed merchants in different countries.

Nellie was kept cheerful by regular visits from a gin-bearing Cockie, who had recently left the philandering Bror Blixen and was now living with the brilliant and temperamental architect Jan Hoogterp* (called 'Hookie'), assistant to Sir Herbert Baker, the designer of the new Government House in Nairobi. Cockie and Nellie went off on a safari, financed by Cockie, to Kericho, Kisii and the Kakamega goldfields, and thence via Eldoret to Kapsiliat. At Kisii they stayed with the District Commissioner, Jack Dawson, formerly a farmer at Njoro, who had lost a leg in the First World War. Recently Dawson had been paid a visit by the famous anthropologist Bronislaw Malinowski, later to be Elspeth's teacher at the London School of Economics, who had spent his stay trying to pinch the bottom of the nursery governess. Five weeks later Nellie was appalled to hear that Dawson had died of typhoid fever, shortly before his second son was born. Kenya was still a dangerous country. Nellie's friend Tich Miles also died prematurely, in April 1934, of something that sounds like meningitis.

Cockie dwelt on the fringe of the Happy Valley set, a small group of people living in moneyed idleness in the Wanjohi valley, on the Rift Valley side of the Aberdares between the mountains of Kipipiri and Satima. Unfortunately their garish image has obscured the picture of the Kenya settlers, greater far in number, who were dedicated to the land and had a capacity for committed toil. They were not Nellie's sort at all, but her friendship with Cockie meant that she saw them fairly frequently. She called them the 'Smart Set' and, though no prude, disapproved of their heavy drinking, drug-taking and sexual promiscuity. Now and then she visited

---

* Hoogterp later left Kenya for Johannesburg, where one of his achievements was to plan and lay out Lusaka, the capital of Northern Rhodesia (now Zambia). He was hopeless with money, got into debt, took to drink and died young.

Clouds, the large thatched house in the Wanjohi valley of the five-times married Lady Idina Sackville, former wife of Josslyn Hay, the playboy twenty-second Earl of Erroll, and now married to Donald Haldeman. Idina's incorrigible affairs meant that her marriage to Donald, whose money came from clothing manufacture, was far from tranquil. After one explosive quarrel he drove off, leaving her on the verandah crying after him, 'You makers of shirts, how can you understand us, who have been wanton through the ages?' Donald once shot out the tyres of her current beau's car. Idina stayed at Gikammeh once or twice, and Nellie also sometimes put up Kiki Preston, a cocaine addict and member of the Happy Valley set, or went to stay with her.

Joss Erroll and his wife Molly stayed with Nellie on the night when he spoke to the Njoro District Association on the subject of British Fascism. Nellie was far from impressed by his lecture, or by the fact that whenever he declared that British Fascism stood for complete freedom, Molly could be heard at the other end of the room saying that within five years he would be dictator of Kenya. Erroll had divorced Lady Idina to marry Molly, possibly in order to move into the magnificent Oserian, a splendid white and minareted house on the shore of Lake Naivasha in the Rift Valley.

Oserian came in useful for 'parking Pa', a scheme Nellie and Elspeth discussed in detail. Stung by the shambles over his Azania holiday camp affair, Jos had returned to live with Nellie at Gikammeh. In 1934, undeterred by his lack of success with short stories, he decided to go to live cheaply in the Seychelles and write a book about them, but it was tartly turned down by the London literary agents Curtis Brown and never published. With that, his literary experiments came to an end. He was unhappy living at Njoro, which was rendered too chilly by both the weather and Nellie's somewhat contemptuous attitude towards him – she told Elspeth, 'I've been very near signing off Pa's kipande lately but I don't suppose I shall.'[2] She tried to find a farm at a lower altitude which would take him as a paying guest – hence the brief and unsuccessful sojourn at the Errolls' house.

Ever energetic, Nellie had joined the East Africa Women's League,

founded in 1917 'to take an interest in, and action on where necessary, all matters affecting the welfare and happiness of women and
children of all races'. She also belonged to the Natural History
Society and the Race Improvement Society, though pieces she tele-
graphed for the latter were garbled by the Njoro postmaster trans-
cribing her 'population' as 'copulation'. This somewhat negated the
effect of her argument. She was very wary of the more extreme
members of the Race Improvement Society, including Ewart Grogan, the womanising proprietor of Torr's Hotel in Nairobi and a
domineering character who brooked no opposition. She also
derided Lord Delamere's successor Lord Francis Scott for his
'stupid' idea of a British East African state from the Limpopo to
the Nile, run by whites.

Rather than contravene natural justice by limiting African fertility, Nellie wanted the EAWL to work at the eugenics of whites,
some of whom, she lamented, were breeding 'like rabbits'. Three
hundred white children in Kenya were getting no education at all.
Kenya's 'poor whites' were mainly Afrikaners, but there was also a
group who had emigrated from Britain and failed at farming, and
were forced to live in very poor circumstances. Eugenics was a
fashionable subject in the 1930s, before the actions of Adolf Hitler
made it taboo, and no more is heard of Nellie's interest in it after
1939. As if she did not have enough to occupy her, she was also a
member of the Squatters' Committee and on the board of Nakuru
hospital, which entailed frequent, often acrimonious quarrels with
the doctors. In April 1935, on the occasion of George V's Silver
Jubilee, she was awarded a silver medal from Buckingham Palace
for social services.

Nellie's finances were still dire and she asked Elspeth to guarantee
an extension to her overdraft in order to plant more pyrethrum.
She also converted the Ford car bought for her and Jos by Aunt
Vera to run on paraffin, for economy's sake, because she could not
afford to license and run the new Ford V8 Elspeth had bought
them. Anxious that Jos should not borrow money from Elspeth,
Nellie told her to write business letters to her separately, and to
type the address on the envelope so that he would not know what

they were discussing. Elspeth was so concerned at their financial situation that Nellie mocked her for going all filial and shouldering the white child's burden of old, unpleasant, indigent parents. Elspeth sent money to replace the old car's tyres, and dresses from England and New York. She also offered cash, but Nellie said it would make her too miserable to take her daughter's money. However, eventually necessity made her swallow her pride and accept.

Nellie still envisaged Elspeth and Gervas building a house on the ten-acre plot she had given them, and plans were drawn up for one by the architect Dorothy Hughes. The Huxleys arranged for a cage for fruit trees to be constructed on their plot, and in 1937 Nellie bought several cows to start a dairy herd for them.

In June 1935 Nellie had a windfall – Trudie Denman paid her fare to England, gave her money to employ a manager in her absence,* and paid to 'park Pa', who had recently had a heart attack, in the Seychelles, where he was writing his ill-fated book. Nellie stayed with Elspeth in the London flat, with Aunt Blanche in Wales and with Trudie at Balcombe and Thorpe Ness. Seeing her daughter and husband on their own ground, she began to realise that they might never make their future on the farm in Kenya, particularly as colonial policy under the Labour and subsequent National coalition governments was hostile to the idea of settlement as whites in Africa had known it. With considerable gloom she began half-heartedly to look for alternative places to live, now that she had failed to make a go of the Njoro farm. In August Elspeth and Gervas took her on holiday to the south of France, and she wondered about settling there, but Elspeth squashed the idea.

Nellie and Elspeth were utterly interdependent, despite behaving like two pieces of sandpaper rubbing together when they were in each other's company. To the outsider the relationship between the two women can seem odd – for instance, mother and daughter

---

* In fact she left the farm in the hands of Muchoka, a light-skinned Mkamba from Machakos, south-east of Nairobi, with slanting eyes, wispy moustache and a little jaw-defining beard, who had become her headman on Njombo's retirement. Literate, honest and charming, Muchoka was also good with dogs – essential in Nellie's household, which now boasted six dachshunds.

exchanged risqué jokes, Mae West being the butt of many. For example: 'What is the difference between Mae West and Mount Kenya? Only eight men have ever been up Mount Kenya.'

At the end of September Nellie returned to Kenya, flying from Cairo in a biplane which crash-landed at a tiny aerodrome in the Sudan desert. While awaiting rescue, the passengers heard on the radio that Italy had invaded Abyssinia (now Ethiopia), on Kenya's northern and Sudan's eastern border. They were rescued after two days and Nellie made her way back to Njoro, where Muchoka had been an excellent manager in her absence.

The Italian invasion of Abyssinia prompted a short-lived boom in Kenya's economy, because Italian troops needed the provisions Kenya's farmers could supply. Nellie's financial worries were temporarily suspended, although the pyrethrum she was drying and selling affected her skin, making her eyelids peel and her hands very sore. Nevertheless, her crop won first prize at the Nakuru Show.

Elspeth assuaged her guilt about not joining her parents and living in Kenya by visiting whenever she could. Gervas would sometimes snatch a fortnight or more there, but his work precluded more prolonged visits. The main event of one of Elspeth's stays was a safari with her parents and Ingrid and Gillis Lindstrom to Serengeti in Tanganyika in 1936. 'Ingrid,' said Elspeth, 'possessed a quality hard to define; I would not call it placidity since that suggests a certain torpidness, and she was anything but that; her sense of humour was as lively as Nellie's and in her deep, slow, well-articulated voice she would deliver pungent comments which never crossed the border from shrewdness into spite. In all the ups and downs of life – and the Lindstroms had a good many downs – she remained calm, tolerant and good-humoured; I never saw her fly into a temper or give way to despair.'[3]

The party, including Kibushu (as general factotum) and Karoma (as cook), all piled into two decrepit cars and progressed three miles down the road before their first breakdown. Faulty wiring was the problem, and after it had been fixed by the local German mechanic they proceeded on their way through Nakuru on to the Narok road, the local wildlife putting them in mind of Cockie's definition of a highball as part of a giraffe. They successfully crossed two rivers – five miles before Narok the Sabaya running into its huge rocky gorge, and beyond Narok the southern Uaso Nyiro – and when the road petered out they camped for the night. The Tanganyika border, distinguishable only by two little dukas, was crossed in the early afternoon of the next day. Soon Fish Lindstrom disappeared beneath the crimson bonnet of the Model A Ford and threw away the brake rod, saying the car would be better off without it. None the less, they finally reached Loliondo, and looked down on the magnificent Serengeti plains.

The weather was breaking up so they retraced their steps to nearby Soysambu – a two-duka settlement, not Delamere's farm of the same name in the Rift Valley. Steady rain fell all night, but they had a fortunate encounter the next morning, with Tak Singh, a burly Sikh with a huge black beard, a charming smile, a ready laugh and delightful manners. They built a road of sticks and branches to get through the mud, then came across a huge concourse of Maasai, the inhabitants of this stretch of Africa, dancing in lion head-dresses as they moved pastures. As the safari's aim was to see lions, they shot a zebra, leaving it out as a kill. Alas, hyenas rather than lions demolished it. Fish picked some hairs from a thorn, claiming they were lion hairs, whereupon Nellie, when he was not looking, put some from her own head on another thorn. Fish duly determined that they too were lions'.

A Maasai told them they should go on twenty-five miles, to Njoro Eibor, for lions. There was no road and the mud was so sticky that they hired an Indian to take them in his lorry, at 75 cents a mile. Fish and Elspeth sat perched on the luggage in the back. When it started to rain they covered themselves with a tarpaulin full of holes, leaky as a colander. The lorry broke down just after they crossed the Pollilet river, which now became a swirling, raging torrent. They were cut off, soaked and frozen, and the mosquitoes fed on them mercilessly. Two donkeys arrived, the river dropped a little, and the bedraggled party managed to cross it and walk back the way they had come, leaving the Indian working on his lorry on the other side of the river.

After a long trek through drizzle, and one mile from Soysambu, where they had left their cars, the lorry, having been restarted and eased across the river, caught them up. There was no point in continuing the safari, and Tak Singh, whom they met up with again at Soysambu, said he would escort them back with his lorry. The first ten miles took two hours and then the cars stuck fast again, so camp was made. Ironically, unseen lions sniffed around their tents all night. Tak Singh was laid low with fever and had to be nursed; when he was better they left him to take his lorry back and proceeded onwards into Kenya. Elspeth had borne all the costs of this rather disappointing journey, though her verdict was that even when getting stuck all the time it was a marvellous feeling to be absolutely away and cut off from everything, quite self-contained and self-reliant in your own unit.

Gervas flew from South Africa to join Elspeth at Njoro, and in May 1936 the pair travelled to Uganda, staying with the Governor, Sir Philip Mitchell. They then flew up the Nile to Egypt, where they spent two weeks while Gervas tried to convert the Egyptians from hashish to tea. Material gathered along the way by Elspeth provided the basis for an article on General Gordon of Khartoum, which was accepted by *The Times*. This may have been the trip on which they had to wait for several nights at a landing strip on the Nile while spare parts for their plane were brought from Cairo. The temperature was 110 degrees Fahrenheit in the shade, but a hospitable detachment of the Egyptian army took them in. One of the passengers, a Belgian with his own whisky supply, toped all day, snored raucously at night and broke into frequent, tuneless, obscene song. The strictly Muslim Egyptians were most upset and the other passengers profoundly embarrassed.

Elspeth and Gervas were back in England at the end of May, and on holiday in Scotland in August. Elspeth had only a week or two in the London flat before she travelled to Kenya again in December. By now Nellie had terraced Elspeth's plot on the farm and planted trees. As well as providing irregular donations of money, Elspeth was sending quarterly payments to her mother, so it appears that she was buying the plot from her.

At this period Elspeth was thinking deeply about the anti-white-settlement views of Margery Perham, though she believed she was under several delusions about Kenya. For example, when the wife of the Nyeri Provincial Commissioner took Miss Perham into the Kikuyu reserve and chatted to Kikuyu women outside their huts, Margery was astonished to see that a white woman could be treated with friendship by the Kikuyus. Elspeth decided to write a book purely about the Africans, partly in answer to critics, including Margery Perham, who felt she had ignored the African point of view in her *White Man's Country*, and partly because of her growing interest in African responses to colonialism. According to Elspeth the idea for such a book had been germinating for a while from its seed as a sort of biography of Karanja, who had worked for Nellie for years. It is not clear which Karanja she meant, because there were two men of that name who worked for Nellie. Elspeth interviewed both of them about their backgrounds.

Karanja, son of Mukoro, was a small boy when Nellie came to BEA, and his first job was to lead the oxen under yoke. He graduated to helping turn the coffee beans while they were being dried, to prevent overheating. He had a vivid memory of Elspeth as a child playing with a stick to represent a gun during the First World War, saying she was going to shoot all the Germans. From bean-turning he moved to carrying young trees for planting. Tired of this work, he returned to his home in the Kikuyu reserve four miles away. After working for a while on another farm he returned to Kitimuru, where he stayed until he was circumcised, the mark of entering manhood. He then went back to the reserve to help his mother while his father rode over the Aberdares to Njoro, upon Nellie's move to Gikammeh. Karanja joined him there a year later, decided to stay, then returned to Thika to fetch the girl he wished to buy as a wife. His wife joined him in 1928, the year named 'Ithingiria' for its earthquake. He was still paying for her, having already given fourteen goats, three cows, two heifers and a young bull. He now worked for Nellie as a herdsman.

The second Karanja, son of the affluent Kinoko and his eighth wife, lived in the Kikuyu reserve as a boy. In the famine of the 1890s the only one of Kinoko's wives to survive was Karanja's mother. Kinoko then went to work for Fawcus and a clerk called Smith at Kishobo, the farm of Nigel and Lilian Graham at Njoro, where he became a squatter. When the First World War broke out he was seven years old. All the whites went to war, he said, except Smith, who was left to look after four farms. Karanja worked as a kitchen boy for 'Bwana Gatuni' (unidentified) for three years, then went to Beryl Clutterbuck (Markham) until she left Njoro, and subsequently to Reginald Pelham Burn, Nellie's partner in the ploughing business. One of his duties was to keep an eye on Pelham Burn's mentally disturbed brother, who kept running away. The Grahams at Kishobo used him as a shamba (garden) worker while he learned to drive oxen and plough. When tractors supervened he became a tractor driver for a year.

After Nellie's arrival at Njoro, he worked in her house, and he accompanied her to Piggery Nook. When she visited England in the late 1920s he looked after her house and chickens, and used the opportunity to go to school at the Unga Flour factory, to learn to read and write. He accompanied Nellie on a trip to Meru in 1929 and on safari to Tanganyika. He married, but when his wife's children died he took another wife. In 1935 Nellie paid ten shillings for him to go up in an aeroplane. He was now her cook.

Elspeth was also encouraged to write a book about Africans by Nellie's burgeoning interest in the Kikuyu people, fostered by her recent acquaintance with the archaeologist and anthropologist Louis Leakey, born in 1903 of missionary parents, Canon Harry and May Leakey, at the Kabete mission near Nairobi. When Nellie met him, Leakey and his wife Mary were excavating ancient skeletons in the Rift Valley, just over two miles from Nakuru. Leakey's magnum opus, a study of the Kikuyu people, their pre-history, culture and customs, planned as a three-volume work, was in preparation, the first volume having already reached a million words (it was finally published in 1977). Leakey told Nellie he wanted to meet Elspeth, but was nervous because he had been informed she 'had a fierce hate against him ... I assured him ... that nothing was further from the case, that you were practically a wrecked soul from the hopeless passion you cherished for him.'[4]

Although Leakey and his son Richard were to hold important posts in Kenya after the Kikuyu Jomo Kenyatta became President in 1964, at this time he believed Kenyatta, who was campaigning for African political rights, to be a malign influence. He regarded Kenyatta's writings on Kikuyu religion as inaccurate and entirely his own invention, an opinion confirmed to him by some Kikuyu elders, and saw his childhood friend Peter Koinange, son of senior chief Mbiyu Koinage, as the up-and-coming Kikuyu leader. Leakey wanted to stand for election to the Legislative Council in order to have Koinange as his lieutenant and train him in the ways of politics. The plan proved impractical, as all Nairobi's hotels and restaurants said they would refuse to admit Koinange even if he was accompanied by a white man. Impressed by Leakey, Nellie started to take private Kikuyu lessons from him. She also began a school on her farm for the children of her Kikuyu squatters, importing mission-educated Africans as teachers. One of them, Jehosophat, attracted eighty pupils. This was not entirely an altruistic measure on Nellie's part – she had forbidden her squatters to keep goats, important animals in Kikuyu rituals but devastating to the land, and feared they would leave her unless she provided an incentive to stay.

Nellie and Elspeth decided to go to live for a month or so in the Kikuyu reserve, to research Elspeth's book on Karanja or perhaps the Kikuyu in general, as her riposte to critics who pigeonholed her as a colonialist author. First they had Christmas at Gikammeh, with Nellie holding a beer party for the neighbours and Elspeth giving Njombo a present of the January 1937 issue of the *Geographical Magazine* containing photographs she had taken of him and the farm. Jos, Nellie and Elspeth spent New Year's Eve at the Muthaiga Club, which was overflowing into tents pitched in the garden, such was the number of people flocking to Nairobi for the races. At midnight the sky was lit up by a huge bonfire and rockets.

Elspeth danced all night, but a day later it was time to tear herself away from reading *Gone With the Wind* and get down to work. At Nellie's request the Nyeri PC had put at their disposal a camp, named after the local chief Murigo, nineteen miles from Nyeri and seven from Karatina, and had engaged an interpreter to be at their disposal on 2 January 1937. Just before they left for the camp Elspeth wrote to Gervas, who was spending Christmas with his father at Wootton near Oxford, 'I believe there *is* a really good book there – I am still in a complete fog as to how it is to be handled, but a lot of nebulous ideas are beginning to float about . . . I can't hope to get a real insight into the native mind.'[5]

On 2 January Nellie, Elspeth and Karanja the cook set off in the old Ford. They found Murigo's camp to be atop a ridge and ringed with wattle, 6,500 feet up and with a wondrous view of Mount Kenya towering beside it. On rich red soil stood a banda (a grass-roofed hut, usually with only three grass walls and an open end) which would be their living quarters. There were three other huts roofed with banana leaves, which would serve as bedrooms for Nellie, Elspeth and the interpreter. The interpreter, named Robert, had graduated from high school and was now a teacher at the nearby Church of Scotland mission, Tumu Tumu.

They went to meet Chief Murigo, a great warrior in his youth who proved to be half Maasai and half Kikuyu and had fourteen wives and innumerable children. Every day he went in his handsome Chevrolet to Karatina six miles away to preside over the kiama, or tribunal. He explained the recent abdication of Edward VIII to the kiama by saying that the King wanted to marry an unsuitable woman, and the kiama stuck their toes in so he resigned. He assigned one of his bodyguards, an old man in a red blanket, to look after Nellie and Elspeth and guard their camp. One of Murigo's many sons was assigned to help Karanja.

That evening Nellie and Elspeth went for a long walk in the reserve with Robert, and were followed like the Pied Piper by a retinue of curious onlookers. When an old man gave them a present of a chicken they invited him to their camp, in the hope that he would tell them stories of former days. That night, as they sat round the open fire, the old man gave it as his opinion that customs were changing so rapidly that young boys who went to school no longer even knew of them.

Elspeth's letters from Murigo's camp to Gervas, whom she addressed as 'Gerry', began by being girlish: 'I do hope all goes well with you, my poor pet. You'll be pleased to hear we gave Murigo a present of a teapot, a kettle and a pound of tea.'[6] The only European novelties that had caught on in the reserve were tea, coffee, cocoa, salt and onions, and Karatina had a whole row of little teashops. Although Elspeth kept saying to Gervas, 'You are a lamb for letting me do this,' she soon began to be irritated by what she considered to be the whining tone of his replies: 'I wish you would go out and about more and really you would miss me less.'[7] It was distracting to be getting such depressed letters from her husband every mail, for it made her feel she should go dashing back to him. She was sorry the plan had not worked out for him, but told him he would soon be on his way to America, where he might have some fun: 'At least you won't have to crouch over a smoking fire to keep warm – did you ever get that larger size electric fire we agreed we needed?'[8] Eventually, to calm Gervas, she promised never to go off and leave him again. It was a hollow pledge, never kept.

The days dawned bright and sunny. Elspeth and Nellie interviewed medicine men, smiths, elders, even progressive farmers who were beginning to apply European methods of soil conservation. Elspeth attended the trial for murder of a Kikuyu who had hit a friend over the head with a piece of firewood during a beer-drink (a ritual beer party). The charge was reduced to manslaughter and he was given five years' imprisonment. After a week the proximity of the magnificent Mount Kenya proved too tempting, and Nellie and Elspeth decided to climb to its snowline. They organised six porters from a forest officer, and a headman to supervise the safari. The first part of the journey was a trek through forest swamps in which they sank to their knees in thick black mud. Then they entered the steep bamboo belt, stumbling over the spiky, slippery bamboo stalks and having to cross rivers. Camp was pitched among the bamboo and they endured a very chilly night. The next day they hit moorland extending to the rocks of the two peaks of Mount Kenya. There was of course no path, so they made their way as best they could over the boggy ground covered with giant heather and giant groundsel.

The second camp was made at 11,000 feet, giving them a spectacular view over the Kikuyu reserve. On the third day they slid and stumbled through shoulder-high grass, forcing themselves up the steep slope. At 15,000 feet the grassland gave way to sheer rock and scree. Lack of oxygen began to affect them: Nellie was sick, while Elspeth's head swam and her chest felt as if it was bound tightly by an iron belt. When they were forced to stop every two steps for breath they realised they would have to turn round if they were to get back to camp before dark. It was disappointing not to reach the snowline, but they had seen remarkable panoramas, the whole of the greenly lush Kikuyu reserve and the plains of Laikipia stretching away into the rocky desert of the Northern Frontier District. Elspeth ran down the mountain to Murigo's camp, leaving her mother to descend more sedately.

Reluctant to waste a minute, as soon as Elspeth was back at camp she bought a goat for a purification ceremony and took it to the medicine man's house. She was purified the next day – 'I'm glad to say with a deputy, who had to eat a lot of raw goat's inside and spit it out again.'[9] Another visit to Murigo resulted in an outpouring of stories of his brave young days and the display of a shield of a Maasai youth he had killed.

Cockie wanted to join mother and daughter in the reserve but was firmly repulsed from the sober, simple, clean-living camp. It was not, however, teetotal – before the missionaries at Tumu Tumu came to supper the ladies had a tremendous clear-out of beer and whisky bottles, and even Nellie was sufficiently daunted to have only one weak whisky and water at the meal. Nellie and Elspeth were invited to a meal by a Kikuyu family, and dined off mealies, beans, bananas, potatoes and nettle spinach all stewed up together in a big black pot and ladled out with calabashes. They attended a day-long beer-drink and a dance at night. Elspeth came to the conclusion that the Kikuyu people lived as nearly an idyllic life as was possible, the only shadow in their lives being the taxes imposed by the government.

Her book was taking shape in her mind. She decided it was to be a novel, though 'if you come to think of it the idea of writing a book entirely about an alien race and people as *characters* (not therefore as objects being observed from outside, but people interpreted from within) after five weeks among them and not speaking their language, is somewhat fantastic'.[10] She had learned enough to realise that the whites would soon have to make big adjustments in their view of Africans, perhaps greater than they were capable of making. She saw that Africans deeply resented the whites having taken their land.

Nellie had arranged for a reluctant Elspeth to give a talk to the Njoro Settlers' Association, so there was an interruption to their camp as the two women crossed the 11,000-feet Aberdares on foot to meet Jos, who was awaiting them with a car on the Rift Valley side of the mountains. They followed the old track used in former times by Maasai raiding the Kikuyu and by Arab slaving caravans. One night's camp had to be made in the bamboo belt, with the bamboo on their cooking fire exploding like gunshots into a night sky made pale by a full moon.

After three days' absence they returned to Murigo's camp for another fortnight, before packing up. Although she had written pages and pages of notes, and felt 'fit as a female Viking', Elspeth complained to Gervas that it was hell not being able to speak Kikuyu, not to understand what the porters were chatting about, not to get a line on ordinary casual conversation. There is no doubt that the part Nellie played in the origin and gathering of information for the book that became *Red Strangers* was significant. Elspeth could not have lived in the Kikuyu reserve without her, and Nellie's interest in Kikuyu customs spurred on her daughter. Indeed, Elspeth dedicated *Red Strangers* 'To my mother, who first suggested this book, and helped to bring it into being'.

On their return to Njoro Elspeth continued with research for the book. Through an interpreter, she questioned all the farm squatters on their histories. That of Kagama was particularly interesting. From his home at Maguga he had gone to work as a policeman for John Ainsworth, a simple and dignified man who became Nairobi's first Commissioner in 1899. He fought rebellions of the Ndia, Embu and Meru, after which he was taken by train to fight the Nandi rebellion of 1905,* and there he stayed for four years to help keep the peace. When his father died he returned to Kikuyuland, but there was not enough land there for him, so he went to Galbraith Cole's farm at Njoro to work and cultivate a shamba as a squatter. Cole sold the farm to Black Harries, whom Nellie hated.

In 1911 Kagama watched the great Maasai trek when the northern Maasai were moved from their lands at Laikipia by the government, to join the southern Maasai around Narok. The Maasai went on the Njoro side of Menengai mountain to Rongai, but farmers there refused them permission to pass through their land so they had to turn back to Njoro and go through Harries's farm. In payment for watering at a spring there, they paid Harries two cows for every herd of 180 cows. Very indignant at being moved by the government, they wanted to return to Laikipia, but the askaris (African policemen working for the government) drove them onwards. They took four days to pass. The moran (young Maasai), painted red and white, carried spears and shields and wore full war headdress. The elders walked in front, then came the cattle, then the young men driving them, then women driving donkeys loaded with pots and skins, then children. Some of the moran cut a broad path for the cattle with their pangas (machetes). About a year later, during a famine, the Maasai women came back over the Mau hills to look for food. As they had no money, they had to work in Kikuyu shambas in return for food which they took back home. Kagama stayed on the Harries farm during the First World War. His son ran away aged

---

* This was the rebellion Richard Meinerzthagen was sent to quell. He arranged to meet the laibon (leader) of the Nandi, and when he stepped forward and shook hands, Meinertzhagen pulled out a gun with his left hand and shot him dead while he was clinging to his right hand. The Nandi regarded this as a normal act of war. The Nandi, fifty miles from Njoro, resisted British rule in the early years of the century, whereas the Maasai seemed to accept it, because the Maasai had been severely weakened by cattle disease, smallpox and famine. In contrast, the Nandi resented the British presence and the imposition of hut tax.

twelve to the Kijabe mission, not returning for six years. Elspeth used the stories of both this mission boy and the Maasai trek in *Red Strangers*.

As for Nellie's squatter Karioki, who hailed from Chura in Kikuyuland, he could read and write. He followed the customs of his fathers until 1926, piercing his earlobes in Kikuyu fashion and extending the holes so they swung almost to his shoulders. In that year he heard about God, started wearing European clothes and, feeling his distended earlobes looked ridiculous, had them sewn up.

Nanga, somewhat older than the others, remembered the wars between the Maasai and Kikuyu. He and hundreds of other Kikuyu followed the Maasai to Mau and captured their cattle and goats. He also remembered the great famine of the 1890s, in which his mother died, and knew the small boy who tended sheep and became the powerful chief Kinyanjui after he co-operated with the whites. Nanga was the offspring of a Maasai–Kikuyu marriage, his Maasai mother having been captured as a little girl by his father. All this, and several other stories, were absorbed by Elspeth and woven into the plot of *Red Strangers*.

Elspeth also gathered Kikuyu proverbs, such as 'The bushcat skips in the dew' (The early bird catches the worm), 'To get the fire's warmth one must first stir the embers' (No gain without pain) and 'Food in the mouth is not yet in the stomach' (Don't count your chickens before they're hatched). She listed all the names of male circumcision groups, as far back as the old men could remember. Groups were named after an event in the year in which the circumcision took place – for example, the 1933 group of boys was called the 'Kenyabus' group, because that was the year buses were introduced to Kenya.

As part of her preparation for writing *Red Strangers* Elspeth enrolled in an anthropological course at the London School of Economics from October to December 1937. She thought the academic rigour of studies under Professor Bronislaw Malinowski would prepare her for writing the book, and the people she chose as her particular study were of course the Kikuyu. She drew up elaborate Kikuyu kinship lists, relying on what she had learned at Murigo's camp, information sent by Louis Leakey, and what she gleaned by talking to Johnstone (later Jomo) Kenyatta,* who spent several years studying in England and was a member of the same seminar. She lunched with Kenyatta on 26 October 1937. Elspeth also wrote a short thesis on the Kikuyu with the title 'The Influence of Environment on Land Tenure and Kinship Grouping with Special Reference to the Akikuyu', and read it to the seminar, in front of the anthropologist Raymond Firth, Malinowski and Kenyatta, well aware that she was dealing with a subject on which Kenyatta was expert. She was terrified of his response, but he spared her, 'adopting an aloof, paternalistic, benign approach, wrapping up his few remarks in a swaddling of words with little bearing on the subject, like the skilful politician he was'.[11]

At the conclusion of the seminar Elspeth felt ready to begin work on her Kikuyu saga, though she was aware that 'no person of one race and culture can truly interpret events from the angle of individuals belonging to a totally different race and culture'. She began writing on 14 December 1937, working solidly until May 1938, spending the last two months with Aunt Blanche at her house in Wales, while Gervas was in the United States. At times she felt the strain – 'what a bore and waste of time this book-writing is'.[12] The hills of Wales were temptingly lovely, and she 'would much prefer to walk on them all day than scribble at a desk'.

Elspeth continued the book at Gikammeh, which she and Gervas visited at the end of July 1938. In March Hitler's troops had marched into Austria, so the political scene was uncertain. They found Nellie, as usual, embarking on new schemes, this time the raising of turkeys, hens and pigeons, and the cultivation of grenadillas (a sort of passionfruit). She had maintained her friendship with the Leakeys, who arrived with many dalmatians to stay on the farm while they excavated a cave in the forest nearby. This site had been discovered

* The future President of Kenya worked as a carpenter in his youth. On his trips to Nairobi he wore a wide ornamental beaded belt called a kenyatta. As he stopped along the way to give children sweets, they took to calling him 'Kenyatta', and the name stuck.

by Nellie, who found some prehistoric tools there. The Leakeys, not always popular among the settlers because they were considered to have pro-African views, found a marvellous stone vessel and several bones. They discovered the site to be a place of ceremonial cremation, containing the bones of pygmies among others. At his camp in the garden, Louis Leakey taught Elspeth the Kikuyu game giuthi* and how to make Kikuyu string figures. Then there was another safari with the Lindstroms to Serengeti and Ngorongoro in Tanganyika. The Huxleys were back in London on 1 December.

Red Strangers is the story of three Kikuyu men, the brothers Muthengi and Matu, and Karanja, each of whom reacts in a different way to the coming of Europeans – that is, the red strangers, their skin crimsoned by sunburn and dust. Muthengi co-operates with the District Commissioner and becomes rich, partly by betraying the trust of his fellows; Matu works on a white farm at Njoro; and Karanja becomes educated and a Christian, abandoning some of the traditional beliefs of the Kikuyu. The three stories are skilfully interwoven, and each man becomes a symbol of what happens when cultures meet and clash. The novel describes Kikuyu ceremonies and their meaning, wealth as measured by goats, and breaches of traditional courtesy, together with the introduction of money and machinery, horses and carts. Ancient rites of male and female circumcision are put into context and their significance revealed, beer-drinks are accorded their true importance, and marriage by traditional means is shown to be kinder to women than more recently introduced forms. The inhumanity of Christianity in sneering at traditional ways of life is revealed by Elspeth, never a believer herself, who felt that European religion had done much damage to Africans.

In the first sentence of the foreword to *Red Strangers*, Elspeth told her readers that although the book was a novel, most of the incidents it related were true. A vein throbbing through the book

---

* The Maasai called the game, which was played with beans in holes in the ground or rock, 'bao'. It was known all over Africa. Leakey had found 'boards' scooped out of rock which showed it was played in 2000 BC.

is African resentment of whites. The cajoling of thousands of Africans to fight the white man's First World War, many of them never to return, is one grievance; but it is whites taking their land which creates the most bitterness among the Kikuyu:

> Why then do we allow the Europeans to steal from us what the Masai could not? . . . Have not the Europeans taken away our land, and made their own shambas on stolen property? Are not many of our people homeless, because Europeans have driven them from land rightfully belonging to their clans? And who cultivates the same shambas now? Are the Europeans able themselves to plough the land, to weed it, to reap the crops? Why then do you work from sunrise until late in the afternoon in order that Europeans may become rich on land they stole from your fathers?[13]

Elspeth's ideas had clearly moved a considerable distance since she had expressed in *White Man's Country* the opinion that whites walked into empty land and took it without protest from local people. Henceforth she would be much more sympathetic to the African point of view.

She sent the book to Macmillan, publishers of *White Mischief*. They agreed to publish *Red Strangers*, but Harold Macmillan wanted considerable cuts, as it was far too long. He also wanted Elspeth's graphic description of female circumcision omitted, arguing that the practice was unfamiliar and abhorrent to European readers. Elspeth reacted sharply:

> The whole of native life is unfamiliar to European readers and it is the purpose of this book to make them a little more familiar with it than they are at present. To do this it is, in my opinion, utterly impossible merely to present those aspects of native life which are pleasant and acceptable to the European mind and to omit those which do not commend themselves to Europeans. This destroys the whole basis of the book which is to present it as it is, not as certain people in this country would like to think it is, whether some aspects are abhorrent or not is beside the point.[14]

On receipt of this letter, Macmillan refused to publish the book. Elspeth then offered it to Harold Raymond of Chatto & Windus, whom she had met before. Raymond asked for cuts of 40,000 words (not including the passage on circumcision), which was more than Elspeth expected. However, she was about to sail once again for the USA, and made the cuts with exemplary speed. Thus began a long and fruitful partnership between Chatto & Windus and Elspeth Huxley.

Red Strangers was published on 1 June 1939. Elspeth was not above altering the blurb to say she had spent 'a few months' in the Kikuyu reserve rather than 'a few weeks', which was closer to the truth. Gervas had put his marketing skills at the service of Chatto & Windus and had obtained quotations for the jacket from his cousin Julian Huxley ('It would be hard to find a more vivid and yet dispassionate portrayal of the tribal African's life and mind, and of his bewilderment and exasperation when confronted by the incomprehensible ways of white men and white rule') and from Lord Hailey, of *An African Survey** fame ('I have found it of absorbing interest, and I feel that anyone called upon to take up work or residence in East Africa would be the poorer if he omitted to read it').[15] Jan Smuts thought the book even more impressive than *White Man's Country*, writing to Elspeth:

> You have succeeded in producing a marvellously realistic picture of a primitive African people suddenly confronted in our day with the most advanced civilization. This story as told by you of the impact on the native culture forms a wonderful human drama, full of humour and pathos, of comedy and high tragedy . . . [It is an] intensely interesting account of the contemporary destruction of a primitive civilization of Africa. Here is entertaining diversion. Here also is the deeper note of *lacrimae rerum* which accompanies all our human story.[16]

Louis Leakey said *Red Strangers* was the best book on the Kikuyu he had ever read, and Margery Perham was 'immensely struck by

---

* A huge book, containing a commentary on each African country. It was repeatedly updated and reprinted.

the imagination and insight about native life and ideas'. She thought 'this book has a definite part to play in making race relations more sympathetic'.[17] Other comments were similarly enthusiastic. The book was reprinted twice, but then the Second World War broke out, and paper rationing put a stop to further impressions until 1944, when permission for a reprint was finally given after supplications to the government committee which decided such matters from Margery Perham, the Colonial Office and the Church Missionary Society bookshop in Nairobi. There were further subsequent reprints, and in 1999 the book joined the Penguin Twentieth Century World Classics series. Elspeth was well on the way to making a literary reputation for herself.

Before the publication of *Red Strangers* Elspeth had brought out two crime novels under the Methuen imprint – *Murder at Government House* (1937) and *Murder on Safari* (1938). In the year *Red Strangers* appeared she published a third, *Death of an Aryan* (called *The African Poison Murders* in America, and now generally known by that title). All three received favourable reviews in the *Times Literary Supplement*. That she could be a writer of fiction as well as fact had occurred to Elspeth soon after she completed *White Man's Country*. Hers was no dry pen, and her ability to find the perfect word or phrase was ideally suited to storytelling. She had researched the crime novels in Kenya, and wrote them while accompanying Gervas on his travels in the mid-1930s, during stays in the USA, and at Gikammeh – she read the proofs of *Murder at Government House* while deep in the Kikuyu reserve at Murigo's camp.

Elspeth always had decided ideas about her dustjacket designs. For *Murder at Government House* she wondered about having an aeroplane on the cover, but admonished Methuen not to make it a Puss Moth, as the book specified a Vega Gull. Eventually her suggestion of a drawing of the Governor slumped dead at his desk was adopted. She kept her publisher up to the mark by listing the East African and South African newspapers to which review copies should be sent, and herself visited the bookshops of Nairobi to persuade them to stock copies. To her delight Jocelyn Gibb, her editor at Methuen, sent *Murder at Government House* to Hollywood, leading Elspeth to speculate, 'Do you think there might be a chance of really making some money out of this writing racket at last?'[18] Alas, nothing came of the venture.

Immediately after their stay at Murigo's camp, Nellie and Elspeth had gone on safari to Samburu with their friend Major Harry Barron Sharpe ('Sharpie'), and Elspeth had picked up all she could about safari life. Sharpie, the cultivated and outspoken homosexual DC at Rumuruti, was viewed with suspicion by his superiors, who feared he would land himself in some epic scandal, and kept out of the way by the administration, which consigned him to spend his working days in remote places where he could do little damage. He was a spectacular horticulturist, using the inmates of his jails to make famous gardens around his houses. His garden at Rumuruti was a beautiful oasis in the middle of a brown desert.

On the way to join him, Elspeth and Nellie stayed in Meru with the gossipy Roy Whittet (Kichanga), who had shared Nellie's house at Thika at the beginning of the First World War. They were joined on their safari by Nellie's great friend Rose Cartwright,* formerly the wife of the Algy Cartwright who had sold Nellie her land at Njoro. Rose lived with her daughter Tobina in a large, stone barrack of a house on a farm in the Rift Valley, at constant war with her ex-husband, now bankrupt, over the custody of Tobina. Tall and willowy in physique, and quietly amusing, Rose courageously farmed all by herself while simultaneously producing intricate and beautiful needlework. She also took two Dorobo trackers for a fortnight at a time to camp by herself in the forests of the Aberdares. In later years Elspeth remembered her:

> I can see her in her house at Gilgil scattering seed on the polished floor of the living room for the birds, those little

---

* Rose went to Kenya after the First World War to be with her brother Geoffrey Buxton. In 1923 she met and married Geoffrey's friend Algy Cartwright, but he was an odd man and the marriage, which lasted ten years, was unhappy. They had a son, Giles, and a daughter, Tobina. Rose was a friend of Denys Finch Hatton, who had known her brother at Eton. She loved Ferdinand Cavendish-Bentinck, later the Duke of Portland.

finches which my mother called animated plums, the dogs paying no attention, and she perhaps getting on with that wonderful embroidery. She had a lovely, even, melodious voice. Simple tastes, yet appreciation of luxury. Calmness, no false attitudes, a twinkle in the eye.[19]

The safari started from Isiolo at the end of September 1937, with Sharpie travelling in comfort and style in a brand new Ford V8, followed by Nellie, Elspeth and Rose in Nellie's car, and a government lorry piled high with camp kit and armed policemen. They passed a camp of Italian prisoners, deserters from Abyssinia, lunched on the banks of the Uaso Nyiro river, and made camp that night at four thousand feet on the Wamba river, at the foot of a long, tall, forested range of mountains called the Matthews range. The next day Sharpie held a baraza (meeting), which the women attended. There had been forty-six murders in his area, including, three years earlier, that of Theodore Powys, son of Theodore Powys (the writer) and nephew of Llewelyn, Will and John Cowper Powys,* which gave rise to a parliamentary inquiry in Britain. When the DC rounded up Samburu cattle in punishment for the murder, thus causing great hardship, the Samburu chiefs turned up with some young men and said, 'These are the murderers of Powys.' The men were arrested but acquitted, though the judge said he was pretty sure they were guilty.

The safari visited Maralal, at an altitude of seven thousand feet and in an ideal climate. There a charming tribal policeman took Elspeth, Nellie and Rose to the Leroghi escarpment, and Sharpie told them he was one of the murderers of Theodore Powys. Elspeth loved Wamba:

The freshness of the morning is unbelievable, and in the evening there's that glorious golden light – *pure* gold – followed by a marvellous sunset, and then a cool dusk period, and then drinks round a blazing camp fire, with a sky overhead fairly bursting with stars, and crickets and owls calling.[20]

---

* Llewelyn Powys wrote *Black Laughter* (1925), a lyrical account of farming in the Rift Valley, after he joined his brother Will Powys, who spent his life in Kenya.

The ladies climbed to the top of the range of hills behind Wamba, Sharpie having arranged thirty-three (far too many) Dorobo porters to carry their loads. None the less, they gave every man some small item and streamed off in a great cavalcade. Whenever they stopped the Dorobo rushed off to find honey, returning smeared with the sweet substance. From the top of the hills they could see the distant silver of Lake Rudolf (now Lake Turkana). They also accompanied Sharpie on his official expeditions, guarded by dozens of askaris in full uniform, plus askari-kanga (tribal retainers in red and blue blanket uniforms), all armed with enormous rifles. They saw several elephants, but rhino were already becoming rare due to poaching.

Elspeth took the opportunity to talk to Rose about safaris, for she was plotting her next crime novel, *Murder on Safari*, which was set in this region. Later she also had much discussion at Loresho with Alistair Gibb, Glady Delamere's lover, about the mechanics of safaris, and he got her interviews with two white hunters. She interviewed other people, too, making a point of seeing Neil Stewart, who had known her as a child in Thika and was now head of the Kenya CID. He had started a crime museum, and lent Elspeth several books on crime detection. He told her stories of important criminal cases in Kenya, and directed her to the local gunsmith, who treated her to lectures on ballistics. So impressed was Elspeth that she modelled the book's hero on Stewart. She obtained useful details about elephants and poaching from Cecil Hoey, an ivory poacher in the early days of BEA, but now a respected member of the Legislative Council. Others filled her in with information about African arrow poisons. That used in the relevant area came from a tree of the acokanthera species, small and gnarled and looking somewhat like an English oak. Its twigs and roots were boiled for days to produce a thick, tarry substance which was applied to the arrowhead to kill animals (and, in *Murder on Safari*, people).

Later in life Elspeth said that the books she had most enjoyed writing were her crime novels, because the end always had to be worked out before writing could begin. It was the finite nature of crime writing that appealed to her. All of her early crime novels were set in Kenya, thinly disguised as 'Chania' (the name of a real river in Kenya). Her sleuth was the Canadian Superintendent Vachell. In *Murder at Government House* the Governor of Chania is found dead at his desk, and the heroine, a female anthropologist with shades of Margery Perham about her, uncovers atavistic ceremonies and settler intrigues. The book has a wonderful setting, but is not as polished as *Murder on Safari*, in which Elspeth is at the height of her command of background material, character and plot, cleverly laying traps for the reader in a yarn which gathers pace until the triumphant dénouement.

Elspeth often inserted her theories about African society in her light-hearted books, in order to reach the profound through the trivial. In *Murder in Government House* one of the characters, Olivia, says:

> In many ways . . . the functions of a detective in our society resemble those of a witchdoctor among native tribes. The witchdoctor's job, like the detective's, is to hunt down the enemies of society and prevent them from doing further harm. In my opinion there's a good deal of nonsense talked about the barbarity of witchcraft . . . Sorcerers are killed, of course; but we kill murderers, and that's what sorcerers are, in native eyes. The conviction of a sorcerer is by no means arbitrary. There has to be a long record of suspicion by responsible people – not just an unfounded accusation – followed by a properly conducted ordeal, before a verdict is given. Of course, there are abuses, as in all systems, but in nine cases out of ten I believe the victim has been genuinely guilty of anti-social designs. In many ways it's a very efficient method of eliminating the disruptive elements in society. And it has enabled African tribes to maintain for centuries a large measure of social stability, without anything in the nature of a police force.[21]

In *Murder on Safari* Elspeth made use of Sharpie, thinly disguising him as Peto, the District Commissioner, the tribes under whose control found him

capricious, but just and firm. His superiors in the Secretariat
disapproved of him; they found him outspoken, independent
and deplorably lacking in the three sacred virtues: respect for
seniority, devotion to precedent, and discretion ... His ruling
passion in life was plant collecting ... So far he had steered
clear of trouble, and left for each of his successors a reasonably
peaceful district and a perfectly irrigated garden ... Natives
who had done time in jails in Peto's district were much in
demand by Europeans as head gardeners when their terms of
imprisonment were over.[22]

Death of an Aryan (*The African Poison Murders*) has a strange
theme – that of a Nazi *Bund* in Chania. It is true that some whites
in Kenya, among them Joss Erroll, had belonged to Oswald Mosley's
British Union of Fascists for a while in the 1930s, but many of them
had left it when there were rumours that Britain might appease
Germany by returning Tanganyika, which had been ceded to Britain
at the end of the First World War. The book is more violent than
Elspeth's previous crime stories, with strange slashings of dogs and
decapitations of delphiniums. She made good use of her researches
into African arrow poisons in the story – indeed, she is positively
dangerous in revealing the plants and trees they come from. Perhaps
she felt that most of her readers would never set foot in Kenya,
where 'the climate was fine. Living was cheap and easy; the country
still free from the more rigid fetters of convention, still with a
twinge of the frontier about it'.[23] The victim, Munson, is murdered
by a poisoned nail in his shoe in a pyrethrum-drying shed; but he
is not the only one to suffer, and the reader is treated to an epidemic
of killings. Although macabre, the book is lighthearted and somewhat gothic in tone. It has an excellent description of a typical
white farm in Kenya:

> It looked as if it had been reproduced by budding, like certain
> kinds of bacteria. The nucleus was the living-room, with a
> stone veranda in front: a long untidy welcoming room,
> warmed by a big open fire stacked with cedar logs ... The
> walls inside were plastered with a mixture of skim milk and
> flour, and distempered a bright cream. The roof was corru-

gated iron, concealed from within by a celotex ceiling . . . The kitchen quarters were out at the back, and a series of thatched mud huts of varying shapes and sizes was dotted inconsequentially about, like weavers' nests around the crown of a tree. One of them was connected by a covered way and a cement path to the veranda of the living-room.[24]

These three novels were published by Methuen, but Harold Raymond tried to get Elspeth to move her crime books to Chatto & Windus, which had accepted *Red Strangers*. Initially she thought it would be better to have two different publishers for the two different types of book, but she was tempted by the prospect of being the only pebble on the beach at Chatto, which did not normally publish crime novels. There was, however, a hiccough in her relationship with Chatto when she found that the proofs of *Red Strangers* had developed a rash of commas, which she insisted on striking out – 'I know little or nothing about punctuation and rather wondered if I had gone nuts when the proofs appeared with a comma before every and, which I'd thought was the one place they shouldn't go.'[25] Harold Raymond blamed the printers and the commas were withdrawn, though in fact it was Elspeth's typist who had inserted them.

By the end of the 1930s Elspeth had established herself as a writer, a task that had taken her only five years and five books. She had also become known as a journalist, with articles on such subjects as agriculture, erosion and tropical soils appearing in many British and African papers. She was soon to break into another medium – that of radio. But war was about to interrupt everyone's plans for the future. The British government was coming to the inescapable conclusion that Adolf Hitler must be prevented from dominating Europe.

FIVE

Domesticity, War and Secret Service

After Elspeth and Nellie's sojourn at Murigo's camp and the Sharpie safari, mother and daughter travelled to England together in April 1937. Gervas and Elspeth's reunion would have been undemonstrative, for neither of them was ever openly affectionate. Elspeth suffered depression and soul-searching about leaving Kenya. She was now thoroughly reconciled to the country she had repudiated when she left it as a student, and she viewed England with dread. Gervas's dismay at having been left alone for so long had caused her to write to him bitterly, 'I realise it was terribly selfish of me ever to want to come to Kenya, even though it was because of writing books . . . I haven't the slightest idea when, if ever, I'll be able to come back, but realise now it won't be for many years when you are ready to retire and I've ceased to be young – if then.'[1] She said she did not have a single friend in England except for two (something of an exaggeration), and that the older she got the more she disliked London.

The solution to her restlessness and dissatisfaction was found in a joint decision with Gervas to buy a house in the country. While Gervas continued with his job, Elspeth went to stay with his father at Wootton to look for a suitable property. She thoroughly scoured the villages round Oxford, but her search was unsuccessful – 'Damn it, I wish we could find something.'[2] She nearly bought the Old Mill at Newbridge, but that fell through. Then one day, having been to Cirencester in Gloucestershire to visit her former nanny, Nanny Newport, now infirm and in her seventies, she stopped off to see friends in the nearby village of South Cerncy. She was much taken by the countryside there, and a year later found what she considered to be the perfect house in the village of Oaksey, a few miles from South Cerney and within easy reach by car of Gervas's father at Wootton. Kemble station was only four miles away, with frequent trains and an hour-and-a half journey to London. On 13 June 1938 the Huxleys bid successfully at auction for Woodfolds, a seventeenth-century stone farmhouse with fifty acres of land. They got it for a remarkably low price because it lacked all amenities, having been lived in by two bachelor brothers who had led spartan lives.

Oaksey is in a corner of Wiltshire on the edge of the Cotswold hills, in a level expanse of dairy country halfway between Malmesbury and Cirencester. It stands on higher ground just north of Swill Brook, which flows on to join the Thames. 'It's always been,' said Elspeth, '. . . a borderline case. On the border between Wiltshire and Gloucestershire, between the Cotswolds and the vale, between the midlands and the south-west, in the Middle Ages on the borders of the Forest of Braden; before that, of the kingdoms of Mercia and Wessex; almost on the borderline between the Thames flowing east and the Avon going west.'[3] The village, whose inhabitants numbered about three hundred, consisted of a main road, called 'The Street', flanked by stone houses, with some side roads leading from it, and boasted a shop, a pub and a thirteenth-century church. There was a village pond, called Bendybow because in winter the ice covering it failed to crack, instead bending like a bow. In due course the name would be inherited by a housing estate built there. In the Middle Ages there was also a castellated house in the village, belonging to John of Gaunt, Duke of Lancaster.

Woodfolds, built in approximately 1670 of Cotswold grey stone, with a stone-tiled roof, lay on the edge of Oaksey village. Formerly it was part of the manor's estate, but the agent to whom the manor owner sold the estate in 1938 divided it into separate lots, and the Huxleys bought Woodfolds and a nearby cottage. Three-storeyed Woodfolds, with a little porch and twin gables at its west or entrance front, stood among fields, with tall trees to its north and west.

There were several outhouses. The main block, flanked by long outhouse ranges, had a wing projecting at the back containing the staircase, kitchen and two bedrooms above. Altogether the house contained six bedrooms. The ground floor of the long south range had three rooms used for smoking bacon, storing grain and cheese-making. Elspeth and Gervas determined to knock these through, to make an elegant long sitting room. Outside this room, on the east side, ran a loggia. They decided to make the north range into a maid or nanny's room, boiler room and dairy. As the house was in a primitive state, lacking water, drainage and electricity, these would have to be installed, together with three bathrooms. There was much rot in the roof timbers, and all the flooring had to be repaired, windows replaced or repaired, walls grouted and parts of the roof rebuilt. So much had to be done that it was a year before the house was ready, at a cost of £3,000, and the Huxleys could move in.

Much of the intervening year they spent abroad, despite the rumblings of a possible European war. They spent mid-January to 10 March 1939 in the USA, then took a chance and went to Sweden from 1 to 12 April, hoping war would not be declared while they were there. They had a few days' sojourn at Lee Abbey Hotel at Lynton in Devon. After another voyage to the USA in May, Elspeth returned to England to face the upheaval of moving into Woodfolds. She and Gervas were installed by 10 June, although Gervas still spent weekdays in London, staying with his brother. Elspeth commuted to London whenever required.

The neighbouring manor house and its Park Farm had been bought by a German sect, the Bruderhof, a Christian community expelled from Germany by the Nazis. They made a living from a milk round and selling eggs in Swindon. The Bruderhof women wore long blue kirtles girded at the waist, and the men knee-breeches and beards. On the outbreak of war in September 1939 they were hounded out by the Oaksey villagers, taking refuge in Uruguay. Park Farm and the manor house were sold to the Ciren-cester Conservative Benefit Society for £12,000. Jim Woodhouse and his wife Renée came as tenants of the farm, while the manor house became RAF billets and later a failed hotel. The Woodhouses later bought it and knocked it down in 1956. They themselves lived in the adjacent farmhouse.

With the Huxleys settled into Woodfolds, they could turn their attention to a problem every couple faces sooner or later – whether to have children. They had been discussing this spasmodically for years. While she was in Kenya in 1937, Elspeth had encouraged Gervas, left behind in England, to look for a stone house in the country, possibly to rent, with attics that could be used for a maid 'if we really got around to this family business'. She was now thirty-two years old, with few maternal feelings, but Gervas wanted a child. He regretted not having had children with his first wife, but while Elspeth was at Murigo's camp a turn of events left him in a quandary. He was advised to move his office to the United States for a couple of years, and Elspeth's view was that if this meant more money he would be a fool to turn it down, though she added in a letter, 'and what about this family? You really must think it over soon!' As it happened, Gervas stayed in London.

From Kenya Elspeth had written, 'The more I'm away the more I realise how lucky I am and how lovely it is to feel that you are there and that we get on so well – it gives me a sense of security which makes everything else a thousand times nicer. I shall never want anything else!'[4] It may have been when they moved into Woodfolds that the decision was taken to have a child. Elspeth, however, failed to conceive.

A factor in this may have been that she was working so hard. In the late 1930s she had a variety of schemes to make money and develop her career. She continued with her writing, widening the range of newspapers for which she provided articles. When in Nairobi she had been fiercely critical of the local newspaper, the *East African Standard*, and had plans to take it over, possibly with the help of the Maggs Group in South Africa. She regarded its ownership as 'more and more awful': the proprietor, Claude Anderson, had 'got religion in a big way', while the editor, George Kinnear, 'gets worse and worse and the whole thing is going to pieces, yet coins money'.[5] Elspeth envisaged buying it, or alternatively, since the *East African Standard* did not cater for an African readership, starting an African newspaper, to be issued in both Swahili and English. This idea, somewhat impractical given that Elspeth's main domicile was in Britain, was soon shelved. Nellie then put a proposal to her. Frank Couldrey, deputy editor of the *Kenya Weekly News*, based in Nakuru, wanted to go on leave to England and asked Nellie whether Elspeth could take over from him for four months in 1938, at £25 to £30 a month. Elspeth turned the offer down.

She had found another interest – broadcasting for the BBC. She had been mentioned to the corporation in 1935 by Stephen Tallents, former head of the Empire Marketing Board, who heard that Elspeth had set off alone in a small car to tour America. He told the BBC that while at the EMB she had written up popular accounts of scientific research with extraordinary skill, obtaining a wide market for her articles overseas, and suggested she might be good for a broadcast talk. Nothing came of this at the time, but the BBC kept her in mind, and approached her in February 1938. She agreed to broadcast a talk on *Soil Erosion in America's Middle West* for the Schools Programme's 'History in the Making' course. Sent eight guineas in payment, Elspeth displayed a trait that was to continue all her life. She quibbled over the amount, saying she understood the usual fee was ten guineas. The BBC courteously replied that that was the payment for experienced broadcasters, and she was a novice. Elspeth's frequent requests for raised remuneration were always politely phrased but tenacious, such was her memory of her poverty-stricken childhood.

After her broadcast on 22 March, a BBC internal memo by the Schools Programme producer noted that 'her voice, though slightly metallic in parts, would be suitable for Scottish schools. She seemed hurried in parts. Scottish schools prefer a man's voice, but I could use her.'[6] Elspeth had hurried, slightly clipped speech, without a trace of a colonial accent, but she modified her pace for broadcasts. In December 1938 she did two talks for the Schools Programme, on *Mud and Flood: the Mississippi, Friend or Enemy?* and *Misunder-*

standing Climate: the Dust Bowl. For both she had to provide photographs and maps for schools' work packs, and suggestions for music. This time she got her requested ten guineas for each talk. In December 1939 she gave another two talks, for the *Travel Talks* series, on *A Boy's Life in Kenya* and *A Pride of Lions.*

Elspeth was also involved in another broadcasting operation, this time one with highly secret aspects. At some stage after January 1939 Trudie Denman, Nellie's friend and benefactor, asked Elspeth to join the Joint Broadcasting Committee, on whose board she sat. The JBC, a mainly secret organisation, was set up to broadcast to other countries in the event of war, preparing material for use in neutral and enemy countries. It also aimed to prepare programmes directed primarily at the German public, to be broadcast from clandestine stations both inside and outside Germany; the discs on which such programmes were recorded would be delivered by the security services. The JBC defined itself as arranging 'for broadcasts from Stations abroad of British information and opinions, to supplement the BBC service. It is a small, flexible and informal organisation, in which expertness in such matters as selection and rehearsing of speakers, preparation of scripts and the production of records can be combined with knowledge of broadcasting conditions and the specialised requirements of listeners in countries abroad. The Committee is directly responsible to the Ministry of Information for its overt activities, though it has other activities on behalf of another organisation.'[7] The covert activities, distinct from those openly carried out by the JBC, were financed by Section D of the secret service, MI6, under Laurence Douglas Grand, until war broke out, whereupon they were transferred to the Foreign Office vote. Funds were provided in gold sovereigns. A specially designed mobile recording unit was constructed for the JBC, and German-made musical records were bought.

Since one of the main tasks of the JBC was to diffuse British propaganda through broadcasting, it was not surprising that it clashed with the BBC, which jealously regarded it as a rival. However, the BBC's attempt to crush it failed, and when war broke out in September 1939 Hilda Matheson, formerly BBC Talks Director and now the head of the unit, temporarily installed the JBC at her home, Rocks Farm at Withyham, Sussex. But after a few months it was evident that it was safe to work in London, and the JBC returned to its premises at 71 Chester Square. Elspeth, who worked part-time for the JBC, was one of the seven members of the unit, among whom were Guy Burgess, not yet unmasked as a spy, who was formerly a member of the BBC Talks Department and was now liaison officer between the JBC and the Ministry of Information. She was paid a monthly salary of £33.6s.8d, had an office at 71 Chester Square and used JBC notepaper for her official letters throughout the third quarter of 1939. 'The organisation was totally chaotic,' she said, 'and I sat for some weeks, or months, at a desk with absolutely nothing to do. My main memory is of Guy Burgess going downstairs to lunch about 12.30 and staggering back quite drunk and reeking of brandy at about 3.30 or 4 p.m. – later I thought he couldn't have been a reliable spy.'[8]

In September 1939 war broke out between Britain and Germany. Elspeth never talked about her secret work for the JBC, but she was there only a short time before she accompanied Gervas on a final journey to the USA to put his tea affairs in order before he could begin working for the wartime Ministry of Information, which had recruited him as an adviser on publicity. Elspeth organised unpaid leave from the JBC and they sailed across the Atlantic at the end of October 1939. It was a highly risky voyage, for German U-boats were in command of the seas, but America was reached without incident. In January 1940 Elspeth cabled the JBC from the United States to say that she was reluctantly obliged to resign. While in America she was invited to become a British correspondent, providing a monthly letter about anything likely to be of interest to women, for a New York organisation which sent out radio scripts to about four hundred radio stations in all parts of the USA. She felt she would be more useful doing this than twiddling her thumbs at the JBC, and when she returned to England the Ministry of Information arranged appointments for her to supply material for these monthly letters. Not for the first time she found her husband's job most useful in providing contacts.

She continued, however, to write occasional talks for the JBC on a freelance basis. In May and June 1941 she provided for its Empire section two talks on *In the Country*, and two more on *The Life of an Englishwoman*, which were broadcast in several parts, including *Getting Married and Having a Baby*, though she knew nothing about the latter. She also composed scripts for East and West Africa on the English housewife, again hardly her speciality, and these were adapted for use in the West Indies (broadcast in December 1940). Her scripts were also broadcast in Malaya, Aden, Baghdad, Bahrain and several African countries. Her skill at communicating some-times difficult ideas clearly and succinctly stood her in good stead, and she was adept at making her scripts interesting to the listener.

One repercussion of Elspeth's time in the JBC was a request from Hilda Matheson that she write a book for the series 'Britain in Pictures', instigated by Miss Matheson with the assistance of her lover Dorothy Wellesley and the journalist and critic Walter Turner, and launched in March 1941. Part II of 'Britain in Pictures' was 'The British Commonwealth in Pictures', for which Elspeth wrote *East Africa* (March 1941), receiving the standard fee of £50. The books in the series, published by Collins, were beautifully produced and illustrated, with distinctive dustjackets and paper-board covers; Elspeth's book contained several paintings by the Duchess of Glou-cester, Lord Francis Scott's niece. The series was gently propagan-dist, and was intended for a readership chiefly abroad, such as in the United States, Latin America and the Commonwealth, who needed to be persuaded that Britain was worth supporting and saving. In her text of 12,000 words Elspeth is frank about East Africa, unhesitatingly pointing out some disadvantages of British rule and of the treatment of the land, which was increasingly becom-ing subject to erosion. Over 13,000 copies of her book were sold. At the same time Elspeth wrote two short books for the Foreign Literature Committee of the Sheldon Press, owned by the Society for the Propagation of Christian Knowledge, *The Story of Five English Farmers* (1941, 64 pages) and *English Women* (1942, 60 pages). These were intended for use in East African schools during a time of scarcity of teaching materials.

Another book Elspeth undertook in 1941 was *Atlantic Ordeal*, the true story of the rescue of six children and a teacher, Mary Cornish, from a torpedoed ship, the *City of Benares*, which was transporting evacuated children from Britain to America in September 1940. Elspeth sought out Miss Cornish, who was now teaching music at a Wokingham school. She came to stay at Woodfolds for a weekend, and told Elspeth the whole story. After the ship had been torpedoed, Mary, six children, a priest and a Pole were in a lifeboat with thirty-seven seamen, thirty-two of them lascars (Indian seamen). In her book Elspeth stuck to the facts but toned down the profane language and bloody-mindedness of a naval gunner in the boat, making him out to be fatherly. The Ministry of Information, to which the book was submitted under wartime rules, approved it, and Mary Cornish and Elspeth both gave their royalties, which were split half-and-half, to charity because they did not want to exploit a tragedy in which seventy-seven children had been killed. Over 6,500 copies of the book were sold by Chatto.

Simultaneously, Elspeth continued to work for the BBC. She undertook a mysterious journey to Belgium in early February 1940, for unknown reasons, possibly as a companion to Gervas on Ministry of Information business. After her return she wrote to the BBC to let them know she would now be settled in Britain for some time. As a result the BBC's Evelyn Gibbs and Mary Somerville went to Woodfolds in September and asked Elspeth to contribute to the series *Meet the Empire*, for which she provided thirteen scripts between October 1940 and January 1941. She also provided scripts for the *Bill and Bob* series of Army Education broadcasts, for *Travel Talks* (on American farms turned to dust and on science's fight against the tsetse fly) and for the Schools Programme (the tsetse-fly problem in East Africa), which earned praise from one school as 'a very good lesson, useful, interesting and practical. The children were thrilled throughout.'[9] Evelyn Gibbs of the Schools Programme found Elspeth 'quite excellent to work with in that she is able to write very quickly and to incorporate such teaching points as we want in a really lively dramatic script'.[10] In March 1941 she wrote the *Our Allies* series for Army Education broadcasts – twenty-minute talks on Norway, Holland, Belgium and the Netherlands East Indies. For the 'British History' series she composed two 2,600-word plays for children aged eleven to fifteen on 'Stories of West Africa': *White Man and Black Man* (June 1941) and *Indirect Rule, or a New Way of Governing Backward People* (July 1941).

More exciting possibilities lay ahead. Winston Churchill took over as Prime Minister, to head a Britain and its Commonwealth now deeply embroiled in the war on several fronts. In May 1941 Elspeth was enrolled as part of a team preparing a new series, *Radio Reconnaissance*, covering despatches from the front, extracts from regimental history and snapshot sketches of people in the news. After the USA entered the war on the Allied side in December this expanded into *The United States and Ourselves*. She wrote three character sketches of Americans living in different parts of the States and their attitudes to Canada, South America and Japan. Elspeth's frequent and lengthy visits to the USA came in very useful for material for such programmes. But she was restless. By now Britain was finding it hard to feed itself. The squeeze on imports meant that all available land had to be commandeered to grow crops, and every able-bodied woman without children had to play her part in replacing male labourers who had gone to fight. Elspeth had been trained for farm work at university, and felt bound to participate in practical work on the land. In May 1941 she engaged herself to Jim Woodhouse at Park Farm, next door to Woodfolds, for part-time work. Willing to put her hand to anything, she spread dung with the dung-cart, helped in the dairy and assisted with the potato machine and the harvest.

This meant she had to withdraw from Evelyn Gibbs's team, which needed her for two or three days a week. But she still did occasional programmes, and after the harvest was brought in she returned to more BBC work. There were further *Radio Reconnaissance* and *Travel Talks* programmes, mainly on Africa and the USA. Among other scripts, Elspeth wrote a dramatic presentation of the building of the Canadian-Pacific Railway, as well as *The Commonwealth at War*. She was criticised twice for what she wrote about Africans: once by the historian W.N. Macmillan, who found one script too patronising; and once by her BBC producer, who objected to a remark she had made and told her, 'Where African natives are concerned we want to get over the fact that whether they are dressed in European clothes or in skins, they are live people, thinking and feeling about life much as we do, though with interesting differences.'[11] The attitude of the BBC towards the peoples of the Empire, now waging war together whether black, brown or white, had undergone a change as colonial armies left their own shores to fight far afield. The old stereotype of the 'uncivilised' African or Indian, which Elspeth to some degree retained, was no longer admissible. All soldiers were to be treated equally in broadcasts, and there was no place for derogatory or patronising remarks.

At the end of 1941 Elspeth was commissioned to write six scripts for the London Transcription Service, into which the overt part of the JBC had been absorbed, for broadcasting and demonstration from mobile units in Africa. A most interesting enterprise on which she embarked in April 1942 covered what women were doing to help the prosecution of the war. Elspeth was given a month's absence from farmwork while the Air Ministry arranged for her to visit a fighter station, a bomber station and a balloon station. She was allowed into operations rooms and to conduct interviews with members of the Women's Auxiliary Air Force, and followed this up with visits to the women's branches of the army and navy, the ATS at Bristol and the WRNS at Harwich, hurrying to fit them in before haymaking in mid-June. She did not have an entirely free hand – the BBC wondered whether she might tone down her account of grumbling among the WAAFs, and her words 'uniformed unemployed' were removed. Elspeth much preferred the WRNS to the two other services and was unable to hide this in her broadcasts, to the dismay of the ATS and the WAAF. When the WRNS talk was broadcast on another programme, *Calling Africa*, Elspeth wanted to include a mention that the WRNS were in Mombasa, and to cover the work of WRNS on submarine supply ships, but she was denied permission to refer to either subject.

Elspeth thus played a full part in Britain's war effort. She had to go to London frequently for broadcasting purposes, and so witnessed the Blitz at first hand. Gervas had the bright idea of setting up tea cars, five hundred of which were eventually in use, to provide refreshments to people fighting the nightly fires in a London set ablaze by German bombs, or trying to rescue those buried in the rubble of bombed or burning buildings, and Elspeth sometimes drove one of these at night to newly burning areas to distribute tea and buns.

Elspeth tried to write a book of her own at this time, but, unsurprisingly in view of all her other activities and the disruptions of wartime, it was the only one she ever failed to complete. Its subject was America, and it was intended to entertain and consisted of three parts: a description of life at an American university, interspersed with a few passages about the history and associations of parts of New York State; a description of the South, including Kentucky hillbillies, Negro colleges, poor whites and sharecroppers, based on the two motor trips she had made to the region, with some history and biography thrown in; and a description of other parts of the United States, mainly the south-west and Pacific coast and the Dust Bowl, based on her trip across the USA to California and back to Chicago in 1937.

When she completed the first part of the book she asked Harold Raymond of Chatto & Windus for his thoughts on it. He found it lively and informative, though he felt it needed more fact and opinion. Elspeth disagreed, but his view appears to have led her to abandon the book, though she did use the first part in her later *Love Among the Daughters*. Harold Raymond and his wife Vera stayed at Woodfolds for both Easter and Christmas in 1942, and the families became firm friends. Harold laid a flagstone path, ever afterwards known as 'Harold's Path'. The Huxleys' friendship with the Raymonds would be of great value to both Elspeth and Gervas in their future relations with Chatto & Windus.

In mid-1942 Elspeth was recruited to a new job by the indefatigable Trudie Denman, now national head of the Women's Land Army, who liked to draw her friend Nellie's talented daughter into whatever organisation she was involved with. She persuaded Elspeth to become one of the organisers of the Women's Land Army in

Wiltshire, to restore order to the chaotic situation in the county.

From 7 January 1943, at the end of her contract with the Women's Land Army, Elspeth was engaged by the BBC's Home News Department as a part-time (three days a week) member of staff, on the understanding that she was paid full rates for any work done outside BBC hours – in other words, for scripts written at home. The arrangement meant that she was ineligible for payment for the scripts she prepared in her office (Room 133) in Broadcasting House, where she worked from Monday morning to Thursday midday, though those she wrote on a freelance basis earned her twenty-five guineas each. Examples of her work at this time were the talks *War Against the Locust* (5 June), *War Against Superstition* (12 June), *The Kenya–Uganda Railway* (16 June) and *War Against the Bush* (23 July) – all for the Home Service. She also wrote scripts for the Senior History and Senior English series for schools. Lady Grigg, wife of a former Governor of Kenya, inveigled her into doing a talk on the Women's Land Army for the Eastern Service in the series *Women Generally Speaking*, and Eric Blair (George Orwell) organised its translation into Hindustani. There was a new departure for Elspeth when she wrote a specially commissioned thirty-minute radio play, *Eternity in an Hour*, which was broadcast on 21 April 1943.

In June 1943 Elspeth resigned from the BBC on her appointment to a new job. The Colonial Office wanted to keep some control over what was being broadcast to the colonies in time of war, but the BBC was refusing to issue any material it broadcast for prior checking. The CO also wanted to be given advance warning of the BBC's broadcasts about colonial affairs, and insisted on seeing the scripts. 'It should be made known in the BBC,' went one memo, 'that anything touching on the Middle East or colour discrimination or colour prejudice was potentially troublesome.'[12] The BBC, as usual guarding its independence, was unhappy, but a compromise was reached when Gervas Huxley, who in July 1942 had been appointed head of the Empire Division of the Ministry of Information, suggested his wife as the perfect person to solve the impasse. He proposed that she become the liaison officer between the BBC and Colonial Office, her role being to stimulate the provision of information and publicity material necessary to the effective coverage by the BBC of the affairs of the colonies and the work of the Colonial Office.

Elspeth signed a full-time contract and was allocated Room 313 in the Colonial Office in Whitehall. She was allowed to see incoming telegrams from the colonies – other than secret defence ones – so she had the raw material of publicity before the CO machine got to work on it. All divisions and departments of the BBC were told to make maximum use of this liaison channel for all material affecting the Colonial Office and to keep her informed of any relevant matters. She was to act as a sieve as well as a channel, and was also to be available as a speaker for any service on colonial questions. It was at this time that she began her talks on *Calling East Africa*. Her subjects included *Working in London*, *Mass Education in African Society* and *Indian Shopkeepers in East Africa* (approved by the Colonial Office as 'commendably tender to the Indians'). But Elspeth found that not as much use was made of her as might have been by the BBC Overseas Service, and concluded that the existence of her post would not be justified if it confined itself to satisfying requests from the BBC for colonial material and getting scripts passed, because very few were received. On the other hand, if her job was – as she was making it – actively seeking out and collecting colonial material and writing and instigating scripts, its usefulness would increase as time went on. The trouble was that the BBC was still insisting on its independence. The Controller (News) wanted 'to be quite sure that the CO are not claiming the right to see in advance everything we may broadcast about the colonies – an important point of principle'.[13] Elspeth regretted that her liaison with the BBC News Department was limited.

Shortly after taking on the liaison job Elspeth discovered she was pregnant. She had been trying without success to have a baby ever since it became clear that she and Gervas would be settled in England for the duration of the war. Eventually a small operation by a gynaecologist fittingly named Dr Beckett Ovary rectified the problem. She resigned as liaison officer on 30 September 1943. In their letter of farewell the Colonial Office said:

> That you have ... [broken new ground] with such marked success is, believe me, due far more to your own tact and powers of persuasion than it is to that kindliness in the Colonial Office of which you made so much yesterday. You have certainly convinced a large number of people here that the BBC is essentially a human and approachable body and we have every reason to expect that, with the excellent start which you have given to them, our arrangements for liaison ... should continue to the mutual satisfaction of both parties.[14]

From the end of 1943 Elspeth confined her work for the BBC to weekly *Calling East Africa* talks. Thousands of miles away in Kenya, Nellie avidly listened to her daughter's voice on these programmes (indeed, she was so impressed by their content that she concluded that if Elspeth came to live in Kenya after the war she would be its Prime Minister within two years).

Nellie and Elspeth had continued their weekly correspondence during the war, although sometimes they were obliged to resort to a not entirely satisfactory method of communication imposed by the government. Nellie had to write on special sheets, which were then photographed by officials. The film was sent by air to Britain, where it was developed on to small pieces of photographic paper three inches square and sent to the addressee, who would use a magnifying glass to decipher the occasionally blurred result. In one of Nellie's letters she told Elspeth of the sensational murder of Josslyn Hay, Earl of Erroll, whose body had been found in a car on the Ngong road near Nairobi in January 1941: 'I know no news about it, but it is said he was playing around with some woman. It is indeed ironic that the Ngong road should have proved more dangerous than Tobruk or anywhere else.'[15] She made reference to Elspeth's detective sleuth when she said, 'Joss Erroll's murder is still unsolved;

it appears rather to be a choice of angry husbands. Many have wished that your Mr Vachell was here to help ... it is all very sordid and foul ... I hope to God they will all be kicked out of the country forever, it has done an infinity of harm.'[16] Nellie had no time for wastrels.

Within the constraints imposed by the censor, Nellie told Elspeth about the war in East Africa. On Kenya's northern border lay Abyssinia, now in the hands of Hitler's ally Mussolini and 200,000 of his Italian troops. On 10 June 1940 the Italians opened hostilities, driving westward to the Sudan (then in British hands), southward against Kenya's frontier post of Moyale, and eastward into British Somaliland.

The siege of Moyale, guarded by only two hundred Kenyan troops, lasted a week until the garrison made a dramatic escape. Fortunately the Italians, faced with the hostile terrain of the Northern Frontier desert, paused in their attempt to invade Kenya and turned their attention to British Somaliland, which they overran. This gave Kenya a breathing space, and columns of troops gathered in the north of the country to march into Abyssinia. In addition to the King's African Rifles and similar units such as the East African Reconnaissance Squadron, there were West Africans from Nigeria and the Gold Coast, and South Africans of both Dutch and British extraction. A corps of Cape Coloured transport drivers arrived, and thousands of exiled Abyssinians were trained into a guerrilla force called the 'Ethiopia Irregulars'. In December 1940 the British forces attacked. As the troops fought their way northwards through Somaliland and Abyssinia they had to be supplied with provisions from Kenya. Endless convoys of supplies and troops, going to the front or returning from it on leave, passed through the Northern Frontier District, and all farmers had to play their part by increasing production to provision them.

The British emerged victorious from the Abyssinian campaign, taking the capital Addis Ababa and sending thousands of captured Italian troops and civilians south to internment camps in Kenya. Some were distributed among farms to provide skilled labour, and Nellie found that those she was allocated, who numbered seven at one stage, were very useful in the vegetable industry and in the spinning and weaving training centre for Africans she had set up in a workshop on the farm with government assistance. She also took over a vegetable canning factory at Njoro, employing for a year and a half a young Swede, Hans Stjernswärd, who had been helping the Lindstroms on their farm and who married their eldest daughter Viveka. He described Nellie as always the centre of everything, the moving spirit in all conversation, the constant source of witty remarks: 'In a country that was very farmery and dull, she was intellectually head and shoulders above almost everybody else.'[17]

At this time Nellie was deeply involved in learning more about the Kikuyu, not only for intellectual satisfaction, but also because she genuinely wanted to understand the people who worked on her farm, among whom she lived. She had several language lessons from Louis Leakey, who told her that the standard Kikuyu grammar, by Barlow, was wrong in many places. Barlow's word for heat, for example, meant sexual heat, 'so what the gentle wives at Tumu Tumu [the Scottish mission in the Kikuyu reserve] really say to their servants, after being taught exclusively by Barlow, we *would* like to know', Nellie wrote to Elspeth.[18]

To amuse her daughter in war-torn Britain, Nellie recounted the news of everyone she knew in Kenya – how Lady Eileen, Lord Francis Scott's wife, when rather the worse for wear started to undress in the royal box at the races, only to be bodily borne away by Joss Erroll; how Boy Long had been left by his wife Genessie because he shouted and screamed all day in his drunkenness; how Bror Blixen's third wife, Eva Dickson, had been killed in a car accident near Baghdad; how poor Bobby Roberts had died of burns after attempting to save his sister-in-law from a bushfire. There was also great drama on the farm: Nellie had received a pencilled note from H.M. 'Black' Harries, the Welsh owner of the neighbouring farm Larmudiac, saying that Wakuha, a Kikuyu living on the Grant farm, had knifed his European assistant Jack White to death in the Harries farm butchery.

Years before, Harries had got into trouble for ill-treating an African boy he caught torturing his pigs. The boy died, and Harries was jailed for six weeks. He was so disturbed by this that he left Kenya for South Africa, having sold his farm to Ben Birkbeck, Cockie's husband, on easy terms. Birkbeck was too idle to send Harries the quarterly cheque, and the farm reverted to Harries, who returned to Kenya. Immensely strong, he once pulled a wounded leopard backwards by its tail from a bush, maintaining that as it was a cat it would pull away from him. It did, and he struck it dead with one blow. He had a passion for horses, letting them run wild on his farm and never breaking them in. Several of them starved to death. Nellie could not abide this ill-treatment of animals. She also thought Harries and his wife lived like pigs, ankle-deep in animal bones, pushing ducks off their Chippendale chairs before they could sit down. An indescribable stench belched from their kitchen.

Harries made an impassioned speech by Jack White's graveside at Nakuru, demanding public meetings and the Governor's attendance. A meeting was called of the Njoro Settlers' Association, to which Harries did not turn up, and it was agreed that the liquor laws and the growing incidence of violent crimes on farms would be investigated – there were illegal beer shops on both the Harries and Lindstrom farms. But the murder had nothing to do with drink: Wakuha had not gone to work on a Sunday because he was at church, and Jack White had punished him for his absence by striking him when he appeared on the Monday, whereupon Wakuha picked up a knife and stabbed the white man. Wakuha ran away, but gave himself up. Such incidents, and her growing concern about her father, troubled Elspeth, separated by war from any possibility of visiting her parents and helpless to assuage their troubles.

Nellie, too, was very worried about Jos throughout the war. She felt she should look after him, but found him impossibly irritating to be around. Whether she had extramarital affairs is a matter of speculation. In later years Elspeth wrote in a letter to Tobina, Rose Cartwright's daughter: 'I daresay my Mama and Rose had a few off-the-record chats, coded, perhaps, about their lovers.'[19] In 1940 Jos had got a job on a tea farm at Kericho, but he grew restless and applied to the Occupied Territory Administration, which had taken over Italian Somaliland following the defeat of the Italian forces there. He was appointed to the intelligence section and left for Mogadishu in March 1942. He transferred to a new job in May, taking army recruits from Tanganyika, Nyasaland and Northern Rhodesia northwards by lorry to Egypt via Uganda and Sudan. This lasted only a few weeks until his age (sixty-eight) began to tell and he was hospitalised in the Belgian Congo with influenza and malaria. He was invalided out of the army in April 1943 and returned home to Gikammeh in May. Jos never felt well when he lived at Njoro, which was too high for his weak heart, and once he was back there he behaved, said Nellie, like a sore-headed bear, and developed a bad case of eczema, until he went once again to Kericho to run another tea farm. There he suffered from bronchitis, influenza and emphysema, which forced him to seek a lower altitude, staying in Lawford's hotel in Malindi, on the coast. But the humid climate there gave him prickly heat, and he had to return to Gikammeh.

Nellie, at her wits' end, begged Elspeth to come out to Kenya after the war, whenever that should be, to take over the farm, or part of it, so that she and Jos could live at a lower altitude to reduce the strain on his heart. 'It is his passion for enterprises which is so wearing,' she confided to her daughter in 1944, when Jos wanted to join Rex Fawcus in a fish supply scheme.[20] Pa was useful only when it came to winding the wool spun on Gikammeh, having too superficial an attitude to any of the other activities he undertook. He had few friends, apart from an old soldier called Steele who lived in Nairobi. The fact is that age had eliminated the charming, exceptionally handsome man of his youth. He was rather a conversational bore, and was very hurt when, at an Njoro Club evening at which people invented and sang rhymes about each other, that concerning him ran:

> Here's, here's to good old Jos
> Drink him down, drink him down,
> He is not the man he wos, etc.

At Gikammeh he was mercilessly nagged by Nellie. She was also looking after Rose Cartwright's daughter Tobina, who was attending

Egerton Agricultural College near Gikammeh. Tobina later remembered the awkward scenes:

> Nellie was perfectly horrible to Jos when I was there. He liked reading detective stories and she didn't approve; probably like my mother, who thought reading books before dark was extremely idle ... Nellie wouldn't let Jos sit down when he was reading and I am haunted by this figure in slippers shuffling round the room, wheezing from his bad breathing while Nellie berated him.[21]

Nellie was relieved that her house servant Mbugwa appeared impervious to being castigated by Jos for stealing things Jos had mislaid.

Jos tried another sojourn at the coast, this time in the Mombasa Club, but Nellie was paradoxically guilt-ridden at not being with him in his needy old age. Elspeth sent him books, but he could settle at nothing and still pathologically yearned for a job. He found himself unable to abide the Mombasa Club, or the Jadini Hotel at Diani beach, or other coast hotels he tried, and toyed with the idea of buying a plot at Kilifi, halfway between Mombasa and Malindi. Sometimes Nellie parked him with some old Thika friends, the Ridleys, as their daughter Pamela remembered in a letter to Elspeth:

> From time to time your mother used to send your father, Jos, to stay with my parents on the farm at Makuyu when, in his old age, we suspected that his splendid schemes for turning ideas into gold became too much for her. He and my father, always an irascible character, would spend the morning fighting happily about the merits and demerits of the latest scheme until one or other of them became tired and querelous [sic] and would withdraw to confide in my mother. To Mama and me he was always charming – I was overawed by his considerable erudition.[22]

In contrast to her husband, Nellie flung herself into activities during the war. She started a sort of Women's Land Army in Kenya, a somewhat risible affair which consisted of herself as the CO, assisted by Tuppence Hill-Williams, and as recruits the two

Lindstrom girls and Hans Stjernswärd, whose sex apparently did not bother her. Eventually the machinery of the canning factory she ran with Hans wore out, no spares could be obtained and the enterprise had to be closed down. Nellie then started breeding white mice for the veterinary laboratories at Makerere College in Uganda, an institute of higher education for East Africans of all races on whose council she sat. She also cosseted sailors galore at her now somewhat worn farmhouse, which she threw open to servicemen on leave. Nellie remained absolutely tireless, with a terrific sense of humour. One guest found her entering the room in the early morning with a bowl of plaster of Paris which she proceeded to slosh on to a crack in the handbasin. Nellie said it would dry in five minutes, and her guest would then be able to wash without getting her feet wet.

Nellie was thrilled to hear that Elspeth was pregnant, and immediately started making garments for the baby. 'My first reactions,' she said, 'were to have all available lambs fallen upon and shorn in season and out as I think they will contribute very satisfactorily to the tiny garment situation.'[23] She evolved a very soft wool from mixing corriedale lamb with angora rabbit, and began knitting and weaving, though she worried about protruding hairs and told Elspeth that if her child was a clothes-eater she must muzzle it. She also tactlessly said that if the baby was deformed it would fit her garments better, and wondered whether the patterns she was following were for children with malnutrition. Soon she had posted four vests, four pilches, three pairs of bootikins, one jacket, one shawl, a pram cover and a pram suit (for which she removed the buttons from her polo breeches) and bonnet, together with two cot blankets woven by the deaf and dumb boy she was teaching in her weaving workshop and dyed in the canning factory's pea-and-bean-green colouring. For several years Elspeth's child was dressed with clothes Nellie had made.

Nellie received a cable from Gervas on 13 February 1944 telling her that a son, Charles Grant Huxley, had been born to Elspeth on the tenth, in a nursing home in London. Soon she received some photos. 'I showed them,' she said, 'to the Seychelles postmaster at the PO and he said "Intelligence personified". Candidly, I think Charles looks rather drunk in some of them.'[24] She told her daughter that deep blue eyes and auburn hair sounded devastatingly lovely, and made it her duty to find help for Elspeth – she wanted, somewhat impractically, to send her cook Karanja and house servant Mbugwa (Njombo's son) to England to give her a hand. Then she came across Miss Lily Clague, whom she persuaded to agree to go to England as Elspeth's nanny. Miss Clague had arrived in East Africa from England seven years before, had worked in Infant Welfare in Uganda, and then spent five years as a nanny to two settler families. Nellie estimated her age at fortyish, said she was not attractive to look at but not bad, and was 100 per cent trustworthy and good with children, taking great care of their health and manners. Most importantly, children adored her. She kept herself to herself but liked food for the mind. However, war was still raging, and there was no hope of Miss Clague, 'who is Truby King not Norland', getting a passage to England. Nellie even raised with the Governor the question of a berth, to no avail.

Despatching tea and jam to Woodfolds (the Huxleys also received many food parcels from America, which were stored in a vast storeroom at the top of the house), Nellie continued to beg Elspeth to consider coming to live in Kenya after the war. But whereas Elspeth had been reluctant to return to England after her sojourn in Murigo's camp in 1937, by now she had suffered the London Blitz and the upheaval and disruption of a war-torn country. Her experiences had made her British. She had contributed to the secret services' effort to maintain loyalty abroad, and had been a member of staff at the BBC and the Colonial Office as part of her wartime duties. What she had undergone made her identify more profoundly than previously with the British, and she began to see her future in Britain. Having a child confirmed her in this, because she wanted him to avoid the limitations of her own education. Nellie understood: 'It is the very greatest error being seperate [sic] from your young.'[25] Elspeth was also thinking about having another child – her mother congratulated her with the words, 'It is thrilling you mean to have another Charles or Charlotte and most praiseworthy of you.'[26] This never happened, possibly because Elspeth became absorbed in other projects, but more likely because she failed to conceive.

Elspeth's acquaintance with Margery Perham, now Reader in Colonial Administration at Oxford University, had blossomed after she attended a Colonial Conference at Oxford in the summer of 1941. Margery was the queen of colonial studies at Oxford. An impressive woman, with an incisive mind, she was consulted by people in government, administration and academia about the British Empire and its future. She lived in a house in the Woodstock Road with her sister Ethel, who housekept for her but went senile fairly early, thus reversing their roles. While she did not take kindly to the demands of caring for her sister, she coped with fortitude.

When Margery suggested an interchange of letters with Elspeth, possibly for publication, Elspeth went to see her and agreed to open it with a challenging letter. Margery also spent a weekend at Elspeth's home. Perhaps Elspeth's motive was that she felt the white settlers in Kenya had had an unjustifiably bad press, and she wanted to put forward their side of the argument. For her part, Margery wished to proclaim the view that Africa should fundamentally be for black Africans, though whites could help them along until they were ready to take control. The correspondence was designed by the two participants to be formal and structured, and was published by Faber & Faber in 1944 as *Race and Politics in Kenya*.

The book consisted of fifty-five letters between the two women, written between March 1942 and August 1943, in which they discussed white settlement in Kenya. Elspeth's attitude was that the white settlers were there, for good or ill, and no amount of hostility would cause them to vanish into thin air. She failed to see how the country and all its inhabitants could make progress unless the settlers were made partners in the enterprise, instead of being antagonised and attacked by armchair critics.

Margery Perham, who had visited Kenya, even going on safari

with that inveterate womaniser Bror Blixen, whom she liked very much, appreciated the settlers' point of view to some extent:

> I think I now understand the 'immigrant community'. To own a bit of this lovely, virgin country; to make a house, and, still more; a garden in which you can mingle all the beauties of Western and tropical flowers; to have a part share in this thrilling sunlight; to have cheap, apparently reverential, impersonal labour; to feel the sense of singularity, of enhanced personality that comes from having a white skin among dark millions. You leave behind the fogs, the conventions, the problems of the old country: your resulting sense of freedom and joy is increased by the space and the sun. If you find the native to be a problem at least he is a fascinating one. You feel there is a future to be made and that your head and hands will count in the laying of its foundations. And – almost best of all – just round the corner is the wild Africa that not even the commercialization of big-game hunting for American tourists has spoiled, the majesty of the wilds, their strangeness, loneliness and danger. Here, in the effort to kill or to see the animals, you spend long days, matching your endurance, skill and courage against theirs, with evenings round the camp fire, and nights in a tent into which, as you turn over on your camp-bed, comes the occasional music of the animals' own night-hunting in the bush.[27]

None the less, she felt strongly that further white settlement should be stopped and the settlers' attempts to dominate politically the three and a half million Africans in Kenya should be abandoned.* Indeed, there should be no further development of the whites' political power, but a period of rapid political and social advancement for Africans. Needless to say, Margery was not popular among Kenya's whites. The staff at Makerere College in Uganda found her 'no more use than a sick headache', and Louis Leakey's wife Mary could not even bear the mention of her name. At times Margery also irritated people by her propensity to discuss serious

* In 1940 there were 24,596 whites, 44,200 Indians, 15,800 Arabs and 3,447,700 Africans in Kenya.

matters long into the night when others, used to the tropical day of early to rise and not too late to bed, wished to retire.

Both correspondents agreed that there had been drift, contradiction and muddle in the British government's attitude towards Kenya, and that this had been exacerbated by the inferior quality of many of Kenya's Governors. There were some matters on which they saw eye to eye – for example, that racial discrimination, whether socially or in the ownership of land, should no longer be allowed to persist. Margery Perham did not want Imperial control weakened lest the settlers, bent on obtaining political domination, got the upper hand, while Elspeth favoured an extension of local government and devolution of responsibility to local bodies.

Margery thought the Africans would for a long time be incapable of self-rule, so Kenya would have to remain a Crown Colony until they were ready to share in government. Elspeth, however, felt the whites should be given the share in control that was their due, that they were unjustly denied a greater part in running Kenya, and that those who did run the country (Parliament and the Colonial Office) were inefficient and often ignorant. She was impatient of armchair critics of colonial affairs. Margery, herself an armchair critic, thought such people were important watchdogs of the rights and interests of Africans, which should be paramount. In the future Elspeth wanted to see large constitutional changes which would give both Africans and whites a bigger share in running Kenya, but Margery preferred no change for twenty-five years, after which the Africans would be capable of meeting the whites on equal ground.

Lord Lugard, former Governor-General of Nigeria and a proponent of indirect rule in Africa (rule by the British through the medium of local chieftains, regarding as he did traditional native institutions the surest foundation on which to build), wrote the introduction to the book, his words being fine-tuned by both correspondents, who did not wish him to be seen to take sides. In actuality he was much more sympathetic to the magisterial Margery's point of view, but he managed to conceal this to a certain extent. Initially he said to Margery that Elspeth 'belongs to the era of the slave-drivers! . . . White and Black she says "have got to live together whether they like it or not". Would it not be more accurate to say whether the 3 million Blacks like it or not?'[28] Yet, when persuaded by Margery actually to read their letters, he grudgingly admitted that Mrs Huxley made so plausible a case that it might carry weight with some people. What Lugard really would have preferred in Kenya was a small settlement of whites, circumscribed in area and numbers: 'If the settlers accepted such limitations there is no reason why a prosperous model little settlement should not exist in Kenya, instead of the present perennial controversy with H.M.G. That a small oligarchy of employers should legislate for and control the great majority is repugnant to British and American opinion . . . It cannot last . . . when the native population increases in numbers and in education, and also want to run *their* own show.'[29] Elspeth contemplated writing a short life of Lord Lugard in 1944, but when Margery Perham revealed that she was working on the same subject, Elspeth dropped the idea.

Race and Politics in Kenya had a second edition in 1956, to which Margery and Elspeth each added a postscript, unseen by the other, indicating how far their views had been modified by the events of the intervening twelve years, and how they now saw the country's future. The two women remained friends, occasionally visiting each other. After the war Nellie found Margery, who was on a trip to Kenya, entirely mellowed and speaking of Elspeth with real affection. Towards the end of her life Margery became very disillusioned about Africa because things had not worked out as she had hoped. She felt the pace of change had been too fast, whereas Elspeth knew that it was unstoppable. In effect, therefore, they had reversed their points of view, Elspeth now becoming the more radical of the two. Elspeth said to Margery thirty years after the first publication of their book: 'And remembering those times. How remote they now seem! It might be a different age. The pace of change may seem slow at the time, but looking back, how enormous have the changes been.'[30]

After the war Elspeth had a further opportunity to put forward her ideas in the 128-page book *Settlers of Kenya* (1948), part of a series published under the auspices of the Royal Empire Society to provide a forum for discussion of questions relating to the British Commonwealth. In *Settlers of Kenya* Elspeth provides a history of white settlement, concluding that the settler population could not indefinitely expand and that dreams of a white dominion embracing the whole of East Africa, or the whole of Kenya, had faded for good.

In the same year (1948) she wrote a pamphlet called *African Dilemmas.* This is less measured in tone, and in it she used emotive words that would be frowned upon today, among them 'primitive' and 'savage', while examining the question of self-rule for African countries of the British Empire. She saw whites and blacks going forward in partnership:

> Our task is to know more clearly what it is we seek to propagate and then to fire the minds of Africans, so to strike sparks from their souls, that their own leaders will take things into their own hands and talk less of negative self-government, which may yet be seen as a reactionary ideal, and more of a positive alliance with us, and not against us, to raise the mind and soul as well as the body of the African by hard work, honesty, faith and brotherhood to a level where the best may become good citizens and servants of the Commonwealth, and through it of the world.[31]

Events were to show that this was an impossible ideal, although after the Second World War, as after the First, the British government strengthened white settlement in Kenya by giving a year's training at low cost and providing land for five hundred white ex-servicemen to buy on favourable terms.* Most of the land they were given was already alienated and in the white highlands, some of it being bought from existing white owners. This was typical of the ambivalent attitude Britain had towards Kenya. On the one hand, it declared that the interests of the Africans should be para-

---

* In order to attract British ex-servicemen the Settlement Fund provided loans of £1.5 million at 3 per cent. Ninety per cent of those chosen by selection committees in London and Kenya succeeded in establishing themselves on farms.

mount; on the other, it poured in white settlers who would inevitably disrupt African progress. The Troup Report of 1952 also advised that there should be more white immigration.

Nellie was much involved in the ex-servicemen's scheme because the training was done at Egerton Agricultural College, close to her Njoro farm, and she got the contract to supply the college with a thousand pounds of fresh vegetables a week. She also sent parcels of food to Elspeth and Gervas to combat post-war rationing in Britain. Her own political ideas were evolving thanks to the anthropologist Audrey Richards, then teaching at Makerere College, who often came to stay with her. 'Talking to people like Audrey Richards,' she said, 'makes one indeed realise how deep felt is the point of view that Africans are happier without white settlers. I think she is right as I admire her psychological wisdom. It makes for depression to feel we've all been so mistaken.'[32]

Elspeth was now living at Woodfolds looking after her baby and her three dogs, including the dachshund Spickit, who produced seven young, having evidently, opined her owner, heard the appeals for manpower. She employed a gardener, Sid Cook, and intermittent people who helped her in the kitchen. After the nurse hired to look after the newborn baby had left she had to rely for babysitting on the vicar's wife and the baby's godmother, the teenaged Cherry Gibbs, who lived with her parents on the Woodhouses' Park Farm next door to Woodfolds. It was a difficult period for Elspeth, who was used to having her time to herself, and she complained that her mind was going soft under the effects of baby-minding, dishwashing and bed-making. On 7 April 1944 the BBC asked her to do one broadcast a month for East Africa, but she said she would have to refuse unless she could find another nurse, 'which in these days is rather like searching for a case of grapefruit or some silk stockings'.[33] Nevertheless, she continued with her BBC talks and her writing, her domestic situation being eased in July 1945 when she employed Mrs Mills as a cook/housekeeper.

When she could get away to London she frequently stayed with

Harold Raymond and his wife, braving the V2 bombs raining down on the city. Gervas, working at the Ministry of Information housed in London University's Senate House in Malet Street, helped at Woodfolds when he could, but he was only in Oaksey at weekends. He was besotted with his son, walking up and down with the baby over his shoulder, singing 'Charlie is my Darling' again and again. During the week Gervas took a room in the Cumberland Hotel or shared his brother Michael's Earl's Court flat. Apart from the tea cars, he was the begetter of the National Catering Services, which provided hot meals for those working long shifts. He was also heavily involved in managing civilian relations with the large numbers of American troops now arriving in Britain.

In early 1945 Nellie was staying at Government House in Nairobi when the Governor of Kenya, Sir Philip Mitchell, broached to her the subject of starting an African University Press, and asked her to write to Elspeth to persuade her to take it on. Nellie leapt at the idea, which would bring Elspeth out to Kenya to live. 'It would be a supreme job,' she told her daughter, as, apart from overseeing the publication of books engendered by Makerere College, she would be director of East African literature, and would have to spend a lot of time in England. Then, in May, came the more than welcome news of the ending of the war in Europe. Mother and daughter would be able to see each other again.

Gervas demurred at the idea of settling in East Africa as Nellie wanted, and instead made a generous gift to his mother-in-law to help with her finances. Nellie was hurt, writing to Elspeth: 'I've lost interest in the future of this farm as you are not going to take it over.'[34] This caused a flurry of activity at Woodfolds, both Gervas and Elspeth writing to reassure Nellie that she should not sell the farm or their site upon it. They asked her whether Gikammeh had ever paid, to which she responded, 'Yes, but you wouldn't notice it, as everything has always gone back into the farm as is the case with so many.'[35] This was the great dilemma of white settlers in Kenya, whose stake in the land was all they had, which denied them the possibility of leaving. Most of Kenya's farmers ploughed all their profits back into their farms, making them miserably poor in material things. Many years later Elspeth tried to define what had held Nellie and her friend Rose Cartwright in Kenya:

> I think it was, among other things, a love of the country, which did possess many people in those days, and of its plants and animals and seasons and moods. There was a constant struggle to overcome its challenges, they both bounced back from all the disappointments, they both went on trying again.[36]

Things were looking brighter for Elspeth's father. An assistant game warden named McArthur opened a roadhouse (Mac's Inn) at Mtito Andei, halfway along the 340-mile road between Nairobi and Mombasa, and asked Jos to run it for £15 a month. It consisted of a petrol pump on the road and, a hundred yards back in cleared bush, a bar and dining room and three cottages of two rooms each, with their own bathrooms and WCs. Nellie jumped at the opportunity to Pa-park, though she recognised that Jos was temperamentally unsuited to run the establishment, with all the attention to detail that would be required. She took him down to Mtito Andei herself, but he was soon back at Njoro after developing bronchitis again and falling out with the housekeeper. Nellie wanted to visit Elspeth and Gervas in Britain and see her grandchild, but felt it would be too unkind to leave Pa. She parked him with the Delaps at Ol Donyo Sabuk, with Kit Henn at Ruiru, with Mary Cuninghame at Thika, with the Ridleys and others, complaining to her daughter, 'Except in the war, what has he ever done?' This admixture of exasperation, hostility and responsibility is common in spouses caring for infirm partners, but Nellie felt a particular vexation when she contemplated Jos's past life and its failures.

Then she heard that her daughter was coming to Kenya. Elspeth had been appointed by the British government to report on the availability of books of all sorts and in all languages in East Africa. She was to advise the East African Governors' Conference whether the normal processes of publishing by commercial firms would provide what was needed for the production and distribution (by sale and loan) of the kinds of reading material, educational and other, that were required in a changing society. The emphasis was to be on the needs of Africans and the development of a local literature. She was to go to West Africa to see what had been done there, then fly across the continent and report on the situation in East Africa. To allow herself to do this she engaged Dorothy Harcourt as nanny for her seventeen-month-old baby, who was to be left behind at Woodfolds. The presence of Mrs Mills as housekeeper also made leaving her husband and baby more feasible.

Elspeth set off by plane for Gambia at the beginning of October 1945. As she was on government business, she was put up at Government House wherever she had an overnight stay. This was luxurious after the stringency of rationed Britain: 'it seemed very odd,' she wrote to Gervas, 'to have several courses at dinner! And plenty of gin . . . A special kiss and hug for my Charles. How is he behaving?'[37] From Gambia she flew to Sierra Leone, where the man on the spot told her it was inconceivable that such untrustworthy people as Africans could be allowed to take charge of things without supervision. The town of Lagos in Nigeria, her next stop, she found sprawling and overcrowded, indescribably filthy and lacking in sanitation. Nigeria's Governor did not believe that self-government was a possibility for many years to come, if ever, because of entrenched corruption and venality.

In Lagos Elspeth found a fortnightly African newspaper, and school books and readers in the Hausa language. It was arranged for her to go to northern Nigeria, to the old, walled, red-mud cities of Zaria and Kano. Intrigued by these self-contained, inward-looking cities, she later used them as the model for her novel *The Walled City*, published in 1948. In an evening market she was sold a crocodile bag for twenty-five shillings by a veiled Tuareg from the Sahara desert. At Zaria she was able to take a good look at the recently installed newspaper publishing presses and offices financed by money from the Colonial Development and Welfare Fund and designed to counter the 'scurrilous and anti-British rags' of young political agitators such as Nnamdi Azikiwe, who later became President of Nigeria (1963–66).

Elspeth then flew across Africa to Khartoum, where she was staggered by the amount of fruit and fish, cream and cheese. She flew onward to Kisumu on Lake Victoria, where she was met by Nellie. It was seven years since they had seen each other, and Nellie was visibly older, with grey hair. Pa was awaiting her at the farm, looking much older and thinner. Everything was very different from before the war. Gikammeh now had a 550-foot borehole, a 25,000-gallon water-tank, and various flumes and channels built by the labour of Italian prisoners of war. Nellie's spinning and weaving centre was a hive of industry, and she was keen to clothe all the Huxleys in wool and tweeds made on the farm. Because Elspeth and Gervas had declined to take it over, Nellie had sold half her land, keeping 520 acres, and was busy dealing with Adams and Anderson, two settlers who wanted most of the rest on a seven-year lease, with the option of purchase. She herself would keep only 120 acres.

Adams and Anderson also wanted the Huxleys' plot, but Elspeth was reluctant to let it go. She consulted Gervas by letter:

> All this links with our undetermined future plans. Ma realises you will never want to farm here but is less clear (as I am) whether you will ever want to come here for long enough at a time to make it worth building a house ... We could always return here for a winter now and again – or all come for summer holidays, if air travel gets cheaper ... If we sell it you would get all your money back I suppose. I am trying to put this fairly, though personally I feel it *would* be sad to lose it ... It depends on how many children we have.[38]

In every letter she wrote from Kenya, Elspeth asked Gervas whether they should keep their plot, and his refusal to reply to the question led to considerable irritation – Gervas was always one to postpone decisions in order to avoid conflict. Elspeth hated the idea of everything going, but her mother was now sixty, and thoroughly dispirited by the Huxleys' reluctance to take on her farm.

Meanwhile, Elspeth's mind was taken up by the project in hand – reporting on the state of literature in East Africa. She stayed in Nairobi with Sir Geoffry Northcote, the Principal Information Officer of Kenya, and began investigations and interviews, establishing herself in an office in Nairobi overlooking an avenue of jacaranda trees in full blue bloom. One of the first people she saw was Charles Granston Richards, manager of the Church Missionary Society bookshop in Nairobi. A first-class operator with a scholarly mind, he impressed on her the substantial need for newspapers and books in vernacular languages, despite disputes over which language should be used and disagreements over orthography. He showed her a card index of manuscripts which were awaiting publication when he had the capital available. Richards had already met Nellie, whom he thought a 'great woman',[39] and she had encouraged him to start a lending library of books on African history, current problems and related matters. He told Elspeth there was a growing demand for simple, informative books about science, history and current events in Swahili (in which enormous numbers of Africans were literate), Kikuyu, Luo, Luhya and Kamba. Any publishing concern would find the twenty vernacular languages too large a number to cope with, but a start could be made with Kikuyu, Luo and Kamba. Something would also have to be done to improve on the three vernacular newspapers already in existence, very crude anti-white efforts printed by Indians.

As well as calling at missions in the Kikuyu and Kipsigis reserves, where she found the missionaries had strong views on literature and orthographies, Elspeth visited African schools and Makerere College in Uganda. She found Uganda seething with political intrigue. Tanganyika was also on her itinerary. There she found the tropical heat in the lovely Dar-es-Salaam, with its gracious avenues of flamboyant trees, too much to bear, and government officials gloomy about the hopelessness of the Colonial Office.

Elspeth began to see the outline of a scheme, but had doubts about its implementation:

> It will need money and a good director to get it going, with enough drive to cope with three quarrelling and inefficient governments, enough intuition to understand how to get things across to Africans, and enough administrative ability to cope with a fairly complex organization. Where is he or she to be found?[40]

She advised that the developments needed would not take place without government action. One of the problems was that Sir Philip Mitchell, Kenya's Governor, had upset his counterparts in Uganda and Tanganyika by being too pushy and trying to run the other two territories as well as his own. Elspeth thought the only hope was unification of the three countries, because it was too difficult to manoeuvre things through three jealous, separate governments. At the same time, it was crucial that a Literature Bureau be established as soon as possible, to produce and distribute books (especially textbooks) and pamphlets in vernacular languages, and to settle linguistic controversies in orthography. An expansion of printing facilities was also essential.

Elspeth was coming to the conclusion that the only hope for East African countries was European enterprise and capital, whatever disadvantages they brought with them, on a far bigger scale than before. She was depressed by the soil erosion in the Kamba reserve, about which nothing had been done for eight years. The Kikuyu land, too, was being ruined by over-population. Staying at Government House in Nairobi, she discussed all these matters with Sir Philip Mitchell, though he was having a nervous breakdown brought on by overwork during the war.

Christmas 1945 was spent with her parents at Njoro, away from her husband and child. In her honour Nellie arranged a Boxing Day party for 160 adults and seventy children. Elspeth returned to England in January, torn apart by having to leave her unhappy parents, her father depressed about his health and feeling he would not live much longer, and her mother worried about her husband and anxious about selling the farm: 'She hates to see everything go as an end to thirty-five years of effort, and an end to her hopes that we would take over the farm and carry it on.'[41]

Depressing as Elspeth's trip to Africa had been, it had tangible and important results. Her report proposed the intervention of government in the development of vernacular literature. Consequently Charles Granston Richards was given leave of absence from the Church Missionary Society and appointed to the East African Governors' Conference for a year from April 1947 as adviser on literature for Africans. His report, suggesting the establishment of the East African Literature Bureau, was accepted and the CMS granted the government's request to release him to set up the bureau, as a department of the new East African High Commission which had taken the place of the Governors' Conference. From 1948 to 1963, when Richards retired as its director, the EALB produced an average of one title a week, in one of twenty-seven vernacular languages. Elspeth's report also recommended the publication of a magazine to convey material of an educational and development nature. The result was *Tazama*, published in Nairobi, which occasionally shocked its readers – for example, when it included a picture of an African woman on a beach wearing next to nothing. Elspeth's report played a crucial part in the development of African literature in East Africa.

SIX

Motherhood and Post-War Austerity

It is the lot of every working mother to have to juggle time and childcare, and if she was to continue to contribute to the family budget and have money of her own to help out her parents, Elspeth would have to find a solution to this problem. At the start of 1946 she saw her first duty as the employment of a nanny to look after Charles, now almost two years old. As a committed writer, she did not wish to spend all her time caring for him, and indeed she had been brought up as a member of a class which would not have dreamed of doing so.

But the world had changed during the war. The former class system was imploding, and people were no longer willing to work in master–servant relationships. There was also a new egalitarianism under a Labour government led by Clement Attlee. The Conservative Winston Churchill had led Britain during the war, but – surprisingly to a few but inevitably to the majority – had been defeated in the post-war general election. Now the railways and other utilities were being nationalised, and a universal and free health service was about to be introduced. It was not going to be easy to find a highly qualified, live-in nanny.

It was still impossible for Lily Clague to get a passage from Kenya to England. The travel situation was chaotic, with returning soldiers and people rejoining loved ones separated from them by long years of war, and immigrants and emigrants to every country. Nellie kept Miss Clague interested in the prospective job with the Huxleys by occasionally having her to stay on the farm, and she also took temporary jobs with other settler families. When Elspeth arrived in Kenya in late 1945 on her assignment to investigate the establishment of an African publishing press she interviewed Miss Clague, and found her 'very nice, small, quiet and competent – probably not a very chatty companion, but very easy with no tiresome mannerisms'.[1] But it looked as if Charles might be a schoolboy before Lily Clague could start her job, for no ship had sailed from Kenya for England since April. Then, while Elspeth was in Kenya, a berth was secured for Miss Clague on the liner the *Cape Town Castle*, called by its passengers the 'Belsen Castle', so overcrowded and unpleasant was the vessel.

Elspeth, always inclined to fret even when things were going well, was concerned about how the new nanny would get along at Woodfolds with her housekeeper Mrs Mills. On balance, though, she thought Miss Clague would be a success, because she was so good with children that her training of Charles would be better than Dorothy Harcourt, the current nanny, could offer. It had been arranged that Miss Clague would not go to live at Woodfolds until Elspeth returned to England, and Elspeth wrote to tell Gervas that she still had qualms: 'Obviously it would be awful to lose the wonderful Dorothy and upset Mrs Mills. I do feel rather pledged to Clague – she is very nice. But I can't bear to think of Dorothy going. Let's leave it till my return and if we decide to jettison Clague we must ask her down to stay and break it very nicely ... Her reason for wanting to come to us was to free me to write books. How difficult it all is.'[2]

Having left an easy life in sunny Kenya for the rigours of an English winter, Miss Clague would have been dismayed to hear of this potential treachery. A fortnight later Elspeth compounded it by telling Gervas, 'It is going to be very difficult about Clague. We may have to abandon her. But I do *hate* the idea of Charles getting spoilt by Mrs Mills – as he gets older he'll need more handling and firmness and she is *not* a disciplinarian. If I do it myself it is goodbye to all idea of writing books. I *do* want to get one or more done before I die.'[3] Three weeks later she confided, 'I am so afraid of Master C. getting terribly spoilt under a purely Mills regime.'[4]

Elspeth was beginning to express her decided ideas about a firm upbringing for children, a point of view which conflicted with her husband's more laissez-faire approach.

Over Christmas in Kenya Elspeth busied herself sending food parcels to her family and friends. Exhorting Gervas not to spoil Charles with too many presents, she herself bought several gifts to take home to the child, including a beautifully iced birthday cake made by the Sinhalese cook at the Molo Hotel. Nellie added bootees and a home-woven scarf. Elspeth missed her son while she was away, though she valued the freedom she had to write. In every letter to her husband she asked after Charles. Was he talking? Was he feeding himself yet? She asked for his height, as 'a matter of interest and comparison', and wanted Mrs Mills to write with 'some of the quite unimportant details of his progress'.[5] Mrs Mills obliged with the news that Charles was now talking.

Elspeth got back to a wintry England in January 1946. Fortunately for Miss Clague, she decided to overcome her doubts and appoint her as Charles's nanny from 4 February, and gave notice to Dorothy Harcourt. Initially things did not go well – Nellie sympathised with her daughter with the words, 'I AM sorry that the C is so dour, damn her, and fancy that muttering over the wash, the ruddy limit. She was all so full of being helpful out here. But it must surely be something for Charles to have really intelligent handling.'[6] Nellie was delighted with Elspeth's report that Charles had pointed to a black woman and said 'Granny!', which she thought extremely bright, as he had linked up Africa, black people and Granny, a very advanced concept. She had been reading a book on child psychology and gave Elspeth the number of nouns, verbs, adjectives, pronouns, adverbs and prepositions a child should know at twenty-eight and thirty months. Poor Charles. Elspeth began trying to socialise her son, inviting other children to tea, because he was 'dictatorial . . . and obstinate as hell' and led altogether too sheltered a life.[7]

With a nanny installed, Elspeth was able to pursue her career. In 1946 she wrote several talks for the BBC, often giving them herself. On 10 March, having insisted on being paid the first-class fare from Kemble to Paddington so that she could work on the train, she broadcast a talk about her impressions of East Africa on revisiting it so soon after the war. Other talks in 1946 included *The Colonial Empire* (May), *England After Africa* (June) and *With the Masai* (*Travel Talk*, September).

She still hoped to have another baby. Nellie wrote in October: 'Doesn't it happen, or what? I remember the slight scare – or hope? – just about a year ago.'[8] But there was no sign of a pregnancy. In the first week of November Gervas's father died. Gervas was in America at the time on tea business, having resumed his former job at the end of the war, and Elspeth went alone to the simple funeral, held with a minimum of fuss and ceremony. She and Gervas inherited some of his father's furniture, which she installed at Woodfolds, and his dinner service.

When Elspeth realised she could trust Miss Clague to raise her son in the manner she expected, she was free to go abroad again. She felt obliged to visit her mother and ailing father, and was also drawn to Kenya by her idea of writing a sort of travel book on East Africa, which would need considerable research. She decided to combine the two and arranged to be away for four months, which stretched to six, from just before Christmas 1946 to mid-1947. This was a long time to be parted from her son, now two and a half years old and in a period of rapid development. She admitted she would miss him – 'he is such a companion now' – but she was unsentimental about partings, not surprisingly in view of her own experience as a child. She was resolved to pursue her own career, and believed she had made the best provision she could for her son's welfare. Prolonged absences such as this made Charles gravitate emotionally more towards his father than his mother, and the removal of his mother at this vital point in his life must have been very unsettling for him.

Before Elspeth arrived in Kenya, Nellie had been obliged to remove many of her squatters under the provision of a new law. The number of goats kept by squatters on white farms had risen to absurd heights, largely because bride-price had increased to eighty goats. The government had intervened in order to curb the resulting devastation of farmland and now insisted on squatter registration, to limit their numbers. Even Ingrid Lindstrom next door to Nellie was delighted to be rid of some of her squatters, many of whom were illegal, after they tried to steal maize they had already sold to her husband Fish by sending up to the farm a wagon with building sand and reloading it at night with the maize. Even after the removals, Nellie still had 142 Africans living on her farm. She held on to Karanja as her cook, Kupanya as headman and Mbugwa, Njombo's son, as house servant. Njombo, with her so long, had finally retired and left her farm, to Nellie's distress because she regarded him as an old friend. Contrary to later opinion, it was common for firm bonds to be forged between white Kenyans and their African employees. Mbugwa had been a baby when he came from Kitimuru to Njoro. A very hard worker and possessed of a sunny and considerate nature, he rose from kitchen toto (the cook's skivvy) to house servant. 'He can turn his hand to anything,' said Elspeth, 'from cleaning out a carburettor to ironing tender fabrics, from planting maize to whipping up an omelette, from mending the refrigerator to arranging flowers, at which his touch would not displease Constance Spry.'[9]

Nellie hardly knew which way to turn. She was in a quandary because Jos's health was deteriorating at the same time as she had been appointed to an exacting position on the Settlement Board, which oversaw the welfare of ex-servicemen allocated land in Kenya. Pa's illness worsened, forcing her to take a bungalow for May and June 1946 at Likoni, at sea level on the south mainland of Mombasa, from where her little dachshunds amused themselves by barking at the ships sailing past to Kilindini harbour. Ever seeking intellectual stimulation, she used the time while Jos convalesced to take Swahili lessons. It was a depressing time for her. She was still bitterly disappointed that Elspeth would not take over her farm. Pa failed to improve, and she returned to Njoro, leaving him at the Muthaiga Club near Nairobi, where he immediately became very unpopular for storming at the servants, accusing them of cheating him over chits.* He fell over in the bath and ended up in hospital. Nellie was therefore relieved and delighted to hear that Elspeth was coming out to Kenya.

Following the usual air route to Kenya at the time, in December 1946 Elspeth flew to Paris and travelled by train through Italy, then flew across the Mediterranean to Alexandria, and from Alexandria to Khartoum, a distance covered in one day, a great improvement on pre-war journey times. The British Overseas Airways Corporation tried to keep its passengers comfortable, which made Elspeth, a supporter of the Conservative Party, conclude that the airline's recent nationalisation under the Labour government was harmless. On the plane she read the Indian tales of Rudyard Kipling, and experienced a fear not uncommon in authors: 'Reading these really good writers makes me feel it's quite useless ever trying oneself to write a word.'[10] She took the flying boat service from Khartoum, landing on Lake Victoria at Kisumu, where Nellie was awaiting her.

The situation that faced Elspeth was dire. Her mother again had pyrethrum poisoning, a painful rash on the face and eyes suffered by those who handle the powerful insecticide, while her father was in Nakuru hospital having injections to reduce the excess fluid in his body caused by a failing heart. Jos was feeble, frail and shrunken, and the doctor was not optimistic about him getting better. Elspeth had a pang of regret about her projected travel book before deciding she wanted to be with her father as much as possible, even if it meant sacrificing the book she had come to East Africa to write. She had always had a soft spot for her gentle father, who had treated her patiently as a child, in contrast to the somewhat peremptory and bossy, though ever stimulating, Nellie.

Although it was less than a year since she had last been there, Elspeth found Njoro much changed. It was full of newcomers, the ex-servicemen and their wives who were learning how to farm at the nearby Egerton Agricultural College. The 'township' of Njoro consisted of a single row of Indian dukas facing a little 'park' of

---

* The chit system was universal in Kenya. No money passed over bars or other counters, people instead signing chits which were paid later. It was a system which led to bankruptcies when bills were not paid.

young flowering trees, an Indian-owned 'European store'* and a post office. Elspeth visited Egerton and discovered that passages of her *Red Strangers* were read to the newcomers' wives and girlfriends, to familiarise them with local customs and discourage them from kissing their husbands and boyfriends openly, which offended the Africans. One woman was almost disappointed because the country was not as wild and pioneering as she had expected, while another felt let down because it was much too wild. An Njoro neighbour, Mrs Keane, whom Elspeth visited appeared at her door with her hands and arms covered in flour, apologising with the words, 'Please excuse me, I've been making the bread, as the cook went to hospital this morning with leprosy.'

Pa left hospital in the third week of January, but it was arduous to nurse him at home because he was weak and 'wandery in the head', as Elspeth put it, and needed help with his bodily functions. He was a difficult patient, seeming older than his seventy-two years, dozing much of the time, but liable to get up and lose his balance. Sometimes nothing he said made sense. There was no alternative but to hire a nurse, a somewhat voluble white South African, Mrs Lomax, who got on Pa's nerves. Nellie and Elspeth decided to take him to Malindi, on the coast north of Mombasa, to relieve his breathing. It was easier than before to leave the farm, so shrunken in size since Nellie had disposed of much of her land. She had kept a bit of pyrethrum, and bred angora rabbits and angora goats for their wool. There were turkeys in a playpen and muscovy ducks under the house. Kupanya could cope with all this, and the house now had a telephone which could be used in emergencies – if Karanja, who appeared to spend all morning on it, would free the line. Gikammeh was also about to be provided with mains electricity instead of the unreliable generator previously used.

---

* Initially the store had been owned by Mr and Mrs Hawkins. Mrs Hawkins would sometimes take a holiday with friends up the line at Molo. She knew Mr Hawkins's little habits, so when she got into the train she chose a carriage well at the back. The train would pull out, then take a long drink of water prior to the haul up the Mau. Out would skip Mrs H., and dash back to the store to find Mr H. in the very act of opening his first whisky bottle for supper.

On the first day of the journey to Malindi Elspeth drove her parents and Mrs Lomax to the Muthaiga Club in the farm's ancient Ford, a vehicle so decrepit that she had to keep looking round to see if bits of the bodywork had dropped off. She had bought it for her mother in 1938 for £130 and it had done thousands of miles in the war. But the trip went smoothly, not least because the road from Nakuru to Nairobi, save the last twenty miles, had been tarred by Italian prisoners of war. Nellie and Elspeth reckoned it would be a one-way journey for Pa, for he would be unable to return to the altitude of Njoro. In private, Elspeth thought he might die at any minute, or hang on for months.

From Muthaiga Nellie went to Mombasa by train and Elspeth drove Pa and Mrs Lomax to stay the night at Mac's Inn, the hotel at Mtito Andei which Pa had tried his hand at managing. It was now run by one of the Hartleys, an extensive Kenya family, who provided them with an excellent five-course dinner. They were remote from other human beings and surrounded by bush, and as night fell around their stone cottage, cicadas began to whistle and wild animals to grunt and roar.

The following day Elspeth completed the car journey to Mombasa and took them to the newly built Nyali Beach Hotel, on the mainland north of Mombasa, where Jos and Nellie had stayed in a sweltering corrugated-iron hut beside a sisal plantation in 1912, on first arriving in East Africa. The sisal had long gone, and the beautiful beaches of fine white sand had begun to attract hotels for holiday-makers. The Nyali Beach Hotel was romantic and luxurious, with steps and pergolas sloping down to coconut palms and coral sands. Pa was too ill to enjoy any of this, though he survived the remainder of the journey to Malindi, sixty miles up the coast. Malindi's flame of the forest trees (*Delonix regia*) were in their full scarlet glory and its sea was coloured chocolate by the topsoil washed along the Sabaki river from Kikuyu country far inland. In the moonlight the creamy crests of the breaking waves were the colour of Ovaltine.

Nellie had rented a tiled cottage on the bay, beside the beach fringed with casuarina trees sprung from seeds which had drifted over the ocean from India. On their first night the moon was round and full, a lighthouse blinked wildly on the right and thousands of little pink crabs danced on the beach before the waves. Mother and daughter thought it a peaceful place to end one's days. Nellie asked Mrs Lomax to stay till Jos died. But die he did not. He rallied to such an extent that he was able to sit up for meals at table. His brain, though, had been severely affected by his illness. He could not read, and rambled incoherently all the time, chuckling to himself.

Mrs Lomax came to the end of her promised stint and was replaced by a Mrs Bell, who promptly suffered a virulent bout of malaria and had to be nursed herself by Elspeth and Nellie. Pa's money, which mother and daughter needed to pay for his care, could not be accessed because he could not or would not write a cheque. They took it in turns to sleep in his room at night, lest he get out of bed and fall. At least shopping was easy, with hawkers bringing fresh fish and vegetables to the door. One day an African turned up with a basket of live crayfish, with shining blue armour and red spots, at only three shillings each. This provoked Elspeth to show everyone her ration book, and she must indeed have felt pangs of guilt about the plenty before her eyes in contrast to the restricted diet of her husband and son left behind in England. One curiosity was that in this stifling heat every Indian duka offered for sale rubber hot-water bottles, still unobtainable in Britain.

Tempers grew frayed in the Malindi cottage. Elspeth looked around the local whites to see if there were any congenial people among them, to help while away the time and relieve the tense tedium. John Carberry, a passenger on her recent train and plane journey to East Africa, had begun Carberry's Club, beside which a new hotel, the Malindi, was being put up by one Holmes, a fellow inmate during Carberry's year-long sojourn in Fort Jesus, Mombasa's prison, serving a sentence for flouting wartime Defence Finance Regulations. The two men had gone into partnership when they were released. Holmes was most unappetising, a huge man like a large white boar, with a vast torso and always naked save for a pair of shorts. Then there was Rex Fawcus, who was staying at Carberry's Club, a man of nearly seventy with a 'deed-poll' wife who had changed her surname to his, a young woman with legs like mountains.

The Lindstroms arrived from Njoro for a holiday, with Ingrid's sister Henriette and her husband Nils Fjastad. Nils (a 'mahogany Viking', as Elspeth described him) took Elspeth out in a small boat made from a seaplane float, to see the reef. She found a fascinating Walt Disney world of waving corals of all shapes and colours, like heads of upright hair on pink calcified brains. Also in Malindi were the Lawfords, friends since Elspeth's childhood days in Thika and now the proprietors of Lawford's Hotel on the beachfront. Elspeth renewed her acquaintance with their daughter Marjorie, who had shared her governess at Thika. Marjorie was dressed like a girl of eighteen, with dyed hair and carefully tended complexion, in contrast to the more sober Elspeth, who never had much interest in clothes or make-up. Everyone loved her father, 'Pop' Lawford, with his halo of white hair, merry black eyes and light-hearted bonhomie.

The dawns were lovely and always observed by Elspeth, whose lifelong practice was to rise at about five o'clock and do her correspondence before others were awake. This early rising made her a superb correspondent, who placed great value on the letter as a means of communication. She thought it unmannerly to make a correspondent wait more than a day or two for a reply, and her letters, often long, were filled with wit and perspicacity. At first the Malindi dawn was monochromatic, in all shades of indigo, with the sea like grey silk. Then salmon pink intruded, and all became bichromatic until the sun rose over the horizon.

One day an early walk took Elspeth to Malindi's cemetery for whites – even in death the colour bar operated. There she found the grave of a child of five. Asking about the circumstances of the boy's death, she was told that in 1940 a woman married to a German came to stay at Lawford's Hotel with her small son. Her husband turned out to be a Nazi and was interned, which left her shattered. One morning the boy ran down to bathe, fell and knocked his head on a stone. He drowned in a foot of water before anyone could reach him. The woman blamed herself, and a week later, at the same time and in the same place, she walked out into the sea and was drowned.

Elspeth soon grew restless at Malindi, writing to Gervas: 'I can't stay here for ever and it is too much for Ma single-handed. One is more than ever convinced that a quick ending is the thing to pray for from every point of view.'[11] It may have been at this point, witnessing the long-drawn-out death of her father, that she developed the ideas about euthanasia she was to hold in later life, when she became a stalwart member of the Euthanasia Society. She tried to revise the typescript of her novel *The Walled City*, written in 1946 before she left for Kenya, but came to the conclusion that it was terribly poor. The travel book she had hoped to research in Kenya looked less and less likely to materialise.

Nellie had taken the cottage only until the end of February, but she managed to extend the let to 21 March. Apart from nursing Pa, she had nothing to do but sit around and knit. As inactivity was abhorrent to her, the atmosphere became very strained. Nellie was exasperated and quarrelsome, Jos obstinate and slow. To escape, Elspeth decided to go to Nairobi for a week to do research, then return to Malindi while Nellie departed for a week to attend to farm matters. She was feeling less troubled about her projected East African travel book since she heard that Arthur Creech Jones,* the Secretary of State for the Colonies, had told the three East African Governors to afford her facilities and generally be of assistance to her. In Nairobi, which was packed with so many people that no hotel beds were available, she stayed with Sir Geoffry Northcote, the Chief Information Officer, and saw the Governor, Sir Philip Mitchell, of whom she had a high opinion, thinking him twice as brilliant as anyone else, despite being worn out. Mitchell told her he had a hopeless lot of administrators, blocking him on all sides.

Elspeth made a series of non-stop appointments in Nairobi, cramming in as much work as she could. Her intention was to write a sort of travel book on the three East African countries,

---

* Creech Jones and his great ally the anthropologist Lucy Mair, whom Margery Perham disliked intensely, wanted to increase the pace of freedom for the colonies. Elspeth was amused by this because in his early days Creech Jones had been a lion-hunter.

analysing their politics and infrastructure, describing their econo-
mies and societies, prognosticating their futures. Intended for the
general reader, it was to be a book of a type that does not exist
today, but was reasonably popular when the British Empire was
engaging in post-war navel-gazing.

Elspeth had lunch at the United Kenya Club, to which all races
could belong. Having always abhorred the social colour-bar, believing that with enterprise, tact and common sense the races could
co-operate and meet together, she followed this by taking tea with
some Indian professionals. She found the Muslims more moderate
politically than the Hindus, whom she thought 'rather silly'. Then
she interviewed Frederick Muiruzi Nganga, the Executive Officer
of the Kenya African Union, a political organisation which Eliud
Mathu, a Kikuyu product of Balliol College, Oxford, who became
the first African member of Kenya's Legislative Council, had helped
to found in 1944. Nganga gave her an example of the sort of incident
which gave rise to African resentment of whites – if a white man
was stuck in a car on a road, instead of politely asking Africans to
push, he beckoned them with his finger.

Elspeth also went to Nairobi's Coryndon Museum, which to her
surprise was packed with African visitors, to renew her acquaintance
with the Leakeys, Louis now being its curator. He put before her
his theory that human life had begun at Rusinga Island on Lake
Victoria, where he had found the 'Proconsul' skull, older than any
unearthed before. She found him very conceited and a bit of a
firework who was always putting ambitious archaeological schemes
to a government too poor to authorise them.

Her week soon over, she returned to Malindi on the Nairobi–
Mombasa train, always a slow journey with lengthy stops. Back at
Malindi she found swimming no longer possible in the bay, which
was now full of banana trees torn up by the Sabaki river in flood.
African women were drawing mud rather than water from the river,
such was the amount of silt washed down to the sea from far inland.
While Elspeth was away Nellie had arranged for them both to sail to
the ancient Arab town of Lamu, on an island to the north of Malindi,
for fifty shillings each way. It was an opportunity too good to miss.

Lamu was famed as a harbour for dhows sailing on the monsoon winds southwards from Arabia to Zanzibar and beyond. It consisted of distinctive Arab houses of coral rag, the width of whose slender rooms was determined by the length of the mangrove poles which supported the ceilings and cement roofs. The houses' elegantly carved wooden doorways faced each other across streets whose narrowness afforded shade from the relentless sun. The sole wheeled vehicles were hamali carts pushed and pulled by Arab vendors in kanzus and embroidered caps, and the only method of transport was the donkey. The shore was lined with dhows and smaller lateen-rigged fishing boats, while further along the island at Shela the bleached skulls and bones of men fallen in a grand battle a century and a half before poked through the even whiter sand. Lamu's women swathed themselves in black buibuis, all encompassing robes that could be raised to cover the face at the approach of any member of the opposite sex.

'Lamu,' said Elspeth, 'seemed like some ancient vessel becalmed in the seas of history, its sails furled, unrocked by tempests, even the barnacles on its keel fast asleep . . . No crude or impoverished culture had given rise to this architecture, which combined simplicity with elaboration, stark design with graceful decoration.'[12] It was a place where homosexuality was no shame, and it thus attracted a few white men like Nellie and Elspeth's old friend Sharpie, who had a house there, and the gentle Swiss Henri Bournier, with whom they stayed. Like Bournier, who had become a Muslim (his brother became a Hindu), the other five white men on the island were also bachelors. Three of them, Percy Petley, Coconut Charlie (Charles Whitton) and the DC Daddy Cornell, so fascinated Elspeth that she devoted a section of *Out in the Midday Sun* to them.

With Pa refusing to die, and the impossibility of staying at Malindi for ever, mother and daughter decided to move Jos up-country again. Reinvigorated by Lamu, Nellie went ahead to Njoro while Elspeth put Mrs Bell and Pa on the Mombasa–Nairobi train. She herself stayed in Mombasa for a couple of days to do research for her book. Again she came up against the social colour-bar, having to entertain three African civil servants to lunch in an Indian hotel because European establishments would not serve them. The Africans pointed out the unfairness of the system in which Indians and Arabs doing the same work as Africans received higher pay. There was also resentment at the lack of any government school for Africans, who had to rely on the missions for their education. Inspecting, under a blazing sun, new housing designed for African occupation, Elspeth remembered her family in England, suffering the most bitter winter for decades, and felt resentment of her own:

> Where . . . does the money come from? At the moment, very largely, from that patient, plodding, acquiescent milch-cow, the British taxpayer. This housing scheme is mainly paid for by the Colonial Development and Welfare Fund, the £120 millions voted by Parliament as a free gift to finance good works in the colonies . . . The British, shivering with meagre fuel and docked electricity, struggling into overcrowded transport, returning to arctic houses to exist on their two weekly ounces of butter and bacon, shorn by vicious taxes of what they should be putting by for a little comfort in their old age, and themselves grossly overcrowded in patched-up houses, are paying for these Mombasa Africans to live almost rent free on their own sun-warmed island, all but unrationed, never cold and seldom hungry, a six-hour day the most that is ever asked of them.
>
> Fair enough, perhaps – restitution for past neglect, fulfilment of colonial responsibilities? – but it does seem hard that the British should be accused of exploiting Africans.[13]

Elspeth tried to suppress her impatience at cant, but there is some hard-hitting in the book which emerged from this trip to East Africa, *The Sorcerer's Apprentice*, which was published by Chatto in 1948.*

Elspeth well understood the wrongness of Britain's sense of moral

---

* The title, which came from *Der Zauberlehrling*, a poem by Goethe, provoked an erudite correspondence in the *Sunday Times* in January 1948 involving the subjects of Goethe, Lucian and books of necromancy.

and spiritual authority over other races and nations, and she knew that if you scratch beneath the surface of politics you often uncover wounded racial pride, for little personal slights enter the soul and fester; but at this stage of her life she failed really to understand the inevitability of eventual African political supremacy. At the opening of her book she warned her readers that there were still wild places to be found in Africa, deserts and empty forests, but they were vanishing, and it was not of them that she would be writing. The reader in search of jungle-noises would have to go elsewhere, for she had talked with clerks – less romantic, perhaps, but more potent harbingers of the new Africa. She revealed the alarming increase in Kenya's population, laying the blame at the foot of the white man: 'Like a blundering rhino horned with a desire for good, the white man charged on the scene. He made war on death.'[14] Consequently Kenya's people were protected as never before against epidemics, tribal warfare and starvation.

Now that the reserves were becoming overcrowded, African political leaders were calling for the return of land occupied by white farmers, who themselves stood on the boundary of the reserves and saw productive land, improved by their sweat, money and efforts on one side, and devastation and erosion caused by bad husbandry on the other, and said, 'Look what will happen if we give you our land.' 'Gone are the days,' wrote Elspeth, 'of "veranda farming", and with them the type of settler – always in a small minority, but gaudy enough to catch the eye – who lived on private means and whisky and now and then made the headlines with scandalous exploits.'[15] The present white farmer was a man of altogether different mettle, whose whole capital and therefore future was sunk in Kenya's land.

In Elspeth's opinion, Kenya's vernacular newspapers fostered race hatred, and not enough was being done by the government to counter this. The almost total failure of the government information services, tardily started, inadequately staffed and ill-conceived, to instil a grasp of the harsher economic facts into the minds of the people was a failure, she said, for which a cruel price would be paid. Moreover, the education syllabus, with its English literature and British history, was irrelevant in African schools and should be replaced. She found members of the African intelligentsia growing progressively more politically minded, increasingly unrealistic and 'more and more impatient to snatch from European hands the promised reins of power'.[16]

Those who believed Africans were always in the right, she said, 'surely propagate racialism no less than the exponents of white supremacy . . . Were their assumption valid, Africans would not be human, but of another order, inherently superior to us and therefore inherently different; true equality means that they are also, like ourselves, as predatory, self-seeking, irrational, obstinate and lazy as circumstances permit, and as all history proves.'[17] This is a constant theme of Elspeth Huxley's writings – that those who reach out for the gifts of Western materialism are heirs to its malaises as well as its triumphs. This did not mean that she shared Jean-Jacques Rousseau's view of the 'noble savage', but she acknowledged that there was much evil as well as good in Western civilisation, and the assumption by Africans of Western ideas and trappings was a mixed blessing. It might be better for them to stick to their own traditions and cultures to warm and nourish the soul, without which a healthy mind is not possible.

In *The Sorcerer's Apprentice* Elspeth wondered whether in truth one race could pass on to another its own experience: 'Can you change natures moulded over centuries by their environment in the wink of an eye? . . . Even were all the answers negative, that would not be to damn the attempt as wasted. Men and assemblies of men make efforts, when all is said and done, not to meet the wants of others but to fulfil needs of their own.'[18] She understood what she called 'the natural and gathering impatience of the half-educated, fed on the vapour of our own philosophy, to be done with an alien ruler', but warned of hurricanes ahead:

> Because the African now covets more and more the material goods of his so-much-richer masters, and because he has no idea in his head that the money you earn must depend in the long run not on the organisation of your discontent but on

the worth of your labour, and because he feels himself to be shut out from the esoteric circle – for these and for other reasons, the situation is full of danger.[19]

The Sorcerer's Apprentice was researched at a difficult time in Elspeth's life, while her father was dying. Mrs Bell and Nellie took Pa back to Njoro, freeing Elspeth to travel to acquire information. She covered thousands of miles on her own, staying with Governors and DCs, every day visiting one, if not more, new school or government enterprise or agricultural settlement or housing estate or factory or research institute in Kenya, Uganda, Tanganyika and Zanzibar. She would rise early to do some notes and her correspondence, spend the day gathering information by means of interviews and visits, be as sociable as was required of her in the evening, and then settle down to write up her notes for the day. It was a punishing schedule, and it is no wonder that Elspeth wrote to Gervas that actually she was a bit despondent about it, as she thought that writing the book was impossible if she had only six weeks in which to do the whole of Uganda, Tanganyika and Zanzibar. 'One is very superficial,' she said, 'and gets so muddled.'[20] In fact, the book is a model of clarity and incisive thinking in its attempt to examine and understand the African condition. Elspeth was ever capable of seeing the world from other people's point of view, and could express complex matters with simplicity. Christopher M. Harris wrote in the *Times Literary Supplement* (5 February 1949): '[The] book is most entertaining and is full of exceptionally good pictures of life in East Africa. It is also good politics, and a book to be recommended strongly to all concerned to help ... The author writes objectively, accurately and amusingly with an impeccably liberal generosity and balance ... It is important to appreciate the thoroughness of this journey.'

In Tanganyika Elspeth's first port of call was Moshi, at the foot of Mount Kilimanjaro, where the DC and his wife took her part of the way up the mountain rearing from the African plain like a man's head topped with a bald pate – the snow. The intention was not so much to climb the mountain as to meet a chief of the local

Chagga tribe and examine the African methods of husbandry in the highly fertile soil of the region. The Chagga cultivated coffee and were growing very rich, displaying their wealth in proud car-ownership. Notwithstanding the tiring day, in the evening Elspeth drove twenty miles to dine with the leader of the local settlers, Frank Anderson, a tough Australian. He told her there were strong rumours that the United Nations was allowing Germans back into Tanganyika. The rumours were not unfounded. In 1936 Hitler was demanding the return of German colonies taken at the end of the First World War, and this was considered by the British government as part of its appeasement policy. Hitler rejected some half-hearted proposals, and there was also opposition from within Britain and the colonies.

After a night of wakefulness caused by loud dance music at the Lion's Cub Hotel in Moshi, Elspeth was taken by Indian taxi the next day to Tanga. A man three feet tall with a goatee beard showed her sisal plantations before she embarked for Zanzibar, where the British Resident, Sir Vincent Glenday, put her up for two days. She was there when she was handed a telegram from her mother telling her that Jos had died in Nakuru Hospital on 8 April. As Elspeth wrote to Gervas on 12 April:

> he had a stroke on Sunday and died on Tuesday without regaining consciousness. I very much wish I had been there, but [Ma] says the Hospital people were marvellous and arranged it all . . . I shall always regret not being on the spot to help. Poor Pa, he must have started to go downhill almost the day I reached Kisumu, as he was not normal really when I first saw him, though of course he knew me all right then.[21]

She did not curtail her trip and return to Njoro. Perhaps she felt there was no point in doing so, though Nellie might have appreci-ated the gesture. Instead, Nellie leant on Ingrid Lindstrom for sup-port in the immediate aftermath of Jos's death and at his funeral at Nakuru cemetery. A year later, once the earth had settled, Nellie erected a Celtic cross over the grave – 'Jos was really always a Celt in spirit,' she wrote to Elspeth[22] – designed by Aunt Vera, the widow of Jos's brother Robin.

Probably to keep emotion at bay Elspeth continued her schedule, going on to Dar-es-Salaam to see the Governor of Tanganyika, Sir William Battershill. She then left the splendours of Government House for a tent erected in the mud of the ill-fated groundnut scheme,* travelling in Galloping Dick, a guards' van (attached to a freight train) believed to have square wheels by the government officials forced to use it in the wet season when roads were impassable. She also had meetings with Tanganyikan African intellectuals, whom she found far less advanced than those of Kenya and Uganda. By now the rains were well established – Dodoma had to be excluded from her schedule because the roads were too wet.

Elspeth was getting fed up: 'There is too much talk and too little seeing about this trip; distances are so enormous.'[23] She regretted the lack of opportunity to snoop around alone, off the beaten track, and reminded herself of the danger that the book could read like a pepped-up series of official reports. Her last stop in Tanganyika was Tabora, where a welfare officer squired her round a rushed day which included a visit to the Williamson diamond mine.

On 29 April a car met her to take her to Uganda, the richest of the three East African countries. A terrifying schedule had been prepared for her by Ugandan officials. She spent two and a half weeks travelling by staff car right across the country in constant rain storms. The DCs along the route had been asked to book hotel accommodation for her or, where there were no hotels, to put her up. They were young, white, university-trained men who administered huge areas, being responsible for thousands of Africans – the one at the tsetse-ridden Mbale had 700,000 local people under his wing. Previous to their appointments their only administrative experience had been as prefects at their public schools.

Elspeth stayed in Government House in Kampala from 15 to 16 May. Her hurried itinerary in Uganda left her with the impression

---

* A post-war project intended by the British government to invigorate the economy of Tanganyika. It was a miserable failure.

that the country was 'a world at once bustling and languorous, easy-going and suspicious, credulous and scheming, peopled by men with dreams too vague to follow and too glorious to renounce'.[24] From Uganda Elspeth returned to Njoro, seeing her mother for the first time since her father's death. She completed her travels with a tour of Kenya which lasted until the end of the month.

Elspeth's long journey, punctuated by the sorrow of her father's death, left her with ambivalent feelings. She approved of African advancement and education. She also maintained that it was not necessary to be literate to have the right to vote. But she was afraid of the influence of the 'spivs', as she called them, young African political agitators who whipped up hatred against the whites. She was distressed at the erosion and bad husbandry of some African areas, such as the Kamba reserve, and feared white farms would deteriorate if transferred to African hands. She hated the social colour-bar and wanted it abolished. Like many moderate whites, she favoured gradualism and an ultimately multi-racial state, though she avoided postulating how Africans could be admitted to the electoral roll and what power they could wield. 'The coach's progress may seem painfully slow to those pulling it up the hill,' she said, 'but, in the perspective of history, seldom can a vehicle have rushed forward at such breakneck speed.'[25]

If her ideas are contrasted with those of Lord Francis Scott, one of the leaders of white opinion in Kenya, the gulf is wide indeed. Scott was of the opinion that 'However much in a minority of numbers we might be, our ideas will always be the dominant ones. This is what our British race has proved throughout the ages.' He thought the African 'bone idle, no doubt the result of centuries of living under a hot sun, he has little or no ambition, he has no idea of "the dignity of labour", he sees nothing wrong in stealing from his employer, and in fact he has not the elementary qualities of a good citizen'.[26]

Elspeth spent a fortnight with her mother before leaving for England. Nellie had painted Gikammeh with red oxide mixed with tractor sludge while Elspeth was away, a necessity forced upon her by lack of paint, but with pleasing results. Mains electricity and a new electric cooker had been installed. The African staff were nearly always semi-drunk on tembo (strong African beer), which was now readily available. Crime around Njoro was increasing, probably because so many squatters had been laid off. Pyrethrum, which had been a labour-intensive crop, was now being abandoned owing to over-production and the refusal of the Americans to buy any more.

Elspeth began to pack with a heavy heart. She admitted to Gervas that she hated leaving her mother, and her mother hated it too: 'I am worried about Mama being all by herself and I feel rather depressed. Write and invite her home this summer. I've told her she'll be very welcome, but she has taken to heart about Toby's having refused to have Aunt Blanche [Nellie's sister] any more at Eggington and I think feels you might think the same.'[27] Elspeth flew up the Nile to Cairo, where she caught a flying boat which landed at Poole in Dorset on 16 June 1947. She had been away from her husband and child for six months, and Gervas was there to meet her.

While she was away England had suffered a bitterly cold winter, the worst for decades, which lasted into April. Gervas had been forced to spend time off work by the onset of tonsillitis, though he had recovered enough to have Harold and Vera Raymond to stay at Woodfolds for Easter. Charles had had whooping cough. In Kenya Elspeth had feared her son would forget her, and longed to see him. She had issued instructions about her household from afar. She hoped Sid Cook, the gardener, had been made to clean up really thoroughly in the potting shed and dairy while the snow lay so long on the ground. She was annoyed when Gervas paid Mrs Mills while she was off sick: 'Of *course* you shouldn't pay Mrs Mills while she is away. It is never done. She is not on her annual paid leave. You shouldn't have paid her anything at all and I am sorry you have as it is not really right and she isn't entitled to it. I hope you are not doing so any longer?'[28] She reiterated the point in her next letter: 'I hope Mrs Mills has come to life and you have stopped paying her! It really *was* wrong.'[29]

There was no doubt that Gervas was being reprimanded. Elspeth was the dominant partner in the marriage, though at the same time she was emotionally dependent on her husband. She was fortunate to have married such a tolerant man, one who did not mope or retaliate in the face of censure or rebuke. When Elspeth got back she found Mrs Mills still not back at work, and Miss Clague (now called 'Cleggy' by one and all) behaving maddeningly. In fact Mrs Mills decided to leave. Cleggy would assume some of her duties.

Elspeth settled down at Woodfolds to prepare a paper for the Cambridge Summer School she often attended, and also a talk for the Royal African Society. Then there was a family holiday in Swanage, Dorset, before Gervas went to the United States on business in September. He came back in low spirits, and was depressed for the rest of the year. Elspeth answered questions on 'solving household problems' on the BBC's *Woman's Hour* on 15 October, a strange departure for her, and never repeated.

She was engaged in writing *The Sorcerer's Apprentice* throughout the latter half of 1947, and was disturbed to hear that the American journalist Negley Farson was in Kenya doing a similar book at the request of the Governor, Sir Philip Mitchell. Both Elspeth and Nellie felt this was disloyal on Mitchell's part, especially as he had asked Nellie to put Farson and his wife up for Christmas. She had them for several days, cunningly insisting that Farson read Elspeth's *Red Strangers* and *White Man's Country* while he was there, both to stop him working and to dishearten him by Elspeth's superiority. She reported delightedly to her daughter that the more he read Elspeth's books, the more depressed he got about his own: 'He has written a bit, but has nothing like your industry. He reads the damned thing aloud at breakfast and lunch. He's all right really, but a childish show-offer.'[30] In the New Year Nellie was implored by Mrs Farson to have them to stay again, because Negley, always prone to over-indulgence, had broken the spell of teetotalism he had maintained at Gikammeh over Christmas. He had drunk the Nairobi Club dry of whisky and was doing no work. Nellie demurred, and on the appearance of *The Sorcerer's Apprentice* later in 1948 was delighted that Elspeth had stolen his thunder by getting her book out first. The BBC asked Elspeth to introduce a Farson script on 28 June 1948, for the *Commonwealth and Empire* series, but Farson refused to allow this, and the idea had to be scrapped.

Nellie had thrown herself wholeheartedly into the cultivation of vegetables for Egerton College students, and had begun breeding poultry on quite a large scale. She also took in two families of paying guests when Egerton had insufficient accommodation, but of course she managed to fall out with both of them, though she preferred the Cockney couple to the county lady and her husband. She was heartened when old Njombo turned up and asked to spend the remainder of his days on her farm. Through Nellie's sharp intolerance thrust shafts of kindness, and she was glad to have her old retainer set up home on her land. She tried to sell Jos's clothes, but the only interest aroused by her advertisement was in his polo jodhpurs; she could not think what to do about getting rid of the remainder, though Fish Lindstrom took a suit.

While at Malindi when her father was dying, Elspeth had worked on *The Walled City*, a novel she had written in 1946, making corrections suggested by Cecil Day Lewis, the poet employed by Chatto & Windus as reader and poetry editor. Describing it as a remarkable novel, the firm had been enthusiastic about the book and offered an advance of £150, with a royalty of 12½ per cent for the first thousand copies. Day Lewis, however, thought it had a certain lack of selection or economy, 'five words . . . always being used when one would have done, particularly in the interior monologues scattered all over the book'.[31] He felt the pace would be improved if most of the soliloquies could be halved in length. Elspeth always acted upon suggestions from publishers and their readers. Seldom did she send a book to her publishers in its final form, always intending to cut and alter as they advised. She now reduced the length of the book considerably, and Day Lewis approved it.

It is interesting to compare *The Walled City* with Margery

Perham's earlier novel *Major Dane's Garden* (1925), which covers similar themes and indeed may have inspired Elspeth's book. *The Walled City* is set in northern Nigeria, which Elspeth had visited in 1945, in an old walled emirate such as still existed because of the British policy of indirect rule. The African scenes alternate with ones set in a cool, green England. The plot covers love and jealousy, rivalries in work and marriage, intrigues within the city's walls and witchcraft in the bush. Elspeth's exploration of character has unusual depth, as men and women face the task of ruling and responding to an empire. She makes many jabs at the Colonial Service, which the character Freddy Begg, with his self-seeking ambition and scheming mediocrity, exemplifies, although there is another type of colonial civil servant portrayed – Robert Gresham, who inspires trust and respect in Africans but is dogged by an integrity too stalwart for him to compromise and rise in rank. Again, Elspeth examines the effect of two cultures on each other, that of the black man who is torn from his centuries-old balance with nature, and of the white man who applies spiritual, moral and political ideals to people who have their own beliefs and codes of conduct. The Africans' reaction to the white man's attempts to change them has a profound effect on the white man himself. A selection of quotations from the book illustrates its wisdom:

> The idea of integrity in the western sense, as applied to affairs of taxes and money, did not enter the picture. Taxes were tribute, paid to the Emir by right of conquest . . . they certainly were not contributed by the citizens to a common fund. That the Emir's agents should dip their fingers into the honey-pot as it passed from hand to hand was considered not reprehensible but plain common sense. The object of authority was to enrich yourself and to enjoy privilege, not to part with a large share of your riches for the dubious benefit of sweepers and slaves.[32]
>
> In Africa many things may occur, or be made to occur, to reduce the impetus of the best-rolled hoop to a point where it wavers, loses direction and topples over in the dust.[33]
>
> Time meant so little in this continent that even the Euro-

pean-trained could not be relied on to remember the vast difference that distinguishes, in the European's mind, one identical sunrise from the next.[34]

Men are divided with greater potency by faith than by race and pigment.[35]

Free your women, we said: and those that had done so we rebuked for their prostitutes and beggars.[36]

He was hers still, and she might be ready to die for him if need be; but to live with him, that was another matter.[37]

A thousand years of history, of a balance struck between man and his nature and man and the desert, were caught by the twin forces of this western invasion: the secular force that undermined and uprooted from without, the Christian force that bored away from within.[38]

In every age and among every people the same tales appear to satisfy the same needs. Man fears death, so he invents life after death; he needs authority, so he bows to God; he is bound by the seasons, so he postulates resurrection; his impotence in the face of nature drives him to create a calendar of saints and spirits he can propitiate with prayer or sacrifice.[39]

A flower out of place in a field appeals more to the imagination than its sister nurtured and fussed over in a garden.[40]

How closely . . . children invest a piece of landscape with their dreams and memories, until it becomes a very part of their lives! The child and the landscape grow together, and afterwards he cannot look on it unmoved; though so much of the meaning has faded, he is looking back into the making of his own soul.[41]

Were we . . . too sure that our own values held for all peoples and places, that we could destroy selectively the evils of the primitive without also damaging its virtues?[42]

If love was a burden, then he travelled light. As water to the body, so love to the spirit; you could carry a little with you but must find it or perish as you went along, and the route, like the tracks of caravans, was lined with the skeletons of the unsuccessful. But love rose from many springs, and as the dourest and most blistering desert concealed oases where birds sheltered in the shade of trees, so it was to be met with in the harshest of places, and no journey need be without hope.[43]

Elspeth did little work for the BBC in 1948, though on 19 July she participated in *The Brains Trust*. She must have been a success because she was asked again for October, but had to refuse as she had planned a holiday with Harold and Vera Raymond in Florence and wanted to go 'while the Iron Curtain is still the other side of Italy'.[44] However, she did find time to join the panel of the current-affairs programme *Any Questions?* on 21 December.

Elspeth spent the year 1948 at home in Oaksey, unusually not paying a visit to Africa. She became more involved with her son's life, now that he was becoming more interesting as he left babyhood. His nanny was not an unalloyed success. Cleggy was like a thunderstorm about to break, and could be sullen and rude on occasion. When Gervas was away, as he was for two months in the Far East in January and February, Elspeth felt duty bound to sit with her in the evenings, though she found the experience a trial and welcomed the weekends her nanny went away. A glum Cleggy, continually interrupting with trite remarks, 'wasted' Elspeth's evenings, which she preferred to spend sitting by the fire, enjoying her supper and listening to the radio. Cleggy was in charge of Charles during the day, though the boy elected to spend much of his time outside 'helping' Sid Cook with the gardening. Elspeth felt 'Cookie' was over-indulgent with the boy and that it was time to send Charles to school, because he had too little contact with other children and 'though very sweet, is too self-centred and cannot bear not having his own way in everything'.[45] Dancing classes brought him limited contact with others, so Elspeth continued to invite other children round for tea.

She told her husband, away in the Far East, that Charles was getting more and more obstreperous, was seldom in the company of people under the age of forty, and the sooner he went to school the better. He was certainly physically big enough, being taller than average for his age. On his birthday Elspeth took him for a long walk, in the course of which he had a ride on a tractor, played football with Michael Woodhouse, son of the neighbouring farmer, collected sticks, and told most of the village that he was four. The next day Elspeth had a birthday party for ten local children, the food being prepared by Cleggy, who was an excellent cook. 'It is sad he is a little boy rather than a tot,' said his mother, adding that she was treating him like a boy now, who should be learning a few things.

At this time an incident occurred which soured the Huxleys' relations with their neighbours Marjorie and Geoffrey Lawrence, who lived across the fields about five hundred yards away. Geoffrey Lawrence, first Baron Oaksey, was a distinguished judge who had headed the Nuremberg war-crime trials. One day someone at Woodfolds picked up a gun and peppered with shot a dog harassing Elspeth's chickens. Apparently this was not the first time the dog, which belonged to the Lawrences' daughter, had perpetrated the crime. No one confessed to the misdemeanour, but the culprit was probably Elspeth. Well acquainted with guns from her childhood days in Kenya, she was ruthless in protecting her farming interests, and was more likely than Gervas to lose her temper and shoot. Thereafter there was no love lost between Marjorie Lawrence and Elspeth Huxley, although the Lawrences' son John would later help to heal the rift between the two families.

In January 1948 Elspeth urged Gervas to confine an eastern trip he had to make to a visit to Ceylon (now Sri Lanka), and not to go to the Indian mainland, where communal riots and massacres had followed independence and partition in 1947. In fact Gervas did go to India, despite his wife's strictures, and was there when Mahatma Gandhi was assassinated. '*Poor* old boy,' wrote Elspeth, 'it seemed a great tragedy. I suppose he will go down to history as a saint and I suppose he was in some ways, though whether you can really square a preaching of non-violence and brotherhood with continual inflammation of nationalist feelings in the masses I don't know.'[46] The fact that Britain had given India its independence was an indication of what might happen to the African colonies, a matter of concern to Elspeth.

Although their relationship had degenerated into breakfast bickering and sporadic outbursts from Elspeth at other times, Gervas and Elspeth were very fond of each other, and never abandoned their mutual respect. A more robust character than Elspeth's father, Gervas would not tolerate too much provocation from his wife. Friends and staff could not help but notice the squabbling, mainly over silly things. Elspeth's energy was responsible for much of her frustration – not only was she writing full-time, but she ran Woodfolds' poultry farming and had been appointed a magistrate, which required her to attend court about once a month. The cases she tried, at Malmesbury and elsewhere, concerned matters like petty theft, shoplifting and motoring offences. Once a youth appeared before her accused of 'causing unnecessary suffering to a cat' and having an air rifle in a public place. She also sat in judgement on a man accused of throwing a Ministry inspector into a dung heap. Elspeth remained a magistrate for thirty years.

Most days Elspeth spent in her study writing. She was always looking for new subjects, and she turned her mind in July 1948 to a proposal from a group of fauna-minded old-timers in Kenya who wanted a book compiled on the habits and migrations of game animals, 'most of which have been exterminated, and the old soaks who knew all about it thirty years ago are also fading from the scene. We ought to record this information before the old soaks drop off the perch.'[47] Chatto & Windus said they would like to consider the book, which they thought might sell two to three thousand copies. But when Elspeth thought more deeply about the matter, she worried about obtaining the material for such a book, relying as she would have to on the reminiscences of various rather bibulous old gents. She was nervous that there would be too much 'How I Shot my First Lion' and not enough 'How the Lion Attracts its Mate'. Donald Seth Smith, a neighbour and acquaintance of Nellie, was putting up the money, and Elspeth told him the publishers wanted something more scientific and austere than chatty. She went to book an air passage to Kenya for 3 January 1949, only to find on her return home a letter from Seth Smith, who had got cold feet and wanted to call the whole thing off. Harold Raymond then relented a little from his strictly-nature-book position, agreeing to allow personal reminiscences, providing they were relevant to the central theme. The project was, however, dropped.

By now Elspeth was publishing all her full-length books with Chatto & Windus, with whom she had an arrangement giving them first option on any such manuscript she produced. During the last quarter of 1948 Norah Smallwood, originally a secretary in the firm but a woman of many talents who had assumed much responsibility in the war years, took over Chatto's correspondence with Elspeth from Harold Raymond. Norah was a slim and elegant woman of medium height with a cloud of hair, penetrating blue eyes and a rosy complexion. She was inclined to wear loud shades of scarlet and black, broad-brimmed hats. Her husband, who was in the RAF, had been killed a few months after they were married, and she was now assuming a powerful position in Chatto & Windus. Elspeth liked and respected Norah, who in turn could not do too much for her feisty female author. Contrary to the fierce and domineering aspect she often presented to the world, Norah was kind and patient with Elspeth, became a firm personal friend, and steered her books through the process of creation. The Raymonds also remained close friends of the Huxleys and invited Elspeth to go to Florence with them in October, where for an idyllic fortnight Elspeth found a pre-war world, with a non-stop blend of culture and chianti. Harold Raymond was 'a perfect Pasha, conducting his two women every-where with just the right mixture of indulgence and authority'.[48]

The publication of *The Sorcerer's Apprentice* on 4 November 1948 led Elspeth and Norah to commiserate with each other about the iniquity of booksellers, whom they reckoned did not even *try* to sell books. This is a constant theme of Elspeth's letters throughout her life. Following a habit common among writers, she perpetually went into bookshops anywhere in the world to see if her books were on sale; if they were not she created a fuss both in the shop and at Chatto. The reception of *The Sorcerer's Apprentice* opened Elspeth's eyes to one of the dangers inherent in the writing of travel books – the people encountered in the course of the journey frequently failed to appreciate how they were subsequently portrayed in the book. No matter how remotely situated and unlikely to read the book they were, somehow news of what had been written about them always seemed to reach them.

One indignant letter arrived on Elspeth's desk in January 1949. On page 127 of *The Sorcerer's Apprentice* she had written: 'It is a curious commentary on human nature that Torr's, Nairobi's largest hotel, is Indian-owned, and most of the others belong to Indians or Jews.' The letter thundered that this was libellous to Torr's, all of whose shareholders were and had always been British-born Europeans. Torr's Hotel was still owned by Elspeth's old adversary Ewart Grogan, who in 1902–03 had helped scupper a British plan to make thousands of square miles in the Mau region of BEA a national home for the Jews. Chatto & Windus had to publish an apology to Grogan in all the East African newspapers and *The Times*, and Elspeth was obliged to omit the offending sentence in subsequent editions of *The Sorcerer's Apprentice*.

She was less prepared, however, to change her text in response to another complaint. In Tanganyika she had met Gladys Rydon, a crackpot member of the British Israelite movement who believed the millennium (in the sense of the apocalypse) would start in 1953. Mrs Rydon was clearly dismayed by Elspeth's reproduction of her view and by her dry comment that 'To British Israelites, all is pre-ordained. One can but admire the serenity which their faith induces.'[49] Believing she might be ostracised by the Israelites, Mrs Rydon maintained that she had been misquoted, and that Elspeth's remarks harmed the movement. Elspeth wanted to stand firm. She told Chatto that she wrote nothing down while talking to people, but made full notes in the evening and the early morning of the following day, while all was fresh in her mind. Ultimately, however, Mrs Rydon's millennial beliefs were removed from later editions of the book.

The Walled City was published in March 1948. It became a Book Society Choice, which absorbed 14,500 of the 25,000 copies issued. Anthony Powell, writing in the *Times Literary Supplement*, disliked the book, finding its chronology difficult to grasp. But elsewhere it was much appreciated, and it has become recognised as a classic work of British literature of Africa, on a par with Joyce Cary's *Mister Johnson* (1939). Oliver Prescott in *The Times* said: 'Mrs Huxley writes extremely well. She knows Africa intimately. She knows human nature. She knows how to give her characters solid life and individual force, and how to keep a story moving. Her book, without being emotionally powerful, is constantly interesting. Its appeal is to the mind; but is made in direct fictional terms without pretensions or needless obscurity.' Today it is still read as an extraordinary insight into the minds of the colonial administrator and the emergent African politician.

Elspeth perpetually experimented with new forms of writing, and now tried a satirical light novel, whose object was merely to entertain. She was inspired by stories told by her gardener, Cookie, about old times in Oaksey and the odd characters who had populated the village. Harold Raymond found the wittily insouciant book funny, vivacious and charming, but regretted that it wobbled between genteel comedy and fantastic caricature. Elspeth admitted this fault, blaming it on the plot, which she had simply slung together – 'I'm *lousy* at plots.' 'Humour,' she said, 'is a sort of quaking bog into which one can tumble at any moment and die a horrible death . . . [but] even a horny-handed attempt to be cheerful is called for by the circumstances of 1949.'[50] She thought her new novel was really two books rather than one, without much connection between the two. The first covered the heroine's life as a girl who befriends the daughter of the manor house, a creature enveloped in hunting and snobbery, while the second dealt with her return to the village after several years, having run away with her friend's beau, when she takes a job in a progressive school in the old manor house.

After some revision Harold Raymond liked the book sufficiently to accept it. When Elspeth gave it to Nellie to read, the older woman, picking up a trivial point and remembering her own background, made her daughter shave off the coachman's moustache, as no such employee would have been permitted to sport one. The book was published as *I Don't Mind if I Do* in 1950, and became a Book Society recommendation, rather than a more prestigious choice. One or two critics picked up on the book's weakness – that while the first part was witty, charming and delightful, the second was implausible and slapstick comedy. None the less, the book was an engaging outlet for Elspeth's well developed sense of humour. All her friends remarked on her quick wit in conversation and correspondence, and she had at last put it to commercial use. There are also shades of the real-life adolescent Elspeth in the book, for example:

> With Mrs Skinner I always felt ill at ease. Her competence in all she undertook emphasised my natural clumsiness, her resolute honesty made me feel, by comparison, an ineffective cheat. It is no more logical to compare oneself with another person than to match a primrose with a cedar, saying that both are plants; yet most adolescents do so; later on, they learn not wisdom but a greater measure of indifference, with which wisdom is so often confused.[51]

The sales of the book from September 1950 to February 1956 were a respectable 11,448. After Elspeth submitted it to Chatto she put her pen down for a while, because in summer 1949 Nellie came to England for the first time in twelve years to visit her daughter and the grandchild she had seen only in photographs.

SEVEN

Fame, not Fortune

Being an only child may have advantages in youth, not least the benefit of the undivided attention of one's parents, but it can become a trial in later years, when the cares of a remaining parent are particularly burdensome to the sole heir. Not that there was much to inherit from Nellie, so all Elspeth had was the cares. She would have preferred her mother to live in England near her, but Nellie adamantly adhered to her independence and penury in Kenya. Neither could she abide the English climate.

Why did Nellie's farming never become prosperous? She continued to experiment with animals and crops, as ever envisaging the best of times in a resurgent future. Tragically, the best of times were never in the present for Nellie. She failed to stick at her projects, to see them right through. This is a characteristic typical of the pioneer, who looks always to the future. Pioneers are not constitutionally inclined to consolidate. Nellie recognised this failing in herself – she was once moved to tell Elspeth that observing wealth depressed her, for 'what a hellish misfit one has always been'.[1] Eternally hopeful, Nellie the inveterate experimenter continued to send for new seeds, plants, information and products from countries as far afield as the United States and South Africa. None of her enthusiasms lasted long. The dawn of 1948 found her deciding to sell her geese and most of her ducks and rabbits, and to wind up her weaving school. Chickens were her new enthusiasm, and Elspeth was obliged to contact poultry breeders and arrange the despatch by air of fertilised Light Sussex eggs from England to Njoro. She also bought and sent two incubators, which arrived with both their thermometers broken. By June Nellie had 573 chickens, as well as the rather smelly white mice she was still breeding for the laboratories at Makerere College.

Elspeth obeyed her mother's time-consuming commands if not blithely, then at least with fortitude. The jobs she undertook for Nellie even included the interviewing of English applicants for the posts of sisters at Nakuru Hospital, on whose board Nellie served. This was only one of Nellie's many public duties – another reason she felt she could not abandon Kenya. As a member of the council of Makerere College, an institute of higher education for East Africans of all races, she regularly went to Uganda, noting while she was there the value of higher education for Africans. She also served on the Advisory Council for European Education, which met regularly in Nairobi. In the course of this work she had befriended the headmistress of the Kenya High School in Nairobi, Janette Stott, who named one of the school houses 'Huxley', after Elspeth. Nellie rather gleefully reported to her daughter that Huxley House did abysmally at one school sports day to which she was invited.

Nellie was, moreover, a leading light in Egerton Agricultural College (now Egerton University) at Njoro. In 1938 she had been instrumental in establishing this institution, as Egerton Farm School, only a few miles from Gikammeh. It grew out of her suggestion that money being raised for a memorial to Lord Delamere should be put towards a training centre for young European farmers in Kenya. With the assistance of her neighbour Sandy Wright she drew up a scheme to establish such an institution on land at Njoro presented free by Lord Egerton of Tatton, who had earlier settled in the district. It provided training in the principles and practices of agriculture, as well as courses on animal husbandry, dairying and forestry.

Nellie's public responsibilities meant that she was often beset by visitors. She always took a prominent part in the annual Nakuru Show, when her house was full of guests. The Randall Swifts, her polo partners before the First World War, came to stay – not an enjoyable time, for Randall, at seventy-seven, was muddly in the head. Dolly Miles was another frequent though not entirely welcome visitor, on account of her irritating non-stop chatter. Unfortunately Karanja, Nellie's cook, was now so often intoxicated that she had to do some of the work of caring for the needs of her visitors herself.

Much was changing in Nellie's life and views. She was developing a far more sympathetic attitude towards Africans and their aspirations, and she invited African visitors, including students from Makerere, to come and stay at Gikammeh. At first they slept separately, and not in the house with her, but in 1948 she took the step, radical for a white settler, of having an African, the artist Ntiro, to stay in the farmhouse. She also asked Elspeth to entertain the Kikuyu Chief Waruhiu's son David, who stayed at Woodfolds for three days. One of the few whites besides Nellie to welcome Africans into their own homes was Charles Granston Richards, the head of the East African Literature Bureau which Elspeth had played such an important part in setting up.

Nellie was a popular hostess, with her rapid brain, wit, intelligence and capacity to transmit energy and enjoyment. Negley Farson described her as

> a unique personality . . . that astonishing woman, the mother of Elspeth Huxley, the Hon. Mrs. Nellie Grant – one of the most sensible, lovable, industrious women I have ever encountered; with her eight dachshunds and unorthodachshunds, her two boxers, her tame hornbill, household of black servants who just would not work for anyone else, her poultry, and the Angora rabbits she raises for their fur; that delightful little home on the slope of Njoro, with the Goya over its fireplace . . . The Hon. Nellie Grant has been practically the patron saint of the Egerton Agricultural College. She probably knows as much about what *not* to do in Kenya as any man in it.[2]

The impression her visitors got of Nellie contrasted with her views of them, set out in her weekly letters to her daughter, which give the reader the impression that she despised most of the human race. Her comments are almost invariably scathing. If this is what she really felt (and cattiness and kindness are not necessarily anti-thetical), she hid it well from her friends and neighbours. Realising she had been at Njoro for twenty-five years, an anniversary which deserved a celebration, she invited all her neighbours to a party, for which one of them, Kate Petrie, made a magnificent cake sur-mounted by a figurine in icing of Nellie indulging in many of her activities – polo, almonds, cattle, white mice, pyrethrum, poultry and spinning.

Hoping to wear down her mother's resistance, Elspeth continued trying to persuade Nellie to relinquish her farm and retire to Eng-land. Elspeth herself seems to have abandoned by now all plans to have her own place in Kenya, and she was anxious that Nellie should at least give Britain a try. This irritated Nellie, who refused to visit England in 1948. When Elspeth tried to use her son as bait, Nellie couched her reply in petulant terms: 'Re Charles and his growing up, as he and I are not likely to meet anyhow for more than a few weeks in his lifetime, it is probably better that his Granny should remain an idea to him.'[3] Disinclined to abandon her assault, Elspeth got Charles, just beginning to master a pencil, to write to his grandmother. Nellie was impressed, comparing him with Els-peth, who had not written until she was six, when she penned her first poem, which ran:

> Swallow, swallow
> Little Swallow.[4]

In a further attempt to induce Nellie to move permanently to England, Gervas suggested she take a smallholding near Woodfolds and come over for a year's trial. Nellie was tempted, though she eventually demurred at the thought of the winter work involved. Believing she might be able to let Gikammeh, she proposed that she come to the Huxleys for a year from summer 1949, in part to relieve Cleggy, who was doing all the cooking now that Mrs Mills had gone, from her kitchen duties. Or she might be able to find a working partner and spend half the year in England and half in Kenya. Unfortunately chickens were labour intensive, and she would have to teach someone how to manage her incubators and egg delivery while she was away. She was selling fourteen cockerels a week by August 1948, and forty dozen eggs a fortnight. And of course she was still busy with her public activities.

Beginning to weaken under Elspeth's assault, Nellie advertised in British papers for a farm manager. Mr Sinclair, a Scottish ex-prisoner-of-war, replied, and Elspeth was detailed to interview him in England. He seemed suitable, and Elspeth despatched him to Kenya. At first Nellie liked Sinclair and his short, stout, pretty wife and disabled son, largely because they were dog-lovers. But it was only a few days before Nellie's personality asserted itself and she was reporting to Elspeth that Sinclair was gaga and unable to remember a thing, his wife was 1000 per cent Conservative, and the boy a workshy little rotter. None the less, the farm was left in their hands, and Nellie departed for England on 27 April 1949.

Nellie had had the foresight beforehand to send a parcel of a sheepskin waistcoat and mittens, made for her in Nakuru, to Woodfolds concealed in an old red dresssing-gown to bamboozle the customs. She had also booked a Bedford Utilivan, because she wanted to have her own transport in England. Elspeth, hurrying back from Stratford after seeing 'that penny dreadful, Macbeth',[5] met her mother at Victoria station on 28 April. It was a different England to which Nellie had come. One of the first things she noticed was the amazing health and well-nourished look of the children – many of whose diets had, paradoxically, improved dramatically as a result of rationing – compared with when she had last been in England thirteen years before, and the high standard of post-war 'utility clothing'.

Seeing her grandchild for the first time, Nellie thought Charles 'a very seductive child, there is no doubt about it; hugely tall but not weedy; genuinely affectionate nature, violent temper but it doesn't last long. *Horribly* spoilt by Father. He is so bright and advanced that it is difficult to remember he isn't six till February.'[6]

Elspeth was now forty-two, and may have abandoned hope of having another child. She joked to Norah Smallwood that a friend who was having trouble with female relatives in the forty-five-to-fifty age group who were going a bit batty was thinking of starting a small hotel where ladies of that age could retire for a year or so at ten guineas a week, to be called Menopause Manor. Perhaps she was making light of something painful in order to keep emotion at bay.

Nellie's arrival put an end for a while to Elspeth's writing. 'It tends to go off in the summer, like milk,' she told Norah Smallwood.[7] Since it was warm and sunny and Nellie had to be entertained, mother and daughter visited historical attractions like Longleat and Tewkesbury Abbey. At the end of July the whole family went to the seaside, and Elspeth then drove Nellie to Edinburgh for a week at the Festival, for an intensive dose of the culture she so missed in Kenya. Nellie wallowed in a surfeit of plays, ballets, operas and concerts, treats she had lacked for thirty years. Elspeth took care to visit four booksellers in Edinburgh to ensure that they were stocking *The Sorcerer's Apprentice*. Afterwards they motored northwards because Elspeth was curious about her paternal ancestors and wanted to meet some of them, while Nellie wished to tell Jos's relatives about his last months.

They went deerstalking at the old haunt of the Grants of Shewglie, Glen Urquhart near Inverness: 'I shall long remember the cloud-shadows stalking slowly across the crevassed hills, the deep-steel-blue loch, and the smell of bog myrtle, and the eagle up a lofty crag,' one of them wrote in a notebook of the journey.[8] Nellie also did some fishing, reporting to her friend Ingrid Lindstrom at Njoro, 'I got some salmon fishing but although huge things leapt about all around me, nothing thank goodness attached itself to my fly or hook, so I had all the fun and no responsibility.'[9]

The Scottish relatives proved to be odd characters, decrepit and peculiar. Elspeth wrote to Harold Raymond of one of them: 'the female member weighs eighteen stone, has brilliant carroty hair (at over 70), wears a jockey cap draped with chiffon, and plimsolls, lives in a huge caravan and conducts long conversations with spirits by a sort of planchette. She can also be very witty in a quite malicious way.'[10] This was Lady Sybil Grant, wife of Jos's cousin Sir Charles

Grant and daughter of the former Prime Minister the fifth Earl of Rosebery. Ever the author on the lookout for copy, Elspeth took notes throughout the trip.

Since they were in Scotland, they decided to visit some friends Nellie had met in Kenya – Captain John ('Jock') Hay and his wife Eve, who lived on the outskirts of Lerwick. They flew from Inverness to Shetland, where there were no trees, and the sheep, dogs and ponies were dwarf – perhaps, thought Nellie, in response to the gales that blew relentlessly most of the year. There was a smell of burning peat in the air and gulls everywhere. They met two people who insisted they had seen the Loch Ness monster, and impoverished lairds presiding over immensely gloomy slit-windowed houses on acres of peat permeated with the smell of herrings. An inveterate knitter herself, Nellie found the women on Shetland disgruntled at constantly having to knit the Fair Isle patterns in vogue at the time, with half a dozen needles on the go at once.

Another friend they went to see was Charlie Dawson, the widow of Jack Dawson, the DC at Kisii who had perished of typhoid fever shortly after Nellie and Cockie had been to stay with him in 1935. This required a flight back to Inverness from Lerwick and a drive across Scotland, turning off just before Oban into wild and rocky land. Charlie Dawson told them of her travels across Central Africa and the Sahara desert with the notorious Lady Idina, formerly Joss Erroll's wife. Then it was on to Oban, a miniature Naples, and a startling sunset over the islands and multi-coloured lights above the bay at night. They drove home through Campbell country and the outskirts of Glasgow, where Nellie remembered launching ships on the Clyde as a child. In the car they had a haunch of venison which made its presence smelt increasingly as they continued south and back to Oaksey, though they blamed the odour on manurial experiments and tanneries they passed along the way.

This journey to Scotland was pleasurable for both mother and daughter. Nellie was able to tell Jos's relatives about his life and death in Kenya, and Elspeth explored the Highlands, whence half her genes had come, and the places her father had lived and played in as a boy. Mother and daughter were also able to tighten the bonds between them, stretched loose by the war. They got along better when they were alone together, with no one to witness their snapping and bickering, their little emotional skirmishes and self-deceptions.

Elspeth enjoyed the time away from her desk, and it appears she had come under Nellie's influence. She wrote to Norah Smallwood ominously: 'It is heaven not actually having a book in hand – I wasn't cut out to write the things. We are going to start a small farm now, only twenty acres [on the land which came with the house when the Huxleys bought Woodfolds], just enough to mean a lot of extra work and not enough to make much if any money, but I am tired of looking at all this land and not being able to farm even a tiny bit of it.'[11] The effect of being with Nellie can be seen here, and it is unlikely that Elspeth was serious about the smallholding venture. But for the moment she threw herself into it wholeheartedly, which may have been in part a ruse to persuade her mother that farming in England was preferable to that in Kenya. Nellie certainly did a lot of the work, tending day-old chicks, washing eggs, and making use of her rented van to transport bales of hay and pigs to the boar.

Apart from helping with the new farming activities, Nellie felt she would have to domesticate herself if she were to consider settling in a post-war, ration-dominated and servantless England. She borrowed a flat in London from Judy Burrell, the daughter of her old friend and benefactor Trudie Denman, and enrolled in a brides' course run by the Good Housekeeping Institute in order to learn cookery, housework and laundry. Her chief companion in the cookery class was a jolly Jamaican lady with five children, so, said Nellie, 'her bridal status is no better than mine. We have long cracks about things like yams and sweet potatoes and feel we could teach the instructors a thing or two, which is good for morale. The cooking side, actually, is easy, but with washing woollens and scouring pans my touch is less sure.'[12]

After the course, Nellie intended to spend a fortnight with her sister Blanche at Lodge Park, near Machynlleth in Wales, but it was not a success. Blanche's notorious sulks surfaced soon after Nellie's arrival, and she spent only a day and a night there. Then her brother Hugh died on Christmas Eve, which spoilt Christmas and necessitated a journey to a damp Dorset for his funeral. If this was not depressing enough, the British winter was taking its toll of Nellie. She was reaching the conclusion that the weather was a deciding factor in her life, and that she would have to return to warmer climes to be happy. Moreover, she loved Kenya and its extraordinary beauty, and her farm and the Africans who helped her run it. She felt she would be letting them down if she sold her land – an attitude common to Kenya's white farmers, who never doubted that what they were doing was right and proper and of benefit to Africans. Nellie had been at Njoro from the beginning, trying to make something of the land, creating a rich and lovely garden, building a house for her family, struggling to help make the country prosperous. The words of Robert Bridges rang in her head: 'I too will something make/And joy in the making:/Although tomorrow it seem/Like the empty words of a dream/Remembered on waking.'[13]

When her year in England reached its end in spring 1950, Nellie returned to Gikammeh and Elspeth had to face the fact that she had failed to persuade her mother to live in Britain, where she would have been much easier to care for as old age took its inevitable and cruel toll.

From 1949 Elspeth became more involved in her work for the BBC. There was considerable need for sensible discussion on the airwaves of the new subject of self-government for Britain's colonies. African soldiers had returned to their homelands from overseas after the war, demanding equal rights and encouraged in their ambitions by the independence Britain granted India in 1947. They had fought alongside white soldiers, and seen places with no colonial yoke. Why should they not aspire to the same freedoms and participate in choosing who would govern them? West Africa, with its non-settler colonies, was in the van of the independence movement, with the Gold Coast (later Ghana) pushing hard for liberty.

There was plenty of opportunity, therefore, for Elspeth to talk on subjects close to her heart – on 7 February 1949, in the *Enterprise and Achievement* series she expounded on *What Next in the Colonies?* and three weeks later in the *London Forum* series her subject was *Colonial Policy – Is Britain Advancing Self-Government at the Right Speed?* On 9 June 1950 she took part in a discussion programme on *The Colour Bar*, and on 23 November in a *Taking Stock* broadcast, *Whither Africa?*, centring round the possibility of handing African colonies over to the Africans. She also joined a *Younger Generation* 'Question Time' on race relations for the Light Programme. Her contributions were characterised by a sort of wry detachment, as she introduced notes of warning against rushing headlong into dismantling British rule. She was conservative by temperament, and usually voted Conservative. In the general election of February 1950 she went to vote with her dog Spickit wearing rosettes of red, blue and yellow on her collar lest any of the three main candidates should feel unfavoured, 'but as the Labour candidate is called Mr Drain I'm afraid [Spickit's] vote is a foregone conclusion, and her motto is now Dig for Drain'.[14] But Elspeth did not belong to the far right, and in 1964 she voted Liberal.

She was well remembered in East Africa for her radio contributions, in wartime and after, to the *Calling East Africa* series, and the Kenya government asked her to do a BBC talk on trees for Arbor Day on 1 May 1949. She also pre-recorded a Christmas Day programme for *Calling East Africa*, in which she compared Christmases in East Africa with those in England.

Elspeth's BBC contributions and growing fame had caused her to be invited in 1947 to serve on the BBC Advisory Council, the first meeting of which she attended on 27 October that year. The purpose of this body was succinctly described to its members by the chairman, who acknowledged that executive responsibility lay elsewhere:

> If they were unwisely zealous they could be an embarrassment to those whom they purported to advise, while if they were excessively prudent they could become rather decorative than effective.[15]

At a meeting on 11 October 1949 Elspeth asked whether the BBC was satisfied that no more could be done to interest listeners in colonial topics, in view of the fact that over 50 per cent of those questioned in a recent opinion survey had been unable to name a single colony correctly. This plea fell on deaf ears. She was more successful with an intervention in 1953, when she asked whether the BBC was satisfied that it was attracting all the talent it needed, especially in the field of drama, and whether it was providing adequate facilities to persuade experienced writers to write for radio, and especially television. This stirred the BBC into developing better methods of dealing with scripts submitted. Another successful contribution, on 16 June 1954, was her criticism on the grounds of cost of the BBC's internal *Quarterly Magazine*, which was subsequently terminated. Her membership of the council ceased in 1959.

In May 1950 Elspeth returned from a five-day trip to Holland to see the tulips to find a letter asking her to take part in *The Critics*, a weekly programme which reviewed books, films, plays, radio broadcasts and art exhibitions. She was both appalled and tempted, replying to the BBC: 'My critical judgement lacks incisiveness, I fear, not to mention the omniscience born of long immersion in the waters of culture,' and claiming that her only recent reading was the *Farmer and Stockbreeder*.[16] None the less, the prospect of six weekly programmes at fifteen guineas each was attractive, and she agreed to take part. For the first programme, on 24 September, she was required to select a book for review out of several she was sent by the producer. She also had to attend a film and a play, listen to a radio programme and visit an art gallery (chosen by the other four members of the panel, each of whom had their own speciality). The book she chose was Angus Wilson's novel *Such Darling Dodos*, which she thought accomplished and brilliantly told:

> He pins down human specimens and delicately exposes their shams and shoddiness, their raw nerves and unattractive insides, with a civilised and sardonic humour and quite without pity or sympathy.[17]

The trouble was, she said, that Wilson picked third-rate specimens for his vivisections, so she did not find the book moving.

The BBC need not have feared that Elspeth would falter on *The Critics*. She was a superb critic, wise and crisply incisive, and throughout the 1950s was repeatedly asked to undertake six-week stints on the programme. Before each recording she would send the producer a script of what she intended to say about the selected book, and this formed the basis of what was actually recorded. One disadvantage of the work was that it required her to spend two days and a night in London to see the films, plays and exhibitions. Gervas was still staying in his brother's box-like flat in London during the week, but although she occasionally stayed with him there, it was not really big enough for Elspeth as well, and she preferred to spend the night in Norah Smallwood's flat or at the Oriental Club, of which Gervas was a member. Since from May 1951 the BBC gave each of its critics two tickets for every film and play, Norah frequently accompanied Elspeth to evening per-formances.

At the same time as undertaking more broadcasting, Elspeth expanded her journalism, which was far more lucrative than the writing of books. She was now writing regular articles for the weekly magazine *Time and Tide*, which brought in welcome funds, and was also contributing to the *Geographical Magazine*, edited by Gervas's brother Michael, the *National Review, Round Table, Foreign Affairs* and *African Affairs*. She gave a paper at the Cambridge summer conference she liked to attend, on the subject 'Must Africa Starve?', and reviewed several books, including C.S. Forester's *The Sky and the Forest*, Alan Paton's *Cry, the Beloved Country* and Negley Far-son's *Last Chance in Africa*, the book he had been writing when he stayed with Nellie, which had finally appeared in 1949.

In his book Farson takes a position further to the right than Elspeth in her similar *The Sorcerer's Apprentice*. He approved of aristocratic settlers who had come to Kenya to try to continue a life they knew was doomed in Britain. Whereas Elspeth thought the Happy Valley circle had done considerable harm to Kenya, Farson's view was that they had done a great deal of good, because they gave the colony its exhilarating sense of adventure, the only thing that had allowed it to weather many a crisis. This was, of course, nonsense. Elspeth was far more realistic and hard-headed, understanding that the real work had been done by the ordinary white farmers and their African workers. She also pointed out that settlers must change their opinions if they were to continue to be tolerated by Africans.

Elspeth found that combining journalism and broadcasting with caring for the small farm Nellie had encouraged her to develop was more work than she had imagined, particularly when she bought nine Jersey cows in August 1950. She had to employ a girl to look after them, and so Vera Norris from the village entered her life. All the outgoings forced Elspeth to review her financial situation: 'After the corn harvest I hope to get down to work to pay for cowsheds, water supplies, feeding stuffs, fertilisers.'[18] The cowsheds had to be improved, and Woodfolds was crowded with builders and electricians. Elspeth watched thousands of pounds disappearing at a horrifying rate. Despite having Vera to help, Elspeth still regarded herself as overworked on the farm, and in 1951 she took on a lad to do all the farm jobs she had been doing.

Charles and Cleggy were despatched to Studland Bay in Dorset for a summer holiday in 1950, while Gervas and Elspeth went to Jersey for a fortnight in September, not for a holiday but to look around its farms. Elspeth thought it would be an ideal place to settle, for food was twice the price as in England and drink half as much, so one would eat less (very necessary on her part, she thought) and drink more (an admirable state of affairs). Elspeth was not a heavy drinker, but she did like a gimlet. Gin was one of her favourite drinks. Later on her son Charles disliked her drinking because he thought it made her more aggressive, though others did not notice this. While the Huxleys were on Jersey their best cow died of milk fever, and Elspeth wrote to Harold Raymond that keeping cows was a nice quick way to get rid of £130 if he was looking for one outside publishing.

With the farm proving less profitable than she had hoped, Elspeth thought she would have to take on more writing work. She felt both oppressed and depressed, suffering from a realisation of the tyranny of time and the futility of future pretensions. The truth is that with a young child, a writing and broadcasting career, a large house, pigs, chickens and cows, she had overstretched herself. She should have concentrated on her writing, journalism and broadcasting and given up farming, though it is likely that she offset her farming losses against other income and thereby reduced her tax burden. She also had farming in her blood, and disliked seeing land lying idle.

In October 1949, only a fortnight after she had told Norah Smallwood that she was not cut out for writing, Elspeth wrote to Macmillan to ask if they would publish an abridged version of her two-volume *White Man's Country*. Much of the book had been devoted to a study of the early colonial history of Kenya, and Macmillan suggested that she remove this from the book, update it, and recast it as a modern history of Kenya. Elspeth was attracted by the idea, though she had 'not much enthusiasm for returning to one's vomit'. But the project would not require too much research, and would be less mental effort than a novel. 'I'll try to slip in female circumcision to give them a pursed lip or two,' she told Norah, recalling Macmillan's refusal to publish *Red Strangers*.[19] Eventually, though, the project was abandoned.

Chatto & Windus had tried to augment her earnings from *I Don't Mind if I Do* by offering it to Hollywood and to the Associated British Picture Corporation in London, but both turned it down as not really suitable for making into a film. Now Chatto tried to suggest ideas to Elspeth for other books. She rather wanted to do another biography, and Harold Raymond proposed Gladstone, but she was appalled at the prospect of reading all his speeches. Norah suggested Thomas Coke, the late-eighteenth-century first Earl of Leicester. This was more appealing, and Elspeth began reading round the subject. She wrote to the present Earl of Leicester at Holkham Hall in Norfolk to ask if there was any new material, but his reply, while full of encouragement, informed her there was none.

Moreover, she was reluctant to embark on the book unless she had a housekeeper who could maintain Woodfolds while she herself was doing research at Holkham Hall. Apparently cooling on the idea, Norah Smallwood told Elspeth that such a book would only sell about four thousand copies, and that it would perhaps be better for her to choose a universally known figure, such as Jan Christiaan Smuts or Cecil Rhodes. Smuts would not do, Elspeth replied, because he had handed all his papers over to Sarah Gertrude Millin, who was writing the official biography.

Norah thought Elspeth might earn a reasonable sum if she undertook a book about West Africa on the same lines as her East African *The Sorcerer's Apprentice*. Not convinced, Elspeth wondered about a biography of David Livingstone or the nineteenth-century colonial statesman Edward Gibbon Wakefield. Either would need research, for which she would have to spend time away from Woodfolds. Although it would increase the total of dependants to be paid from four (Cleggy, the gardener Cook, Vera and the cleaning lady Dolly Jennings) to five, Elspeth went as far as advertising for a housekeeper, but no one replied.

Exhausted and indecisive, and feeling uncertain about the world and her place in it, Elspeth decided to have a holiday to contemplate the future. In early April 1951 she and Gervas embarked for Madeira. Sea voyages could be agonising for Elspeth if the weather was rough, as she would be prostrated by seasickness, but Norah Smallwood sent her some Dramamine tablets, with the admonition, 'I send eight – four to take you there and four back. If the Customs spot you furtively inserting them in your mouth they will probably search you for snow and strip you to the buff.'[20] Elspeth thanked Norah lugubriously, pointing out that the name of the man who prescribed the pills was Dr Coffin (and she had just been reading a report on sterility in cattle by a Dr Barron). Elspeth ran various ideas through her mind during the holiday. She wondered whether she might write on Thomas Arnold, the historian and headmaster of Rugby, because 'there is a lot in the public school motif', but concluded 'I wish he was a more exciting man', then considered the traveller and writer Gertrude Bell instead.[21] Elspeth's indecision was typical of the professional writer. Those who earn their living by writing books have to weigh up the amount of research and work a subject requires with the possible financial return, and are more frequently than not guided in their choices of subject by publishers' suggestions.

The voyage out was calm and untroubled, and Elspeth had to spend only the first day prone in the cabin. Madeira, where they stayed in Funchal at the New Avenue Hotel, was indistinguishable from paradise, thought Elspeth. She loved the wonderful flowers and the beautifully terraced mountains. The hostess in the hotel, which served English food, was a fat, dreamy Englishwoman, while not a person among the guests was under seventy, which made the Huxleys feel very spry. Elspeth wanted Gervas to eat more. He was extremely thin, practically rattling as he went down to the swimming pool, but his tall, ectomorphic body shape did not take kindly to excess food. Elspeth, constitutionally unable to relax and do nothing, read the lengthy *Middlemarch* and five Ronald Firbank novels. She continued to brood over the Earl of Leicester book, but actually started writing a light novel during the holiday.

After the return voyage Elspeth was approached by the Colonial Office, then producing a series of 'New Colonial Books' under the editorship of Frank Debenham, late Professor of Geography at Cambridge. They wanted her to write a book on Kenya; she would be expected to cover political, economic and social aspects, and the history and geography of the region, in 100,000 words with copious illustrations. She was offered £400 and the fare (first class, by air or sea) to Kenya and a subsistence allowance while she was there of £1.5s. a night, while travel within the territory would alike be included. This sounded a most tempting proposition, and, as she was contractually obliged to do, Elspeth asked Chatto & Windus whether she might take up the offer.

Alarm bells immediately rang in William IV Street. Harold Raymond was most reluctant to lose his promising author, now earning useful sums for the firm. He reminded Elspeth that Chatto had often discussed with her the possibility of another book on Africa, and said they could put forward a more attractive proposal.

Moreover, up to 30 March 1950 she had earned a total of £1,218 from *The Sorcerer's Apprentice*, which was still selling, and up to the end of March 1951 10,346 copies of *I Don't Mind if I Do* had been sold. Raymond pointed out that the Colonial Office were offering rotten terms, and a book published by them (through His Majesty's Stationery Office) would not add to her prestige as a writer. Would the official commission, he asked her ominously, curtail her freedom of speech as a writer? Elspeth was not convinced by Raymond's arguments. She reminded him that the Colonial Office were volunteering to pay her fare and expenses, and asked to come and see him to talk the project over. Raymond then backtracked a little, offering to publish the Kenya book jointly with HMSO.

Although the book was never written, the episode strengthened Elspeth's position with Chatto & Windus. She decided to write for them the West African book she had been contemplating for several months – an account of a journey through the four British West African colonies of Gambia, Sierra Leone, Nigeria and Gold Coast (now Ghana), and of life and politics there, on the same lines as *The Sorcerer's Apprentice*. She could not persuade the firm to pay her air fare, but she got an otherwise generous offer – an advance of £750, with a 15 per cent royalty on the first four thousand copies sold, 17½ per cent on the next four thousand, and 20 per cent thereafter. She did not, however, sign a contract: it was her practice never to do so until she had written the book.

Although women had made major advances during the Second World War, when they had had to assume the jobs of men away fighting, most of them reverted to their former domestic roles when their menfolk came home. Elspeth was unusual for a woman of her time, though far from unique, in insisting on continuing to work, and in her willingness to travel alone to places she had never been before. After a frantic time trying to write a script for the BBC Chinese Service, lift fodder beet, sell pigs and support the tenant of a cottage in Oaksey which Nellie had bought as an investment, a young American Air Force wife whose child had fits and who never stopped telephoning, Elspeth departed from England in the third week of November 1951. Since her last trip to Africa, air transport had made rapid progress. It seemed to her extraordinary to leave London at 2.15 p.m. and be breakfasting in Kano at 8 a.m. the next day in hot sunshine with bougainvillaea in the garden and vultures perched on the roof. Gervas immediately felt her absence from the farm, for his duties increased alarmingly. He realised just how much her days had been interrupted by farming and household matters, and told Nellie he thought Speff (Gervas's and Nellie's pet name for Elspeth) could never do any more writing if she stayed at Woodfolds. He said he felt a brute for having urged her to go, but knew it was essential for her to make the break.

As Elspeth travelled in West Africa she interviewed scores of people, white and black, eliciting their views on the subject of the moment – the appropriateness and timing of the countries' self-government and ultimate independence from Britain. There were moments when she felt doubtful whether it was indeed an improvement that the risks of being in Africa had shifted from the perils of yellow fever to being talked to death about politics, which was slower but more painful. She absorbed the ethos of the lands she visited while noticing too the preciousness of the ephemeral. Part of the charm of her writing was her ability to see both the important and the trivial, and to comment on each alike in perfect prose. In *Four Guineas*, the book which resulted from this trip, she moves from a discussion on the wisdom of imposing a Greek-derived Western democracy on African cultures to a description of a fleeting vision:

The houses were so close they almost touched each other, with narrow alley-ways between, and shallow open drains. In one such alley-way I saw a flock of small, fluffy chickens – all blue. Astonished, I watched them scurry through a hole in the wall. They were gone, and I stood wondering – perhaps a touch of the sun? The driver reassured me. They had been dipped in indigo, he said, to discourage hawks. In the street, a man wearing pink trousers and a gown with broad black and white stripes flew past on a bicycle.[22]

Elspeth's father Jos as a
young man.

Nellie Grant and Elspeth,
1907.

ABOVE The grass hut near
Thika in which the Grants
lived while waiting for
Kitimuru to be completed,
1912.

LEFT Kitimuru, 1913.

BELOW Inside Kitimuru,
1913.

ABOVE Elspeth as a child at Kitimuru.

RIGHT Elspeth feeding her pet duiker, Twinkle.

ABOVE Kitimuru in 1999.

RIGHT Jos and Nellie at Kitimuru, 1920.

LEFT Left to right: Denys Finch Hatton, Jack Pixley, Lady Colvile and Tich Miles, 1920s.

CENTRE Chania Bridge, with the Blue Posts Hotel in the background, 1920s.

BOTTOM Nellie, Jos and Elspeth in the 1920s.

OPPOSITE
TOP The Norfolk Hotel, Nairobi, in the 1920s.

CENTRE AND BELOW Two views of Nairobi in the 1920s.

Elspeth in 1923, aged fifteen.

Elspeth (second from right) as a bridesmaid at the wedding of Roger Money and Charlotte Plowden, Makuyu, 18 June 1923.

Left to right: Joss Hay (later earl of Errol), Bobby Roberts, Jos Grant, Lady Idina Hay, Cockie Blixen, Princesse Philippe de Bourbon and Nellie Grant at Gilgil, 1924.

ABOVE Gachche, a helper at Murigo's camp, in sheep-stomach hat, 1937.

LEFT Left to right: Judith Denman, Trudie Denman, Nellie Grant, Jos Grant and Evelyn Waugh, 1931.

BELOW Jos in the 1930s.

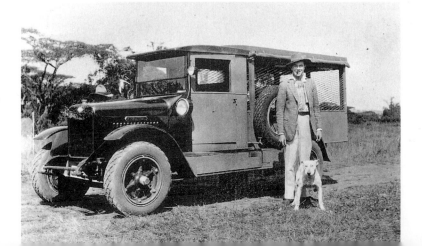

LEFT Elspeth in the 1930s.

BELOW Rose Cartwright, Nellie Grant and H.B. Sharpe ('Sharpie'), 1937.

Gervas Huxley, 1914.

Elspeth in 1935.

Elspeth and Gervas on honeymoon in Cornwall, December 1931.

Elspeth.
Photograph reproduced by courtesy of the National Portrait Gallery, London

LEFT Nellie in the 1930s.

BELOW Njombo in the 1930s.

BOTTOM Gikammeh.

ABOVE Woodfolds, the house in the Wiltshire village of Oaksey which Elspeth and Gervas bought in 1938.

LEFT Gervas and Elspeth with their son Charles at his christening, 1944.

BELOW Left to right: Harold Raymond, Cleggy, Vera Raymond, Charles and Gervas at Woodfolds, 1947.

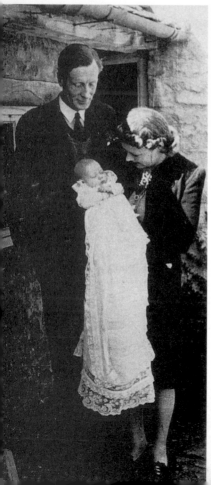

LEFT Karanja and Mbugwa in the 1940s.

BELOW Elspeth and her dachshund
Honey at Woodfolds, January 1960.
© *Topham*

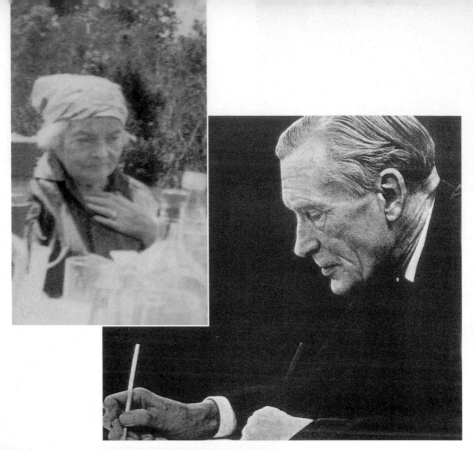

TOP Nellie in the 1960s.

ABOVE Gervas in 1967, aged
seventy-three.

LEFT Charles in the 1980s.

ABOVE Cockie Blixen in old age.

RIGHT Ingrid Lindstrom in old age.

BELOW Elspeth, Holly Aird (who played Elspeth as a child) and Hayley Mills (who played 'Tillie', i.e. Nellie) during the filming of *The Flame Trees of Thika*, 1981. © *Hulton Archive*

Elspeth, Esmond
Bradley Martin
and Peter Scott
at Slimbridge,
1980s.

ABOVE Elspeth on
her last safari in
Kenya.

RIGHT Elspeth and
Michael Blundell
with Kenya friends,
1980s.

As in East Africa, her days were packed with visits, often with a gubernatorial escort, since the Governors and their minions had been apprised of the coming of so well-known a commentator on African affairs, and she worried that she might be gaining too official a slant on things. It was a hectic journey, with only one period of rest, when King George VI died on 6 February 1952,* causing the postponement for five days of a trip up the Gambia river to visit a Conference of Chiefs. Elspeth wished she could have had twice as long in Nigeria, a country so vast that it needed months to see properly. She knew her impressions were bound to be superficial; on the other hand, there was so much that would have to be emasculated for fear of giving offence to well-meaning persons. Preferably, she thought, instead of one book there should be two – one unexpurgated, and one for official perusal. She regretted that she could not also roam around the French and Portuguese West African territories and Liberia.

Elspeth returned to England in the first week of March, having been away three and a half months, to be 'told on all sides that the White Man's Grave has added pounds of flesh and subtracted years of age and observe raised eyebrows when I speak of the toil and sweat and rugged endurance needed to survive the rigours of tropical travel'.[23] Charles had suffered measles while she was away, and was now 'about eight feet tall'. Nellie's cottage in Oaksey was 'clear of Tobacco Road Americans and occupied by a highly sanitary Flight-Lieutenant and houseproud wife'.[24] She found the village much as usual, everybody finding fault with everybody else.

Almost immediately she embarked on another six-week session of *The Critics* for the BBC, simultaneously getting down to writing her West African impressions. She was a fast worker, having no difficulty in finding the *mot juste*, and by the end of June had written 20,000 words. Having to review a bunch of travel books

---

* Princess Elizabeth was in Kenya at the time, and heard of her father's death when she was visiting Treetops to view big game by night. 'She went up a Princess and came down a Queen' was a boast of Treetops for many years thereafter.

on Africa for the *Financial Times* reminded her how dull such tomes could be. Hers, however, was not, despite her lament that there was too little love interest in West Africa. Sent an early draft, Norah Smallwood urged her to put in more about local people – a problem for Elspeth since she had been sent from one District Commissioner to another all along the way, and given little opportunity to steep herself in village life. Norah also wanted her to bare her soul a little more, which elicited the lament, 'As for soul-baring, I'm bad at it. Forward the soul! At the moment the soul is in abeyance. We have Gervas's sister and brother-in-law and their three children. Charles has sprained his ankle and has to be carried for miles over boulders.'[25] It was not that Elspeth suffered from emotional aridity, but exuberance of temperament alarmed her, and she tended to keep her true feelings in permanent quarantine.

That year the family went on holiday to Hartland Abbey in Bideford, Devon. It was the last holiday before the seven-year-old Charles, previously at a local Cirencester day-school, was sent away to board at Westbourne House, a preparatory school near Chichester, thus depriving him of constant parental contact at a tender age, as well as further increasing the financial pressure on the Huxleys. At the same time, Elspeth's tax inspector in Chippenham was pursuing her while she tried to have Cleggy's salary classified as tax-deductible, on the grounds that having a nanny was essential if she were to pursue her profession. Norah Smallwood found her a tax adviser, a Mr Baker, of Chatto's accountants Chalmers Wade, who privately handled many authors' accounts. Elspeth shifted all her tax burdens on to his shoulders and bought a Corgi motor-scooter to get around the village and its environs. It was cheaper than using the car.

Elspeth's attitude to money was frequently irritating to her family and friends. She was ever afraid, quite unnecessarily, of bankruptcy. Her poverty-stricken childhood, adolescence and university days had eaten into her soul, and her mother's perpetual money worries added to her burden as an only child. She wrote a light-hearted but only too true article for *Punch* in the early 1960s which accurately portrayed her concerns. The first money she ever earned, she said, came from opening gates on a common for which, if she was lucky, she would be thrown a penny. She still hated disgorging pennies. 'It hurts me to pass with brass, especially on a small scale.'[26] If the conductor was coming down the stairs of a bus while she was getting off, she would hurry past. She calculated that she had saved over £1,000 by giving up smoking for reasons of economy. This had paid for an 8mm cine camera, books, holidays, one or two watercolours and bits of porcelain, half a washing machine, and part of an all-electric labour-saving kitchen. She saved old envelopes, never travelled first class (not entirely true, as she was happy to do so if others were paying), put twenty-five-watt bulbs on landings, and saved odd nylons to match with others similarly bereft of their pair. She begrudged money for necessities such as writing paper, stamps, shoes and watch repairs. But she did not economise on food, cooked in olive oil or butter and never bought margarine, used strong, real coffee and had heaps of vegetables. She would rather spend a bit extra on food and less on clothes. On the other hand, although she did not enjoy waste and ostentation and disliked expensive meals at restaurants even when not herself paying, she would pare necessities to the bone to get a luxury. She bought pictures, particularly watercolours, not just to look at but as an investment.

Although when young she laboriously wrote down everything she spent, she had never kept detailed accounts since. In order to reduce her anxiety she left the payment of the insatiable bills for light, oil, coal, the telephone, rates and repairs to her husband. They paid cash for food and ordinary housekeeping, and each bought their own wine. Elspeth kept a cash box in a drawer into which Gervas put a weekly sum which was never nearly enough, so they often had to have a whip-round to pay the baker or for the Sunday papers. Costs were ultimately pooled – though not fairly, since Gervas paid the lion's share – by transfers between their separate bank accounts, the secrecy of which they jealously guarded. Gervas did not like Elspeth to know when he was overdrawn, and she kept her own payments private. She explained Gervas's attitude to money, far more robust than hers, as due to the fact that he had always had a salary, whereas her income was much more precarious – every sixpence had to be earned. 'Sometimes,' she said, 'I pretend to earn less than I do because I'm afraid one day it will stop. Sooner or later every writer does dry up.'[27] Consequently, she never borrowed money or bought things on credit. She could envisage being wealthy in an abstract way: 'If I was rich I'd like to be very rich indeed and spend the money partly on large and splendid farms – bulging-uddered cows, sleek pedigree bulls, brightly-painted modern machinery, rich clovery leys.'[28] It is significant that her dreams were farm-based. That longing to make the land produce had been imbued in her during her childhood days in Kenya.

While Elspeth continued with her time-consuming *Critics* assignments for the BBC, 1952 also saw her in demand to write articles for newspapers on the current upheaval in East Africa – the Mau Mau rebellion.* The rise of Mau Mau corresponded with the changeover of a ruling generation (itaki) among the Kikuyu. The Mau Mau belonged to the 'in-between' generation, unwilling to co-operate with the British as had their elders, and suffering from land hunger, frustration, boredom and resentment. The old disapproved of them, the very young were afraid of them. Their womenfolk, who had far less contact with whites, felt they had been left behind, and this also caused deep resentment. Altogether, whites upset Africans profoundly, with their sense of hurry and pushing on with things. Whites' behaviour could also offend the Kikuyu, who were deeply sensitive, with an almost pathological pride. For example, Elspeth recorded an incident when an African Christian minister, on his way to take a funeral at Fort Hall, was stopped by a young white policeman, to whom he gave his pass. The policeman tore it up, told the lorry carrying the minister to drive on, and said

---

* The meaning of the term 'Mau Mau' has been much debated. Some have said it was an anagram of the Kikuyu words 'Uma, Uma', meaning 'Out, out', used by lookouts outside huts where oaths were being taken at the approach of danger. The term was first used in 1948.

to him, 'Run down that road like hell. If you stop running, I'll shoot you.'[29]

Some of the Kikuyu of this new generation had finally decided to do something desperate to make their point of view heard. They wanted the vote and they wanted land, which meant that the white farmers would have to go. They were unprepared to play the waiting game of their chiefs and the four African members of the Legislative Council,* and determined on militant and direct action. Unrest had been simmering for a while, but the Governor, Sir Philip Mitchell, had chosen to ignore or disbelieve police reports. It seemed he was treating African discontent like a tortoise, which had to put its head out before it could be killed.

Now some Kikuyu formed themselves into gangs, armed themselves with whatever firearms they could obtain or steal, and took to the thick forests of the Aberdares and Mount Kenya. At night they came out to harass white farms. One of their favourite tricks was to hamstring cattle, which would be found in the morning bellowing in agony until the farmer could shoot them. It was a sound that, once heard, was never forgotten. Some farmers, too, were attacked and cut to pieces with pangas, the sharp, all-purpose, machete-like knives owned by all agricultural Africans. White men and women, terrified for their families and farms began to arm themselves at all times, and dire penalties were imposed for leaving arms about where they could be stolen. When in 1952 it finally dawned on Britain that matters were serious, a new Governor of Kenya, Sir Evelyn Baring, was appointed, and troops were sent from England.

The Mau Mau was confined to the Kikuyu people and their Embu and Meru cousins – the other Kenyan tribes did not join the rebellion. The rebels decided to involve all the 1.2 million Kikuyu people by making the whole tribe take an oath. Oaths and secret societies had always played a part in Kikuyu life. Whereas in other societies a legal contract might be drawn up, among the Kikuyu an

---

* The first African member, Eliud Mathu, was appointed to LegCo in 1944. In 1948 a new LegCo was introduced, for the first time with an unofficial majority and with four African members.

oath bound the taker solemnly to the promises he made, and magi-
cal retribution could be invoked should he fail to keep to the
agreement. The work of oathing the whole tribe, to present a united
front against the British, was organised on a regional basis and
carried out by divisional committees, each controlling teams of oath
administrators. So powerful were the threats from the gangs that
many Kikuyu farmworkers, lukewarm and unwillling to get
involved, were forced to take Mau Mau oaths to save their lives or
those of their families. The Mau Mau ceremonies went further than
previous oathing practices. Whites who heard the oathing details
considered them atavistic, obscene and bestial. Male and female
genitals figured in the procedures, as did menstrual blood. It may
be that some Kikuyu had reached a point where the only alternative
to their rage was insanity. There were seven levels of oath, each
more extreme than the last. The fourth oath, for example was this:

> To burn European crops, and to kill European-owned cattle.
> To steal firearms.
> If ordered to kill, to kill, no matter who is to be the victim,
> even one's father or brother.
> When killing, to cut off heads, extract the eyeballs and drink
> the liquid from them.
> Particularly to kill Europeans.

To counter the rebellion, the British began an extensive campaign to
round up Mau Mau suspects and put them through an interrogation
procedure to determine their guilt or innocence.

Elspeth was very worried. Nellie, alone on the farm, was surrounded by Kikuyu workers. Her only non-Kikuyu employees were
five Kamba – Muchoka, her former headman, promoted to poultry
supervisor, Manvi, skilled with engines, and three others. Behind
Gikammeh stretched the Mau forest, an ideal haven for Mau Mau
gangs. Elspeth had seen the rebellion coming for years. She believed
Jomo Kenyatta was the movement's mastermind, as did many of
Kenya's administrators and settlers, and Baring decided to have
him interned and tried. Kenyatta was found guilty and imprisoned
in Lodwar, a remote desert post in north-west Kenya, far from

Kikuyuland and other settlements. Elspeth offered to talk about Kenyatta on the BBC, but was rebuffed. The BBC producers, mindful of the delicate question of political balance, thought her not sufficiently impartial, and an internal memo was sent round advising programme-makers not to encourage her. Elspeth was put out, saying she had had in mind more a sort of background piece explaining how and why Mau Mau had erupted. She would have been ideal for this, and the BBC lost a good opportunity.

Letters from Nellie caused Elspeth acute anxiety. She wanted her mother to come to England, but Nellie could find no one to look after Gikammeh. In October 1952 Nellie wrote that white farms around Timau, beyond Nanyuki, had been raided by Mau Mau and 350 head of stock killed. Worse, shortly afterwards the faithful old Kikuyu chief Waruhiu was murdered by Kikuyu youths who regarded him as a British stooge, and the white Bindloss family at Kiambu was nearly wiped out. Utterly unable to contemplate bolting, Nellie employed two aged Tiriki nightwatchmen, but suspected they slept all night. Each evening she was visited at 7 p.m. by men from the nearby Plant Breeding Station and at 10 p.m. by John Adams, her tenant farmer, and an askari. She thanked the Lord for indoor plumbing and advised Ingrid Lindstrom, panic-stricken lest the Mau Mau disturb her in her evening bath, to take her bath in the morning, which neatly solved the problem. In November 1952 there occurred the horrid murder of a Kikuyu timber contractor in the forest behind Nellie, presumably because he had refused to take a Mau Mau oath. She supplemented her two nightwatchmen with two Dorobo armed with bows and arrows, but they were so frightened of her dogs that they spent their time up trees. None the less, they were a great help and enabled Nellie and the nightwatchmen to sleep better. In November the first Englishwoman believed to have been killed by Mau Mau was found to have been murdered by her husband. But in the same month a farmer named Meiklejohn at Thomson's Falls was murdered. Elspeth suggested she go out to stay with her mother, but Nellie thought she would be more of a liability than an asset.

Nellie suffered a great blow on 1 December 1952 when old Njombo died. He had not worked for years, but could always be seen about the farm. His son Mbugwa dashed into Nellie's room very early one Friday to say that Njombo was in great abdominal pain. She sent him hot water and bicarbonate of soda in the hope that it was only wind, but when this proved ineffective she took him down to the local doctor at Njoro. The doctor diagnosed a blockage and sent Njombo straight to Nakuru Hospital with Nellie and Mbugwa. It took Nellie an hour to impress on the staff that this was an urgent case, but finally she got him accepted into a ward. He was operated on that afternoon, and the next day he seemed to be doing quite satisfactorily. However, two days later he suffered a sudden collapse and died. He was a grand old man, said Nellie, and a terrible loss.

Perhaps distracted by the tragedy of Njombo's death, Nellie mislaid the little revolver she always kept with her in case of Mau Mau attack. Penalties for leaving arms about where they could be stolen were dire. Instead of taking the gun with her after her bath to her simple evening meal, during which she normally sat on it, Nellie left it either behind the radio or stuffed down the side of the sofa. Just before the 9 p.m. radio news, to which she always listened, the Tiriki nightwatchman popped his head round the door to say he was very ill. This struck her as odd, but she said she would get some aspirin for him in the morning. After the news she could not find her revolver anywhere. Finally she rang the police to report her loss, and a white policeman arrived to take the details. They hunted everywhere for the gun, but without success. Then Mbugwa and the underlad Waweru were allowed to stage their own hunt, while handcuffed, around the house. At midnight the policeman departed with Karanja the cook, Mbugwa, Waweru and the Tiriki nightwatchman for questioning, leaving an armed askari with Nellie.

The next morning the same party came back at 7 a.m. Nellie went to the sitting-room, to find Karanja handing the policeman the revolver, which he said he had found down the side of a small armchair. But Nellie had definitely looked there the night before. She surmised that Waweru must have caught sight of the revolver while she was eating and passed it to Karanja in the kitchen. Nellie was definitely in danger, but would not admit to herself that her old retainers would harm her. She reckoned that if she turned Karanja off the farm it would merely make a bandit of him.

The murders of whites continued, and Nellie asked Elspeth to send her a large bell. One wonders what sort of ineffectual assistance a plangent ringing would have summoned. Aircraft were circling round Gikammeh during the day, trying to locate a gang known to be sheltering in the forest behind. Nellie was issued with a sheet of instructions from the police, which suggested that she cover all her floors with loose boards, with nails sticking up through them. Staff were not to be told about these, or their surprise value would be lost. She was also advised: 'You must never be in an inferior position, and your revolver ALWAYS day and night should be so placed that it beats the panga by one second.'[30]

Apart from her concern about these distressing developments and her mother's safety, Elspeth suffered another blow when Gervas lost his job as head of the International Tea Board in London. The Board had members from India, Ceylon and Indonesia, and all was going well until in October 1952 India suddenly withdrew, quickly followed by Indonesia. Now consisting solely of Ceylon government officials and representatives of its tea plantations, the International Tea Board became in effect Ceylon's overseas tea promotion agency. In view of his lessened executive responsibility, Gervas became vice-chairman instead of organising director, with a considerably reduced salary, just as Charles was starting prep school.

The loss of Gervas's full salary appears to have spurred Elspeth to renewed energy. During October she wrote *Four Guineas*, her West African book, solidly at her desk, with Cleggy repelling all callers. Chatto & Windus corresponded with her about a reprint of her 1939 book *Red Strangers*, now requiring a subtitle owing to the Cold War imputation of the word 'red': now that the 'red menace' posed by a USSR possessing nuclear bombs was uppermost in people's minds, the title was in danger of being misunderstood. Elspeth tried to hurry along the date of republication to take advantage of the fact that the Mau Mau rebellion was in the fore-front of the news. Chatto also acquired the rights to *White Man's Country* from Macmillan, and Elspeth wrote a new preface for a forthcoming edition.

She continued writing *Four Guineas* until mid-May 1953, writing to Norah Smallwood, 'books are always buggers to get off one's chest as you know, and this one more than most, what with all the other things sitting on one's head'[31] – only to be told upon sub-mission that it was too long. She offered to cut out one country, making the book 'Three Guineas', but Harold Raymond wanted other alterations too: 'You don't sufficiently express your own point of view. You are apt to give an amusing crack at the parties con-cerned, but leave the reader asking: "That is all very well, but what do you think ought to be done?"'[32] Rather hurt, Elspeth told him she had deliberately not given her own point of view, because she had been in West Africa for less than four months, and did not feel it was her place to lay down the law. She had to be careful because an article, critical of some Nigerian politicians, which she had written for the *Sunday Times* had so displeased two newspapers in Lagos that they had called for the banning from Nigeria of all visiting foreign journalists.

Elspeth took a holiday by herself at the Royal George Hotel, Tintern, to be pampered with good food and service and lovely, well-kept countryside, then went to Avebury with Gervas's cousin Julian Huxley. Elspeth was extremely fond of Julian's unworldly brother Aldous, who lived in America, but found Julian, with his ebullience and perpetual conversation, a great strain. She nervously dreaded weekends spent with him, but continued to invite him and his wife to Woodfolds, possibly from a sense of duty.

Back home after the Avebury trip, she revised and cut the West African book. She was in a quandary about what to write in the foreword. She had received a great deal of official help on the trip, with West African governments arranging the tour and providing most of her transport (except air journeys) free. This ought to be acknowledged, while avoiding the implication that hers was an officially sponsored tour, which it was not. Some readers could well feel that it was impossible to see the real West Africa from Government House; Elspeth mused that a better vantage point might have been the doss-house and harem.

The book finished, she was ready to sign the contract, but she quibbled about Chatto's terms, pointing out that while she received only three shillings a copy for books sold at a guinea, the bookseller got seven shillings. This was her usual pattern of behaviour, but for the first time she sent her contract to the Society of Authors to be vetted. Chatto were not to be shifted from the offer they had made prior to her visit to West Africa, and Elspeth was in a weak position to argue, because she lacked an agent at this time, though she had an American representative, Willis Wing, a pleasant, calm man disabled by polio, who endeavoured to sell her books to US publishers.

Like *The Sorcerer's Apprentice*, *Four Guineas* was the type of book open to attack from those mentioned in the text. Chatto had *Four Guineas* read by a lawyer before it was set in print. He asked for only one remark to be omitted – Elspeth's description of the Gold Coast politician Kwame Nkrumah as an 'upstart'. Unsurprisingly it did not occur to him that another comment might be seized upon by its subject, Dr J.B. Danquah, a lawyer and politician in the Gold Coast, when the book was published in February 1954. In reference to a tea party she had attended at Danquah's house, Elspeth had written:

> Over tea and cakes in a well, but stiffly furnished upstairs parlour, decorated in old gold, the reputation of pots was heavily blackened by kettle. Tales of bribes, extortion, threats and thuggery were told which, whether true or exaggerated, do not make the sort of battlecry likely to gather popular support for such an old hand at the political game as Dr Danquah.[33]

Unfortunately Danquah took the first sentence as an insult to his wife's housekeeping. He maintained that she had served her visitor elegantly, with her best tea set. He himself had never seen a kettle cross the door of their electric kitchen upstairs, let alone seeing it along the corridor of what Elspeth had called the 'upstairs parlour'. He asked Elspeth to explain herself to his wife, who was only twenty-six. Danquah wrote to Chatto, the book's printer Richard Clay and booksellers in Ghana, threatening legal action about this and other comments Elspeth had made about him. At first Chatto refused to alter the passage on the grounds that Danquah had misunderstood a metaphor, but when copies of the book were sold to the Reprint Society the same year, the wording was altered (although Chatto's own reprint in 1957 did not contain the alterations). One of the comments about which Danquah complained was Elspeth's remark when he lost to Nkrumah in Gold Coast's 1952 general election: 'Danquah . . . has lived to see the fat chicken he was stalking fall to a hunter even cleverer than he.' A feisty Danquah told her that like Disraeli or Churchill he was made to wait, but the hour would strike not at noon but towards the evening of the struggle, and it would be a glorious 5 p.m. when a patient man was astir at last and at the zenith of his power. This confident prediction was not to prove accurate.

Four Guineas was reviewed reasonably well. Eric G. Hanrott wrote in the *Times Literary Supplement* (12 March 1954): 'Here is a book to be grateful for . . . Mrs Huxley is not an administrator, politician or expert, but she can see what is significant . . . She can paint a word-picture as well as anyone, and it is of the people that she writes with most relish . . . Rarer qualities . . . than intellectual capacity or the gift for language are Mrs Huxley's independence of mind and the honesty and humour of her writing, so free from the cant, conventions and *idées fixes* which characterise most commentators on Africa.' But there were as usual those who would brook no criticism of Africans, provoking Elspeth to retort, '[the reviews] are not bad, but unless one is prepared to gaze with shining eyes on the new Utopia which is arising in Africa, where all our human faults will be avoided and all our dreams come true, one is regarded as a dreadful old diehard quite out of tune and out of touch with the Modern African'.[34] It was her outspoken pragmatism which got Elspeth into trouble. She recognised that life for Africans would be far from rosy once their countries achieved self-government and independence, and the leaders' promises of riches for all were found to be spurious – and she was not afraid to say so. Aware that those who stick their heads above the parapet get shot at, she was none the less determined to speak what she firmly believed was the truth. If the white farmers, with capital and access to modern knowledge and techniques, had failed to farm profitably in places like Kenya, black farmers would be no different.

After her West African foray, Elspeth returned her attention to East Africa. As early as 1951 she had been approached by Ernest Vasey, Education and later Finance Minister in Kenya's Legislative Council, to write a history of East Africa, financed by the Kenyan government. Chatto & Windus reviewed the proposition, decided it was not likely to be profitable and requested a subsidy to publish it. But Vasey would not offer more than £2,000 in toto for a two-volume work, of which Elspeth not unreasonably wanted £1,750, and the matter was left in abeyance. Elspeth was in any case doubtful about the idea, considering a history of all East Africa too wide a brief, and one which would need more research than she was able to undertake. There the matter rested.

Nellie endured another dreadful year in a Kenya torn apart by civil war. The Mau Mau had now turned upon their own, killing their fellow tribespeople if they refused to join them. In March 1953 there occurred the Lari massacre in the Kikuyu reserve, when an entire village was put to flame by rebels and its inhabitants burnt or hacked to death. The much-loved head farm labourer of Nellie's friend Rose Cartwright lost his wife and entire family there, as did her carpenter. Deaths among Kikuyu loyal to the government far exceeded those of whites, but there were still plenty of the latter to keep the farmers on their toes. The murder of the Ruck family in the Rift Valley in January 1953 particularly caught the whites' attention, because it seemed so brutal and ungrateful. Mrs Ruck, a doctor, who had devoted herself to the care of African patients to the exclusion of whites, was cut to pieces with her husband and their seven-year-old son. What particularly offended white sensitivities was that the very man who had carried the little boy home from a recent riding accident had perpetrated the deed. Nellie was told by police to whitewash the word 'GRANT' in letters twelve feet high on her lawn, to assist aircraft patrolling on the search for Mau Mau.

A murder on her tenant John Adams's part of the farm forced Nellie to contemplate life without her Kikuyu workers and their families. If she asked all her Kikuyu employees to go, she would still have Muchoka, Manvi and the other three Kamba, and her two Tiriki nightwatchmen. She determined to move to beef farming, which required minimal labour. This caused an explosion from Elspeth, alarmed at yet another of her mother's experiments, and renewed pleas for her to come to England. No, said Nellie,

> the only real interest I could have in life is trying to get this lovely little farm into proper production . . . If I came back I would just turn up my toes and not be bothered. You see, besides the impossibility of having any real interest in U.K. ever again, there is also the inevitable feeling that any time you spare me is an encroachment on *your* real interests, so things being like that it does make normal 'family life' (at which none of us have ever really been very good) not very normal.[35]

Nellie could no longer make a profit from her vegetables, she added, and if the beef worked it would mean an English holiday every year. Relations were now cool between mother and daughter. When Elspeth suggested coming to Kenya in the autumn, Nellie told her she would be bored stiff on the farm and would disapprove of her farming methods. In reality, she felt Gikammeh was too threatened by Mau Mau in the forest behind it to be a safe place for her daughter. Near the Lindstroms' farm there was a gang of forty Mau Mau who had gouged out the eyes of a cow, and letters were now franked with the legend 'Guard your Gun'. To improve their relationship, Elspeth suggested that she and Nellie write a book together about the old days in Kenya. Nellie pleaded lack of time, though when she made an attempt to recall past times they reminded her of 'a terrible and sad tale of failures all round and in everything'.[36]

Nellie decided against getting rid of her Kikuyu, who had served her so well and whom she saw as friends, and in August 1953 she started a summer school on her farm for African women. Forty-eight signed up, and she took them all to Nakuru to watch a film of Elizabeth II's coronation – hardly the act of a renegade, but the gesture provoked several white settlers, already suspicious of her pro-African views, to suspect her further of being a 'Black European'.

At the end of September Nellie conceded that Elspeth could come and stay on the farm for a couple of months, though she counselled her against bringing an automatic revolver, which was too danger-ous. There had been forty-two victims of shooting accidents in Nakuru Hospital, most of them serious. Elspeth flew to in Kenya in mid-October. For the first time she felt comfortable in the air, because the new BOAC Constellations flew at 20,000 feet, above turbulence. She and Nellie stayed for a few days with friends in Nairobi while Nellie arranged a flower stall at the annual Royal Show. It must have been a thankless task, for everything was very dried up, and locusts were massing for attack. But the show was enlivened by a performance from the band of the Black Watch, the regiment having recently been brought to Kenya to counter the Mau Mau.

All the while Elspeth observed and made notes, having decided to combine watching over her mother with gathering information for a novel about the whites and Mau Mau. She was also still writing regularly for *Time and Tide*, reviewing books, mainly connected with Africa, and producing articles on subjects such as Mau Mau and its roots, Nairobi and Nigeria. In Nairobi she found the African areas of Kariokor and Pumwani wired like cages, and there was an African boycott of buses as the Mau Mau had threatened to kill anyone seen on a European-owned public vehicle. She perceived the absurdity of a notice in a Nairobi shop window advertising the Limuru Hunt Ball while past her walked a fat old white woman in inelegant khaki trousers, bush shirt and broad-brimmed hat, with a huge revolver in a holster strapped to her ample hips. Another woman sported a revolver in a fancy cheetah-skin case. Elspeth had no firearm; her only weapon, if such it could be called, was a whistle which she absent-mindedly left about everywhere. A few days later she was lent 'a horrid little automatic' by the District Commissioner in Nakuru.

She spent a few days in Nairobi talking to people about the current situation. One of those she saw was the unpleasant Ewart Grogan, that radically anti-African thorn in the government's side who had managed to get himself re-elected to the Legislative Council. In his own eyes a hero, he told her, with a streak of sadism, 'You can't kill a psyche with bullets,' advocated that convicted men be publicly hanged, and thought the government should declare all the Kikuyu reserve as Crown Land. Elspeth also had lunch with Michael Blundell, another Legislative Council member and a magnificent gardener, who propounded liberal and conciliatory policies to allow Africans greater power. He was deeply unpopular with the more diehard whites, and the government had insisted on him having a policeman as a bodyguard, but the man twice turned up completely drunk and once came not at all, so Blundell got rid of him. Although Elspeth was later to develop affection for Blundell and they were to correspond regularly towards the end of their lives, at this time she did not like him, thinking him arrogant and eaten up with conceit. He larded his conversation with remarks such as, 'I have a great flair for politics, I know how to put things over;' 'I've got a very quick, clear mind;' and 'I carried England with me.' He had a theory that the colour bar, which he wanted progressively abolished, had come about through the introduction of lavatories. He stressed racial co-operation, and wanted equal pay for equal work. Elspeth, while believing his ideas absolutely right, yet thought he had insufficient confidence in his ability to put them across, and lacked the personality and force to impose his will upon his followers. She was to be proved wrong.

She also saw Edward Windley, the Chief Native Commissioner, who told her that some of the African members of the Home Guard, a body of men now thousands in number, recruited to serve on the government's side, were fifth columnists and in reality Mau Mau members who hoped to acquire rifles. The existence of loyal Kikuyu members of the Home Guard would leave a legacy of feuds and hatreds for many years after the end of what was now, in effect, a civil war. Windley implicated the Indians in encouraging the Mau Mau.

After hearing these views, Elspeth thought far more should be done by whites to wage psychological warfare against the Mau Mau. But when a Director of Information had been appointed he was a brigadier with no knowledge of public relations or of Kenya. There were repeated big raids in search of Mau Mau in the towns and on farms, and thousands of Kikuyu were being arrested and taken away from their work and their homes for interrogation on the word of informers, thus allowing every private score and grudge to be paid back. Many Kikuyu who were suspected for some reason or other were being put into labour camps: in Manyani camp, in the Tsavo bushland between Nairobi and Mombasa, there were 76,000 inmates. On one occasion when the police official Colin Imray took Sir Evelyn Baring and the Colonial Secretary Alan Lennox-Boyd around the camp, the hate emanating from the cages full of Africans was palpable. So apprehensive was Imray that the VIPs would be attacked that he insisted they be followed by a policeman with a Sten gun.

At Njoro, Elspeth felt a pang when she heard again the insistent, fluting call of the nightjar and saw that the site Nellie had given her and Gervas when they were married had been sold and built upon by strangers. She rode a horse for the first time in years. The consciousness of the self-exile she had chosen, uprooting herself from the country of her childhood, was hard to bear. Wreathed in smiles, Karanja and Mbugwa greeted her warmly; indeed, there were no sullen faces anywhere, which made it hard for her to believe the reality of Mau Mau. But there had been trouble while her mother was away in Nairobi – Mbugwa was in disgrace because in Nellie's absence he had brewed illicit tembo, got tight and participated in a general fracas, in which he bit someone's ear. Another man was hit on the head so hard that he was in Nakuru Hospital, and the police had been summoned by one of the non-Kikuyu. A Kenya Police Reserve man called at nightfall, as he did every night, and Nellie's tenant John Adams made his usual evening visit, wearing a heavy uniform coat and a revolver while he incongruously discussed the market for cut flowers, from which he derived his livelihood.

Edward Windley, the Chief Native Commissioner Elspeth had talked to in Nairobi, arranged for her and Nellie to visit the Kikuyu reserve. They stayed with the Fort Hall DC Penney before being put up at the Church Missionary Society mission at Weithaga, where Elspeth experienced a touching atmosphere among the Christian Kikuyu, all of whom refused to take the Mau Mau oath, thereby putting themselves and their families in great danger. Indeed, many had been murdered. Then they moved on to stay with the Provincial Commissioner at Nyeri, in the middle of Kikuyuland and crawling with soldiers, before being taken into the Kikuyu reserve. It was dotted with strongpoints, each manned by two young members of the Kenya Regiment and the Kikuyu Home Guard, a queer-looking assortment of warriors, none in uniform, some with shotguns, others with swords and bows and arrows. Distinguishable from their enemy only by pink strips tied round their heads before battle commenced, some of them were fighting a gang nearby. Elspeth's car was turned back to a guard post from where she watched the action. She wrote to Gervas:

> It's all exactly like a buffalo hunt, or even a grouse drive, with beaters advancing in line and whacking the bushes. The captive [recently taken] was a lad of 17 or 18 in tattered clothing with long, matted hair and a very grim and depraved look and it does exist, a look of complete thuggishness. He had cartridges on him, a capital offence, so he'll hang. It's an extraordinary sort of war – incredible quantities of troops with all their tabbed Generals and armoured cars, lorries and jeeps, huge camps, engineers, aircraft, modern guns and heaven knows what, ranged against a few groups of thugs armed either with home-made swords or home-made rifles made out of a piece of lead piping and fired with a door bolt or a nail and elastic. It all makes a fool of us really and is almost pathetic.[37]

As in most guerrilla wars, the guerrillas, who had fanaticism on their side and a burning sense of grievance, were easily able to escape into difficult terrain – in this case the thick forests of Mount Kenya and the Aberdare mountains – to evade their enemy.

The battle in the reserve over, Elspeth went on to the district headquarters, where she met an attractive, enthusiastic young Colonial Service cadet, John Nottingham. Later he was to write a book on the origins and growth of the Mau Mau, but now he was busy laying ambushes every night to catch gangsters leaving the forest or women entering them with food for Mau Mau gangs. Elspeth went on through veld and whistling thorn to Nanyuki, with Harvard aircraft droning overhead on their way to bomb the forests, and visited farms in the heart of Mau Mau country. Every farmer told the same story: there was excessive stock thieving to feed the Mau Mau. One farmer had had 390 sheep taken; another locked his labour into the wheat store at night to prevent them being harassed by Mau Mau gangs into taking part in oathing ceremonies; another told the story of Mrs Meiklejohn, the farmer's wife slashed by Mau Mau and left for dead. With one hand almost severed she crawled to the car and drove eight miles in the rain in bottom gear to the police station to get help for her husband, who died from his injuries.

At Ol Kalou, with its broad, cultivated farmlands stretching north to Lake Olbolossat, Elspeth heard of the Fergusson and Bingley murders from Kit Hendrey, who found the bodies of his neighbours chopped into bits. He had to gather up the pieces and roll them in a carpet, because all the sheets and blankets had been stolen. In retaliation some whites, including many Afrikaners, wanted to go and kill the first hundred Kikuyu they could find. Hendrey dissuaded them, but the Governor agreed that they could seize all the African sheep in the Wanjohi valley (Happy Valley). Five thousand sheep were taken, and it was after this that the Ruck murders, including that of the little boy, were perpetrated. After the killings all the women and children in the area came to stay in the Hendreys' house, Mrs Hendrey having to feed thirty-five people. Twelve of them stayed for several weeks. Hendrey, who was in charge of screening Africans in the region to discover whether they were members of the Mau Mau, thought that almost all Kikuyu had taken Mau Mau oaths. Elspeth spent a day watching the screening teams at work. Then she visited the Friesian king, Bruce Mackenzie, who later became a minister in the African government of Kenya, on his thousand-acre stock farm at Solai. She went on to see Louis Leakey, who gave one of the main reasons for the outbreak of Mau Mau as lack of security among squatters and town Africans. He thought industrialisation was vital, as was the establishment of villages (an idea alien to the Kikuyu) where people could buy their own homes.

Elspeth was invited to stay at Government House twice on this trip. She found the new Governor Sir Evelyn Baring a weak man not up to dealing with the Mau Mau, exuding a confidence born of ignorance. His relations with the military leader, Major-General Sir George Erskine, were unclear – Erskine insisted on running his own public relations without consulting anybody else. Lady Mary Baring, the Governor's wife, seemed the more lively of the pair. A cocktail party was given in Elspeth's honour at the New Stanley Hotel in Nairobi by the African Affairs Committee of the Electors' Union and the elected members of the Legislative Council. It was an inter-racial affair, and for the first time she witnessed Africans and whites mixing freely in a social setting in a hotel. Michael Blundell's views were beginning to prevail, and for the first time there seemed to be a genuine desire and heartening efforts by some whites to work out a common future with the Africans, and diehards were being sat upon.

There was also an inter-racial cold lunch given by Nell Cole, Galbraith Cole's widow and a staunch member of the Moral Rearmament movement, who had built a church at Naivasha at which four hundred Africans worshipped every Sunday. On the day Elspeth visited it the preacher was David Waruhiu, the son of the Kikuyu chief murdered by the Mau Mau, who had stayed with her and Gervas at Woodfolds. He was a padre at the huge Athi River Mau Mau detainee camp, run on Moral Rearmament lines. The MRA was influential in Kenya, Nell Cole and Tuppence Hill-

Williams being among its original members, and had created the Torchbearers, an inter-racial society. At the Athi River camp, where Tuppence was in charge of five hundred women, Elspeth found the MRA workers very sincere and devoted, although she doubted whether they could really change black hearts. The inmates were rather fat, because they were fed on Geneva Convention rations four times as heavy as the normal Kikuyu diet. At intervals they were given pep talks and called to God.

On this trip Elspeth also had an opportunity to visit the East African Literature Bureau, which her 1945 report had been instrumental in establishing, and its director Charles Granston Richards, in whose house she stayed in Nairobi. Richards lamented the subversiveness of some African newspapers, and was trying to counter it by popularising his own Swahili magazine by introducing pin-up girls to its pages. Then there was a visit to the Tugen reserve, outside the area of Mau Mau operations, with Abrams, the District Officer at Eldama Ravine. They drove to Kabarnet, with its bare, dry land ruined by over-grazing, up the hill to Tugen. 'It's a region,' wrote Elspeth, 'that looks as if the gods had fallen into a fury and torn up all the earth and hills and scattered them about. All cleft and steep and bumpy, its outlines are jagged and harsh. Every bush has to cling on for dear life. Below lie the Baringo plains, bush-bespattered and hot as hell.'[38] The road ran along a knife-edge at the top of a ridge, one of the scenic wonders of the world. On one side was the huge Kerio valley across which could be seen the steep Elgeyo escarpment, with the little village of Tambach perched perilously halfway down. Abrams was the first born-and-bred white Kenyan boy to join the administration, and Elspeth wished there were more like him. He genuinely liked Africans and had no hint of patronage about him, only friendliness. Like most white children bred in Kenya he was slower, quieter, calmer than his English counterparts, closer to the tempo of Africa. If people such as him were allowed a voice, thought Elspeth, the future with Africans would be settled amicably.

Before she left Kenya Elspeth listened to as many points of view as she could in Nairobi. She thought the African members of the

Legislative Council a poor lot, and went on to see the African trades union leaders at Kaburi House, their headquarters in Nairobi. She had an appointment with Dr Pant, the Indian High Commissioner, said to be highly sinister, a follower of Indian Prime Minister Nehru who was regarded as encouraging Mau Mau by making highly inflammatory statements about Kenya. A pleasant interlude was lunch at the Kenya High School with its headmistress Janette Stott, and a tour of Huxley House (named for her), with much autograph-hunting by its occupants.

Nellie thoroughly enjoyed Elspeth's visit, and was able to see far more of the country while accompanying her than she had done recently. Since returning to her farm after her year in England she had been less sociable than before, indeed describing herself as a recluse. This was far from the truth, but she had perked up in Elspeth's company and was depressed at the thought of her returning to England for Christmas. Elspeth wistfully wrote to Gervas that if she could get some money by writing another book, it would give her mother a tremendous boost if the family flew out to stay with her for the Christmas holidays, and it would be a thrill for Charles, not a delicate child and therefore well able to stand the climate. She very much wanted Charles to see Kenya now he was old enough to take things in. Nellie told Elspeth that it was most unlikely she would ever occupy the cottage she had bought in Oaksey, and that Elspeth should take it into her farm, perhaps with a farmworker as its tenant.

Elspeth flew back to England on 20 December 1953, bearing a Dorobo bow and arrow for Charles, a present from Ingrid Lindstrom. She was just in time for the New Year's Honours list of 1954, in which Gervas was appointed a CMG (Companion of the Order of St Michael and St George), an event which made a friend observe that they had hung something on him at last, a reference to Gervas's normally modest manner.

Elspeth's visit to Kenya had a profound effect on her. It brought home the seriousness of the Africans' desire for power, the strength of their feeling in prosecuting the war against the British, and the variety of opinion among whites. Although Elspeth tended towards the view that a black and white partnership to take the country into the future was possible, she was beginning to have doubts. For the moment, however, she still hoped for a loosening of racial tensions, a pragmatic and tolerant response from whites to African advancement, and a future in which both races went forward together. She tended to ignore the position of the Indians. On a personal level, she was deeply worried about her mother, alone on the farm during a savage war. She had again tried and failed to persuade her to live in England. Nellie was adamant – her future was in Kenya, on her farm, with her African retainers, of whom she was very fond. It was a dilemma which was not to have a solution for another twelve years.

EIGHT

Mid-Life and Mid-Career

While Elspeth was away in Kenya in October and November 1953, Gervas was at home at Woodfolds. Having taken on a less burdensome role in the world of tea, he was in London far less than in the past, when he had come home only for weekends. He now indulged his hobby of collecting eighteenth-century porcelain and spent many hours gardening, planting over five hundred varieties of roses. He also embarked on an ambitious project: he bought Coole's, a 120-acre dairy farm near Minety, the next parish three miles from Woodfolds, and installed there a working manager and a herd of high-yielding Friesian cows.

It is tempting to think that this was a ploy to evade Elspeth's constant pestering about his duties on the small farm attached to Woodfolds. Certainly her letters to him from Africa while she was visiting her mother or doing research are crammed with hectoring instructions about what he should be overseeing on her land. She even reminded him about what he should be doing on his: 'I hope you've got the rest of your corn drilled, as it doesn't do to miss the bus at this time of year.'[1] She told him to get her cowhand Vera more cow cake, to order next year's chicks, to earmark new calves, to give Vera her calf bonus, to plough up the far end of the old pasture in front of the house for kale (an instruction accompanied by a map), to spread the dung, to move the roots and mangolds, to get the winter wood sawn, to see to the Woodfolds drains because if the sewage was forced back up the pipes it was a big job to clear them, to withhold the road payment if water was lying in the field near the cottage septic tank because that meant the drain under the road was blocked, to dispose of forty-three cockerels – the list was endless. In reality, however, Gervas's farm was an attempt to make some more money now that his income had decreased. Sadly, it never made a profit, although the rise in the price of land enabled him to cover his original purchase price and all his losses when he sold his farm ten years later.

Elspeth had thrown herself into working Woodfolds as a farm with characteristic diligence. Unable to envisage defeat, she constantly strove, like her mother in Africa, to make a profit from her smallholding. The Woodhouses, professional farmers in the much larger farm next door, hardly viewed her as a farmer at all (some cream cheese Elspeth gave Mrs Woodhouse had a maggot in it), though Elspeth herself took her farming as seriously as her writing. Her background, university training and experience of rationing during the Second World War made her reluctant to leave land idle. To her a well tilled vegetable patch was more beauteous than a flower garden, a field of kale more lovely than a meadow.

Elspeth's perennial problem was getting sufficient help on her farm. She reflected on the contrast between Britain and Kenya: 'I must say it must be nice to farm in a country where there are always plenty of people to do the work! Everything can be so much better done – hay made on tripods, good fencing everywhere etc. There is not that feeling of always being behind with things.'² As it was, she only had one casual worker, Ronald, and Vera Norris for her cows and occasional ploughing. The two women rubbed along together fairly well. Elspeth complained that Vera was willing but moody (she was hard put to decide whether Vera's or Cleggy's moods were the worse, but thought Vera's were often excusable because of the miserable time she had with her mother at home), while Vera found her employer needed a firm hand: 'I always stood up to her, she respected me for it. She was the boss; Gervas was meek and mild. He was lovely. She got irritated with him. He wouldn't put his foot down with her, so she didn't respect him. She loved him in a way. She'd get fed up with anybody. She was careful with money, but not mean. She was humorous and you could pull her leg. We got on very well – she was nice to work for.'[3] Vera and Cleggy wrote to Elspeth when she was away, and Elspeth reciprocated.

In the house Cleggy was housekeeper and cook, now that Charles was away at boarding school and had no need of a nanny save in the school holidays, and Dolly Jennings, who rode in daily from the village clad in beret, jersey and trousers, was the cleaner. Life at Woodfolds was humdrum rather than inspiring for a writer, with winter tussles against burst pipes and frozen taps, 'one of the quaint old-world customs they know nothing of in places like Canada and Greenland'.[4] It is unsurprising that Elspeth never wrote lyrically about her English house and farm, as she did about other places and other lands. It was as if familiarity prevented her noticing the details of her home life, perhaps as a means of survival or defence against the daily onslaught.

When Gervas contemplated building a cottage at Coole's to house another worker on his farm, Elspeth became very testy and pointed out that it was Woodfolds rather than Coole's which needed more help. 'It is wrong we should have to do so much ourselves – it tires you out and badly hampers my writing, whereas at Coole's they ought to be able to manage as they are, especially if we had a good young man at Woodfolds, who would work in with Ronald and involve both of us in less farm work ourselves. It is all very well for Coole's to run smoothly, but there is not much point if *we* are both worn out.'[5] The trouble was that Vera had hinted she might go, as the job had got too big for a girl, and a man would cost £3 a week more, so Elspeth felt housing should be provided as a bait for Woodfolds, not Coole's. Elspeth said she was too old to carry on with the work herself if Vera went, what with the pigs, cows and chickens. Vera was doing more work than two men did at Coole's. There were eight cows in milk at Woodfolds and only fourteen at Coole's (though Gervas ultimately increased his herd to thirty). As for Sid Cook the gardener, he was getting on and was due to retire in four years. 'We shall then be completely stuck,' Elspeth told Gervas, '. . . we'll have to do something or else be compelled to sell Woodfolds, as we can't carry on with no one to do the work but ourselves . . . You employ a lot of dogs and bark a great deal yourself.'[6] The tirade was stilled by a loving letter Gervas sent Elspeth in Kenya for their wedding anniversary. She replied: 'Thank you for remembering our anniversary – and to feel so full of goodwill after 23 years – no, twenty-two, surely? I can't think how you could have stuck it out. You are full of patience and love.'[7]

When Elspeth returned to her family from Kenya just before Christmas 1953, she settled down to write the novel about the Mau Mau which had been gestating while she was in Africa. She decided to dedicate the book, *A Thing to Love*,* to Cleggy, to inspire her to further domestic efforts and a little mellowing. It tells the story of events in the Rift Valley leading to the murder of a white couple by trusted members of their staff who clandestinely belong to a secret society dedicated to removing the whites from their country. An African chief loyal to the country's white government is also murdered (as was the real Chief Waruhiu). Of his two sons, one is a radical aiming to oust the whites and the other works as a District Officer for the government. By alternately examining each son's thought, Elspeth expresses the essential dilemma every African then faced: whether to collaborate with whites in the hope of gradually attaining a better standard of life, or whether to use violence to oppose them and thereby attain that objective more quickly – or fail utterly. The hero, Sam Foxley, falls in love with the daughter of the murdered couple, who finds herself having to choose between marrying him and becoming a farmer's wife or continuing with her missionary and educative role among Africans.

The book is assured when describing the farming life of the settlers, the details of secret society oaths and the pursuit of terrorists into the forest. Although the Mau Mau is not named, *A Thing to Love* is clearly based on what Elspeth learned about the movement

---

* The title comes from G.K. Chesterton's poem 'To Hilaire Belloc' (*Poems*, 1915): 'Likelier the barricades shall blare/Slaughter below and smoke above,/And death and hate and hell declare/That men have found a thing to love.'

on her 1953 visit to Kenya. Again she reverts to the constant themes of her writings:

> Sam [a white man] saw him [Gitau, a black man] suddenly as a man endowed with pathos because of his beliefs: his belief that all the troubles, frustrations and evils of the world – his world, anyway – would vanish like smoke if only he and his tribesmen could have their country to themselves, go back to the days when their dark forests kept out all people, all changes, all ideas. Then, like a miracle, would dawn a golden age full of wealth and easy living and the respect of one man for another, and free of bitterness.[8]

Elspeth describes in the novel Kenya's tangible problems, such as the influence of 'subversive news-rags' written by scoundrels and believed by Africans 'credulous as babies', and the lack of anything for young men to do with their leisure. She remarks upon the inadequacy of the teaching by Christian missionaries of the need for Africans to be patient and to earn the respect of others. At the same time, she constantly keeps in mind the Africans' point of view, achieving a sympathetic understanding of why they thought and acted as they did.* Matthew, the black District Officer, muses on Christianity and his former tribal beliefs:

> When Matthew became a Christian, he had been told not to believe in such things [spirits]. Yet Christians believed in spirits and in the vengeance of God and in the punishment of the evil-doer, and God had different ways for different peoples, just as he did not expect the eagle to swim or the barbel to rest in trees. Matthew had seen with his own eyes rain-clouds fill the sky after sacrifice, he had known a man die within three days of swearing falsely on the sacred stone, he had heard sticks knocking against the thatch at night when all men were shut into their houses: it was no good saying that these things

---

* There is a good commentary on the book by Michael Harris in *Outsiders and Insiders* (1992). But his view that Elspeth is nostalgic for the old days when colonial life was simpler is not correct. If anything, she is nostalgic for pre-colonial Kenya, though her view was that all schemes to remake the world, such as colonialism, socialism and environmentalism, were doomed to failure.

were superstitions, or devil-sent. Europeans were strong and their knowledge beyond the bounds of comprehension, yet to some things they were deaf, blind and insensitive.[9]

Elspeth is remembering the Ruck family's murder when she tries to explain the dangers faced by whites who treat Africans well, 'the soft Europeans, who try to win us round with smiles and medicines',[10] for they are the ones terrorists will try to eliminate in order to keep hot the hatred of the European. She understands the power of oaths for Africans, oaths which 'were now within each man, they had merged into his body and no power on earth or beyond it could free him from his bond. It did not matter whether he agreed or did not agree with what was to be done, any more than it mattered whether he agreed with the falling of the rain or the hatching of termites; it was something that must happen for good or ill, and he must acquiesce and participate.'[11]

Once again, Elspeth points out the paradox of the whites' belief that Africans could not rule their own country because they were too 'uncivilised', while Africans themselves found the whites uncivilised:

> Gitau ... read many letters and speeches by Europeans, full of the spirit of impatience, which abused Africans who, they said, could not hope to run their own affairs because they lacked two thousand years of Christian civilization. If the Europeans had really had two thousand years of Christian civilization, ... they had not been very successful, for they still had wars and killed each other, they still needed policemen to stop thieving and, if their books and films were to be trusted, they were fonder of adultery, and got drunk more often, than most Africans.[12]

A Thing To Love explores with equal sympathy ideas held by whites and blacks. Many questions are asked and many themes explored, but no answers are given. Although Elspeth later described it as 'an early, light and not very interesting novel',[13] it is an intriguing book which displays the complex relation between fact and fiction, as Elspeth retrieved and refashioned what she had recently seen and heard in Kenya. The inevitability of a conflict engendered by the clash of ways of life and religions is made plain. Neither side is right or wrong: things simply are. It is clear that Elspeth was puzzled about what the dénouement of the conflict in Kenya would be, and the unsatisfactory ending of the book reflects this. Her original ending was disliked by Chatto & Windus, who asked her to change it, whereupon she merely cut the final chapter out altogether. The book therefore comes to an abrupt and unsatisfactory halt, with Sam saying to the woman with whom he has fallen in love: 'I'm coming back . . . You mustn't think you've had the last word.' Yet *A Thing to Love* was Elspeth's most humane work to date, an example of the hurt bafflement felt at the time by both whites and blacks in Kenya and of the sorrow of a people, the Kikuyu, divided by civil war.

Apart from not appreciating the original ending, Norah Smallwood worried about Elspeth's use of the word 'arse', lest it affect the book's sale to Boots libraries. Elspeth changed the word and ever afterwards referred to the incident as 'the arse into bottom transmutation'. *A Thing To Love* was a success when it was published on 11 October 1954, selling 16,000 copies, and was later compared to Kipling's books on India. In the month before publication the Secretary of State for the Colonies, Alan Lennox-Boyd, made a personal request to read the manuscript before he flew to Kenya to try to sort out the Mau Mau rebellion. 'I hope,' said Elspeth tongue-in-cheek to Norah Smallwood, 'Lennox-Boyd's flesh creeps all the way to Nairobi, that you had the press photographers on the job at the airport, and confidently expect to see some reference to This Great Work in his first public pronouncement.'[14]

Elspeth was amused to learn in March 1955 that a scene she had invented for the book had actually happened in a Kenya cathedral, and she told Norah: 'Did you see Mau Mau have been copying *A Thing To Love*? Shall we sue them for plagiarism? Only they went one better and held their ceremony in a full-blown cathedral. I love the idea of the Bishop scurrying around afterwards with *his* mumbo-jumbo to counteract theirs.'[15] Nellie read the book and told Elspeth that on page 59 she had erroneously made the sun rise in the west, over the Aberdares, but it was too late to do anything about this.

Altogether Elspeth felt cheerful at this time. Her book of letters exchanged with Margery Perham, *Race and Politics in Kenya*, was republished by Faber & Faber in November 1954, with a new seven-thousand-word preface by Elspeth; a Frenchwoman who lived in Mombasa wanted to translate *Red Strangers* into French; and Penguin were reissuing *Murder on Safari*.

At the end of August 1954 Elspeth had a fortnight's holiday with Gervas at the Hotel Edelweiss in Adelboden, Switzerland, where they spent their time rambling in the countryside. After a winter of the usual burst pipes at Woodfolds, in January 1955 Gervas went to South Africa for two months on business. Elspeth worked rather aimlessly on another novel while anticipating a visit from Nellie, who arrived in England on 7 April.

Nellie had experienced an extremely difficult sixteen months since Elspeth had left her at the end of her last visit, and what she endured profoundly affected her daughter's work and thought. There had been a brief interlude of laughter in December 1953 when the Njoro Club put on a pantomime Elspeth had written at their request while she was in Kenya – 'We're very grateful to you for the giggle,' said Nellie.[16] Then Nellie braced herself to face the Mau Mau, whose murders continued throughout 1954. She thought she might teach her employees American square dancing in order to distract them from joining the Mau Mau movement, and visited the American Embassy for instruction sheets. This optimistic scheme came to nought. At one point Nellie was greatly disturbed when she found she had lost nineteen rounds of ammunition. She could not bring herself to tell the police for fear that Karanja and Mbugwa would be carted off and imprisoned for life – a fortunate hesitation, because she eventually found the ammunition.

The murders of whites persisted, including that of a four-and-a-half-year-old child. The Kenya Regiment and British troops retaliated. Operation Anvil was begun on 24 April 1954, and put 24,000

Kikuyu through screening camps in Nairobi in an attempt to discover which belonged to the Mau Mau. Still the Rift Valley swarmed with Mau Mau gangs, and 350 of them continued to operate in the forest behind Nellie's farm. The Mau Mau were blamed for burning down Treetops, the viewing platform from which tourists watched wild animals in the forest near Nyeri, but Nellie thought its owner burnt it down himself for the publicity, because he had removed its furniture the day before.

Njoro was given its own screening station, and Nellie feared for her employees. When she discovered that Karanja her cook was an oath taker, she was both frightened and deeply hurt. He was taken away by the police and charged with being the Mau Mau clerk and keeper of the books for the whole district. Nellie was informed by the authorities that her farm was stiff with Mau Mau members, and her ox driver was an oath administrator. He got five years' imprisonment, while two more of her employees were also incarcerated. Furthermore, Mbugwa was interrogated and found to have probably taken the second of the seven Mau Mau oaths. So many Kikuyu had taken this oath that white farms would be denuded of employees if all were imprisoned, so Mbugwa stayed with Nellie and the pair tried to do Karanja's kitchen work between them.

In September Nellie returned from a visit to Rose Cartwright to find Karanja back on the farm. Regarding it as monstrous that he had been released, she sent him straight to his hut to wait until she received the police report on him. After four days he was removed by the police to Dundori screening camp. There he was found to have taken the third Mau Mau oath, but the screener regarded him as fit for re-employment so back he came to Gikammeh. Determined to play him at his own game, Nellie held a de-oathing ceremony, in which Karanja made a fine speech, denounced the Mau Mau, and told everyone else to do likewise. Then Mbugwa was taken away for screening. Elspeth, helpless in England but severely alarmed, offered to send Cleggy to stay with her mother, but Nellie demurred. So Elspeth asked her to come to Woodfolds for Christmas, but again Nellie said no, because she felt she could not leave her dogs and her stock. Nellie's spirits sank further when she heard of the murder of Gray Leakey, Louis' uncle, and his wife. His body was never found, but it was thought he had been buried alive.

Only the prospect of Cockie Blixen coming to stay for two weeks in October and November cheered Nellie. Cockie proved to be on excellent form, a little stouter over the hips, and with a cornucopia of new jokes. She had only recently left Gikammeh when in dashed a young white policeman who blurted out that he wanted to use Nellie's phone. He had had a running battle with Mau Mau and chased them on to the farm, where he shot one dead. Nellie had to help him load the corpse into her van and transport it to the police station. Matters were also in disarray on the Rift Valley farms of Rose Cartwright and her daughter Tobina, who suffered nightly slashings and killings of valuable animals – hardly encouraging news for Nellie, now building up her own stock. She was persuaded by the local police to establish her own Kikuyu Home Guard group on her land, whereupon Karanja was made to renounce Mau Mau all over again. Members of other tribes on Gikammeh were invited to join, but were reluctant to do so, Muchoka refusing point blank. Nellie was so broken-hearted by the involvement of her employees in Mau Mau, despite all her attempts to treat them fairly, that she began to believe a firmer hand was required: 'I am convinced that the velvet glove is all wrong for their psychology which is close to the beast as ours is too when aroused. Until they are CONQUERED there's no hope of making a people out of them.'[17]

She soon heard even worse news: Mbugwa had confessed to allowing Mau Mau ceremonies in his hut right into 1953. 'I just don't speak to him any more except for orders,' she wrote to Elspeth in December 1954.[18] She decided to scrap the Christmas celebrations and lucky dip she normally held for her staff, because she no longer had the heart to be pleasant to people who had betrayed her. Yet a surprise awaited her:

> I have withdrawn from any attempt to foster friendship, under-
> standing etc with the African after their defection to Mau Mau,
> but I must say I came very near to it again when, on Xmas
> morning, Mbugwa staggered in with my morning cuppa and
> laid a huge box of potatoes on my bed tied up with (my)

brilliant violet crepe paper. This is a very special sort of spud called 'Mweri umwe' (= one month) which he knows I love and have looked for in vain for a long time now; he had got some and grown it on specially for me. Disarming? Especially as I didn't give anyone one single thing for Xmas.[19]

She relented and organised a paper chase at the beginning of January 1955, only to find that the caves at the end of her proposed trail were a Mau Mau hideout stuffed with oranges and peppermints. Fortunately no one was about when she stumbled on them.

Nellie's good friend and neighbour Ingrid Lindstrom had a nervous breakdown caused by her anxiety about Mau Mau on her farm. Nellie was given two members of the Home Guard from the Elgeyo tribe to protect her, but they proved a disaster when one of them shot dead a little Kikuyu farm child. She was shaken to the core, blaming herself for not being around when this happened (she was in Nakuru at the time), because she might have been able to save the boy by getting him to hospital quickly.

Nellie had suffered a further blow when Trudie Denman died in the summer of 1954. There was, however, a silver lining. Trudie left Nellie £400 for a trip to England, which she undertook at the beginning of April 1955, and a legacy of £150 a year. While she was in England her friends Jean and Francis Drummond invited her and Elspeth to come on a motoring holiday on the Continent. They set off in the second week of May, five people in a Jaguar car. The journey took them through French wine country into Italy, where they explored Turin and Genoa, Pisa and Rome. Nellie loved the trip, but Elspeth found her companions uncongenial, and by the time they reached Ravenna she wanted to go home. But she was forced to suffer for a further nine days while they saw Venice, the lakes and Lausanne. In Venice their sleep was so disturbed by the caterwauling that Nellie produced a theory that all the toms lined up on one side of the Grand Canal and all the she-cats on the other. Unable to swim across, they communicated by shrieking.

*   *   *

On their return to England Elspeth undertook another six-week session of *The Critics* for the BBC. A popular contributor who could be relied on as the voice of sanity and good temper, she had participated in several sessions of the programme in the previous two and a half years. She had the rare gift of never getting riled on air, however much opponents of her ideas provoked her. Later she transferred this ability to television, though she was never as happy in that medium as she was on radio. Harold Raymond once described her to a colleague as having 'one of the liveliest and, at the same time, most critical intellects of any woman I have ever met, and also a very pungent power of expression'.[20] Elspeth found the programmes an ordeal, as she told the producer Elizabeth Rowley:

> One suffers agonies first wondering what to say and how to say it, and agonies after wishing one had said something different, or said it differently. But it's a tremendous stimulant and I am most sincerely grateful to you, both for including me and for your gentle and discreet production. It makes all the difference to have a calm and confidence-inspiring captain at the helm and I am sure we should all burst into tears and start biting the table if a producer of a harsher nature (and the temptation to be harsh must at times be [sic] almost overpower you) and more discordant personality were to take over.[21]

By now the pay had risen to twenty guineas a programme, with first-class train fare and expenses of £1.15s. As preparation Elspeth had to keep her eye on book reviews and new publications, a few of which she would then ask the BBC to send her. She had to do a phenomenal amount of reading each week in order to choose one book for review on air. For example, on 20 August 1954 she asked for Joyce Cary's *Not Honour More*, Laurens van der Post's *Flamingo Feather*, William Sansom's *Lord Love Us* and Eudora Welty's *The Ponder Heart*. In September 1954, to her annoyance a rival programme, *Talking of Books*, got its hands on the review copies publishers sent to the BBC before Elspeth could have them.

She herself, however, was not above participating in *Just Published*, another similar programme. Her judgement of which books to review was sound for *The Critics*, which catered for middle- to highbrow taste. For the six weeks beginning 28 March 1954 she chose *Go Tell it on the Mountain* (James Baldwin), *Reach for the Sky* (Paul Brickhill), *The Bridge on the River Kwai* (Pierre Boule), *Don Quixote de la Mancha* (a new translation of Cervantes), *The Spanish Temper* (V.S. Pritchett) and *The New Men* (C.P. Snow). Her fellow panellists varied – for example in October 1954 they included Michael Ayrton the painter, Colin MacInnes the writer, Basil Wright the film-maker and author, and Walter Allen the author and literary journalist.

The year 1955 saw Elspeth undertake only one six-week session of *The Critics*, in June and July, but on 26 June she appeared on a *Calling East Africa* programme on which she discussed the new East African Royal Commission report with the Labour MP James Johnson. She had recently seen Margery Perham, and they agreed that parts of the White Highlands of Kenya should be opened to African tenancies on certain terms. Tongue in cheek, Elspeth also suggested, though not of course on air, that the White Highlands should be offered as a testing ground for the British hydrogen bomb.

Elspeth, regarded by the BBC as being 'on the Left of Right', was not always as careful with the written word as she was on air. In *Kenya Today*, a thirty-six-page booklet published by the Lutterworth Press in 1954, she set out her vision of a future Kenya in which the three races lived together in partnership – 'That is the goal; it remains to be seen whether it can be reached.'[22] She pointed out that as yet none of the races was willing to accept intermarriage, that there was bitter feeling about different rates of pay for each race and this practice should be stopped, and that white settlers could be intemperate in their political demands. She regretted the lack of social mixing of races: real progress towards a multi-racial state would never be made until all three were educated together in the same schools. These proposals were too radical for many of Kenya's whites.

To assuage land hunger among the growing African population

Elspeth advocated that marginal land be developed, proper husbandry methods be introduced to African land areas to make them
more productive, and the system of African land tenure be altered
to one of consolidation of scattered holdings. She favoured the
continuation and support of European farming and settlement, but
suggested a partnership with Africans. The liberal tone of the booklet is marred by her assertion that Africans had lived 'for many
years the crudest kind of life, encased in magic and superstition'.[23]
She saw the appeal of Mau Mau as strong to 'people whose beliefs,
religion, way of life and sense of security were crumbling, and who
had not found their feet in a new world which seemed at once to
offer them bright visions of power, wealth, sophistication and ease,
and to deny them a place in that world in keeping with its
promises'.[24]

Elspeth continued to develop her ideas on race relations and the
emergent political African in a new novel. Having used both East
and West Africa for previous novels, she now decided to set her
story in a central African country, the French or Belgian Congos –
the book is confused about which. She started to write this book,
The Red Rock Wilderness,* before Nellie arrived in England in April
1955, but laid it aside for the summer. After Nellie returned to
Kenya in July, Elspeth went on holiday with Gervas and Charles in
Mull, and it was not until September that she resumed writing. But
in November Gervas became ill. His doctor forbade him short
drinks and spirits, and advised him to stay in bed for three weeks
to ward off incipient ulcers. Though Cleggy served him dainty
puréed meals he behaved as if he had been sentenced to twenty
years in the salt mines, and succumbed to gloom. To amuse him,
Elspeth bought their first television set and placed it at the end of
the bed. Although by then both their farms were fairly well organised with sufficient staff, still Elspeth complained that never a day

---

* The title comes from 'The Wilderness', a poem by Sidney Keyes, which contains the
lines 'The red rock wilderness/shall be my dwelling place'.

went by without some obstacle to the progress of her novel rearing its head. She concluded that one could not work at home.

Besides attempting to continue with her novel, Elspeth also became a regular book reviewer, particularly for the *Sunday Times*, which brought her name before readers who had not read her books. Among the books she reviewed at this time were John Gunther's *Inside Africa* and the memoirs of Lord Altrincham (Sir Edward Grigg, former Governor of Kenya). The latter she thought 'rather pathetic', though she forbore to say so in a radio discussion with the journalists and writers on African affairs Colin Legum and Ferdinand Joelson in February 1956. Altrincham had died on publication day (to the sorrow of Nellie, who loved his simple and sweet nature), but his son John Grigg began an acrimonious correspondence with Joelson, accusing him of treating the book unfairly. Elspeth was drawn into the dispute – an awkward position for her to be in since at that very time Joannie, Grigg's widow, was staying with her, and she also frequently opened her house to Anthony, John Grigg's brother. When John sent Elspeth a copy of the correspondence to ask for her views, she agreed with him that Joelson's summary had not been fair.

On 7 March 1956 Elspeth at last delivered to Chatto & Windus the first draft of her novel, which she described as 'a sort of adventure story, not to be taken very seriously'.[25] She was therefore somewhat surprised to receive a barrage of criticism from Harold Raymond, Norah Smallwood and Cecil Day Lewis, still the firm's reader. Very protective of his wife, Gervas went to see Norah to find out whether, since the firm had 'hitherto been disapproving rather than enthusiastic ... perhaps you might be expressing, in a typically tactful manner, a certain reluctance to publish the book'.[26] This proved not to be the case, though Elspeth was asked to tighten and shorten the first hundred pages and to alter the end so that not all the villains emerged unscathed. Norah was particularly dissatisfied with the book's ending, which left evil triumphant and the disappearance of a world-renowned scientist unresolved. She was also perturbed that the scientist, Clausen, was too like Albert Schweitzer, and she wanted the scenic descriptions, normally one of Elspeth's strengths, improved to her previous standard.

Cecil Day Lewis felt the description of Colquhoun's journey to the scientist-missionary's jungle station at the beginning of the book was overlong, but Elspeth refused to change it, saying the book 'was meant to be more (or less?) than a pure adventure story, and to give, as well, a view of the background against which these events could conceivably take place'.[27] She did, however, change the ending, introducing a rhino chase and a more definite dénouement. Reviewers criticised this ending as too fortuitous a climax, and later in life Elspeth maintained that her original ending was better, if less dramatic. But on the whole reviewers liked *The Red Rock Wilderness*, describing it as a literate thriller, long on insight and short on gore, a particularly enriching work which examined uneasy race relations, a rising tide of nationalism, the impact of Western ideas, secret witchcraft rites, and lush and ominous vegetation – many of the things, in fact, which Elspeth had made especially her own. A number of reviewers compared it to Rider Haggard and John Buchan, the *San Francisco Examiner* finding that it made '*Prester John* and most of its successors look as ungraceful and uninspired as a herd of warthogs' (26 June 1957). It was recognised that the book was beautifully written: 'Here is an innocent-seeming story that changes almost imperceptibly into a tense, frightening tale of the mystery and magic of modern Africa, rich in atmosphere and irresistibly compelling' (*Retail Bookseller*, June 1957).

Elspeth's longing for what she had forfeited by forsaking Africa as her home and choosing to live in England is palpable in the book, the 'craving for colour and brightness . . . the open, lazy land of Africa with its blaring sunshine, the tempo of the siesta, the slipshod make-this-do attitude and the blaze of bougainvilleas, the glory of the flowering creepers and trees'.[28] She missed 'the hard, wide, rocky plains of Africa, the sharpness, the pale dust, the red rocks, the spiky stunted bushes, the wind-twisted acacias, the sparse coarse struggling grass, the mountain-forming clouds, the occasional tall cattleman with his spear and tribal scars and lofty, indrawn look'.[29] By making Colquhoun journey to central Africa through Kenya, Elspeth is able to revisit in prose her beloved Rift Valley:

> On top of the escarpment ... what a view! It's as if you were in the prow of a gigantic ship looking down over an infinite ocean, stilled by some titanic stroke, that shimmers and glitters in perpetual sunlight. Extinct volcanoes stand up like coral atolls from this wide, wide petrified sea. Over the surface of this great expanse of sage-green and silver-grey roll purple shadows of the clouds that pace the sky like mighty tortoises in silent cavalcade. No life to be seen below – no towns, houses, people. This vast landscape, with its heat-pulsating air, dwarfs men to insignificance, and now there's not even game any more. What a sight it must have been when the floor crawled with hartebeeste, zebra, gazelle, wildebeeste, giraffe: and when these craggy mountains, clothed with a silvery bush they call *leleshwa* [tarconanthus], were the haunt of buffaloes. All gone – swallowed up by the Moloch of Progress with its precision rifles and barbed wire.[30]

Elspeth of course knew how it had been, for she had seen the view many decades before when she had ridden as a child with her mother from Thika over the brow of the Aberdare mountains, to see the panorama spread below. And every day as she had woken at Gikammeh on the other side of the Rift Valley, the view was there before her.

After her trip to England Nellie was back at Gikammeh in July 1955, facing a political and military situation which had changed little. Mbugwa was sulky and Karanja in disgrace for having been caught stealing farm eggs and maize. 'I have no warmth of heart for any one of them,' she wrote to Elspeth, 'it has all been killed stone dead by their lying and lying.'[31] And yet she transported a farm boy to Nakuru hospital to be circumcised. This was preferable to the traditional ceremony, she felt, and one would not have known anything had been done except that on the way back the boy was carrying his shorts rather than wearing them. And she was touched that when she stayed with friends in Fort Hall her former headman Kupanya walked there all the way from Kandara, above Thika, to see her. She took the opportunity to visit Chief Nderi, whom she and Elspeth knew from their days in the Kikuyu reserve at Murigo's camp. At the same time there were four gangs of Mau Mau within three miles of her farm, and Nell Cole at Gilgil was losing a beast every night to raiders. Foot and mouth disease had broken out again, and three people in Njoro died from plague.

Nellie briefly contemplated setting up house with her sister Blanche in England, but could not bring herself to come to a definite decision. By now her grandson Charles was old enough to write her letters (though she chided him for not thanking her for presents and for what she considered his illegible and characterless handwriting), and she may have been hanging on to show him her beloved Kenya. While she struggled to prevent Gikammeh running at a loss, ironically she heard that her original Thika farm, Kitimuru, was expecting an eighty-ton coffee crop that year, from bushes she had planted in pioneering days so long ago. Doushka Repton was now making £25,000 a year from Kitimuru coffee. To raise her spirits, Nellie had her hair done in Nakuru by a stylist aiming at a 'windswept look'. 'So far,' she wrote, 'the wind seems to be rather in the wrong direction, and the general effect is owl in ivy bush but it saves all iron waves, all sets and practically all expense, the transformation scene cost me Sh.1 so to Hell with the Owl in Ivy Bush and hail to a free life.'[32] In Nakuru all the talk was of a murder by one Edward Alan Huxley (no relation to Elspeth) of his employer. When he was found guilty Nellie advised her daughter: 'The Huxleys are obviously no good at murder so please keep off it.'[33]

Though she now had doubts about the Africans, Nellie was still considerably more liberal than many whites. She was disgusted that the band for a coming-of-age dance for two white girls at the Njoro Club was cancelled when one of the mothers discovered the drummer was an Asian, and she could not understand the fuss being made in the East Africa Women's League about admitting other races. She was in dire straits financially and, despite having built up her herd to 110 cattle, she was forced to sell them to make ends meet. 'What really bites,' she told Elspeth, 'is not being able to leave you a tickety-boo farm – that was the mainspring of my existence.'[34] She was unable to look Karanja the herdsman, who called all cows 'darling', in the face. She now had to rely on her 'basket trade' of growing and delivering vegetables, which brought in only £15 a month. There seemed no prospect of an end to the Mau Mau rebellion, and her weekly letters to her daughter were not infrequently bleak.

Elspeth was still contemplating a book on Thomas Coke of Holkham, first Earl of Leicester, but had been warned off by a lecturer at Manchester University who was writing a thesis on the topic. At this point Len Spiers, a fellow farmer in Njoro, raised with Nellie the possibility of Elspeth writing a history of the Kenya Farmers' Association and Unga flour mills. Elspeth agreed, largely because it would mean a trip to Kenya to do the research, which would enable her to give her mother moral support.

However, within two months of the offer being made Len Spiers died, and Elspeth expected the proposal to be forgotten. When this failed to happen she arranged to go to Kenya in September 1956, but first there was a holiday in Tobermory on the island of Mull, during which Charles caught a trout and his father a cold, and a weekend with Julian Huxley and his wife Juliette at Woodfolds. As usual, Julian was rude, vain and selfish. The two families gossiped about Aldous Huxley's new Italian wife Laura, whom they regarded altogether as a good thing, as there had been serious deficiencies in his sex life with his former spouse. Gervas had recovered to some extent from his ulcer troubles and was now writing a book on tea (*Talking of Tea*), commissioned by Thames & Hudson, but both their farms were causing the Huxleys anxieties, and Elspeth felt the pressure: 'I am not very business-like, I have no secretarial help or filing system and live in a permanent rush. It would be a good deal nicer financially if Gervas and I were divorced.'[35] She now felt that there was no future for small farms in England.

* * *

Nellie met her daughter at Nairobi airport on 3 October 1956. Elspeth was surprised to see, on the ride from the airport to Nairobi, that Kenya's economy was booming, evidenced by the number of skyscrapers going up in the capital. To her huge relief she heard that the government was at last prevailing in the military and psychological struggle against the Mau Mau, and that most of the gangs hiding in the forests had surrendered or been captured. On arrival at Njoro she was relieved to find no one carried guns any more, and at the farm Karanja and Mbugwa greeted her in excellent spirits. They were very feudal and said they hoped that Charles would become their boss, which hardly squared with the Mau Mau oaths they had taken to rid the country of whites. But Charles as farmer was unlikely, Nellie having concluded, as had Elspeth in England, that small farms did not pay, because they could provide no reserve against bad years. She told her daughter that she intended to sell all her land bar the farmhouse and fifty acres. Elspeth longed to write a best-seller in order to help her keep the land, 'but it doesn't seem very likely'.[36]

She began work on her Kenya farming book. One of her first interviews was with Michael Blundell, whom she had met as a member of the Legislative Council on her previous visit to Kenya, and who was now a fat and prosperous Minister of Agriculture. Then the KFA chairman Maurice Pain entertained her at his house near Elburgon – an unsatisfactory interview since he passed out after a couple of gins. As part of her research Elspeth flew to Arusha in Tanganyika. Passing over the Ngorongoro crater she saw its floor packed with Maasai cattle, to the great detriment of such wild animals as still existed there. It was a defining moment, a sight which shaped her, an insight into the urgent need for wildlife preservation. Again she had tea with the batty Mrs Rydon who had taken her to task for reporting her millennial beliefs in *The Sorcerer's Apprentice*, and this time she had to listen to stories of flying saucers and the people from Mars and Venus living nearby; apparently two space ships had landed at Arusha.

For once, Elspeth found the research for her book deadly dull, consisting as it mostly did of having to study dozens of enormous minute books. For the first time she was uninterested in what she wrote. Her attention wandered and she thought the book would be unreadable. What she did, therefore, was write a lively section on the history of the pioneer white farmers to set the scene. To get the information for this she went to see old timers around Eldoret about their early days in Kenya, including those Boers who came in 1908 ('pretty dumb but very impressive people'[37]). But she reluctantly came to the same conclusion about oral evidence as had many historians before her – that it is time-consuming to collect, yields little and is untrustworthy. None the less, she gleaned enough to fill the section.

Elspeth's visit coincided with a royal tour by Princess Margaret, evidently sent to raise morale after Kenya's long years of discontent. Elspeth was disgusted by the royal mania, and would take no part in the fuss, though she did accompany Nellie to a Government House garden party. Particularly distressing to her were extravagance and pomp. And because she was in Kenya Elspeth missed the publication day and author's tea party given by Thames & Hudson for Gervas's first book, *Talking of Tea* ('Chatto's never had a tea party for *me!*' she said). She was sent a copy of the book and thought it 'a real little gem', with an excellent cover. She quickly hurried round to Nairobi's three bookshops to ensure they took copies.[38]

Gervas's book did not get the coverage it warranted because its launch was interrupted by international events. On 31 October 1956 news reached Kenya of Israel's invasion of Egypt following the Egyptian nationalisation of the Suez Canal. All ships from Kenya bound for Europe were rerouted round the Cape of Good Hope, and the air route was altered to prevent planes having to land at Cairo. Then within a week the Soviet invasion of Hungary took place. Kenyan whites, already dismayed by President Nasser of Egypt cutting off their shortest sea route to England, and by anti-British propaganda pumped out to Kenya by Egyptian radio stations, were delighted when British troops invaded Egypt. 'Taking some action has had a most tonic effect,' reported Elspeth.[39] There were sinking hearts, therefore, when the troops precipitately withdrew. Elspeth thought the international situation dire and saw no solution, though 'with [US President] Eisenhower playing golf in Florida, [US Secretary of State] Dulles equally pleasantly employed, and [British Prime Minister] Eden prostrate in Jamaica our leadership will soon at least be in well bronzed hands.'[40]

She was increasingly worried about Nellie, who was now seventy-one. Upon Gervas reporting that he had a cold she urged him to come to Kenya and take over Gikammeh. The Provincial Agricultural Officer inspected the farm and said it should make £1,000 a year, though Elspeth doubted the figure. If they took it over, she told Gervas, they would need to buy a tractor and implements which Nellie could not afford. Elspeth's revival of interest in Gikammeh was due to her dejection about their farming efforts in England, which ran at a permanent loss. She informed Gervas that they really ought to think seriously about closing Woodfolds farm: 'I shan't be able to afford to go on subsidising it any longer I'm afraid. If I have anything to spare I must help more here – [Mama's] income [is] very small.'[41]

Before she left Kenya, Elspeth took Nellie on a trip with her to do research. They went to Fort Hall, beside the Kikuyu reserve, to see how reconstruction was proceeding now the Mau Mau rebellion was almost over. In that area the Kikuyu, who formerly dwelt in isolated huts, were newly gathered together in villages, and the whole system of land tenure was under review. In Kikuyuland, the watchtowers had been dismantled and their guards and soldiers disbanded. There was nowhere a gun in sight, while the release of detainees was proceeding at a rate of hundreds a day. At a detainees' camp a guard of honour was drawn up for Elspeth to inspect, to her immense embarrassment.

On the way they took Mbugwa to Thika to see what was happening to his Kikuyu land under the government's novel land consolidation scheme. They took the opportunity to stop at their old farmhouse, Kitimuru, which Elspeth had not seen for years. Nellie had revisited her first home in Kenya once before, in the mid-1930s, when she found that Guy and Doushka Repton, the purchasers, had hung up 'a jostling crowd of wild beasts' heads' on the walls, which were now cream instead of Nellie's shocking pink. 'Overcome by sentiment, I had to stagger to the sideboard to accept a gimlet. I found I almost had to drink it in a kneeling position, owing to the interference of a Greater Kudu.'[42] Kitimuru was now a solid mass of productive coffee, a sure example of prosperity and a most depressing contrast to Nellie's current farm.

They visited the twenty-six-acre fishing plot on Berkeley Cole's old farm, a narrow strip along a riverbank at Naro Moru which Elspeth had bought years before with the idea that she and Gervas could spend holidays there. Now she was contemplating selling it in order to buy a new car for Nellie. There deracination took its toll of Elspeth and she experienced again the tearing asunder of the white child raised in Africa who lives elsewhere in later life. The fishing plot would be a heavenly place to build a little cedar house, with the river full of trout and the soil so fertile that Gervas could construct a lovely garden. At this point she failed to come to any decision about what to do.

From there they drove to Isiolo, two short lines of corrugated-iron huts enveloped in a constant cloud of greyish dust driven by a drying wind, to stay a weekend with George Adamson and his Austrian wife Joy. He, meek and gentle, was the game ranger in the region while she, quite the opposite in personality, was a skilled flower- and portrait-painter (many of her paintings hang today in the National Museum in Nairobi). Vivacious and overpowering, Joy bullied George a great deal ('No doubt you have a fellow feeling,' said Elspeth percipiently to Gervas[43]), but she was kind to the visiting pair, taking them out in Land Rovers for two long days to see animals in the bush. Joy identified incredible quantities of wild flowers – the countryside was vivid with lilies and gloriosa, sheets of white heliotrope, blue pentamesia and small thorn bushes with yellow button flowers, like gorse.

When Elspeth got back to Njoro there was a telegram awaiting her from Gervas with heartening sentiments about their wedding anniversary. 'I think you have put up with a lot in the last 25 years,' she wrote in response, 'and thank you with all my heart for your kindness and long-sufferingness and love, which has been a great rock in a world of uncertainty. Let's try and enjoy the next 25 years as much as we can!'[44] This was not to be.

Elspeth returned home to Woodfolds for Christmas. Always happier in Africa in the winter, she morosely faced the English cold again, with petrol rationing caused by the Suez crisis and the farm in trouble as usual. She now had a young man, Charlie Butcher, to help Vera on her land, but she was still able to write only from the early morning until lunchtime, spending the afternoons on farmwork. Calf prices had collapsed, and it was difficult to make a profit from milk. It is hard to understand why Elspeth did not get rid of her farm, since it cost her so much worry and money. One can only speculate that the pain was exquisite and she benefited from its stimulation, possibly as an escape from writing. She may only have felt whole when she was growing food or nurturing animals.

There was one thing to look forward to – Cleggy was due to depart on a prolonged holiday in Kenya. Elspeth was overjoyed. She always had ambivalent feelings about her nanny-cum-housekeeper. Neither servant nor friend, Cleggy bored Elspeth to tears with her trite opinions and melancholy moods. Peggy, Aunt Blanche's daughter and Elspeth's beloved cousin, who lived in a nearby village, came to stay to help in the house while Cleggy was away.* It was a relief to have a cheerful Peggy instead of a dour Cleggy, but the cousins had a bleak time in June when Peggy's sister Constance died from an accidental combination of drugs and alcohol. Elspeth was distressed, too, by the suicide of Frank Tilsley, a fellow-panellist on *The Critics*, a six-week stint of which she undertook in February and March 1957. Tilsley had appeared perfectly normal during the recording of the 10 March programme and had carried Elspeth's bag to the taxi afterwards. Then he went home and killed himself.

* Peggy (Margaret) Green, née Holford. Her marriage was not a success and she went off with a yachtsman, but this relationship soon failed and she went to Woodfolds, then lived in a nearby village, Ashton Keynes. Peggy and Elspeth were very close, no doubt from the 1920s when Elspeth stayed with the Holfords at Cherry Orchard.

'The programme is full of jittery, highly-strung, long-haired intellec-tuals,' Elspeth told Norah Smallwood, 'ready to fly off the handle at the drop of a hat, but the one who goes into the garage with the breadknife is the down-to-earth, blunt, no nonsense Lancashire tough put in to add a bit of ballast and common-sense to the racket.'[45] The BBC did not broadcast the 10 March edition.

While Elspeth busied herself writing up her history of the Kenya Farmers' Association, Gervas too was researching and writing. He found he enjoyed his new career, and hit on the subject of the seventeenth-century courtier Endymion Porter, an influential sup-porter of Charles I. He had developed an interest in Porter when Elspeth inherited a Van Dyke painted in 1632 depicting him and his family. For her part, Elspeth ignored her original remit and broadened her range in order to provide leaven and increase poten-tial sales of her book, which she made largely a history of white farming in Kenya rather than of the KFA. The increased length (85,000 words instead of the 40,000 contracted) proved to be a problem for 'Better Country Farther Out', as the book was entitled at that stage. Disappointed that their author had failed to adhere to her brief, the 'philistines' who had commissioned the book (the Kenya Farmers' Association) wanted to omit the most lively, inter-esting section. F.T. Holden, the managing director of Unga, the Kenya flour mill, said, 'I am disappointed with the historical narra-tive of Unga,'[46] and sent ten pages of closely-typed criticism, includ-ing the request that Elspeth change 'Unga Ltd.' to 'Unga Limited' throughout, and that people's names should be followed by their university degrees.

Elspeth ground her teeth, followed a few of the suggestions and cut some of the historical sections, though a considerable pro-portion was retained, which gave the book a wider sale than it would otherwise have had. Now entitled *No Easy Way* – the winning entry, by Mrs Dan Long of Thomson's Falls, in a competition to find a title which attracted over six hundred entrants – it was published by the *East African Standard* of Nairobi in 1958. The book explained how, in Michael Blundell's words, 'the early settlers, the colonial officers, the Asian duka owners and the rather bewildered

African workers created a country out of nothing'.[47] The following year a specially bound copy of *No Easy Way* was presented to the Queen Mother, in Kenya for morale-raising purposes, when she visited Nakuru.

For the rest of 1957 Elspeth worked frantically on newspaper articles, regular book reviews for the *Sunday Times* (including one on the enormous *African Survey* by Lord Hailey) and BBC programmes. She told Norah Smallwood she was working so hard that her hair was like a haystack, nearly down to her knees: 'I have got to the stage of despondency, boredom, gloom and anguish and Gervas makes matters no better by his running commentary on Endymion which he feels must be finished by the end of next week or the heavens will fall.'[48] Sid Cook the gardener was away for three months with a hernia and Elspeth's writing was affected by '100 futile interruptions a day'.

Journalist, broadcaster, novelist and writer of serious non-fiction books, Elspeth was also a parent. Away at his prep school Westbourne House, Charles, 'never the type to whom school appealed ... was ... as happy there as he could have been anywhere else'.[49] He did well, coming first in maths and third overall, despite being below the average age for his form. He heartened his mother by writing to her in Africa and telling her his marks. But when Harold Raymond told Elspeth his son had achieved a first-class degree from Oxford her reaction, perhaps derived from the experience of her own childhood, was, 'Poor Charles will never compete. His home life is too happy. Only friction creates sparks. Still, he was second in the junior hurdles in the school sports.'[50] Charles was coming to the end of his days at preparatory school and was entered for the scholarship examination to Gervas's old school, Rugby. After being exhorted to work hard by Elspeth, particularly at Latin, he won a scholarship and began his first term in September 1957.

Charles later described his mother as 'always away' and 'not a good parent, or, rather, not a good *enough* parent'.[51] He remembered her as never encouraging, frequently and enduringly critical. And yet she was dearly appreciated by her grandchildren in years to come, offering them a stimulating environment, fun, expeditions, and that most important of all things in childhood – a listening ear and uncritical voice. The two accounts may seem contradictory, but it is far from unusual for people's children to be treated differently from their grandchildren. Moreover, older people are more rarely angry and upset, for too much has gone before and age has introduced proportion into life.

With the reduction of tension now the Mau Mau was winding down, Nellie was regaining her spirits and had a succession of guests in 1957. One was Joan Grigg, widow of the former Governor Sir Edward (Lord Altrincham) and still grieving for her husband. Nellie deprecated the self-absorption which a less critical host would have regarded as entirely normal in one whose husband had just died: 'I am baffled and helpless, and sometimes wonder if Ned was too ... Joannie has the mind of a very obstinate hen canary.'[52] Joan Grigg was not aware of Nellie's opinion – in her thank-you letter she appreciated her as 'a very rare companion ... with ... stimulating and intelligent talk'.[53]

Then Cleggy came to stay at Gikammeh, spry and full of beans, though her visit was clouded by Mbugwa losing a six-month-old baby to pneumonia, despite Nellie's best efforts to get the child to a doctor. Elspeth was anxious that her mother should keep Cleggy till June, but she returned to England in May. 'I don't know HOW you can stick her. WHY can't you be all happy together as you are?' asked Nellie.[54] But she concluded that there was no use in being annoyed with Cleggy, because she was always the same. Another visitor was a regular, the unwelcome Dolly Miles. Dolly raged unjustly and unkindly at Nellie, but when she was leaving and Nellie said, 'For God's sake, drive carefully,' Dolly disarmingly announced, 'I have left you £500 in my will to buy a new car.' 'I was so overcome,' said Nellie, 'that I could think of nothing to say except, "In that case, drive like hell".'[55]

Since Dolly was not to die for a while, it was Elspeth who put up the money for a second-hand car. Those who witnessed Elspeth and her mother in their edgy relationship were usually ignorant of covert gifts like this, and these acts, which must have taken much out of Elspeth because of her extreme carefulness with money, are ones that people never knew about. Nellie continued her public works. She was unsuccessfully proposed as Vice-President of the East Africa Women's League, 'purely to annoy the smug bitches Nell Cole and Sydney Farrar',[56] and she became President of the Royal Kenya Horticultural Society instead of Sharpie.

To reward Charles, now almost fourteen, for winning a scholarship to Rugby, Elspeth decided to take him and Gervas to Kenya for Christmas, now that the Mau Mau uprising was all but over. As Nellie contemplated her grandson's first visit, she wondered whether she should tidy up the house – a notion rapidly rejected lest it give her grandson the wrong impression of the hardships and squalor of true pioneering life. Charles, Gervas and Elspeth arrived in Nairobi by plane on 15 December 1957. They stayed at Njoro for Christmas. Charles played tennis with the family of Ingrid Lindstrom's daughter Viveka at her farm in Rongai, and parties were organised by Nellie and Ingrid. At New Year the family departed for Takaungu on the coast, to take up an invitation from Tobina, Rose Cartwright's daughter who had married Arthur, Nell Cole's son, to stay at their holiday home near Kilifi. Tobina had invited them because she thought Rose would enjoy their visit, but she soon regretted it.

The visitors slept in a cottage two hundred yards from the Cole house, and joined the Coles during the day. The cottage formerly belonged to Denys Finch Hatton, 'a man,' Elspeth later wrote, 'never forgotten or explained by his friends, who left nothing behind him but affection, a memory of gaiety and grace, a kind of melody or aroma, like a trace of the *Lamuria** scent on the air', who had stayed there with Karen Blixen.[57] Nellie and Elspeth ignored social niceties and bickered constantly, so much so that Arthur Cole would disappear on his boat at dawn to escape. 'Nellie and Elspeth,' wrote Tobina Cole, 'both powerful women, argued and fought all day

---

* Growing in Kenya's forests, Lamuria is a shrub whose clusters of creamy pink flowers drench the air with the scent of jasmine.

long, comments like how dare you say that, give reason for your theory, voices rose as more gin poured in. Gervas used to come with me to the market for fruit and vegetables, up the creek for prawns, which was peaceful.'[58] Elspeth and Gervas indulged in further, though more gentle, disagreements, such as whether Charles should be allowed to swim before or after lunch. Elspeth was argumentative in the company of her family, oblivious to the embarrassment this caused outsiders. She and Nellie were both selfish in this respect, while Gervas, not as crushable as Jos had been, added his own little barbs. 'Looking back on it,' says Tobina Cole, 'I think Elspeth and Nellie thoroughly enjoyed their rows, but it was tiring for the rest of us, and at the end of the fortnight I was sick of the whole lot!'[59]

Gervas and Charles returned to England for the start of Charles's new term at Rugby, leaving Elspeth in Kenya for a further three months to work on some newspaper and magazine articles she had been asked to write. The *Sunday Times* had commissioned four pieces on the subject of 'Islam in Zinj' and three on 'Nasser's African Design'. Topical and interrelated themes, they were subjects of profound importance. Would Nasser's tentacles stretch southwards towards Kenya? And how significant in this respect was the fact that the East African coast (called Zinj by the Arabs) had been Islamised for centuries? Elspeth also had deadlines to meet for *Time and Tide* and the *New York Times Magazine*.

Elspeth was allocated an office in the Department of Information in Nairobi. She was always treated so well by colonial governments that one might be justified in speculating whether she worked for them clandestinely. The truth is probably more mundane. She and Gervas had many contacts in the world of public information and relations, and she always made a point of asking for help. Being a woman was also an advantage, and she made use of the protective instincts of British governments abroad. While working in Nairobi she stayed at Karen, at the foot of the Ngong hills, with Harriet, another Lindstrom daughter, and her husband Bertie Geoghegan, 'a bit of a bore, who has a passion for talking about the royal family'.[60]

Elspeth gave lunch to the up-and-coming African politician Tom Mboya, born on Sir Northrup McMillan's sisal estate at Ol Donyo Sabuk. He was a Luo, his father having come from Rusinga island on Lake Victoria, and he attended the small school on the estate before going to a Roman Catholic seminary. He had recently been for a year to Ruskin College, Oxford, where he became a good friend of Margery Perham. An able trades union organiser and a member of the Legislative Council from 1957, Mboya was assassinated in mysterious circumstances in 1969. Elspeth also went to Mombasa to see Arab leaders and more politicians, African and Asian.

Whites were pretty gloomy about the political future, and worried about the effect of the radio propaganda from Cairo on the African population. Egypt's President Nasser was hand in hand with the Soviet Union at a time when the Cold War was getting chillier, and had set his heart on seizing for his country the leadership of the African world. The Kenyan government attempted to suppress his influence by setting up a special radio station, Sauti ya Mvita, in Mombasa to counteract Radio Cairo blaring its anti-British propaganda up and down the coast. 'The propaganda chiefs in Cairo,' concluded Elspeth, 'are seeking to sink shafts of influence deep into East Africa, along whatever faults and cracks their drill will penetrate.'[61] Not all the Africans would welcome Arab influence, for memories of the Arab slave trade were still too recent.

Zanzibar, that lovely island scented with cloves and spices, green and warm just before the monsoon changes, was next on Elspeth's list of places to visit to glean information for her articles. She stayed at the English Club and dined with the British Resident, Sir Henry Potter, fat, red-faced, amiable and, thought Elspeth, probably indolent and therefore quite suited to Zanzibar. In the harbour she was stopped by an old lady who turned out to be the widow of the conductor Sir Henry Wood, founder of London's Promenade Concerts. She asked, 'Aren't you Elspeth Huxley? I've read all your books.' Flattered, Elspeth realised she was now a well-known writer.

She then flew to Mogadishu in Somalia, Kenya's neighbour on her northern border, to examine Egyptian influence there. The town was hot and humid, with sand everywhere as fine and white as icing sugar, and buildings covered in flaking white paint – all of which contributed to intolerable glare and painful eye-narrowing. The long-winded British Consul-General and his sweet and pudgy Bulgarian wife put Elspeth in a flat serviced by a handsome Somali who spoke no English but brought her coffee at 8 a.m. and tea at 5 p.m. She saw Muhammed Hussein, a 'badboy' much occupied with Cairo radio propaganda, the Somali Prime Minister and various ministers. The Italians were due to leave the country in two years' time, though there were rumours that they might pull out before then. 'It is a god-forsaken country,' wrote Elspeth, 'and it would scarcely matter who took it over were it not for the strategic question. If it is dominated by Egypt and hence Russia, they will be on the borders of Kenya and opposite Aden.'[62] She lamented that the British offered Somalis only two scholarships a year to study in England, while two hundred Somali scholarship-holders were being educated in Cairo. Moreover, the Egyptians ran their own schools in every province of Somalia.

Elspeth was relieved to quit Mogadishu to pick up Nellie before leaving on a journey through the deserts of the Northern Frontier District of Kenya, further to examine Arab influence. They spent three days with the Adamsons, now absorbed in their relationship with Elsa, an orphaned young lioness they had been rearing themselves. Elspeth regarded Joy's obsession with the animal as most odd: 'I think she may turn into one herself soon.'[63] Elsa was extremely tame, but, now full-grown, her romping could send people flying. Joy shut her up away from Nellie and Elspeth, to their fathomless relief. During their stay Joy gave Elspeth a typescript of three thousand words she had written on Elsa for a picture-book about the lioness which was to be published by Hamish Hamilton, whom Elspeth reckoned Joy would tear to bits if he argued with her. The writing was all in capital letters in Joy's impetuous, ungrammatical Austrian English, and she more or less bounced Elspeth into rewriting it for her. Far from ignorant of Joy's faults,

Elspeth yet admired her persistence and empathy with animals, and agreed to help her.

Reluctant to revamp Joy's prose for nothing, Elspeth went to see Hamish Hamilton when she was back in London. He asked her to write about four thousand words about the lioness based on the pages of 'somewhat hysterical and very incoherent chatter by the Austrian lady tamer'.[64] Elspeth wrote the text, which Joy approved, but Hamilton wanted it in the third person rather than the first, an idea Joy refused to countenance. There was also an argument about whose name should go on the cover as author. Elspeth, who was not consulted, would have said Joy's, but Hamilton wanted Elspeth's more prestigious name. By August Hamilton was so fed up with the long, overexcited letters from Joy, who never learnt to be subservient to her publishers and was too emotional and difficult for him to cope with, that he withdrew his offer to publish the book. He paid Elspeth off with thirty guineas, which she returned to him so that she could retain the copyright in her text. Elspeth thought Joy 'half way round the bend', but felt that 'rather more tact than Hamish Hamilton showed might keep her under control'.[65]

After their stay with the Adamsons Nellie and Elspeth went on via a lodge on the Uaso Nyiro river to Marsabit, a mysterious mountain oasis in the midst of a waterless flat region, the great, grey Kairsut desert. It was an extraordinary place, a thick, heavy forest hung with ragged beards of lichen, with a whitewashed district office in a eucalyptus coppice flying an incongruous Union Jack. Elspeth went on, without Nellie, to the Beau Geste village of Wajir, which owed its existence to a cluster of wells in an outcrop of limestone which trapped the water. It housed 'highly glamorous Somalis with faces like Old Testament prophets or bronzed Persian gods, who follow their camels all over the desert and chant songs at the wells while they haul up water in leather buckets and the women approach with pitchers like bevies of Rebeccas'.[66] Elspeth travelled the 225 miles in a three-ton lorry containing ammunition and two armed policemen, with a bag of 85,000 shillings at her feet. It was a journey through a grotesque landscape:

To reach Wajir you pass the only objects breaking the monotony – fantastic termite castles of red cemented earth, looking
as if Barbara Hepworth, inspired with a daemonic energy, had
been turned loose on the illimitable plain. And only a protean
Graham Sutherland could do justice to the spare and spiky
little thorn bushes, bare of leaves, that cast no shadow on
the baked sand beneath. Such grasses as exist, ash-blond,
straggle over the ground like the sparse hairs on an all-but-bald
head.[67]

On the return journey to Njoro, Elspeth stopped off at Naro
Moru to see about her fishing plot. She met a potential purchaser,
an ex-DC from Nigeria, who offered £1,000 for it. She was loath
to sell, but needed the money, and sold the land to Charles Norman.
The magazine *Time and Tide*, for which she had written regular
articles, was closing, thus reducing her income by about £300 a
year. And the *New York Times*, for which she had recently written
a piece, was making a fuss, insisting she alter it 'to eliminate ...
anti-African bias, [the suggestion] that Africans despite British educational efforts won't listen to reason – i.e., to eliminate the truth
(as I see it), that African nationalists will not compromise and be
nice to minorities, in favour of (I suppose) some nice flabby general-
ities about everyone being democratic and happy ever afterwards
... I do think the Americans are poisonous.'[68] Elspeth often laid
her head on the block by giving her candid opinion that life would
not be all roses under African governments, as has sadly proved
often the case. The newspaper's editor, mindful of the liberals
among his readers, would not publish such frank opinions.

Elspeth went back to Njoro, to receive disturbing news from
Gervas. Charles had been unhappy in his first term at Rugby, and
things had not improved in his second. Now he was being excluded
from his study by bullies. Elspeth was furious:

I am deeply disturbed about this. Poor Charles. But quite
honestly, it is NOT good enough and I do not agree with you
that we can't interfere. After all, we send him to Rugby at vast
expense, to be *educated*, and Charles will not learn if he is
messed about by these idiotic hooligans. It is the duty of the

school to see that he is given the right conditions to work in. Apart from that, if those stupid boys do things like ruining his suit with boot polish and breaking his chair, that is destruction of property and they must not get away with it. We *must* say something.[69]

Gervas, true to character, did nothing. Matters worsened when Elspeth heard that one of the boys in Charles's study was, as she put it, 'filthy dirty in mind and habits', and she imagined he was making passes at her son. In every letter thereafter she exhorted Gervas to see the headmaster, advice he ignored. Had Elspeth been in England, she would certainly have taken matters into her own hands. As it was, she fulminated impotently in Africa. She also raged about what was happening on her farm, with Vera overfeeding pigs suffering from scour – 'piglet pellets are very expensive and Vera is wildly free with them'.[70] One wonders why Gervas bothered to give her any farm news, when all she did was torment him with bullying orders. It must, however, have been exceptionally frustrating and irritating to be married to a man who had to be urged into action, and she appears to have concluded that he lacked the initiative or drive to do things himself.

Elspeth returned to England in the last week of March 1958. She was now fifty-one, with all hope of having another child past and gone. She went into hospital in July to have an operation, probably a hysterectomy. Before that she sent a manuscript to Chatto & Windus on which she had been working quietly for a few months, called 'The Vertical Rays of the Sun'.

NINE

Flame Trees *and* A New Earth

Elspeth had long been interested in the success of Karen Blixen's *Out of Africa*, an autobiography of life on a coffee farm at the foot of the Ngong hills outside Nairobi, before crop failure forced Blixen home to Denmark – indeed, she wrote the introduction to the 1980 edition published by the Folio Society. The book was originally published in 1937 and became an instant best-seller. Nellie, however, dismissed it, genuinely believing it to be a bad book, over-written and forced, with stilted English and erroneous anthropology. It was 'tiresome and exaggerated' about the visitors to the Blixen farm, such as Ingrid Lindstrom. Both Ingrid and Nellie took exception to Karen Blixen's remarks that Ingrid was so passionate about her farm that she would have sold both husband and children to keep it, that she cast 'deep, furious glances' at Karen for deserting her calves when she had to sell the farm, that Karen and Ingrid were 'a pair of mythical women, shrouded respectively in white and black, a unity, the Genii of the farmer's life in Africa'.[1]

'As a book it fails,' Nellie wrote to Elspeth in 1938. '[It is] terribly self-conscious throughout, and, when she gets reminiscent, really weak. She gives no impression at all of Berkeley [Cole]'s, or Denys [Finch Hatton]'s character – they only appear as they affect her, as do all the Somalis and the absurd scene with Kinanjui – I, I, I all the time and the later bits about Ingrid L. [Lindstrom] are just unintelligible. They don't make sense. I hope you don't think it is the last word in African books. Good God, you can do better than that! She hasn't the remotest conception of Aldous Huxley's term "non-attachment" . . . No, you mustn't think it a great book.'[2] She grudgingly, however, found the imagery beautiful. Elspeth, a finer and more dispassionate judge, immediately recognised the quality of the book, with its vivid and imaginative prose, though she never believed the writing was of the calibre to make Karen runner-up for the Nobel Prize, as she later was. By the mid-1950s she knew she could write one as good, if not better, about her own childhood.

The book she eventually wrote, *The Flame Trees of Thika*, brought Elspeth worldwide fame. It was a Book Society Choice in 1959 and the Reprint Society took 78,000 copies as the World Book choice of the month in 1960. The BBC serialised it on *Woman's Hour*. A year after hardback publication Penguin brought out the paperback in a deal with Chatto, having found it both beautifully written and exciting, with wonderfully creative writing which seemed to have come straight from the author's heart. It was repeatedly reprinted, translated into many languages and filmed as a six-part TV serial in the 1980s. The success of the serial revitalised the book's sales and resulted in many more paperback impressions. An illustrated version was published in 1987.

Elspeth had intended the book to be a work of fiction. When she sent Norah Smallwood the typescript of a novel called 'The Vertical Rays of the Sun' on 29 June 1958 she told her the original plan was to cover the whole of her childhood from about 1913 to 1925, 'but when I got half way there seemed to be plenty of material, so this stops at 1914. I can do another of the same kind, more or less, from 1920 to 1925, if you for your part think it worth while, and if I for mine can muster the energy and resolution.'[3] Norah liked the book immensely, and began calling it an autobiography in her letters to John Willey of Morrow, who were to publish it on the other side of the Atlantic. She also used the word in a letter to Elspeth, from whom she requested some photographs to accompany the text. Elspeth replied that she was not happy about calling the book an autobiography: '[It] occupies only about two years and is mainly a picture of a period and a fragment of a society . . . It's a mixture of recollections and fiction and to tie it down with photos would put it firmly in a class in which it doesn't belong, that of fact and truth, and invite people to pick holes in it and accuse it of lying ... It is more fictional than perhaps you think.'[4] Instead, Elspeth suggested a subtitle, 'Memories of an African Childhood'. This compromise was accepted, together with a new title, *The Flame Trees of Thika*, which gave the jacket designer, Rosemary Seligman,* an opportunity to paint the brilliant scarlet blooms of Spathodea Nilotica, colloquially known as the flame tree, an avenue of which Nellie had planted leading up to the farmhouse Kitimuru at Thika. They are handsome trees which grow up to forty feet, with a rounded crown covered with large, bright, orange-red flowers. They remain in flower for many months.

What had prompted Elspeth to write about her childhood at this time of her life? She was fifty in 1957, and perhaps that had made her aware of how relentlessly time was passing. She also saw, in the Kenya of 1957–58, how different the country had become, and how exotic her childhood there seemed in retrospect. Independence was proceeding along its inexorable route, and the white farming life of her early years would never return. It was time to write a book about the Kenya of her youth, preferably a fictional one without too much fact intruding, as real life all too often lacks narrative drive, proceeding as it does in inconsequent fits and starts between periods of monotony. But to establish a believable fiction, certain incidents would have to have a little of the truth in them.

Elspeth opens *Flame Trees* with a journey made by ox-cart from Nairobi to Thika by herself (unnamed in the text) and her mother, whom she calls Tilly. Her father, Robin in the book, is already at the farm near Thika, supposedly building a house. When Tilly and Elspeth arrive, no house exists and they have to live in tents while one is fashioned from poles and grass. In reality, Elspeth was left behind in England when her parents went to Kenya. She herself arrived at the end of 1913 with Daisy Balfour, her mother's friend who escorted her on the boat, to a house already built. In *Flame Trees* Robin entices Kikuyu youths to come and work for him by leaving a lantern out one night, luring them to cluster round and

---

* She used the surname 'Grimble' professionally.

wonder at the fire entrapped by glass. The Kikuyu were used to only open fires illuminating evening meals and dances. In reality, the farm already had a labour force when Elspeth came, largely provided by the local District Commissioner who bribed chiefs, appointed by himself, with goats to encourage them to send young men as labourers to work on farms.

Elspeth invents fictitious neighbours – the Nimmos, Alec Wilson and the Palmers – and Ian Crawfurd, the safari-leader who falls in love with Lettice Palmer. They are not remotely like the Grants' real neighbours, though some incidents are based on truth. Elspeth goes to live at Molo (true) with Ian Crawfurd's brother and his wife. In reality those people did not exist, there was no ride to Londiani with Dirk, no hunt with the Dorobo for buffaloes in the forest, no death of Kate Crawfurd in childbirth. To give the book authenticity, Elspeth mentions the names of some real white people – for example Harry Penton, Russell Bowker, Randall Swift, Ernest Rutherfoord, Pioneer Mary (Mary Walsh, an itinerant Irish trader), and Berkeley and Galbraith Cole. But the characters of these people remain undrawn, and apart from Pioneer Mary, who was safely dead and out of the way, they are merely shadows in the story.

As for the Africans in the book, some of them are given the names they actually bore, such as Sammy the headman, Andrew the Maasai cook and Njombo the stable lad, but others, such as Chief Kupanya, are fictional. Because Sammy, Andrew and Njombo were dead, Elspeth is able to invent incidents and pin them to the characters. A long section of the book deals with the bewitchment of Njombo by Sammy, who blames the former for causing the death of his wife and an injury to his son. Njombo is snatched from death by Tilly's intercession with Chief Kupanya to remove the spell. This never happened in actuality, though the Kikuyu believed that the power of spells was real enough.

There are also a few incidents which are based on fact, such as the destruction by hyenas of the upholstery of the Grants' buggy; episodes in the lives of Elspeth's pony and her pets (the duiker Twinkle, chameleons and a tortoise); the saving of the old man from pneumonia by Tilly; and the topography of Kitimuru farm and the grass dwelling there – though the Grants' stone house with its Dutch gables is moved to become the Palmers' farm. Ian Crawfurd may be an embodiment of the true-life Captain Jack Kirkwood, though Elspeth makes him fall in love with Lettice Palmer rather than her mother. Elspeth was embroidering a relationship about which she knew little, though children sometimes notice more than adults think they do.

Elspeth weaves the plot, of which the love affair between Lettice Palmer and Ian Crawfurd is the axis, to create tension. Lettice is in a quandary whether to leave her husband, who has given up so much for her, particularly his army career (as, in real life, had Charles Taylor for his Gaiety Girl), to run away with Ian. There is a sub-plot concerning Njombo, who commits murder and suffers retribution from Chief Kupanya rather than from the white DC, to whom another man is dispatched to be tried for the crime, on the wholly logical grounds that if Njombo was arraigned and found guilty he would be unable to pay his fine in goats to the chief. In view of the created incidents and plot, Elspeth felt the book should be classified as a novel.

But what Norah Smallwood detected, and what is the work's true triumph, was the element of sympathy and understanding for Africa and its inhabitants both white and black which runs throughout the book. The manuscript could only have been written by someone who grew up in Kenya and knew the flavour of those times (as is the case with Beryl Markham's *West With the Night*, despite the claims of some who have tried to wrest the authorship from her – Elspeth herself always felt the book was ghosted by Ernst Schumacher, Beryl's husband at the time, because she found its writing 100 per cent post-Hemingway journalese, and was sure Beryl could not and would not have written like that. She found the book vivid and effective, but did not care for the style which jarred on her because it was so plainly done for effect). After a first reading of the manuscript, Norah advised Elspeth to stress the character of the Africans more fully, to express 'a shade more warmth when talking about the natives ... [This is] very necessary for sales. You are too objective in your attitude to farmworkers and servants, rather as though they were on one side of a fence and you on the other. I felt Tilly was the only one who had any sympathy and possible love for them. Highlight their endearing qualities – their gaiety, childishness, crinkly smiling faces, and their occasional flashes of simple wisdom.'[5]

These remarks, though today they might seem patronising and typical of 1950s colonialism, encouraged Elspeth to write more about the Kikuyu and Maasai and their society and beliefs, and thereby give the book its special flavour. The sharp distinction between black and white ways of life and thought, and the two races' mutual incomprehension, as well as the tension between Kikuyu and Maasai, thrusts the reader into another, wholly strange world which fascinates and intrigues. That world is summed up by the child narrator's musings about one African: 'Perhaps he had words for his feelings, and his feelings were like mine, but I could never know.'[6] This is what makes the book so successful. By having both Kikuyu and Maasai in the house and on the farm, Elspeth can contrast one people with another, and employ each tribe's comments on the other's actions to display the elements of their society. The conversation of the Africans is made to conform to a particular pattern, with a variety of conjunctions and more imagery than is common in the English spoken word, and thus the reader is introduced to African ways of thought.

Elspeth's stress on the otherness of Africa is designed to excite readers by removing them, if only for a moment, from their own humdrum lives. They are introduced to it on the first page, when the ox-cart departs along a road which 'was not a thing that had been made, it had simply arisen from the passage of wagons'.[7] The oxen proceed into Africa's vastness, across a tawny plain that makes you feel you could walk straight on across it to the rim of the world, through wild animals still teeming in their millions. The sounds of Africa are everywhere – the calls of the birds, the singing of the Kikuyu, always in a minor key which made it sound plaintive, the incessant cicadas. And there were the mosquitoes, brilliantly encapsulated in the words 'no sound concentrates so much spitefulness and malice into a very small volume as the pinging of mosquitoes, as if needles tipped with poison were vibrating in a persistent tattoo'.[8] Elspeth certainly knew how to make words work. The heat and smells of Africa are present on every page. Elspeth describes how you can *see* heat:

> It seemed that everything was quivering – air, heat, grass, even the mules twitching their hides to dislodge flies who paid no attention; the strident insect falsetto seemed like the voice of air itself, chattering through all eternity to earth and grass. The light was blinding and everything was on a high note, intensified, concentrated: heat, light, sound, all blended into a substance as hard and bright and indestructible as quicksilver.
>
> I had never before seen heat, as you can see smoke or rain. But there it was, jigging and quavering above brown grasses and spiky thorn-trees and flaring erythrinas.* If I could have stretched my hand out far enough I could surely have grasped it, a kind of colourless jelly. But it danced away as I rode uncomfortably towards it, my mule's feet now and then tripping off tufts and hammocks.[9]

The smell of African travel – 'dry, peppery, yet rich and deep, with an undertone of native body smeared with fat and red ochre and giving out a ripe, partly rancid odour'[10] – is present with us when we accompany Elspeth and her parents, as is the strangeness and danger of it all. There is an excitement in wondering whether these incompetent creatures, white human beings, will survive in a country where yaws, bubonic plague, smallpox, malaria, parasites, typhoid, elephantiasis and blackwater fever are all endemic; where ticks and jiggas and siafu (soldier ants that attack sleepers in their beds) live wantonly, where every day seems to bring another of those gruesome little tragedies in which Africa abounds.

Because the whites are trying to tame this treacherous country,

---

* Erythrina Abyssinica, small, stiffly-branched, bushy-crowned trees up to twenty feet tall, with short, corky-barked boles. They are deciduous; when their branches are bare of leaves they produce spikes of brilliant scarlet blossoms. They are also known as flame trees, though to be distinguished from Spathodea Nilotica, an avenue of which Nellie planted at Kitimuru. Nellie thought the trees on the Flame Trees cover should be erythrinas rather than spathodeas, as they were more characteristic of Thika.

there is a feeling that they are bound to be defeated, in contrast to the Africans who have devised a way of living there by becoming entirely one with the landscape:

> They walked about their country without appearing to possess it – or perhaps I mean, without leaving any mark. To us, that was remarkable: they had not aspired to recreate or change or tame the country or to bring it under their control ... the natives of Africa had accepted what God, or nature, had given them without apparently wishing to improve upon it in any significant way. If water flowed down a valley they fetched what they wanted in a large hollow gourd; they did not push it into pipes or flumes, or harass it with pumps. Consequently when they left a piece of land and abandoned their huts (as eventually they always did, since they practised shifting culti- vation), the bush and vegetation grew up again and obliterated every trace of them, just as the sea at each high tide wipes out footprints and children's sand-castles, and leaves the beach once more smooth and glistening.[11]

Modern ecologists would recognise and applaud the Africans' hus- bandry. It is an idea much in vogue nowadays that people should live more closely with their environment, caring for it rather than destroying it.

Africa begins to take hold of the invaders, and Tilly gradually abandons attempts to preserve an appearance of leisured elegance. She comes to terms with the Africans' belief in spirits when she sees that Njombo's life can be saved only by the intervention of those intangible beings. She understands that people who appear quite healthy sometimes lie down and die, convinced they are bewitched: 'All the resources of our civilization were unavailing against the word of some obscure, ignorant and heathen wizard with his beans, bones and powders.'[12] The Kikuyu would not sit with a dying person, and dragged him out of the hut if he was going to die. If someone died in a hut, it had to be burnt down. Since hyenas ate the flesh of the dead and thereby possessed the spirits of ancestors, their howls reminded people of the timelessness of it all, as if they were saying 'It will be your turn one day, your flesh will rot, you shall join the great legion of the faceless and dissolved.' It dawns on the child narrator that perhaps it is a mistake to try to change Africans and their perception of time.

The ingrained European preoccupation with the future, the hope offered by the expectation of 'when my ship comes in', translated into the white farmer's 'when the coffee comes into bearing', sits uneasily beside the African way of life. The spell is broken by the outbreak of the First World War and the mobilisation of the white farmers to fight their German counterparts in Tanganyika. The coffee seedlings sown with much endeavour are left for the weeds to smother, while Robin goes off to war and Tilly and Elspeth embark on a train for Mombasa 'freighted heavily with fear and sorrow' and a ship to Europe.[13] Andrew the Maasai cook wants to go with them, and Tilly finds it impossible to explain to him the great gulf which lies between the ways of life in Africa and England, causing him to dash a clod of earth to the ground in anger. This incident actually occurred. Also truthful is the depiction of Tilly and Robin, who are accurately Nellie and Jos, their characters captured cleverly by their daughter – although when Elspeth sent her mother the manuscript Nellie responded, 'I am NOT like Tilly.'[14] One's estimation of oneself frequently differs from the judgement of others. The death which occurs near the end of the book is a fitting denouement and a symbol of the collapse, if only temporarily, of white endeavour in a hostile continent.

The Flame Trees of Thika aches for Africa, capturing a time and place gone for good. The pioneering days in Kenya were fleeting, and within sixty years the whites would be forced to leave. But the hopes of the incomers, and the reaction of the Africans, who could not understand air making water froth (soda water), and apparent eternal fire contained in glass (paraffin lanterns), explaining both phenomena as the work of spirits, are as butterflies pinned for ever in the pages of *Flame Trees*. There are no longer Kikuyu women with earlobes hanging down to their shoulders and breasts sagging like empty purses, plodding along with heavy loads strapped to their backs, any more than there are arrogant whites splashing them with mud by deliberately driving through the roads' puddles, and this is all to the good. But what had been lost was indicated by the early settler Edward Rodwell, who became the editor of the *Mombasa Times*, in a nostalgic letter to Elspeth:

> How we lived before there were bridges, how we bound our car springs with buffalo hide, dropped dung into the radiator when it leaked, or an egg, mended punctures, filled tyres with grass, could take an engine to pieces, cleaned carburettors, drove the car on kerosene once it was going; some used charcoal and one man from Eldoret even used a drum of cow manure in the boot to provide methane gas. Leaking roofs, white ants, snakes, cut open a snake bite and rub in potpermang, malaria, sloshed with iced water in the bath, 40 grains of quinine a day. Blackwater, tsetse, elephants on the Malindi road, wooden wheels, wooden driving wheels, self-made box bodies, mud, rivers across the road, siafu, leopards in the garden, hyenas taking chickens . . . camping on the road and that godsend Mac's Inn. What a time we had. Money nil or scarce. Posho [a porridge made out of maize meal, the staple diet of many Africans] for dinner.[15]

A week after sending Norah Smallwood the typescript of her first draft of *Flame Trees*, Elspeth wrote again to ask her to drop her a postcard if she thought it worth doing the sequel, taking the story up to 1925. Nothing was done at that stage, and a great opportunity was thereby lost. Essentially modest about her work – her friend James Lees-Milne said she always deprecated her own writing – Elspeth needed encouragement to proceed, and a second magnificent book would surely have resulted, which could have appeared a few months after *Flame Trees*, while it was still in the minds of the public. As it was, the sequel, *The Mottled Lizard*, was not written until a few years later, and although it was a splendid book, it did not reach the heights of *Flame Trees*.

In America, John Willey of Morrow was also spectacularly wrong in his judgement. He thought the readership of *Flame Trees* would be small, and that a book about two childhood years in Kenya before World War I, however felicitous in itself, would seem remote to most Americans. He added that the name of the author, though distinguished, did not in his estimation have the currency in America to overcome that impediment. He agreed to take 2,500 sheets of the British edition. However, when Nadine Gordimer in the *New York Times* gave the book a flattering review, he had to order a reprint of almost ten thousand. The US edition sold very well, even though it had a disappointing jacket, portraying, as Elspeth complained, 'a miserable little flower hovering on the top like an anaemic pimpernel, no resemblance to a Spathodea Nilotica whatever, and a BLACK ground'.[16] But Willey, eating his earlier words, did tell Norah Smallwood to encourage Elspeth to write a sequel.

The reviews upon publication in England in March 1959 were excellent. William Plomer's in the *Observer* was headlined 'Lucky Little Elspeth', causing Norah Smallwood to cable Elspeth, now at Njoro with her mother, 'Congratulations on first reviews stop reprinting forthwith stop lucky little Elspeth love Norah.' The success of *Flame Trees* went far beyond anything Elspeth's previous books had achieved. The British hardback was reprinted seven times, and translation rights were sold around the world, making her more well known, and financially better off, than she had ever been before. When Norah wrote expressing the hope that Elspeth had volume two in mind, Elspeth replied ironically that she was trying to decide between a Rolls-Royce and a Mercedes Benz. Nellie confessed to Norah that although she had seen how superb the writing was, she did not think all that much of the subject matter. She now realised how wrong she was. Apart from Elspeth, she was the one person who knew how fictional the book really was.

Flame Trees was published while Elspeth was in Africa busy researching another book. On one of his foreign tours the agricultural adviser to the Colonial Office, Sir Geoffrey Nye, had visited Nairobi. After seeing the work which had been done to rehabilitate African agriculture, he suggested the Kenya administration engage Elspeth to have a look at it and write a book on the achievement. When Michael Blundell, Kenya's Minister of Agriculture, was in

England in August 1957 he asked Elspeth to write about the agricultural revolution taking place in Kenya, where a tribal system of land tenure was being replaced by individual land ownership. Elspeth accepted the proposal and planned a factual travel book like *The Sorcerer's Apprentice* and *Four Guineas*. The Kenya government paid her first-class air fare, expenses and a fee. Elspeth asked Chatto & Windus whether they would be interested in publishing the book, and they rather reluctantly agreed, pointing out that what they really wanted was for Elspeth to write best-sellers for them – a not uncommon ambition of publishers.

Elspeth arrived in Kenya on 17 January 1959, and went straight to Njoro to spend a few days with her mother before beginning her research. Refusing to leave Gikammeh, Nellie had endured there the last flickers of the Mau Mau rebellion, now almost extinguished by British and Kenyan troops. She had had to sell her cows, her entire 1956 maize crop had been condemned because of mustiness, and a Mombasa greengrocer had cheated her of money for several deliveries of her vegetables. And she had grave doubts about the future of the whites in Kenya: 'What a lot of harm we've all done, so better stop doing it is what I say.'[17] She decided to sell the two hundred acres of farmland she had previously leased out, keeping only her house and fifty acres. Then her old friend and neighbour Fish Lindstrom died of cancer of the lung, and Nellie had to comfort his wife Ingrid. Ingrid insisted on returning Jos's suit which Fish had worn since Jos's death, and it was passed on to Mbugwa, who looked wonderful in it. Many other old friends died, one of them Lucy McMillan, widow of Sir Northrup.

Nellie was feeling, and showing, her age. Her top teeth had all been removed, she no longer found eating a pleasure, and lamented that only drink was left. Elspeth was very concerned about her, for she was getting far too tired and needed help on the farm, and her hearing was deteriorating. Nellie admonished her daughter: 'You mustn't take on so about not producing thousands of pounds from writing to salvage this farm. It is all my fault for wasting so much money and farming so badly.'[18] Intimations of mortality now persuaded her to make over to Elspeth her marriage settlement, worth

£22,000, because no duty would be payable if Nellie lived for another five years.

Now that Mau Mau was over, Nellie attempted to build bridges between the races. The Kikuyu residents of Njoro asked her to a tea party where she saw 'lots of old Mau Mau friends'.[19] She reciprocated by inviting twenty-two African ladies to tea. They asked how old she was, and she said three hundred. Mbugwa, still sweet and faithful and doing what he could to look after her, came in at that moment and Nellie said, ' "You have known me for 200 years, haven't you?" Without batting an eyelid he said, "I think slightly more, Madam." '[20] Elspeth's arrival cheered her immensely, and they flew together to the Masai Mara for a few days, to camp under trees beside the Talek river. Back at the farm, Elspeth organised a baraza with eight elderly African men, at which she served beer and a sheep, in order to gather from them some historical material for her book.

Elspeth began her travels to see the new Kenya, where, in response to the Mau Mau rebellion, almost 60 per cent of Africans were now enfranchised, directly electing eight African representatives to the Legislative Council. She was perplexed as she started her journey – 'I don't know what the answer is, but [white] people seem rather sad and puzzled when they talk about it all; no one has the least doubt that matters would achieve total chaos within a very short time if Africans took over, at any rate for many years. A very nice African D[istrict] O[fficer] came round with us, the nephew of the old chief Mumia . . . Am also to meet one of the very anti[-white] politicians. What a blight they really are, it is very hollow and empty, and one cannot see what they really have to offer the shamba-tillers of the bush.'[21] She believed that if Africans took over in the near future, 'corruption would clog the wheels and everything would slow down and stop'.[22] No one seemed to have any confidence in the Governor, Sir Evelyn Baring, who invited Elspeth for lunch at Government House. She found him 'nice – *too* nice really', and not tough enough. She toured among the Luo, Kipsigis and Kisii, Kakamega, Elgeyo and Suk peoples. As usual, the country entranced her: 'One could have a wonderful life here, if allowed to, politically. Only man is vile is certainly the answer and perhaps it would do as a title of my next book.'[23]

Elspeth then visited Kikuyu areas. As usual, all facilities were provided for her, and she toured in a cavalcade of agricultural officers and fleets of Land Rovers, or on specially chartered planes, to meet groups of Africans assembled for discussions. It was impossible to talk under such circumstances, or at least to get Africans to speak their minds. Unsurprisingly, she detected no visible signs of unrest, except in the African press – the paper *Uhuru* printed race hatred and subversion every day. After a flight to Tanganyika to stay with the Governor, Sir Richard Turnbull, a wise man, among whose *bons mots* was 'You cannot change Africa, Africa will change you,' Elspeth flew south to Salisbury (now Harare), the capital of Southern Rhodesia, to gather material for some articles commissioned by the *Sunday Times*. She found its Prime Minister, Sir Edgar Whitehead, quiet and efficient, dour and down-to-earth. The Governors of Nyasaland and Northern Rhodesia, with whom she subsequently stayed in their Government Houses, afforded her facilities to do research, and her articles were duly dispatched to the *Sunday Times*, before she headed homewards to England on 17 April 1959. It was a problematic journey – all three of the aircraft she boarded collapsed.

At Woodfolds she plunged at once into writing her book, fearful lest her material get too quickly out of date, and she delivered the typescript to Chatto & Windus at the end of November. Ten thousand copies of *A New Earth* were published in June 1960. Written in Elspeth's characteristically beautiful prose, the book analyses the progress which was striding through Africa 'at breakneck speed . . . an elemental force, like wind or sun or lightning, that doles out good or evil more or less impartially'.[24] She examines the new land consolidation; the development of agriculture; dam building; the increase in the African population; enclosure; the contrast between the old men, grizzled and proud, and their grandsons, bright-eyed and curious, sitting blue-shirted and beautifully behaved in the schools, eager for certificates. She sees both advantages and disadvantages in the introduction of European methods:

> It becomes continually more difficult to sustain a conviction that the introduction of money, literacy, taxes, votes, the doctrine of work and the religion of materialism; that the suppression of cattle-raids, magic, dancing, sacrifices and indigenous justice; that the end of contentment and the beginning of *angst*; that all these aspects of civilization have made life happier and fuller for the tribesmen. When they have turned their *kokwet* councils into political parties, their cattle-raids into football matches, their virgins into strip-tease artistes, will they be better off?[25]

Elspeth's doubts about this 'progress' were unfashionable at the time, but she saw what others perhaps did not – the value of a culture developed over centuries, and the unwisdom of overthrowing it. Today this is more widely recognised, but at the end of the 1950s her view was not popular, so eager were progressives to dismantle the past and force a 'liberated' Africa into a Westernised pattern of life, with Western methods of government, often inappropriate to the circumstances.

One reviewer said Elspeth emitted ideas like sparks from a Catherine wheel; she was an ideal observer who shattered illusions but was full of compassion and wonder. James Drew Bishop wrote in the *TLS* (15 July 1960): 'Whatever Kenya's political future there is no doubting its tremendous economic potential. Skimming off the political froth that bubbles impressively but so frequently bursts into nothing, Mrs. Huxley has revealed the true power that lies beneath. The enthusiasm, unspoken and perhaps largely unrecognized even by themselves, of the vast majority of Africans for developing this power spills into Mrs. Huxley's book and finds coherence in her brilliant and sympathetic description of a largely undiscovered country.' *The Times*'s reviewer wrote (30 June 1960): 'When Mrs. Huxley began writing in the 1930s her style had the efficiency of a well-designed machine; lately it has taken on a more human warmth. This glowed in *The Flame Trees of Thika* and suffuses *A New Earth*. No better book about contemporary Africa has been written by any living author.'

The book was also appreciated in America, though John Willey of Morrow cabled, asking Chatto to delete 'An Experiment in Colonialism' from the title page of the American sheets, as it would be 'most unselling' to the readers. The offending subtitle was duly deleted from title page and book jacket of the American edition.

Elspeth was heard on air as a panellist on *The Brains Trust* in June 1959 and in another session of *The Critics* in July. She continued to do occasional broadcasts for *Calling East Africa*, and was invited on to *Woman's Hour* on 8 July as Guest of the Week. Permitted to choose a piece of music for the programme she asked for either 'Jupiter' from Holst's *The Planets* or one of her favourite Somerset and West Country folksongs, from a gramophone record she liked listening to in the evenings, especially one called 'Hares on the Mountain' – in the event, 'Jupiter' was played. She took a short break in August, with a trip to Holland and a family holiday in Mull, to which the Huxleys now went every year.

Weekends were spent as they had been for several years – either having guests to stay at Woodfolds, or going to stay with family and friends. Elspeth enjoyed the company of others more than she did being alone with Gervas (plus Charles in his holidays from boarding school). She preferred to entertain or be entertained. Her circle of friends was large, and she maintained social relationships with many relatives on both her father's and her mother's sides of the family. She was also often visited by Kenya friends on leave in England. Aldous Huxley came to stay from America, and there were regular (and unwelcome) visits from Aldous's brother Julian and his wife. Elspeth was acquainted with other members of the literary establishment, such as Leonard Woolf, Evelyn Waugh, J.B. Priestley and his wife Jacquetta Hawkes, and Laurens van der Post, though on the whole this was not her milieu because she eschewed distinction by association and did not move in literary circles. The work of her fellow Chatto author van der Post she did not like, finding it egotistical and without humour – 'far too little Bushmen and too much Van der Post'.[26] Later she wrote van der Post's advance obituary for *The Times*, although she would outlive him by only a few weeks. Norah Smallwood also introduced her to another Chatto author, Laurie Lee, which led to Elspeth's errant cousin Peggy being given one of his manuscripts to type. And it was at Peggy's new home in Portmeirion that in 1963 Elspeth met Richard Hughes, yet another Chatto author, who was in terrific form, telling improbable stories. She also met Iris Murdoch and her husband John Bayley, whom she described as 'absolutely sweet'.[27]

One Kenya visitor in 1958 was Joy Adamson. She wanted Elspeth to collaborate further on her Elsa the lioness story, but Elspeth was disinclined to get embroiled again. She and Nellie, like many in Kenya's Game Department, disapproved of Joy's relationship with the lioness. Whenever Elsa went into the bush and appeared to be settling, Joy whistled her back. In a letter to Nellie Joy threatened to commit suicide if Elsa had to go to Rotterdam zoo, as had been suggested by the Game Department's head, Mervyn Cowie, who rightly refused to allow the lioness loose in any game park for fear her friendliness towards human beings would lead to disaster. Nellie told Elspeth she wished George, Joy's husband, would quietly put a bullet through Elsa's head.

There was the inexorable work of the farm to be done whenever Elspeth emerged from her study at the top of the house, intentionally far from the telephone so she could not hear its ring. When Vera Norris, the cowhand, got married in 1958, an event much welcomed by Elspeth, she turned up less frequently and her work became more erratic. But the farmhand Charlie Butcher continued to be of great assistance. Elspeth found him 'sweet and faithful and hard-working', though 'utterly unobservant and dense'.[28] Woodfolds now had a bull and a herd of fourteen Red Poll cows, Elspeth having exchanged these for the Jerseys of previous years because they were dual-purpose beasts. Every year she put down two to three acres of kale, and she grew fodder beet and cabbages, having to buy in only cattle cake and poultry food. The farm had three to six sows, some Wessex Saddlebacks and some seven-eighths Landrace, but they were prone to wander and needed expensive fencing. There were four to five hundred head of poultry (Brown Leghorn and Rhode Island Red crosses, and Buff Rock and Light Sussex

crosses), bought in as day-olds, and used solely for egg production
– ninety to 100 dozen eggs were sold weekly. Some of these hens
were housed in a two hundred-bird deep-litter house. As well as
the farm, Elspeth also had to look after three cottages in the village,
in a row near the playing field, one of them belonging to her
mother. All of them were let.

Gervas was now happily involved in his new career of research
and writing, working on his biography of Endymion Porter, which
was published by Chatto at the same time as *Flame Trees*. It got
splendid notices and became a Book Society recommendation. He
then embarked on a duller book, a biography of Nellie's friend
Trudie Denman. Judy Burrell, Trudie's daughter, offered a generous
subsidy to get the book published, and it appeared as *Lady Denman,
GBE** under the Chatto imprint in 1961. Later Gervas began his
autobiography, *Both Hands*, published in 1970, in which he gives
this frank estimation of his own personality:

> My lack of ambition has given no one cause for jealousy and
> I have always had a hatred of quarrelling. This might be
> because I am far too much of a 'yes-man', always seeking
> agreement, always inclined to see the other point of view and
> always reluctant to stand firm in opposition, especially over
> matters of principle. But this is not wholly due to weakness,
> since I have long been convinced that the pragmatic is the
> sensible approach to affairs, whether in my work or in general,
> and that conduct should be governed not by some principle
> for which a line of action is taken but by the practical conse-
> quence of taking that line.[29]

Unfortunately for Gervas, Elspeth took full advantage of the
opportunities to get her own way that such a personality allowed.
She also felt Gervas was not strict enough with Charles, and Nellie
encouraged her in this belief. Nellie thought Charles was bored at
receiving so much love from Gervas, and suffered tension at home
by feeling he had to 'play up to Pa'. Charles was unhappy at Rugby,
not being a good mixer, and Elspeth had to intervene with his

* (Dame) Grand Cross of the British Empire.

housemaster on his behalf. His academic work fluctuated, causing his mother much worry, and she wondered whether he had been put into too high a form. She was anxious that her child should not experience the same educational disadvantages she had suffered, and was determined that he should go to Oxford, his father's former university. She cultivated a friend, John Buxton, who was, she believed, the kingpin at New College in Oxford, in case Charles failed to get into Balliol, Gervas's old college. She wrote to Gervas of their son, 'He is not a great lover of hard work (as indeed who is) and it may well be the making of him to learn that distressing habit.'[30] Elspeth offered to give 'little' Ingrid, daughter of Viveka Lindstrom, Ingrid Lindstrom's daughter, a home base when she left Kenya to study in England, partly because she felt she would be a good influence on and a companion for Charles. And she was delighted when on one of the regular family summer holidays in Mull Charles found a girl he was persuaded to admit he could tolerate.

In October 1959, while absorbed in writing *A New Earth*, Elspeth received a letter from the government. It asked her to be a member of a Commission of Inquiry, under the chairmanship of Lord Monckton, to investigate whether the Federation of Northern Rhodesia (now Zambia), Southern Rhodesia (now Zimbabwe) and Nyasaland (now Malawi), set up in 1953, should remain *in situ*, or whether the three Central African countries should be permitted to go their own ways. The aim of federation had been to avoid the development of an apartheid system like that of neighbouring South Africa and to create a multi-racial society with a viable economy. But the Africans, already troubled by the failure of colonial boundaries properly to reflect tribal and regional realities, saw the Federation as an attempt to reinforce white supremacy, particularly as it tended to be dominated by Southern Rhodesia, which had had white self-government since 1923. They wanted the Federation to be broken up, and such was the clamour that the British government, anxious to dodge a situation that might lead to war, as had recently happened between Arabs and French in Algeria, determined to send a panel to the three territories to look into the situation. Altogether, six months' work was required of the members: three from mid-February 1960, touring the three countries, and the remainder in a London hotel helping to prepare the report.

Elspeth grumbled about the time this would keep her away from her writing – it certainly prevented her from starting the sequel to *Flame Trees* – but she accepted the challenge. Although 'committees were never my scene; if I had a point to make, someone always got in first; if I hadn't, impatience and boredom soon set in',[31] she regarded the invitation as an honour, despite telling the BBC she had been 'nagged and bullied into this ghastly job and must go like a sheep to the slaughter to Central Africa'.[32]

Gervas was relieved to see her off at the airport for a three-month stint in the Federation, surrounded by a posse of secretaries and typists, for she had been difficult to live with recently. He confided to Norah Smallwood: 'I hope three months in Africa will give her a rest – no writing, and every moment controlled by others! She really does need it. She was working quite impossibly hard, which was bad for her and for everyone else.'[33] At Nairobi airport Elspeth gave Nellie, who was waiting for her, some English snowdrops, then flew on to Salisbury and a thunder-battered Livingstone airport in Northern Rhodesia, just to the north of the Zambezi river and the majestic Victoria Falls, the spray from which could clearly be seen from the gardens of the delegation's hotel. Elspeth was taken to see the Falls after tea. For once lost for words, she could only tell Gervas they were 'staggering'.

Elspeth was one of the three non-political members and the only woman on the Commission, which immediately set to work in the Victoria Falls Hotel alongside American tourists and the evangelist Billy Graham. It was divided into three groups, and Elspeth found herself in the one headed by Sir Charles Arden-Clarke, with as fellow members Sir Lionel Heald MP, Aidan Crawley MP, 'a dim Nyasaland man' called Hadlow, Justice Beadle from Southern Rhodesia, and two Africans – Wellington Chirwa, from Southern Rhodesia, and Habanyama, from Northern Rhodesia. Not in her group as yet were Lord Crathorne (formerly Sir Thomas Dugdale), a bright and chatty man who looked the perfect English squire, and Frank Menzies, brother of the Australian Prime Minister, a sound, slow-spoken, easy-going and shrewd man with a lot of common sense. She singled out these two as congenial and bright.

Arden-Clarke, formerly Governor of the Gold Coast, looked hard and had been toughened by surviving blackwater fever, bacillary and amoebic dysentery, malaria and Dr Nkrumah, but he was an excellent chairman, gentle though firm, standing no nonsense but hearing everyone out. Elspeth found him somewhat conceited, too gubernatorial at times, but generally likeable. Habanyama was a 'good' African employed by the Northern Rhodesian government, intelligent and balanced, with a pleasant face and worried expression; Hadlow a tea agent in Nyasaland, deaf and a bit of a stick without any original ideas, but with a hidden passion for science fiction; Heald a lean elderly man with a bony face, sweet and not pompous, balanced and keen to learn (Elspeth told Gervas she had quite fallen for him); and Chirwa, who had agreed to join the Commission only at the last moment, a tiresome monopoliser of sessions, refusing to leave witnesses alone, trying to argue with them and contesting their views. In the plenary sessions Monckton was a patient chairman, anxious to avoid any hint of trying to suppress African views, a man so unassuming and gentle that Elspeth thought he would calm an angry buffalo.

Immediately the Commission was plunged into controversy. Roy Welensky, Prime Minister of the Federation and passionately in favour of its continuance (because Northern Rhodesia had copper, Southern Rhodesia agriculture, and Nyasaland provided the labour force), challenged the terms of reference. He claimed it had never been intended that the Commission examine whether the Federation should break up; rather, the purpose was to see how it could go forward. Welensky was a friendly, frank man with great charm who took the Cold War Russian threat very seriously. Communists in the guise of a Czech mission were already in the Congo, while the Soviet President Nikita Khrushchev was soon to visit Conakry in Guinea. He stressed that the Federation was a bulwark against

Communism, though British rule in Nyasaland was so weak and chaotic that it should be replaced by leadership from Salisbury in Southern Rhodesia. Two days were spent idle while telegrams flashed to and fro between London and Victoria Falls defining the Commission's terms of reference. Eventually Welensky prevailed – to the fury of Chirwa, who was a secessionist and caused trouble thereafter – though Monckton made it clear that they must allow those who advocated secession to give evidence.

Elspeth's group was joined after a few days by the former British Attorney General Lord Shawcross with his attractive, rather wicked face which in repose looked cruel and bad-tempered. He did not last long because a bad back put him in hospital; when he first arrived he told Elspeth that this had been caused by carrying his son's heavy suitcase up the stairs at Eton, but he later blamed the rough African roads and badly sprung Land Rovers, which he had never even been near – presumably, Elspeth surmised, in order to have his medical bills paid by the government. He was not the only casualty – Aidan Crawley developed hepatitis which put him too in hospital, and the Rhodesian Judge Beadle developed pneumonia.

The Commission members travelled by Land Rover and small Beaver and Apache planes all over the three territories, though Elspeth's group spent most of their time in Northern Rhodesia. Wherever they stopped they heard witnesses, both white and black. The African members could not resist arguing with the sillier white witnesses and helping out the sillier Africans, so the interviews took twice as long as was necessary. Inevitably the Commission heard the same things over and over again, but there were some moments of light relief. A bright spot was hearing one Mrs Catchpole expressing the most liberal ideas possible about African majorities, the evils of federation, and the benefits of multi-racial schools, to be followed by Mr Catchpole speaking grimly about fighting for his rights and resisting to the death any attempts by black nationalism to trample on him. At the Sal-Ila-Kaunde Native Authority in Barotseland the elders wore MA robes of Exeter University, which they had bought in bulk from an enterprising Exeter firm. At a demonstration outside a town hall a bare-footed African girl wearing only a cloth and with a baby on her back carried a poster reading 'Vox Populi Multi Vox Dei'.

At a copper mine they were taken round the impressive and alarming surface workings, where the molten copper resembled liquid fire, like something out of a horror film. In the library an African was teaching himself English by going slowly through the two volumes of the *Shorter Oxford English Dictionary* and learning every word – he had got to 'crocodile'. In Northern Rhodesia almost everyone was anti-Federation and blamed it for everything under the sun. In one place elderly Africans walked for miles through swamps to tell the Commission they hated federation because it came between themselves and the Queen and they wished to be ruled by Her Majesty, not by black nationalists. This was hardly what Chirwa wanted to hear, but it was not as troubling as the lunatic white woman with fanatic eye who raved for half an hour about Africans, saying they were a separate sub-species with inferior brains and filthy habits, especially relating to sex, and still practised cannibalism and immoral customs like polygamy. In Bulawayo an African boasted that his father had kept four slaves, so he resented being called a nigger by European boys with slaveless fathers.

Commission members were guarded like crown jewels by police, and whenever Elspeth tried to go for a walk to stretch her legs after sitting for hours hearing evidence, cars would stop and offer her a lift, walking being an unknown pastime for whites in Northern Rhodesia. In Nyasaland she managed to get away by herself to climb Mlanje mountain – it was 'very pleasant and solitary up there, though hardly the solitary lost peak of Laurens Van der Post, as my path followed a telephone and power line which goes to the forest station near the top. There was also a Jeep track most of the way.'[34] At the end of every day there were sundowner parties, which Elspeth hated, finding having to bellow above the noise distressing. The only way she could get through them was on gin and tonic, which soon began to affect her health and her sleep. She would have preferred quieter evenings, with a chance to read the mounds of paper which deluged the Commission members.

Elspeth had a very visual imagination and a sharp eye which noticed all the birds, varieties of vegetation, skies and sunsets, and her diary of these months is replete with descriptions of them. There were excursions to caves covered in ancient rock paintings in the Matopos hills, and the obligatory visit to Cecil Rhodes's grave there. The puzzling ruins of the stone-built palace of the ancient kingdom of Zimbabwe were shown to her, and she saw the Kariba dam being built, being taken six hundred feet below the surface of the earth to a huge chamber containing the turbines. Scooped out of solid rock, it was 'a great underground cavern full of men welding and hammering . . . like some queer armoury of the gods or devils in a nordic myth'.[35]

As the weeks progressed, she came to the conclusion that there was no alternative but a British withdrawal from Africa, to 'give them [Africans] responsibility and let them make their mistakes. What happens to European enterprise on which all depends is of course the key factor and no one knows the answer. But one can't for that reason hope to halt the wave, even if it is going to sweep away much that the Africans depend on.'[36] She began to abhor the views of most whites that Africans were children led by the nose by a small minority of agitators, and that the only solution was to stand firm and keep the native in his place.

It was astonishingly brave of Elspeth to admit that she had formerly been wrong. This was a defining moment, the first time she had expressed such views. Hearing the evidence of so many Africans had convinced her that the British had to leave Africa, and that this had better happen sooner rather than later, to avoid black uprisings. The experience of the Mau Mau rebellion must have coloured her opinions, but she was also sensitive to the climate of the times. Harold Macmillan, Elspeth's former publishing adversary and now British Prime Minister, on a tour of Africa just before the Commission left London, had spoken of a 'wind of change blowing through this continent'.

What had happened to Britain's colonial policy to cause the Prime Minister to express this view? Undoubtedly the nationalist movements in Africa had weakened Britain's will; but there was another factor. The Cold War had polarised the superpowers, the USA and the USSR. African nationalist movements whose demands were not being met could turn to the USSR for help, as had happened in the Congo. Africans could play off one superpower against the other, a most unsatisfactory situation. If Britain gave her colonies independence, then she and the USA helped with development projects, the newly independent nations might maintain their allegiance to the West. Britain also had a forward-looking Colonial Secretary, Ian Macleod, who forced Macmillan's hand. He released the nationalist leader Hastings Banda from prison while the Monckton Commission was in Nyasaland, much to its annoyance, and he also insisted that Jomo Kenyatta be freed in Kenya.

When the Monckton Report was published in 1960, it recommended changes in the constitution of the Federation of the Rhodesias and Nyasaland which would benefit Africans, and changes in the racial policy of Southern Rhodesia. It also envisaged the possibility of secession from the Federation. Elspeth played a full part in the deliberations, and agreed with the conclusion that the Federation should break up. Following the report, Nyasaland and Northern Rhodesia effectively seceded from the Central African Federation; they became independent in 1964. Southern Rhodesia refused to alter its constitution to allow Africans to rule, and in 1965 Prime Minister Ian Smith made a Unilateral Declaration of Independence from Britain. Rhodesia did not emerge as a sovereign state under African rule until 1980.

Was the Monckton Commission mere window-dressing, and had the British government in the guise of the Colonial Secretary already made up its mind about what was to happen in Central Africa? The Labour Party, not in office, appeared to think this was so, for it chose not to participate in the Commission, to Elspeth's displeasure: 'It's a pity Labour have opted out of the Monckton Commission. *Something* has got to be settled and it seems an odd way to help Africans, as they say they want to, by taking no part in decisions about their future and doing nothing to get their case across.'[37] When asked about the Commission in later years, Elspeth said she was unaware at the time of any hidden agenda, but that she did get the impression that they were there to drive a nail into the Federation's coffin. There was nothing one could put one's finger on, and Monckton was 'oily' and never gave anything away. She said the Commission did consider the possibility of breaking up the Federation, which it was not supposed to do, but this was because of Macleod's determination to abandon military commitments in the colonial empire and Macmillan's endorsement of this in his 'wind of change' speech. She personally felt the British government had been devious, and this was not the right way to go about things, but Macleod and Macmillan were probably right that rebellion would have to be put down by force, and it was more sensible to surrender; liberal opinion in Britain would not have stood for bloodshed. She pointed out that Britain's retirement from Africa let down a good many people, mostly white, particularly those who felt they had sacrificed themselves for others only to be told that they had been exploiting them all along.

There was one light-hearted result of the Monckton Commission – Elspeth wrote a very funny novel, *The Merry Hippo* (called *The Incident at the Merry Hippo* in America), about a mythical African country called Hapana (Swahili for 'no'), to which the Connor Commission is sent to report on constitutional changes. Like the Monckton Commission it boasts only one woman, Mrs Tripp, who felt she 'owed it to her sex not to be pushed into a corner'.[38] The right technique was to plunge in at once to speak, otherwise others purloined what you wanted to say. Like its real-life counterpart, the fictional Commission was being used as a delaying tactic by the imperial government: 'The great point about Hapana was to prevent its affairs – always explosive despite the fact . . . that most of it was underwater – from erupting at a particularly awkward moment for the Cabinet. This Commission ought to keep things quiet for six months or so.'[39] In Hapana they encounter Chief Faustus, resplendent in a scarlet robe faced with purple, the MA gown of Llandudno University, which his nephew had attended. The chief likes the gown so much he has adopted it as a royal uniform. The exciting finale of the novel takes place in a copper-smelting plant very similar to the one Elspeth visited in Northern Rhodesia.

Elspeth pokes gentle fun at the members of the Commission, as well as at witnesses both black and white. She later told an enquirer that the following scenes, in which evidence is given to the Commission, were just the sort of thing that had happened on the Monckton Commission, and indeed uncannily similar incidents are recounted in the daily diary she kept in Central Africa:

'Have you given any thought to the question of universal suffrage?'

The president nodded vigorously. 'Oh, yes, we have.'

'You have?' the Chairman sounded surprised. 'And your conclusions?'

'That is what we have. We do not want it any longer.'

'Universal suffrage?'

'*Universal*.' She threw her arms out wide.

'Surely only those with an annual income in excess of a hundred and twenty pounds a year or immovable property –'

'Our suffrage is universal! Among all our women! We feed the hens, we look for eggs, we clean them, we take them to markets and there is no one to buy them. We want these suffrages to finish! To finish now!'

Next came a Mrs. Ruby Grubb, relict of the Keeper of an Ethnological Museum, with a paper on cannibalism, human sacrifice, ritual murders and bestiality among the Chuma which, despite all the Chairman's charm, entreaties and finally bullying, she read from beginning to end. It took forty-five minutes.[40]

'I am the President. I am the President of the Penumbra District Council. First, I tell you the history of my people, the Waguma. You know the great King Chaka and Musuma, his general. Now one day this general came with his *impis* to the country of the Pangani and saw a white bullock there. He said, "I will slay this bullock and take the liver and –"'

'Forgive me, Mr. President, that's very interesting,' the

Chairman said, 'but our purpose here is to frame a new constitution for Hapana. Isn't all this . . .'

'He said, "I will slay this bullock, and grind its liver with the sap of the *mugumu* tree to anoint the warriors, and then God will help us conquer all this country." So he told his councillors to fetch his new spear . . .'

The story went on for ten minutes before Sir Christopher interrupted again.

'Mr. President, we are all very interested in what you have to say, but can you tell us something about the *constitution* of Hapana? Have you considered on what basis the franchise should be framed?'

There was a short silence. The President was not used to being interrupted, and needed time to adjust himself.

'I will consult my council,' he said at length. In low, musical voices and stately periods the five Councillors conferred in their own tongue.

'Mr. Chairman, we have their memorandum in front of us,' Mrs Tripp pointed out. 'It sets out very clearly their suggestions on the constitutional issues. Franchise, composition of Assembly, bicameral legislature, Council of Ministers, reserved powers, relations with neighbouring territories – it's all here. Can't we question them on it?'

'Go ahead, Mrs. Tripp, by all means.'

Amelia Tripp cleared her throat. 'Mr. President?' The Councillors continued their conference.

'They do not understand they can be addressed by a lady,' the Rev. Zaza intervened. 'I will ask them. Chief, will you open your ears? This lady has a question to ask. In England she is herself a Chief. She addresses you as an equal. The Chairman is a cousin of the Queen and he is asking you to hear her. Please, madam, now ask your question.'

Mrs. Tripp felt embarrassed, like someone forced to repeat to a deaf acquaintance for the third time an observation on the weather. 'You demand in your memorandum,' she began, 'the immediate introduction of one-man-one-vote. Also a democratically elected Council of Ministers, independence back-dated to last January, and union with Ghana. These are rather sweeping demands, you know. Take universal suffrage, for instance. Do you really want all the *women* to have the vote?'

The faces of the Councillors looked blanker than before. The President coughed, and said: 'Madam?'

'Is this what you want? Women voting equally with men?'

'What we ask the Government,' one of the other Councillors intervened to say in loud, strong tones, 'is for a new market at Kumbula. Five years ago, Mr. Butler the District Commissioner made this promise. A new market, with latrines. Our market now is very little. Too many come, and the people are cheated. The goats can eat the yams because it is without fences. We ask –'

'Yes, yes, but the *franchise*, Councillor. The vote.'

The Councillor shook his head. Another of the five cleared his throat and spoke.

'We are needing in Penumbra a new school. Our school is too little and many children come. The teacher's house is falling down. We need . . .'

'It doesn't look as if the Councillors' memorandum is an exact reflection of their views,' the Chairman remarked. 'Mr. Zaza, perhaps you could interpret? Did they write this memorandum themselves?'

An animated conversation in a Hapanan tongue followed between the Councillors and the Rev. Zaza, who grew quite excited.

'Mr. Chairman,' he reported, 'these Councillors did not write this paper at all.'

'Then who did?'

'Their clerk wrote it. He is an educated man.'

'It's a very educated paper. Do they know what it says?'

'The clerk read it to them, but not the same as what is written here. It was about markets, schools, a new road and the price of yams. Then the clerk translated it into English.'

'A free translation, evidently. Perhaps we'd better sound them on their real views. Please ask them, Mr. Zaza, if they would like everyone to vote equally, women the same as men.'

The question, once translated, appeared to be involved and long, but there was no doubt about their response. With one accord they thundered a single resounding word.

'They say no,' Goliath Zaza reported.

'Would they like to see a democratically elected parliament with sovereign powers and no reserved seats?'

The Rev. Zaza looked a little dubious. 'That is rather hard to translate. But I will try.'

He did so; surprisingly, the question was much briefer. The response was the same, perhaps even more vehement.

'How did you translate it?' the Chairman asked. 'I asked if they wished to be governed by Mr. Mguu,' Zaza replied. 'They said no.'

'But that isn't quite the same thing?'

'But yes, Mr. Chairman, it is. The Triple-P has bribed most of the electors and frightened all the rest by burning down their houses. That is what I have often told Mr. Butterfield. If my party, the Forever Forward Group –'

'I take your point, Mr. Zaza. Well, I'm glad to have cleared that up. I'm not quite sure how we should record their evidence in the minutes, Hugo? Perhaps they would like to submit a revised memorandum? You might explain that to them, Mr. Zaza. I don't know what we should do, I'm sure, without your help.'

Two nuns were the next to give evidence. They wished to see more religious instruction in schools, an end to female circumcision and fewer child marriages.

'I'm sure we're all in favour of your proposals,' Amelia Tripp said. 'For instance, child marriage. But as there's no registration of births, how can you know a girl's age?'

The nuns looked puzzled. They had soft, white, pudgy faces under their coifs, and amiable expressions; one wore pince-nez and was middle-aged, the other had badly fitting dentures and was younger.

'There could be a law passed,' said the older nun in a soft, high Irish voice, 'to make it wrong for any girl to marry until three years after she was circumcised.'

'But you want to do away with female circumcision?'

'Och yes, and so we do. The Bishop is very strong on that, your Honours.'

'Well then, if the girls *weren't* circumcised . . .'

'It has been a shock to me, I must admit it, quite a shock,' Dr. Rumble intervened, 'to find this primitive rite being practised in our nuclear age right here in the heart of a British colony, where your British flag has flown for over fifty years. I needn't remind you gentlemen – and lady – of the importance of the home in the progress of the human family. Now if in the heart and centre of the home we have these unfortunate girls to whom the benefits of Christianity and the democratic way of life have not yet been extended . . .'

'You're quite right, Dr. Rumble, but if we could get back to, let's say, the composition of the Central Legislative Assembly . . .'

'Mr. Chairman, it is part of the policy of the Forever Forward Group –'

'Mr. Chairman,' said Sir Jeremy, 'may I suggest that we adjourn for tea?' Before anyone could speak again, the Chairman was on his feet.[41]

Cecil Day Lewis's sense of humour appears to have deserted him when he read the manuscript as Chatto's reader. He found the book agreeable up to halfway through, when he felt the story began to sag and lose its grip on the reader. He thought the tone uncertain, with official meetings of the Commission, of which there were perhaps too many, teetering on the edge of comedy and sometimes tumbling into farce. Happily, on this occasion the publisher ignored his opinion.

Elspeth took immense pains to avoid libel in this affectionate satire of an African country approaching independence. The manuscript of 'Shooting Star',* as the book was then called, was sent to Lord Monckton, who had no objections to anything written about

---

* The title had to be changed at the last moment because Chatto's agent in Africa told them that a book of the same name had appeared two years ago from another English publisher who pushed out a vast number of copies to Africa with a fanfare of publicity, only for it to be a flop. Since the booksellers were left with large overstocks, a book of the same title would not endear itself to them.

the Chairman of the Connor Commission. Nor did he think other members of his Commission would object, with the possible exception of Wellington Chirwa who, like Mansfield Matunda in the manuscript, was large and bulky, an African nationalist and politician, and commonly believed to owe a lot of money. Elspeth countered that Chirwa was a jovial character and well liked by everyone, despite a tendency to borrow money from the more soft-hearted members of the Commission. But the lawyer Michael Rubinstein, who read the book for libel, thought she should take Monckton's warning about Chirwa seriously. Since he was chronically short of cash he would probably take the opportunity to make money. He was unhappy about the character's tendency to borrow money, and suggested Elspeth give him some Empire honours, a beautiful, sweet and wealthy wife, and a notable sporting record (before his muscle turned to fat). He added that he thought Lord Crathorne, the Deputy Chairman of the Monckton Commission, might be offended by the portrayal of Lord Bagpuse, holder of the same office in the novel. Elspeth did as she was asked, particularly modifying the character of Matunda, and, for safety's sake, proofs were sent to both Crathorne and the senior civil servant who was secretary of the Monckton Commission. Neither made any objection.

Another modification was made for the American edition. John Willey of Morrow wanted the stupid, pompous American member of the Commission to be made British, but Elspeth would not have this. They compromised at Canadian. Norah Smallwood and Elspeth tended to make fun of John Willey, and their letters to each other, always full of irony, now became peppered with Hallelujas, in reference to a letter Willey had written to Elspeth, who found him ridiculous but rather beguiling. Willey had unwisely added a 'Hallelujah!' to his expression of pleasure that he was publishing another of Elspeth's books in 1962. The badinage ceased when Willey and his wife spent a weekend at Woodfolds in 1963, and Elspeth found him sympathetic and intelligent.

Published in April 1963, *The Merry Hippo* sold about nine thousand copies in Britain. Charles thought it his mother's best novel.

It was not only a novel that resulted from Elspeth's membership of the Monckton Commission – on 1 September 1960 she received a personal letter of thanks from Prime Minister Harold Macmillan, and in 1962 she was informed: 'The Prime Minister has asked me to tell you he had in mind in the forthcoming Birthday Honours to submit your name to the Queen for a CBE.'[42] She accepted the honour, telling a friend in the BBC, 'The unexpected is usually something nasty; it is a lovely change to have the ego boosted instead of slapped down.'[43] She had many letters of congratulation, including one from the Governor of Tanganyika, Sir Richard Turnbull, who said he had 'for so long been a devoted admirer of your writings'.[44] The CBE was the sole public honour Elspeth obtained, despite the efforts of several people to have her made a dame. This was not the climate in which a higher award could be made, however, because the gallop towards independence by African countries and Britain's determination to be rid of her colonies meant that it was impossible to honour someone who had had reservations about that policy in the past.

TEN

A Productive Decade

Elspeth's most productive years, in the late 1950s and early 1960s, were marred by domestic upheavals. It is remarkable that she could write so much with her support structure collapsing, but some of her best work was produced at this time. Perhaps her concentration was deeper as her working time diminished. The pattern of her day was constant. She rose early in the morning, tapping at the typewriter as the birds began to sing. The vying chorus woke guests and family. Then, after breakfast, prepared by Cleggy, she went back upstairs to her study and spent the morning writing. Lunch, again prepared by Cleggy, was the herald of her other work, upon the farm, done in the afternoons. Supper, cooked by Cleggy, ushered in the evening spent with Gervas in the Long Room, reading, each alone or to the other, or listening to the radio, or sometimes sampling television. The television had been given to Gervas when he was ill, to watch in his room, but had now come downstairs to the large hall. The Long Room was divided by a velvet curtain, separating the area at the far end, with open fire and easy chairs and books around the walls, from the colder, more formal end adjacent to the hall.

Apart from being a good cook, Cleggy was skilled with the sewing needle, and made many of Elspeth's dresses. She did other sewing for the family, as well as local shopping. Though Charles was in his mid-teens and no longer required a nanny, Cleggy looked after him when his parents were away. Alas, both Elspeth and Gervas found Cleggy a trial. She could be dour of temper and was a limited conversationalist. None the less, she and Elspeth depended on each other. In 1960 Cleggy began to suffer from back pain, diagnosed by the doctor as arthritis of the spine. Elspeth put her to bed, but in September the pain got so bad that Cleggy entered Malmesbury Hospital. It was the school holidays, and Elspeth was cross: 'I'm hoping she'll emerge eventually but I should think only about 50% of capacity, which was never all that high. Meanwhile I keep the family fed.'[1] Cleggy made no progress, and indeed there was little incentive for her to get better, as Woodfolds was having its kitchen renovated, with men pulling up floorboards, knocking down walls, drilling, hammering and requiring constant cups of tea.

The doctors were at sea over Cleggy, who was moved to Bath Hospital, then an appalling, dirty place – like Scutari before Florence Nightingale, said Gervas. She shared a ward with a patient suffering from gangrene in both feet who raved and moaned incessantly. Nellie, ever the practical provider of help, stepped in with the suggestion that 'little' Ingrid, her goddaughter and Ingrid Lindstrom's granddaughter who was now studying in England, should go to Woodfolds temporarily to do the cooking, and when she had to leave Mbugwa could take over. Elspeth accepted little Ingrid, but wisely refused to have Mbugwa over from Africa. Mrs Mills, Elspeth's former housekeeper, also stepped in to help.

Elspeth, like her mother, found physical pain and illness in others disturbing; she preferred the sufferers to endure them with fortitude. A hard childhood had left her believing that strength of mind was the solution to pain and distress. The thought of having to care for Cleggy appalled her, and she looked into the question of convalescent homes while Nellie nagged her by letter that the break from Cleggy should come NOW. Elspeth ignored her, and found a convalescent home in Warminster. She was reluctant to have Cleggy back at Woodfolds: 'I'm afraid she's bound to need a lot of attention and it just isn't the same with all the responsibility of looking after her and talking to her and so on, which interferes so much with one's concentration. However there it is. It is all going to be very tricky.'[2] And 'FAR her best plan is a home, but she's dead against it ... I just don't feel I could cope, for years to come, harsh as perhaps it is.'[3] Cleggy then suggested she should move into the front room of the cottage occupied by the farmhand Vera and her husband, but Vera was loath to agree to this. Cleggy became suicidal, and eventually upon making some improvement she returned to Woodfolds, far from fit. She continued to work there, but in December 1962 her ailment was diagnosed as a brain tumour. This explained her behaviour, which had become erratic, and her treatment of her employer, which was increasingly rude, though she had never been one to kowtow and repress her own opinions.

Ultimately it was decided that she should live in Green End, a cottage the Huxleys had bought from the Woodhouses next door. It was very near Woodfolds, at the end of the drive joining the lane to the village. But Cleggy was admitted to the Frenchay Hospital in Bristol in January 1966, and, according to Elspeth, had five operations on her brain. She was removed to Malmesbury Hospital in a coma, and there she died in the last week of January, having been with the Huxleys for twenty years. Elspeth was subdued by Cleggy's death. She wrote to Norah Smallwood: 'All is well here though I am feeling saddened by Cleggy's demise. One gets used to people after twenty years under the same roof despite inevitable mutual irritations and I miss her a lot, and she was so very gallant, and basically generous, and it was all set to work out so well for her in the cottage and all. One feels a gap sadly and it is a very small household now.'[4] Charles, whom Cleggy had been brought from Kenya to care for, was working in the USA, and was therefore unable to attend her funeral.

For Elspeth, Charles's teenage years were most trying. Not a natural mother, she found it difficult to understand adolescent moods, lethargy and insolence, all hard to bear even for the most experienced of parents. In letters to Nellie she described her son, now as tall as his father and able to wear his suits, as unambitious and unsociable. She compared him unfavourably with the son of one of the secretaries to the Monckton Commission, who had a girlfriend already and took holiday jobs to earn money. She hoped little Ingrid, a year older than Charles, would bring him out socially.

There were severe parental anxieties about how Charles would do in his A-level examinations in 1961. When he entered the sixth form at Rugby, it appeared he had chosen the wrong subjects. Elspeth thought that even though he was not a born mathematician, he ought to take his A-levels in maths and physics – 'there's nothing else he could take it in, and as he is mentally quite bright, perhaps in the long run it won't do him any harm to have to slog away at something he's not all that keen on. Lots of children are not keen on any form of work and I think he comes in that category! But they have to learn to do it. After A level a lot needs thinking about.'[5] From Nyasaland Elspeth urged Gervas to see that Charles did at least two hours' work a day on maths and physics in the holidays. Gervas, however, realised his son was on the wrong track, and talked to Rugby to get things put right. Any achievement on her son's part immensely cheered Elspeth, with her driven personality. She was delighted when he was chosen for the part of the god Ra in a school play, and his selection for Rugby's first cricket XI did something to redeem him in her eyes, though even in that triumphant moment she found reason for doubt: 'Gervas's dear little one has further lifted his morale by getting his first XI cricket colours for Rugby – I should think at the expense of getting into Oxford, as one can't study physics AND play that protracted game.'[6]

As it happened, Elspeth was right. It came as a body blow, particularly for Gervas, when Charles was rejected by Oxford's Balliol College, his alma mater, in October 1961. Relations between parents and child did not improve, and Nellie commented: 'It is boring for you Charles being so unco-operative. Gervas sounds almost as if he had been drained of paternal love but THAT won't undo the harm of years of utter spoiling.'[7] Both Nellie and Elspeth were firmly of the opinion that Charles had been ruined by what they considered the excessive love and attention of his father. But the situation had to be retrieved, and Elspeth stepped in to do the transporting to a crammer and to interviews and examinations for a second try at Oxford.

Towards the end of January 1962 Charles was accepted by Oriel College. One might have thought his mother would be thrilled, but she commented: 'After tortured months of struggle and defeat,

Charles has got a place at Oxford for next October – at Oriel. I can't think why they accepted him.'[8] He was then sent for six months at considerable expense to Aix-en-Provence, where he learnt to speak fluent French and became friendly with a German girl. Perhaps unsurprisingly, he was markedly reluctant to return home. But he showed up in September, promptly to damage Elspeth's Mini in a traffic accident. Elspeth must have commented on his general attitude to his parents to elicit this from Nellie: 'How awful for Charles to be so bloody-minded for so long – over a year now. It is very bitter for Gervas but – whodunit? He didn't seem to get much out of Rugby – no friends, no interests.'[9]

Charles duly went to Oxford in October 1962. Unfortunately he wrote with youthful bravado to Nellie that he was bored, that university education was pointless, but 'one puts up with it somehow and whiles away the time'.[10] This was as a red rag to a bull for Nellie and Elspeth, both of whom had had their Oxbridge ambitions thwarted, Nellie by the social climate of her time and Elspeth by inadequate teaching. Charles, 'who has never had a country love, nor ever been fond of an animal', both of which were of supreme importance to Nellie, deserved a good spanking from Gervas, she said. She had a French neighbour, one Chauvain, and she organised for Charles and some friends to spend the summer of 1963 as crew on his yacht in the Mediterranean. But Chauvain asked the youths to leave at Marseilles owing to their idleness and inability to get up in the mornings. When Charles got home Gervas bought him a car – 'I suppose Gervas *likes* spending money on Charles,' was Nellie's comment.[11] Nellie visited England the following summer, and found Charles estranged from his family. It appears that Elspeth had temporarily abandoned the attempt to relate to her son.

An only child can so concentrate a mother's hopes and fears that far too onerous a burden is put upon him. Before Charles's birth Elspeth had had no experience of children, never having had siblings and suffered the consequent rivalry for attention that explains much child behaviour. She was an utter innocent as Charles was growing up. No wisdom gleaned from books or study prepared her for what teenagers are like. Charles was behaving normally, but Elspeth found it difficult to cope. Part of the trouble was that she was distracted by Gervas, whose health had been deteriorating for a while. She suggested going to Africa to buck him up, but he refused to accompany her on her visits to Kenya, saying he never wanted to go there again. Nellie was deeply hurt, not recognising that Gervas did not want to come because he so detested the at times brittle atmosphere between mother and daughter, and was frankly bored at Gikammeh.

Gervas was also having difficulties overseeing his 120-acre dairy farm, Coole's, which had never been profitable and from which he no longer derived any pleasure, because his working manager Ted left in March 1960. He became more convinced than ever that he should sell when it was announced in the budget of April that year that farm losses could no longer be set against income from other sources, because many people had 'hobby' farms to reduce their tax burdens. This was indeed true of Elspeth and Gervas, though neither considered their farm a hobby, and both strained for ever elusive profits from their agricultural activities. 'What's the point of voting Conservative if they introduce socialist legislation?' was Elspeth's furious comment as she estimated they would have to pay an extra £2,000 tax a year – £500 which would now be ineligible for rebate, £500 as the loss on Woodfolds and £1,000 as surtax.[12] She failed to see how Woodfolds could possibly be regarded by the tax inspector, who she believed hated her anyway, as being run 'with reasonable expectation of profit' when it had suffered continuous losses for ten years. And she was astounded the following year to be asked to become a general commissioner for Inland Revenue for the Malmesbury district. She had been a thorn in their flesh for years, and suspected the suggestion was probably ironic. She refused.[13]

The profits from the sale of Gervas's farm allowed him to travel to South Africa (without Elspeth) in January 1961, but he returned ill, with an ulcer and low blood pressure. With too few red corpuscles in his blood, he felt depressed and was unable to do much. Then he was plunged into gloom by the failure of the *Sunday Times* to review his *Lady Denman, GBE.* Elspeth was impatient with him, and thought he did not have the temperament to be a writer if the buffetings of fate so got him down. A doctor put him on a restricted diet and in June advised a stomach operation in Bristol Hospital, from which he did not recover as quickly as had been hoped. Festooned with tubes and fed through a vein, Gervas was miserable. He lost a stone in hospital and it was some time before he was allowed home, with instructions that he must be fed every two hours.

He slowly recovered during the rest of the year, but failed to regain complete fitness and began to be irritated by the constant parade of weekend guests. He asked Elspeth to stop inviting them, but Nellie supported her daughter in the matter, arguing that it hardly put Gervas to any extra work, and that members of his side of the family came as frequently as those from Elspeth's. Someone he always welcomed seeing, however, was Aldous Huxley, his cousin and former childhood friend, now very frail and thin, and upset about the accidental burning down of his Californian home with all his possessions inside. 'He looks,' said Elspeth, 'as if the slipstream of a passing moth could waft him out of the world.'[14]

Gervas began to suffer from rheumatic shoulders and neuritis of the arm, and in July 1963 had to enter hospital for a prostate operation. Again, there was no quick recovery: neuritis and a bad back plagued him, and his bed claimed him more and more. He was saddened by Aldous's death at the end of November, and wrote to Norah Smallwood to tell her that without exception Aldous was the nicest and most unselfish person he had ever known, and was just the same delight to be with when he knew him so well as a boy. He showed the same courage when he was sixteen and his eyes went, never complaining.

Gervas had another operation in February 1964, causing the postponement of a party to celebrate Elspeth's quarter-century with Chatto. Receiving a congratulatory magnum of champagne from her publisher, Elspeth remembered that she had moved to them from Macmillan because Harold Macmillan had refused to publish the section on female circumcision in *Red Strangers*: 'It was indeed a happy day for me when our future Prime Minister couldn't take clitoridectomy.'[15] By the following month Gervas was insisting on having breakfast alone, unable any longer to endure bickering with Elspeth at the meal. He turned seventy on 6 April, and by mid-1965 he was ill again and Elspeth was very worried about him.

Elspeth was also coping with her mother, who had finally decided to leave Kenya. There was a time in the early 1950s when Nellie dismissed the idea of selling her farm as out of the question. Kenya still exerted a powerful fascination on her, and her attempt to live in England in 1949 had convinced her that her future could never be there. But in the early 1960s such hope as still existed had disappeared from Kenya's white colonists. Iain Macleod, the Colonial Secretary, was determined to grant Kenya independence, and there was a rapid move towards Africanising the civil service, the professions, indeed all occupations. Sir Evelyn Baring was removed as Governor (Nellie had breakfast with him and his wife on the day they left), to be replaced by Sir Patrick Renison – 'a horrid, smug creature', said Nellie[16] – and Jomo Kenyatta was released from detention.

The freeing of Kenyatta was a moment of national transformation indeed. Although he was hardly a man of the people, having spent years in England and married a white woman, he was certainly a man *for* the people, ideal for leading the country to independence. In August 1963 he would make a speech to a gathering of white farmers at Nakuru, a hostile audience if ever there was one:

> I am a politician but I am a farmer like you. The soil joins us all and therefore we have a kind of mutual understanding. We must talk to each other. There will be suspicion and fear if we do not know what each is thinking. If we must live together, if we must work together, we must talk together, exchange views. This is my belief. And one other thing which I want to make clear is this. That we must also learn how to forgive one another. There is no perfect society anywhere. Whether we are white, brown or black we are not angels, we are human beings, and as such we are bound to make mistakes. But there

is a great gift we can exercise, that is to forgive one another. If you have done harm to me, it is for me to forgive you. If I have done harm to you, it is for you to forgive me. The Africans cannot say the Europeans have done all the wrong and the Europeans cannot say the Africans have done all the wrong. All of us ... can work together harmoniously to make this country great ... Let us join hands and work for the benefit of Kenya ... we must work together, we must try to trust one another ... You are just as much Kenyans as myself.[17]

This speech of reconciliation charmed the hostile audience and earned Kenyatta a standing ovation. But, liberal though she was, Nellie was unable to envisage life in Kenya after the colony was granted independence, for she had expected a partnership between white and black, not African domination. From 1961 onwards she made preparations to leave. What she seemed to mind about more than anything else was that 20,000 dogs would have to be put down as the whites left. To add to her depression, her great companion Ingrid Lindstrom was terribly frail and ill, and her horticultural friend Sharpie was on the point of quitting Kenya.

In mid-July 1960 there had been a massive influx into Kenya via Uganda of whites fleeing from the Congo, which had descended into anarchy when Belgium gave it independence. 'Africa can never have had a more gloomy outlook of chaos and crass stupidity,' Nellie said.[18] Now seventy-five, she decided to sell part of her farm to a neighbour and part to the eight Africans who had been with her for so long: Manthi the engineer, Kangethe the odd-job man, Kariuki the handyman, Gachinka the nightwatchman, Nganga the gardener, Karanja the herdsman,* Karanja the cook and Mbugwa the house servant. To enable them to buy, she encouraged them to form a purchasing co-operative and apply for a loan.

The dilemma was where to live next. At first Nellie speculated about having a cosy caravan in Elspeth's field and doing odd jobs

---

* After Elspeth mentioned while being interviewed for a BBC *World of Books* programme in May 1962 that this Karanja suffered badly from rheumatism in Njoro's cold early mornings, she had many offers of long woolly pants from listeners. 'This must be an unusual response to a book review,' she said.

for her daughter. Elspeth paid for her to visit England in June 1961, and Nellie did indeed stay in a caravan beside Woodfolds – 'I feel very bitterly and deeply about being such an infinitely poor relation crawling home and being a nuisance.'[19] The endlessly weeping grey skies convinced her she could not retire to England. Several Kenya settlers had gone to Portugal, a country tempting to Nellie because it had no quarantine for dogs. Despite her age, when she returned to Kenya she obtained books and tapes in order to learn Portuguese, and also took lessons from a Portuguese-speaking Goan woman in Nakuru. She enjoyed the challenge, Elspeth later wrote, 'as dearly as in the days when only those with stout hearts and strong fingernails dared to challenge her at racing demon'.[20]

Nellie was only one of thousands of whites who were leaving Kenya. In the first three years of the 1960s there was a steady stream of white settlers to Australia, South Africa, Southern Rhodesia, Portugal and Britain. New rules for the ownership of land were introduced; white farmers occupying land designated for African occupation, mostly in the Kinangop area, were bought out by the government, and a few compassionate purchases were made in other areas. The land that was bought was then divided up and distributed to landless Africans. Some large farms were broken up into holdings of only a few acres each. It was heartrending for white farmers to know that all their hard work would be destroyed, their fences would come down, their carefully tended fields would be divided into small units.

If most farmers in a district decided to sell, the remainder would do likewise, for fear of harassment by surrounding African farmers and because their social life would disappear. Many farmers had nothing else in the world but their farms. They had put all they had into them, and two generations of children had been born and bred on them. The younger generation knew no other life, had lived in no other country. 'I am sure,' said Elspeth, 'that the displaced settlers will never find a home they love so well, nor forget the sights and the sounds and the smells of Africa which for some will be the only wealth they can take away when they go. And when the gale of nationalism has spent itself – if it does – some, perhaps, like the wise children in Kipling's poem, will go back to the "look of light" and the "scent of heat", "the naked feet" and the "boltless doors", "and the lisp of the split banana frond that talked us to sleep when we were small".[21]*

To take Kenya up to its independence Malcolm MacDonald, Ramsay MacDonald's son who had known Elspeth and Gervas well in the late 1920s and early 1930s when they worked for the Empire Marketing Board, was appointed High Commissioner, the replacement for the Governor. An election was held, during which, to Nellie's alarm, she had to dip her fingers into a bottle of indelible red ink (a safeguard to prevent people from voting more than once). At independence in December 1963 Jomo Kenyatta was sworn in as Prime Minister. 'I wonder so much,' said Nellie, 'WHY it is now generally assumed that Jomo and Tom Mboya [the Luo politician who had risen to prominence via the trade unions] are utterly sincere and truthful in all they say; surely the first politicians in history to be so IF they are.'[22] Sincerity was not, Nellie believed, one of the attributes of Duncan Sandys, or Shifting Sandys as she called him, the Colonial Secretary of the time.

Gikammeh was not on the list of those for compulsory purchase, but Nellie was given a lot of help by the Nakuru PC, Peter Brown (a most suitable name for the time, she thought, halfway between white and black), to settle the sale of the farm to her retainers. To her chagrin, Doushka Repton sold Kitimuru to a vast French coffee combine for £80,000.

Margery Perham covered the subject of independence for British colonies in the Reith lectures of 1961. Elspeth wrote to congratulate her, saying, 'WHAT a task you had, to thread a way through such a vast maze of fact, prejudice, fancy, hope and fear. You spoke with sympathy of the problems of the settlers and came out in favour of compensation. What a hope.'[23] None the less, Elspeth and Margery got together to write a joint letter to *The Times* to plead for compensation for settlers.

Elspeth wanted Nellie to live in England, where she could keep

---

* The quotations are from Kipling's poem 'Song of the Wise Children' (1902).

an eye on her, but her mother was resolved to go to Portugal. A completely new country and language daunted her not at all. She started winding down her staff, made herself a simple little kitchen (Elspeth sent her the book *Cookery for One*) and told Karanja to try to find another job. Continuing to sport his chef's hat at all times though no longer working for Nellie, Karanja spent long periods on her telephone conducting trading deals. When he answered the telephone he spoke in English with an impeccable Oxford accent. He had been a wonderful cook, at his best when rising to a challenge, and able to produce a complicated dish for unexpected guests with French perfection. Nellie now had to learn not to mind the alarming bang when she lit the gas oven and tried to cook for herself. Muchoka, her farm headman, was also given notice. He had been with her for thirty-three years, and it was a great wrench for both of them. She gave a party on the farm to say goodbye to her workers, but it was all excessively traumatic. Of Muchoka Nellie said, 'I miss him more than words can say – and think I always shall . . . A wonderful, loyal and trusty servant over the years.'[24]

Nellie got herself a British passport, but even the prospect of leaving Kenya as soon as the sale of the farm could be finalised did not prevent her embarking on another of her little enterprises – this time with a new flock of goats. Elspeth was not best pleased. Nellie also continued with her production of fresh vegetables, delivering them daily in sacks and baskets strapped to the roof of her battered Peugeot, its back seat piled high with rabbits in cages for sale to the butcher.

Mbugwa, possibly distraught at the prospect of losing his job, began to drink to excess, but Nellie decided to ignore this. No one left the farm on independence night on 12 December 1963, for fear of trouble in Njoro township. The bronze statue of Lord Delamere gazing above his hooked nose at what used to be the bar of Torr's Hotel, that haunt of the remnants of the Happy Valley crowd, was removed from Nairobi's streets and put on the lawn outside the house at his former farm Soysambu, overlooking Lake Elementeita.

Nellie's despair at having to leave was compounded by the failure of an operation to stitch up a drooping eyelid, the death of her sister Blanche in early March 1964, making her the last survivor of the six siblings, and the fact that her friend Cockie contracted polio. There were the deaths of many old friends in Kenya, and the suicide of others – 'life has become completely pointless here for everyone,' said Nellie.[25] To rid herself of possessions, she began to burn letters and diaries – unfortunately all Elspeth's went up in the flames. She gave away the dark panelling which had sheathed Gikammeh's living room, a relic from Aunt Vera's visit in 1929, when she carved the wood with a pattern copied from Hampton Court.

In September 1964 some Kenya friends found an orange grove and quinta (farmhouse) for Nellie in the Algarve region of Portugal, and it was bought for her for £3,300 by her friend Daisy Balfour, who had financed her so generously and so often in the past. Her neighbour in Kenya, Dorothy Powell, agreed to live with her in the quinta. As a result, the horizon of Nellie's expectations expanded, her spirits rose and she began to see the boulders in the way not as obstacles but stepping-stones. But she felt she could not leave Kenya until she had settled her eight former employees and their families on Gikammeh. She showed them how to form themselves into a partnership, which they called Matagari farm, and on 8 February 1964 she made Gikammeh over to them.

On 31 May 1965 she awoke on her farm to see for the last time 'long streaks of rose and lemon rimming the black mountains, and then the gradual paling of the stars in a sky of royal blue, and the valley with its slumbering lake slowly drawing light from the sky',[26] and to feel the sense of wonder as the dawn shadows raced over the Rift Valley through the arch of the beloved thorn trees outside her bedroom window. For the last time she stood on the verandah of the rust-coloured bungalow, with its walls of wood and mud rammed into wire-netting, its corrugated-iron roof and its door guarded by honeysuckle. She had lived there forty years, looking out 'over treetops to the whole panorama of the great valley, the winking lake, the gentle slopes of the extinct volcano Menengai, the tawny plains of Rongai and a hazy distance enveloping Lake Baringo and, far beyond, the deserts of Suk and Turkana'.[27] Then

Dorothy Powell and Donald Graham* took her on a trip to the Masai Mara, followed by a brief stay at Malindi and Mombasa on the coast.

The day of departure from Kenya, 1 July, found Nellie attending a goodbye lunch at the Muthaiga Club, at which Ingrid Lindstrom wept copiously. At 11.30 that night Nellie flew to Lisbon with Dorothy Powell. It was the end of an era. At times it seemed to Nellie that her life had been wasted; and indeed she had nothing tangible to show for it. To Elspeth, also, it was the closing of a chapter. Her childhood home had gone and she no longer had a base in the country she loved, and in which she had invested so much emotion and effort. She had always felt somewhat culturally displaced as an adult, living in one country but belonging to another, though she had had the comforting support of her mother still living in Kenya. Now that was no more, and she had lost 'the cattle and sleek snub-tailed goats, the green parakeets and yellow weavers and brilliant little bee-eaters, the Kikuyu chanting as oxen hauled at stumps, the smoke of fires, the fresh-turned earth, the smell of cedars and the moon riding high over the forest of the Mau –[. . .]all these would be nothing but memories flickering disjointedly, insubstantially, on the clouded screen of my mind'.[28]

Nellie's departure from Kenya put an end for a while to Elspeth's writing about Africa. But in 1962 and 1964 she had brought out two masterpieces about East Africa – *The Mottled Lizard* and *Forks and Hope*. The first of these was a sequel to *The Flame Trees of Thika*, and continued the story of Robin, Tilly and their daughter from their return to Kenya after the First World War to Elspeth's departure for university. She began the book while incarcerated for three months (June–August 1960) in the Charing Cross Hotel (from which she escaped to the Oriental Club) with other members of the Monckton Commission, busy writing up their report on the

---

* The husband of Kathini, daughter of Charles Taylor and his second wife Katherine ('Kit'), *née* Sanderson.

Central African Federation. Amid interminable discussions on the tangled politics of the Federation it was a relief to remember the childhood feeling of being

> absolutely alone with creation, even perhaps the first man to stand upon this particular rock and set eye on this particular scene, with nothing spoilt or sullied or abused. Grass bends before the wind, a soaring buzzard seeks a nibbling shrew, crickets trill, the hyrax drowses in his hollow tree, the spider waits in a crevice of sun-blistered rock – a whole world revolves in balance with itself, more perfect than the finest symphony. Man alone plays no part here save as a destroyer, who must cut trees to warm himself, kill beasts to feed or to amuse himself, and trample the shining beetle, the fruiting moss, when he moves about. Only man is not content to leave things as they are but must always be changing them, and when he has done so, is seldom satisfied with the result.[29]

She mused about what to call the book, eventually settling for *The Mottled Lizard*, which she took from a verse by Kipling.* She requested that Rosemary Seligman, who had been responsible for the *Flame Trees* jacket, do a painting for the cover of the Agama Planiceps Caudospina Meek, a Kenya lizard with an orange head, blue body and tail of paler, almost turquoise blue.

After Elspeth's release from the Monckton Commission Gervas became ill, and it was very difficult for her to finish *The Mottled Lizard*. There are slight indications of this in the book, which does not have the same uninterrupted flow as *Flame Trees*. But she managed to deliver the manuscript to Chatto in May 1961, before Gervas had to enter hospital for an operation. Unlike *Flame Trees*, *The Mottled Lizard* is more an autobiography than a novel, though Elspeth told a friend:

> A good many of the characters are either invented or are combinations of various people. This was necessary partly because of the laws of libel were people still alive, or of not

---

* From 'The Day's Work': 'Put forth to watch, unschooled, alone,/'Twixt hostile earth and sky,/The mottled lizard 'neath the stone/Is wiser here than I.'

unduly offending descendants if they were dead. However some of the characters are real and others are of course founded on someone, and most of the incidents did actually happen, though not always at the same time and place.[30]

She also told Chatto, when asked about possible libel, 'I hope all characters are either dead or composite and partially (at least) invented characters, as some are (largely for that reason).'[31] Alec Wilson, Harry Clewes and his wife, the Beatties, the Nimmos and Captain Raymond Dorsett the hunter are all invented, but Tilly and Robin (Nellie and Jos), Mr Playfair the bank manager, Northrup McMillan, Dr Burkitt the eccentric physician, Sir Edward Northey the Governor, Frank Joyce the farmer and his wife Mary Early, Trevor Sheen who sold Nellie her farm at Njoro, J.C. Shaw another bank manager, Doushka Repton who bought Kitimuru, Lord Francis Scott and his wife, and Billy Sewall the cereal-growing pioneer with his Chinese servants are all real figures who are portrayed accurately, as are Njombo and Kigorro. However, the defection of Kigorro's wife and the killing of the Dorobo are invented. Elspeth has a pet cheetah in the story, but she never mentioned having had one as a child, though she did have a genet as a pet. The book's description of the sea journey to Kenya at war's end was in fact based on the journey Elspeth and her mother took to England at the beginning of the war, for Elspeth did not accompany her mother back to Kenya at this time, having been left at school in England.

As in *Flame Trees*, Tilly and Robin are portrayed as they were in reality: Tilly reluctant ever to see anything going to waste and reposing great faith in experts, determined to get in on the ground floor, however bare and draughty, when applying new theories, resolved to alter things and then move on to something else, and viewing any kind of illness in herself as vaguely shameful; and Robin careless about losing money but maddened whenever he mislaid, as he always did, small items like socks and matches. In the book Robin is given a role in the acquisition of Gikammeh, whereas in reality Nellie was the sole mover. There are scores of incidents which really happened, such as the exploding marmalade, the outbreak of plague, the Makuyu Christmas party, the ride over the Kinangop, having to move the flame trees because they had been planted too close together, the journey to see the soldier-settler land on Mount Kenya, the loss of the bag of wages (though it was Nellie who threatened to burn down the huts rather than Jos), Cousin Hilary's visit, the stay with the Joyces at Kilima Kiu, the absconding Kavirondo, and the Tana river safari.

But, as in *Flame Trees*, it is Elspeth's knowledge of Africa and her lyrical depiction of that memorable, wild land, its animals and peoples, which make the book unique:

> In European eyes, the lives of Africans appeared simple, carefree and in harmony with nature, and Africans themselves child like in their spontaneous, often naive responses. But when you looked a little way beneath the surface you saw that Africans lived like so many Gullivers, bound by innumerable threads of custom, and allowed so little room for manoeuvre that the individual personality was cabined and confined. Their behaviour, and especially their relations with each other, recalled the complexity of some highly sophisticated, mannered society such as the court of Versailles in the eighteenth century. While people drank from calabashes, dressed in skins or blankets, relieved themselves in the bush and had created scarcely any art, they used special forms of address for each class of relative, a mother-in-law was so respectfully treated that even her name could not be mentioned, ritual purification had to follow a hundred small, daily actions and a complex system of fines and penalties existed to cover every small or great transgression. My own fears of dropping social bricks often embarrassed me, but for the young of the Wakamba and Kikuyu matters must, I thought, be infinitely worse, especially as they had not only the disapproval of their elders to reckon with, but all the malevolent, cantankerous and unruly powers of the spirit world.[32]

Because their behaviour was so constrained, any attempt to apply the English legal system to Africans was bound to fail, like 'groping for the scent of spices with a dockyard crane'.[33] As for the country when Elspeth returned to it after the war,

> it was all just as I remembered it: a film of dust over pale grass and twisted trees and yellow sodom-apples by the road-side, four-wheeled wagons with their eight pairs of humped oxen creaking along, little naked boys with balloon-like tummies herding shiny-coated scurrying goats, women plodding under heavy loads suspended by leather straps that bit into their foreheads, and a baby's head, black and shiny as a croquet-ball, peering out from its sling; high, piled, whipped-cream clouds in an immense blue heaven, blinding sunshine, shrilling crickets, a tinkle of bells, a smell of earth and heat-baked dung, wide-sweeping views towards distant plains. In minutes we were as thick with dust as a working bee with pollen.[34]

Elspeth dedicated the book to Aunt Vera, the widow of Robin Grant, the brother of Jos (himself called Robin in the text), with the ambiguous 'To V.G., who remembers Robin'. She did not obtain the same favourable terms from Chatto as she had for *Flame Trees*, for the firm was tightening its belt due to increased production costs, which led her to expostulate, 'How many man hours are employed in publishing any given book compared with the man hours consumed in writing it? I accept the terms with muffled protest, in the sad knowledge that if I go on strike no one will notice.'[35] She was also annoyed with Norah Smallwood for delaying the book's appearance until May 1962, because by then most whites would have drained away from Kenya.

The review by Ruth Harris in the *TLS* (6 July 1962) compared *The Mottled Lizard* to *The Flame Trees of Thika*, which she found 'one of the few books that really smells of Africa and . . . also has the quality that in it the seeing eye is part of the thing seen'. The new book had the same quality, but now Africa was seen through the eyes of a teenager: 'The magic morning has become broad daylight and the shadows are all rolled up.' Another reviewer found the book memorable and moving, nostalgic for a wild and unspoilt Kenya, while Darrell Bates in the *Sunday Telegraph* (13 May 1962) said it was 'a story brilliantly told . . . She had absorbed the character of the country and the people, white and black, who lived there so well that she can conjure them out of their graves and bring them to life so that we can see them and know their texture and hear them talk.'

As was their wont, Morrow decided to change the title for the American edition, and Elspeth herself suggested that which was used – *On the Edge of the Rift* – as it had a triple meaning: it contained the name of the Rift Valley, where the book was set; it indicated the change from colonialism to nationalism; and denoted her own break from her African home.

Nellie loved the book, which she said made her 'howl'. It was serialised on BBC's *Woman's Hour*, the Reprint Society took 60,000 copies in 1964, and a paperback edition appeared in 1965 under the Four Square imprint (Penguin also did a paperback, in 1981).

The second masterpiece of these years was *Forks and Hope*, which arose from a proposal from the *Daily Telegraph* late in 1962 that it pay her expenses in Kenya in return for some articles. For a last look at Kenya as a colony, and to help her mother wind up her affairs, Elspeth flew out to Nairobi on 29 January 1963. The visit was not a success, with mother and daughter squabbling more than usual. They could not resist criticising each other's way of life, food requirements and eating arrangements, and Elspeth was irritable, as she thought this would be her last visit to Kenya. At the time Daisy Balfour, eighty years of age and somewhat slow and fussy, but alert and generous enough to pay off Nellie's enormous overdraft of £1,500, was staying at Gikammeh. Nellie herself was now muddly, forgetful and rather deaf, so Elspeth had two old ladies to humour. Fortunately they battled away acrimoniously at backgammon every night, leaving Elspeth to get on with some work.

She wanted to obtain material not merely for the newspaper pieces but for what she intended to be her final book on Kenya. It was to follow the pattern of *The Sorcerer's Apprentice* and *A New Earth*, being a mixture of travelogue and analysis of the country's current situation. At this crucial time for Kenya, less than a year before independence, so much had changed that it seemed to Elspeth almost as if she was meeting a stranger who yet reminded her of a person once known. The book which resulted from the trip, *Forks and Hope*, is not only descriptive, but full of insight and wisdom, profoundly analytical about colonialism – the benefits it brought and the damage it did – and prophetic about Kenya's future. Elspeth mixed intelligent analysis with directly expressed emotion and the sort of common sense which is not afraid of pointing out the emperor's nakedness.

Although Elspeth herself regarded the book as scrappy, it is a most thoughtful work, a balancing act on a tightrope which could have toppled into prejudice on one side or over-enthusiasm about the future on another, yet does neither. The curate's egg that is empire has the advantage of allowing the meeting of peoples, goods, ideas and cultures, so the world is never static, but always subject to the push and shove of human beings. The past does not disappear, so the British presence changed East Africa for ever, and sometimes did it good. All this was seen by Elspeth.

The usual journeys were necessary to gather material for the book. As land and property ownership was regarded as a prerequisite for African economic development, many white farms had been compulsorily purchased and divided into smallholdings by the Settlement Board. Elspeth found the resettlement scheme for Africans a muddle, despite the £15.5 million the British government was spending on it, and she doubted the wisdom of splitting up highly capitalised white farms into subsistence smallholdings. Yet it was politically necessary so to do.

Happy Valley was now plastered with little Kikuyu mud huts, while the abandoned houses of the whites, which had seen so much gaiety and dubious behaviour, lay empty and ghost-ridden. Lady Idina's house, Clouds, was unoccupied and its beautiful garden a wilderness. In the new Alice-in-Wonderland world the Settlement Board was paying people to pull down expensive fencing in order to create smallholdings of seven to fifteen acres. 'As we went round, stronger and stronger grew the feeling of unreality, a dream, the clock going back 50 years. Is there anywhere else in the world where fences are being pulled down, houses left empty, pyrethrum left abandoned, machinery giving way to the hand hoe, tractors leaving, women with head loads replacing lorries and trailers, all modern methods being jettisoned in favour of peasant agriculture?' Elspeth asked in her diary.[36] At Mweiga she visited the ruined house of Bror Blixen and at Naro Moru Berkeley Cole's grave, now overgrown with rambler roses and the inscribed stone nowhere to be seen.

Everywhere trees were being burnt and in forest reserves the old podocarpus, with their romantic lichens and liana creepers like bridal veils, were being replaced by regimented, marching lines of cypress and pine. Nellie's farm had been named Gikammeh, the Kikuyu word for the tree hyraxes that screamed all night in the forest behind, but now the nights were eerie with silence. Not a hyrax was left, and the Dorobo forest people had abandoned their bows and arrows and honey hives for tractors and saws.

Elspeth was unimpressed by some of the American academics now swarming into Kenya – it had become a status symbol for every American university to have an African project and ties with an African school, college or university. For example, Columbia University had a 'Teachers for Africa' scheme, and so far had sent out three hundred inexperienced young Americans. US teaching involvement in Africa was, of course, a result of the Cold War rivalry being played out in Africa, where the great powers were competing for the favours of thirty-four independent nations.

Elspeth interviewed the leading politicians, including Michael Blundell, Jomo Kenyatta and Tom Mboya in Kenya, and Milton Obote, Prime Minister of the newly independent Uganda. She travelled to Uganda with Nellie and Daisy, passing the hotel on the border whose former owner had put up the sign: 'H.H. Aitkin, licensed to sell beer, wines and spirits as he likes, when he likes and to whom he likes. Tariff: bed, breakfast and bath 20 shillings, bed and breakfast only 30 shillings.' In Uganda Elspeth was entertained by the Governor-General Walter Coutts, who now had nothing to do, a sad fate for this hard-working Lowland Scot. It was on this trip to Uganda that Elspeth met the young artist Jonathan Kingdon, born in Tanganyika and presently at Makerere. He was an exceptional animal portraitist who was to illustrate *Forks and Hope*, and to become a good friend.

Elspeth also flew to Tanganyika, spending a day in the Ngorongoro crater where for the first time rhino had become an endangered species. Her second day she spent in the Serengeti, where she witnessed the wildebeeste migration from an aeroplane, with 400,000 beasts thundering across the plains like trails of siafu (soldier ants), and her third at Oldovai gorge, where the Leakeys had found Zinjanthropus, 1.75 million years old. Mary Leakey was there, working alone in an open shed surrounded by bones, bits of skeleton and rhino skulls, with a haunch of meat hanging from a rafter.

Tanganyika had obtained its independence in 1961, and Elspeth had an interview with its President, Julius Nyerere, slim and nervy, the only African she had seen so far who had reached the top rank politically and remained thin. He was busy revolutionising his country's society and economy, and establishing a single-party socialist state – he believed, like so many African leaders, that the two-party Western model, with its opposition obstructing everything, was a system no African country could afford. Elspeth pointed out that it was very difficult under a one-party system to change rulers if one became unpopular, though she conceded that 'practically, the African leaders are beyond doubt right; in countries torn by tribalism, the single-party state is a necessity. So pragmatists are not unduly worried; but, for the true believer, the dilemma remains.'[37] She found that the reaction of the older generation to Nyerere's villagisation policy was stupefaction, and of the younger, anger and talk of the rape of the country.

In Kenya, Elspeth visited Tsavo game reserve and its warden David Sheldrick. He took her to the remarkable Mudanda rock, from whose summit she watched the elephants coming to drink at sundown. It was another world: 'We sat there as the sun went down behind the Teita hills. The hills faded to a deep, mournful blue. There was a feeling in the air of eternity and peace. Sitting on the warm rock, we were seeing Africa as the explorers and old hunters saw it, unmarked by man, primeval, only the animals at peace with each other, balanced, content.'[38] A visit to a remote Kenyan farm yielded up riches indeed when Elspeth mentioned to her hostess, Lady Mary Boyd, that Gervas had embarked on a new enterprise – he was writing a book on Lady Elizabeth Grosvenor, Elspeth's great-grandmother who had died at the family home of Motcombe in Dorset in 1891, at the age of ninety-four. Her hostess opened a chest which contained Grosvenor papers dating back two centuries. Alas, white ants had consumed many of them, but Elspeth rescued a bundle, including letters from the Duke of Wellington, and sent them home to Gervas. As it happened, the then Duke of Westminster, Gerald Grosvenor, and his wife Sally were staying with Nellie at the time. Seeing her financial situation persuaded Gerald to settle a small annuity on his poor relation.

After the depressing settlement areas, the formerly dirty and dusty Nairobi was a gleaming surprise to Elspeth. Gone was the down-at-heel shanty town which had arisen from the need for the railway to pause before it reached the sheer escarpment of the Rift Valley. Now there were clean new buildings, skyscrapers, glitter and crowds. The sole anomalies were the cattle still grazing and the maize still growing in the vacant lots between the skyscrapers. Nairobi had become a pretty city, transformed by the horticulturist Peter Greensmith, who had beautified it with blue jacarandas, hibiscuses, and bougainvillaeas grown as standards rather than creepers. Everywhere there was bloom, and spacious parks. Elspeth had a meal with the High Commissioner, Malcolm MacDonald, who told her Kenyatta was moribund and at meetings either slept or did not turn up, and had not contributed a single constructive idea.

Elspeth had known Kenyatta in his London days in the 1930s, and now had lunch with him again. She is polite, even commendatory, about him in *Forks and Hope*, finding him more jovial than ever, 'no longer so watchful and so wary ... but his mind was still alert and sinewy'.[39] With a bead cap on the back of his head and his flywhisk on his lap, he had mellowed and looked every inch the father figure ready to bring his country to independence. But in a letter written to Gervas at the time she called him 'a revolting figure, gross, fat, raddled, with a cunning, peasant look ... jovial and faux-bonhomie, stuffing himself with food, eating cheese off the end of his knife', while the 'ineffable' Tom Mboya was 'fat, sleek and full of self-confidence'.[40] When Chatto took her to task for her evasiveness about Kenyatta's part in the Mau Mau, she responded: 'I *was* evasive about Jomo Kenyatta. J.K. himself, and the other African leaders, appear to be making a real effort to follow a "bygones be bygones" line and avoid recriminations, inquest and so on; I really do believe it would be wrong at this stage to reopen these half-healed sores. And no one has all the facts. And with the present hypersensitive feeling I'd be on the Prohibited Immigrants list. My mother is nearly 80 and I need to go there.'[41]

When *Forks and Hope* was published in 1964 Elspeth sent a copy to Kenyatta, who replied:

> You are partly right in assuming that the ineluctable urgencies inherent in my office may make it difficult for me to find time to read. I do find time to go through some of my books, albeit intermittently. I am looking forward to glancing through yours in the near future.
>
> Since our days at the London School of Economics, much has been written about my life – sometimes for literary and sometimes for other reasons.
>
> I am not unmindful of the necessity to write the story in my own words and also to record my views about the future in black and white. How soon this will be possible will depend on circumstances.[42]

While careful not to criticise Kenyatta in print, Elspeth was at the same time condemnatory of the diehard old settlers at the Muthaiga Club, who were still of the old type, with 'dark red, liver-coloured face, pop eyes, vacant look, drooping jaw, dark blue open-necked shirt' and a 'commanding, wooden-faced bossy wife. One could hear the distant thump of polo sticks.'[43] Out of their mouths came a host of clichés. One white forester, lamenting the lack of Africans joining his profession, said, 'I don't blame them. They have only just come down from the trees. Why should they

want to go back?' The Afrikaner farmers on the plateau around
Eldoret also dreaded independence, and since 1961 the Great Trek
had been occurring in reverse. The journey to South Africa overland,
with everything they could move, took three weeks, and now there
were few Afrikaner farmers left in Kenya. The house of C.J. Van
Rensburg, descendant of Jansen Van Rensburg who had led the
Boers and their wagons to British East Africa in the century's first
decade, was hopelessly neglected, the rooms bare, though there
remained a portrait of the Queen in each. All the internal walls
were darkened by the perpetual smoke from an open fire on three
stones in the kitchen, and the bath had gone.

Elspeth summed up the misunderstandings between white and
black with the conclusion, 'The habit of colonialism dies almost as
hard as that of tribalism. It is the habit of knowing what is good
for others and seeing that they get it.'[44] The expectations of the
Africans were boundless. Would they be fulfilled? Elspeth was
unsure. She chose the title of her book from Lewis Carroll's 'The
Hunting of the Snark':

> They sought it with thimbles, they sought it with care,
> They pursued it with forks and hope;
> They threatened its life with a railway share;
> They charmed it with smiles and soap.

> What are they seeking? Hard to say; something splendid, some-
> thing great. The plan that works, and aid as of right from
> 'the Outside'; freedom without chaos, power without abuse;
> non-alignment, pan-African unity, African socialism; peace
> without conquest, democracy without opposition, nationhood
> without discontent, prosperity without sacrifice; freedom from
> hunger, freedom from neo-colonialism, freedom from inter-
> ference; knowledge without guilt, life without tears; the end
> of an old shame, the dawn of a new dignity.[45]

The road was at the fork. Ahead lay 'Happiness, contentment and
fulfilment, and a small bird singing on a mango tree; or the command: Go, bid the soldiers shoot.'[46] But she comforted herself
with the thought, '*Uhuru* [freedom] comes, empires go; weather

and crops, rain and sunshine, drought and flood, death and child-birth, these remain.'[47]

Parts of *Forks and Hope* were serialised in twelve instalments in the *Liverpool Daily Post* (February 1964) and in four instalments in the *Johannesburg Sunday Chronicle* (September–October 1964). Unusual in its restrained optimism about East Africa's future, the book equalled *The Sorcerer's Apprentice* and *A New Earth* in its intelligent analysis. Again, the penetrating eye and poet's pen had been put to good use, to create a contemporary commentary which reads beautifully. William Patrick Kirkman wrote in the *TLS* (13 February 1964): 'In reading her conclusions – tentative conclusions, as one would expect from someone writing with real knowledge of Africa – the author bases herself firmly on facts observed and assessed by a highly perceptive mind. In a few brief lines she can capture perfectly the atmosphere and flavour of East Africa. She does it with equal skill whether she is writing about the Beau Geste quality of Wajir . . . or about the night life of Kampala . . . she is just as good in her chapters on wild life, or agricultural policy and problems . . . Mrs Huxley's political assessments are as shrewd and well informed as those on the social and economic scene.'

Elspeth returned at the beginning of April 1963 to an England which had seen its coldest and most prolonged winter since 1947. Charles had failed his preliminary examinations at Oxford and would have to leave the university if he failed again at the end of the next term. Happily, he passed at his second attempt.

Elspeth had to go into hospital for forty-eight hours in June to have some teeth removed, leaving her, she thought, with a face like a warthog's. She entertained a notion put forward by her new American agent, Sterling Lord, that she attempt a book on the whites in Africa since 1880, though she admitted, 'I AM getting a bit tired of the Dark Continent. But I seem hopelessly chained to it.'[48] Even *A Man from Nowhere*, a novel she had submitted to Chatto just before she had left for Africa in January 1963 had dealt with African matters. It was a strange story of a vengeful man who had suffered a great wrong. The book, strongly influenced by the Mau Mau rebellion, was disliked by Cecil Day Lewis, but Chatto accepted it none the less. Elspeth said it was not solely a novel of action and suspense; her intention had also been to comment on English life and its present self-deceptions, as seen by someone coming from a totally different setting. There were several attempts to write a blurb to bring this out, but Elspeth kept rejecting them: 'I send you a new draft. I have used the words "unusual novel". If you don't like this, substitute another adjective – preferably NOT boring, trite, verbose, gloomy or repellent.'[49]

Published in 1964, *A Man from Nowhere* is not a whodunit but a whydunit. It tells the story of Dick Heron, whose wife commits suicide after going insane following the hacking to death of Dick's brother on their farm. Dick goes to England to seek out and kill the cabinet minister responsible for giving African countries their independence, but he is away on one of his African jaunts, 'shaking another independent country out of the blanket, or handing out more taxpayers' money to keep sweet the fat black politicians with their posh fin-tailed cars and golden beds and armed bodyguards'.[50] A bitterness pervades the book, which contains several similarly injudicious comments. The African murderer has a price put on his head, but with the coming of independence is pardoned, becoming 'a slimy statesman fawned upon by Cabinet Ministers and wined and dined by businessmen wanting contracts ... and diplomats from Iron Curtain countries wanting to destroy the sordid remnants of British influence'.[51] Although no one suggested Kenyatta murdered anyone, the parallels were close enough for Chatto & Windus to raise the issue of possible libel and to send the book to the lawyer Michael Rubinstein. Elspeth made a few alterations, mentioning Kenyatta as the Prime Minister so that he could not be regarded as any other character in the novel.

Through the book runs a theme of the waste and uselessness of white endeavour in an African country. There is a lyrical lament for the bungalow of slats and shingles, or mud and wattle with a tin roof, built with one's own hands with nails scrounged from packing cases to save money, and therefore loved and cherished.

The misery of having to hand it over to someone who never worked for it at all and would destroy it in a couple of years is tangible: 'There won't be anything left of what we created . . . so we might as well not have tried.'[52] A feeling of futility and retreat pervades the book, of fruitless venture, worthless effort. Elspeth explains why farming in Africa is so different from that in England. In England, nothing really belongs to the farmer, who is more of a trustee because the land was cleared of forest centuries ago and someone has been farming it ever since. The English farmer therefore takes land over as a going concern and carries on looking after it. By contrast, in Africa you start with a piece of forest and alter it and make it grow things it has never grown before. You introduce and breed new kinds of animals. You are creating something new, something that was not there before. The land is yours in a different way, because you have a special affection for things you have created.

And then you have to hand it all over and retreat to an England where the people 'moved like shapes gesturing in a sea of ambiguity. There was nothing clear-cut about them, they were afraid to be sharp and definite, afraid to commit themselves.'[53] In England there was a line you had to detect by instinct and never cross; people buried themselves under civility and decently hid their cruelty – which was yet, like graveyard bones, always present beneath the surface. This is a characteristic cry of the colonial, who had left England to avoid its smallness, neatness and ordinariness, to go to another country for adventure and true endeavour. Elspeth is giving vent to the anger felt by her mother and other Kenyan white farmers, but now was not the time for such sentiments, and she risked being categorised with those diehards she herself despised. Perhaps it was with this in mind that she included the words, 'Of course it's hard on individuals. Of course it has its personal tragedies. No man on earth can stop these great waves of history from sweeping away good and bad together. They not only can't be stopped, they shouldn't be. It's right, you know, it's right that people should be free.'[54]

Reviewing the book in the *TLS* (11 June 1964), Marigold Johnson wrote: 'Miss [sic] Huxley has always been recognised as a writer sympathetic to the European minority [in Kenya], and in her new novel she cleverly pleads the outsiders' case by choosing not Africa but rural Home Counties as her setting – a setting in which the newly arrived colonial, direct, embittered, and unsophisticated, is likely to feel more of an alien than anywhere else ... Miss Huxley skilfully disguises her political theme ... under a fast and complicated plot ... the most interesting parts of *A Man from Nowhere* are those where Miss Huxley lets Heron ponder on how and why he can never belong to the country which has sacrificed his happiness for the sake of abstract political ideals.'

ELEVEN

False Starts, a Social Conscience, and Australia

In order to maintain a steady income, Elspeth usually had ideas for her next book before she had completed writing her current one. This meant that she often had to shuffle the reading of proofs and the research for a new book. Now that she was well known, ideas for books came from many sides. Towards the end of 1961 she contemplated writing a popular guide to the contemporary situation in Africa, where three empires, the British, the French and the Belgian, were disintegrating. Norah Smallwood even found someone to do the devilling for facts before Elspeth decided that the book must be a paperback *ab initio*, whereupon Chatto referred her to Penguin. Reluctant to deal with a publisher she did not know, Elspeth cooled on the idea and no more was heard of it.

She also wanted to collect some of her newspaper articles into a book, but Chatto was distinctly lukewarm. They were, however, keen on another of her ideas – that she write a biography of Dag Hammarskjöld, the United Nations Secretary-General recently killed in a plane crash in Northern Rhodesia. This proposal foundered when Elspeth discovered that most of the papers she would need to consult were secret, and could not be opened for years. Then, early in 1963, Sir Charles Arden-Clarke's widow asked Elspeth to write a book on her husband, who had been Governor of the Gold Coast (Ghana), which in 1957 had become the first African colony to gain independence from Britain. Elspeth had served with

Arden-Clarke on the Monckton Commission, and was tempted by the idea of writing about him. As she put it to Norah Smallwood: 'He rode the wave very successfully, and bowed to the inevitable ... I don't think he could have done less without serious trouble. He was a cynic, a bit of an old rogue, a great one for the girls ... he was quite ruthless and unscrupulous. Ideals my backside, he would have said. He was really a sort of latter-day Palm Oil Ruffian in cocks' feathers and shiny buttons. But very little of that could be got past the widow.'[1] Norah was unenthusiastic, which put an end to the project.

Elspeth then had an idea for a picture book on the Kikuyu. Having always been a keen photographer, whose study doubled as a darkroom, she had scores of photographs from the 1930s taken at Murigo's camp and elsewhere. She suggested she write captions to some of these while an African composed an accompanying text, posing such questions as: Had the Kikuyu dropped their old way of life in favour of Westernisation? What had they lost and gained, and were their customs being abandoned or preserved? Elspeth suggested the Kenya High Commissioner in London, Dr Karanja, write the text, but Chatto wanted Elspeth herself to write it. She demurred, because 'Africans so easily take offence at anything which might carry the suggestion that their culture was at all primitive or savage ... [There] is also the feeling that African culture has been much maligned and was a better thing than its rather crude material aspects suggested.'[2] She added that it was almost impossible for a white person to put this across without being patronising. Chatto suggested Kenyatta write a foreword to the book, but Elspeth imagined he would refuse, 'as he is an old man and pretty harassed, not to say preoccupied'.[3] Peter Calvocoressi of Chatto did approach Dr Karanja, but made a grave error. He proposed the Kenya government guarantee to take two thousand copies of the book. Elspeth was annoyed, because she knew perfectly well that the government would not promote a book solely about the Kikuyu, as this would make its impartiality between the country's tribes appear suspect. Calvocoressi's mistake in not consulting her, and Karanja's indignation at Chatto's suggestion, put an end to the project.

Elspeth now turned her attention to what she hoped would be a profitable new genre – stories for women's magazines – and had two accepted by *Woman's Own*. Acknowledging that it was 'not, perhaps, the highest form of literary life',[4] she yet increased her output for newspapers and magazines in the early 1960s. Norah Smallwood suggested to *Homes and Gardens* that Elspeth write a piece on what moment in her life had been most influential, leading the writer to quip, 'It should obviously be the moment I met Mrs Smallwood.'[5] She dismissed her American agency Sterling Lord when it failed to acquire commissions for her in US newspapers and magazines, but her journalism in England flourished. The year 1964 was particularly remunerative, partly because *Punch* engaged her to do a series of pieces on immigrants in England.

Eager to slough off Africa, Elspeth threw herself into the hectic but fascinating research for her *Punch* articles. She visited Birmingham and Bradford to gather material, and when she found she had far too much she suggested that Chatto issue her findings in extended form as a book. This led to the publication, in November 1964, of *Back Street New Worlds: A Look at Immigrants in Britain*. Elspeth was adamant that it was not a sociological work; rather, it was popular reporting designed for the man on the Underground and not the pundit, and for immigrants themselves. The book covered the subject of racial prejudice in Britain, which had arisen in response to the influx of Indians, Pakistanis and West Indians encouraged to come to Britain to provide extra manpower in the post-war economy. West Indians and Pakistanis often became bus drivers: 'Like so many Jonahs,' said Elspeth, 'these adventurers have got into the belly of the British whale; but, unlike that ancient Hebrew prophet, it is unlikely that many of them will ever get out again. They have come to stay, and so, perhaps, the time has arrived for us to get to know them a little better.'[6] Since England was a land of the wall, high fence and privet hedge, there were many misunderstandings which Elspeth tried to put right.

One of these was the different living patterns and needs of the immigrants. Generally they had large families – two and a half times as large as the English – and this led to overcrowding. They also had a different tradition of hospitality; but the crux of the matter was 'sex . . . The ultimate test of all good intentions in regard to integration is the corny old question: would you like your daughter to marry a black? Or, no less, would you allow your daughter to marry a white? Few honest fathers, British or coloured, would return to this question a genuine, unhedged "yes". Most Asian fathers react as if stung by a snake.'[7] Coloured immigrants were not the only newcomers investigated by Elspeth – she talked to Italians, Poles, Greek Cypriots and people of other nationalities who had been displaced by the Second World War and washed up in Britain. She examined the questions of integration or assimilation, and restricted immigration, coming to the conclusion that what was needed was a common cause to unite across dividing lines of community and race. Immigrants had created few new problems; rather they had underscored those which already perplexed British society. The book displays great sympathy towards immigrants without patronising them. Elspeth felt it should be compulsory reading for MPs. Nesta Roberts in the *TLS* (3 December 1964) found it a 'clear-sighted and wide-ranging – surprisingly so for a short book – survey of the problems posed by the refugees in our midst'.

No sooner had she completed the twelve articles for *Punch* than Bernard Hollowood, its editor, asked her to write another six, for £500 and all expenses, this time on factory farming and allied subjects, including wildlife matters, the contamination of habitat, food quality, land usage and aspects of nutrition. Again, Chatto suggested issuing a book of the articles. By now Elspeth had made the acquaintance of Peter Scott, conservationist and son of the Antarctic explorer Captain Scott, and he agreed to write the foreword. He lived not far from Elspeth, at the bird sanctuary Slimbridge, and they had dinner together at Woodfolds to mull over the wording of the foreword. It was the beginning of a significant friendship which encouraged Elspeth to develop her work on nature and ecology, an interest which was to dominate her next few years. Norah Smallwood came up with the title *Brave New Victuals*, which Peter Scott did not like, thinking it too gimmicky and light-hearted, potentially off-putting for scientists and pundits, who would not take it seriously. Norah, however, would not be dissuaded.

Morrow, Elspeth's American publisher, rejected the book, because Elspeth tried to remain impartial on the subject of insecticides, whereas a hugely successful and influential recent book by the American Rachel Carson, *The Silent Spring* (1962), had come down heavily against them. Chatto issued five thousand copies of *Brave New Victuals* in November 1965, and it went into paperback two years later, under the Panther imprint. The magazine *Here's Health* serialised the book in fourteen instalments between January 1968 and October 1969. A copy of *Brave New Victuals* was sent to the Director-General of the World Wildlife Fund, the Duke of Edinburgh. Elspeth attended a conference on the countryside in November 1965, and 'goggled at the Duke who was oozing charm'.[8]

As an inquiry into modern food production, *Brave New Victuals* ranges widely over various types of factory farming. When dealing with hens, Elspeth asks how much the birds *mind* being confined. Can their brains feel pain, frustration, misery, pleasure? She draws the analogy of penned animals pacing in zoos, which is now known to be a symptom of distress and boredom. A solution she proposes is the keeping of small family farms (rather like her own), which allow animals free range while at the same time enhancing the beauty of the countryside, at present being denuded by the ripping out of hedgerows to create huge fields. 'I recall,' she says, 'my own feeling when a young bull reared from birth to enjoy, perhaps, more freedom than a bull should enjoy (he was of a placid breed), was sold to a neighbouring farmer, kept tightly tethered in a stall night and day, and never released except to perform his function.'[9] She then introduces an argument that, had it been heeded, would have prevented the outbreak of BSE in cattle in the late 1980s. She deplores the fact that unused parts of bullocks are made into meat and bonemeal and then fed to cows, which she prophesies would go mad. The lament running through the book is that 'safety first, that unheroic maxim, has never been our guiding light'.[10] She advises long-term research into synthetic oestrogens fed to cattle, to determine the extent to which they enter the food chain and what effects they have on human beings. *Brave New Victuals* also deals in some detail with chemical compounds, including DDT. Elspeth acknowledges that we cannot just let the weeds and insects rip, but correctly foretells that insects would develop immunity to chemicals. L. Amey in the *TLS* wrote (2 December 1965): 'Mrs. Huxley's inquiry into the subject is distinguished by a remarkable objectivity and a refusal to come to easy conclusions. Her readers are left . . . with a plain dilemma before them . . . The issues are many-sided . . . This multiplicity is not evaded by Mrs. Huxley and her examination of their diversity is carried out with wit, percipience and sympathy.'

All in all the book, though published more than thirty-five years ago, is extraordinarily far-sighted and modern in its appreciation of the dangers inherent in intensive and chemically controlled farming. Elspeth was one of the first popular ecologists, trying to attract the ordinary man and woman's attention to the need for balance, for 'treating men, animals, plants, the soil and the entire habitat as one whole, living process, the life-cycle; and considering always the relationship, the balance, between them'.[11] She had always been a pessimist, but now she became a firm one, declaring that only a fool would be an optimist. In a conversation with her friend James Lees-Milne, she opined that there must be millions of earths such as ours in the universe, and saw no good reason to look upon our world as important. Its ultimate destruction was of little moment, and would be no bad thing: 'Our earth is like an apple being eaten by maggots. The maggots increase by devouring the apple which then falls to pieces, hollow and empty. The maggots then die for lack of sustenance. The sun sees to the remains.'[12]

Her pessimism did not mean, however, that she sat back and did nothing about the path of destruction the world was upon. That was not her way, for she was determined to fight. Elspeth had always been a lover of nature and animals, as was her mother before her. Her public concern was new, but it had been developing for some time. In her youth she had enjoyed hunting and shooting wild animals in Kenya. She tries to explain this in *The Mottled Lizard*, which has a graphic account of her killing a cheetah:

I still looked upon the graceful and abundant animals as game to be shot. To know a thing is beautiful and yet take pleasure in destroying it seems, in retrospect, an odd frame of mind, but the best hunters were the best naturalists; they loved the lives they extinguished, and enjoyed nothing more than to watch a buck at play, a herd of impala leaping, a lion on the kill, an elephant searching the wind with his trunk – unless it was to bring them down with a well-placed bullet.

There was, of course, a code to make this blood-lust respectable. You must not kill females or youngsters; you must shoot only when you felt reasonably sure of killing cleanly; and if you hit an animal you must follow and despatch it ... By killing only males, hunters argued ... [they] merely culled older males – the best heads were normally to be found on fully mature animals – and so kept up the vigour of the breeding stock ... For my part, I was obsessed with the importance of an eighth of an inch on the end of a horn ... I knew the record length of horn of every species.[13]

It was partly the ambience of the shoot that Elspeth enjoyed – the excitement of the stalk, the camping in rocky hills, the sunrises with mile-long shadows across the golden plain, the crackle and woodsmoke of the campfires at night, the movement half-seen in the riverbed 'which freezes you into immobility and strips your senses bare, to discover with whom you share the silence and the solitude – a rhino or a leopard, a bushbuck or oryx or just the humble duiker; or even, perhaps, a trick of light and shade. And the knowledge that, while you see nothing but a starling on the sand, a lizard on the rock, all the while other secret eyes are watching you.'[14]

When she was seventeen the pleasure of shooting left her and she never went big-game hunting again. She could remember the exact moment this happened. She had been at a party all night, and went at dawn to look for a bushbuck along the ride cut to mark the boundary of Gikammeh with the forest reserve. Buck crossed there every night to raid the maize on the farm, returning to the safety of the trees at dawn. Just as the sun came up Elspeth saw a fine male bushbuck standing against the sky. His dark coat was wet with dew, bathing him in a film of translucent light which hovered around him. His twisted horns were black against the pink horizon. He saw Elspeth a hundred yards away and stood ready to leap. When her bullet hit him he jumped high in the air and sprang into the forest. She found him lying dead in a little glade, and thought: 'Why should I take the life of this magnificent creature and rob the world of something that can never be replaced?' She turned against animal slaughter very strongly, a feeling reinforced as she grew older, 'partly I suppose because we (humans) have wiped most of the animals out, partly perhaps advancing years, partly the climate of the age and the loss of faith in humans as splendid creatures endowed with wisdom and made in the image of God'.[15] But she was wise enough to realise that the hunting instinct was inborn in human beings, and that anyone who denied this was wrong.

Although Elspeth had enjoyed shooting, she had never had anything but contempt for zoos: 'How people could condemn animals who had done no harm, and who trusted them, to the slow agonies of life imprisonment I had never been able to understand. A grim enough fate for men who had deserved punishment, it was far worse for animals who had not, and whose freedom was their element, as cardinal to them as the sea to porpoises.'[16] However, at the same time as she was displaying concern for tightly penned farm animals in *Brave New Victuals*, she was writing a book about a tiger cub born in London Zoo, whose mother had abandoned it. The idea for the book came from Norah Smallwood, who had seen photographs of the cub taken by Laelia Goehr, and imagined that Elspeth, who had often bent her ear with her love for animals, might be interested in writing the text to accompany the illustrations. In August 1963 she showed the pictures to Elspeth, who was immediately enthusiastic about the project. Suki, the cub, had been born on 26 March 1963. At eleven inches long and weighing under two pounds, she had to be bottle-fed when her mother rejected her. By thirteen weeks she weighed eighteen pounds, and went to a small zoo in Southampton run by Jimmy Chipperfield, a brother of Dick

Chipperfield, the circus owner, whose daughter Mary looked after her.

Chatto arranged appointments for Elspeth to see Mrs Goehr, Desmond Morris, then curator of mammals at London Zoo, and the head keeper at Southampton Zoo. Elspeth also began to correspond with a German naturalist who specialised in cats. Aiming to write about 5,400 words, she did further research and went to see both the circus-owner Bertram Mills and the lion-tamer Chipperfield in his winter quarters at Great Tew, in Oxfordshire. Elspeth was slow to deliver her text, but the resultant picture book, *Suki: A Little Tiger*, was published on 22 October 1964 in an edition of 15,380, of which 7,659 were sold to Morrow. 'To fashion this brick,' said Elspeth, 'I've had to gather straw from some pretty distant barns. A zoo-bred tiger has a pretty uneventful life. So little is known about tigers except as targets for rifles.'[17] Obviously the book, the third of four she published in 1964, was not the place to display her disapproval of zoos, and Elspeth confined herself to including the quotation from William Blake,

> A robin redbreast in a cage
> Puts all heaven in a rage,

and to the comment that it was surely more honest to admit that men caged animals in circuses for one reason only, their own amusement, and confined them in zoos for their interest, and that the feelings of the beasts did not enter into it.

The first half of the 1960s was for Elspeth a time of upheaval, with the illnesses of Gervas and Cleggy, the anxieties about Charles's education, and Nellie's move from Kenya to Portugal. Yet it was also a time of great energy and productivity, with the publication of one book after another, scores of newspaper articles, and continuing work for BBC radio. Given this chameleon productivity, Elspeth should have been secure about her finances, but she was not. In order to reduce the burden of tax, she left most of her advances and royalties with Chatto & Windus, only occasionally asking the firm to make payments into her bank accounts when she needed some money. Her difficulty was that at that time married women's incomes were added to those of their husbands, which in Elspeth's case meant that what she earned was subject to surtax. She bitterly resented the lumping together of the two incomes – 'I certainly do a hell of a lot of work for nothing and purely from the money point of view it just isn't worth it.'[18] For example, in the tax year 1965–66 the Inland Revenue wanted £1,800 from her, which was two-thirds of her total income for the year.

Elspeth would have been wise to acquire a literary agent in Britain, but she had not done so. Instead, she relied on Norah Smallwood to be fair. She almost invariably challenged any fee or advance she was offered for books, articles and broadcasting. Sometimes the offers were raised and sometimes not, but she could have saved herself much trouble by handing over this aspect of her affairs to someone else and concentrating on her writing. Her unhappy experience with the American agent Sterling Lord was not conducive to persuading her to employ an agent in England. Yet she began to suspect that perhaps she was not getting the best of deals from Chatto, and displayed her restlessness by querying the firm's invariable option on her next book, which she felt tied her to them for ever. It is significant that this disquiet began to show itself around the time of the arrival of new staff at Chatto, who took over certain aspects of the publishing process from Norah Smallwood. Whereas Norah had had an excellent relationship with Elspeth, and their correspondence was full of irony, jokes, family news and general chat, now remarks in hands other than Norah's were written on Elspeth's long letters – such as 'What shall we do with this?' answered by 'God knows!', 'This writer has verbal diarrhoea,' and 'What a fusser she is – ignore her enquiries.' If there was one thing Elspeth could not abide it was the discourtesy of not answering letters. Perhaps Norah should have told her that she was passing on some of her letters to be dealt with by others.

Elspeth felt she should be making more money from her efforts. The work of writing and finding the material about which to write was then – and still is – inadequately rewarded, although Elspeth was one of the better-paid authors of her time. In 1965 Chatto & Windus held £8,235 for her – about £80,000 at today's value – but a large amount of that money would have gone in tax if it had been transferred to her.

Elspeth's anxiety about both her finances and Gervas's health was such that she decided to sell her collection of books on Africa and her farm, though not Woodfolds, and buy a rundown cottage in Wales. Unburdening herself of the farm would solve the perennial labour problems and mean that the man who had tended the pigs would be freed to mow the lawn and do other garden chores which were beyond the strength of Gervas now that Sid Cook had left. In the second week of October 1965 all the animals and machinery were sold. It was a sudden and sad ending to all the effort Elspeth had expended over the years.

Elspeth's collection of African books had been built up over the years but had outgrown its quarters and now languished in the attic. She owned 110 books published before 1938, plus government Blue Books, and 150 published since, many of them review copies. She had owned some of them since she was a child, so it was painful to part with them. Their sale was not solely for money, but was also a gesture by Elspeth to prove to herself that she had finished with Africa and would not write about it again: 'I don't suppose I shall write any more about Africa now, as there seems no prospect of going there, and one gets so very quickly out of date.'[19] The money the books raised would pay for kitchen units in the Welsh cottage. She advertised the collection as a whole, and accepted an offer from the University of California, Santa Barbara.

An attempt in 1966 by Boston University to establish an Elspeth Huxley room devoted to her books and manuscripts and every other detail of her career as a writer foundered when Elspeth replied to the request for contributions, she told Norah Smallwood, 'coldly and truthfully that I'd never kept the MS of any book and destroyed everything as I went along'.[20] This was not strictly accurate, as papers she later gave to Rhodes House in Oxford include some typescripts of her books. It may have been a combination of modesty, a desire for privacy, and lack of time to sort jumbled papers that made her refuse to help. 'Things have not been the same since the front fell off the filing cabinet in the 50s and a mouse nested in Land Tenure Systems among the Lilalongwe,' she said.[21]

Elspeth had never had a secretary to work for her in her own home, preferring instead to look after her letters and papers herself, and things inevitably got into a muddle. Periodically she would put papers into sacks and burn them in the garden. Her practice was to type her books herself. Her typewriters, which she occasionally replaced with new models, frequently required repair, which caused her much frustration, particularly when the shop she used for this purpose went bankrupt in 1965 because so many mechanics had been filching money from the till. Her typed drafts, with their many corrections, were sent to a professional typist for fair copies to be made.

By 1965 Elspeth was feeling the lack of a personal secretary: 'I do find it increasingly difficult to manage with absolutely no secretarial or other help at all, and the home situation deteriorating in various ways, which needs more time from me, and still fit in a little actual writing in the early hours of the day!'[22] One solution she suggested would be if Chatto & Windus did her photocopying for her, but when she approached the Chairman Ian Parsons about this she was firmly rebuffed and given the name of a copying service.*

Perhaps it was the thought of her mother leaving Kenya and thereby denying her daughter a haven in the vastness of Africa that stimulated Elspeth to buy a cottage in a wild and lonely part of Wales. Or she may have regarded the cottage as an investment, to be let to visitors in holiday periods. In 1965 she bought eighteen acres of

---

* Elspeth's relationship with Ian Parsons never developed the warmth of her friendships with Harold Raymond and Norah Smallwood. This was possibly due to the fact that she could not invite him to Woodfolds for weekends because she would have had to include his wife in the invitation. Norah's relationship with Parsons was close – there were some who believed she was having a long-standing affair with him – and Elspeth's loyalty to her would have precluded her getting to know Mrs Parsons.

Welsh hillside and a hovel 1,100 feet up the steep southern slope of Gaer mountain (1,400 feet) in Gwent's Black Mountains. The place was seven miles from Abergavenny, off the Crucorney to Llanthony road, and overlooked woods falling to the Honddu river in the Vale of Ewyas. The view from Middle Gaer, as the cottage was called, was magnificent. Across the valley to the south-west rose the Sugar Loaf mountain, and to the south the Brynawr with its slopes blanketed in bracken. To the south-east lay the ridge of Skirrid mountain falling away to the Herefordshire plain and the far-off Forest of Dean. Behind the cottage Gaer mountain, like a shield warding off the northerly and easterly winds, rose steeply to a summit guarded by the earthworks of an ancient pre-Roman fort from which could be seen to the west the Patrishow and Hermitage valleys and the lofty Black Mountains.

Middle Gaer was approached by a very narrow stony lane, lined by crumbling stone walls and far too tight for builders' lorries. None the less, a builder was essential to make the ramshackle dwelling habitable, for all it boasted was a downstairs room with a tiny, narrow kitchen scooped from the bank at the back, from which a ladder mounted to a bedroom divided into two by a flimsy partition. The roof was rubberised felting nailed to rotten rafters. There was no ceiling or bath or lavatory. Water came from a well and the only warmth from an ancient, filthy, wood-burning stove. The door did not shut properly, and all the windows were cracked and rotten. Leaning against the thick walls was a tumbledown shed, roofless but for a few sheets of rusty corrugated iron and called 'the vicar's room' because it had once been occupied by a reverend gentleman who lived there as a hermit. In former times the land had formed part of the demesne of Llanthony Abbey.

Several builders turned down Elspeth's attempts to woo them. She was offered salvation by Harold, a rover who more or less came with the place, the brother-in-law of the postman and the nephew of Middle Gaer's former owner. He arrived on the back of a pony, stocky and fresh-complexioned and blue-eyed with a shock of white hair and perfect manners, and he knew of some builders with a van which just fitted the lane – the Jones brothers of Llanbedr.

They took on the job, creating a well proportioned, stone-fireplaced living room with big, double-glazed windows facing south to frame the view. At one end of the living room they constructed a modern kitchen with an electric cooker, fridge and double sink, and they also installed a larder, a little hall and a cloakroom with toilet. They made a downstairs bedroom, and new stairs up to two small bedrooms and a linen cupboard. They built a garage and toolshed and small patio, created by scooping out the hillside and paved with flagstones from an abandoned dwelling miles away in the bracken which Harold knew about. A new roof, drains and an immersion heater were installed, and water was piped from a spring in the mountain behind.

Elspeth's farming bug had clearly not been eliminated, for she decided to go in for sheep farming in a small way. Harold cut the bracken and repaired the fences so a ram and thirty-six ewes could be put on the field, and they soon produced their first crop of lambs. One of Harold's sons dug up the old nettle-choked garden, which became a little orchard with three plum trees, three apples and three pears. A National Park warden arrived with a gang of boys to remove the carcasses of several cars dumped in the dingle, and a Canadian-Norwegian neighbour who looked like Danny Kaye transformed a pig-wallow between the cottage and the barn into a miniature terraced garden.

Elspeth and Gervas spent their first weekend at Middle Gaer in September 1966. It was perfect, apart from the fact that the bath water rose in floods from beneath the floor instead of taking the usual exit. After this was fixed they tried to go to Middle Gaer for a week every month from April to October. The cottage's remoteness and the mountain air were a complete change from Woodfolds: 'It is a place in which to relax,' said Gervas, 'with Elspeth's household chores cut to the minimum, with no telephone to answer and no garden for me to feel compelled to tend.'[23] With them went their dachshund, who loved the freedom of the hills.

Elspeth paid for the 'terrible financial maelstrom in Monmouthshire',[24] as she described the cost of the cottage and its renovation, with £2,500 Chatto had been hoarding for her so she could avoid tax – she thought it 'rather awful to think of working quite so hard for Mr. Wilson and Mr. Callaghan'[25] – the Prime Minister and Chancellor of the new Labour government. Later, after Gervas's death, she let Middle Gaer from Easter to mid-September, allowing tenants to take only dogs guaranteed to be safe with sheep. Ridiculously, after each tenant left, she went to Wales to clean the cottage herself.

Elspeth's astonishing creativity in this period included work for radio and the ever more popular television. Never wholly satisfied with her appearance and caring not a jot for make-up and clothes, she was more at home with the former. She also disliked being photographed, contriving to have her back turned if anyone pointed a camera at her. She once asked that a particular photograph Chatto was using for publicity purposes be suppressed, 'not that I'm under any illusions that even a flattering picture can equate me with let's say Ava Gardiner [sic] but it might make one look a bit less like something dredged out of the local sewage farm'.[26] She had to endure ordeal by television when *Forks and Hope* was published in February 1964:

> I was whisked off at 3.30 in a taxi by a charming ex-bandmaster sergeant-major who never stopped talking both ways (three hours each way), given (I'm glad to say) two stiff whiskies on an empty stomach (had had hair done in the lunch hour), got into a heated argument with Mr. Allsop* who obviously had cast me for the role of a sort of female diehard Lord Salisbury which I wasn't going to wear, tottered drunkenly into a studio which appeared to be nothing but a haze of lights still clutching my glass (I THINK my third whisky) and can remember absolutely nothing at all about what went on.[27]

There was another television interview for the book, this time in Bristol, which caused Elspeth to fulminate about how much time

---

* Kenneth Allsop, critic and TV interviewer who mistakenly doubted his own talent and committed suicide in 1973.

and manpower was wasted in TV studios. It took a whole day to record what emerged as four minutes of playing time. She had a similar experience when a BBC Educational TV team arrived in Oaksey to do a four-minute interview and took two-and-a-half hours over it. Seven men drew up in a motorcade of five cars. The sole task of one of them was to clap two pieces of wood together and say 'Take,' and of another to hold a light meter against her face. At infrequent intervals she muttered a few words, at one point using the word 'feudal', which required that bit to be done again, as the producer said it was a word the audience would not understand.

Elspeth was far more confident about her performances on radio, where she remained unseen. She continued to appear regularly on *The Critics*, and occasionally on *The World of Books* and *Woman's Hour*. She interviewed the wild-life film-maker Armand Denis for *Frankly Speaking* (July 1963) and spoke for eight minutes on Henry M. Stanley for the Overseas Talks and Features' series on great explorers (January 1964). After the publication of *Forks and Hope* she gave a talk in May 1964 on 'The Return of the Hoe', about the regression of big European farms in Kenya, now divided into small plots of land. Her theme was 'all change is a mixed bag and there are aspects which are sad'. For the white settlers the sadness was that a lifetime's effort had been wasted and the work of several generations thrown away, as carefully built-up soil fertility was squandered in the new Kenya.

Elspeth attempted to break into creative writing for television and radio with a play, 'My Friend, Mr Macdonald', but the BBC refused it in January 1962, giving as their reason that it was below her normal high standard. The plot was too sketchy and rapid, and the sub-plot too thin to carry conviction. Val Gielgud, who was in charge of radio drama, added that plays about politics in Africa were extremely touchy, and this one did not present a sufficiently distinguished and exciting picture to justify the BBC doing it. Elspeth seems not to have repeated the experiment.

Although happy to talk on radio, where she did not have to face an audience, Elspeth was nervous about lecturing or giving public talks of any sort. She tried to avoid them, but sometimes they were unavoidable. She was persuaded by Norah Smallwood to talk at a literary lunch in Leeds in November 1964, but asked her friend never to let her in for such a thing again. Writing the talk, she said, took as much time as writing 20,000 words of a book, and 'I've no suitable clothes either. However, if Iris Murdoch doesn't worry, why should I? I am digging out an old sack from the cowshed.'[28] A more congenial affair, which she described as a 'frolic', was a talk she gave in June 1962 for the Ditchley Foundation at Ditchley Park in Oxfordshire, a Vanbrugh mansion magnificently endowed by the Wills tobacco family as a centre for off-the-record Anglo-American conferences.

Having temporarily sloughed off Africa as adroitly as a snake its close-fitting skin, Elspeth turned her attention to a proposal to expose another continent, Australia, to her particular brand of intelligent scrutiny and ruthless analysis. A friend of hers, Jock Gibb of the publisher Geoffrey Bles, thought Australia was far too little understood by the British, and suggested that she give it the same treatment as she had Kenya in *The Sorcerer's Apprentice*, *A New Earth* and *Forks and Hope*, and West Africa in *Four Guineas*, in order to present the exciting image of modern Australia to the world. Elspeth as usual haggled over money, leading Gibb to exclaim wearily to Ian Parsons of Chatto that he recognised the usual authors' tactics, with which publishers were so familiar. Authors always said that if publishers made it worth their while they would go to the moon. Chatto offered a generous £3,000 advance and agreed to pay Elspeth's expenses, estimated at between £1,250 and £1,500, which they would recoup by taking 50 per cent of serial rights until they recovered the sum.

With the comment 'I think Africa and I need a rest from each other,' Elspeth accepted the challenge, even though she was told to her dismay that she would need to take evening gloves, and she made plans to go to Australia for three months early in 1965.[29] Her only doubt was the lack of interest in Australia in Britain. Jock Gibb arranged a dinner for her to meet Bill de Lisle, Australia's

Governor-General, while he was on holiday in England. De Lisle offered to put her up in Canberra when she arrived, and promised her every assistance from the Department of the Interior with introductions and other matters. Chatto's agents in Australia made all the travel and hotel arrangements, though the Department of the Interior provided her internal travel by air and motor transport in and around the capital cities. They stressed that they did not seek to influence or over-organise her; this suited Elspeth, who did not want to operate at a VIP level.

Ian Parsons asked Elspeth to enquire into what the Australians had done, were doing and proposed to do about the preservation of wildlife. He also requested a plan of the book, which bothered Elspeth, who never really knew what she would write about until she put her fingers to the typewriter. In the past she had persuaded Norah Smallwood to accept her books without any synopsis, and for this reason she would not sign a contract until the book was completed and submitted to Chatto. But in this case Ian Parsons insisted, and Elspeth sent him a sketchy plan with the words,

> I am sure there are writers who map everything out in advance, make a plan and stick to it and I only wish I was one of them. I'm not. I really have very little idea of what I am going to write about until I see what is there, what strikes me at the time as interesting and/or entertaining and so on.[30]

She intended, she said, to visit every state, to come to rest at likely spots and sink a deeper shaft, to concentrate on the outback rather than the seaboard cities, to see as much as she could of the Aborigines, to describe scenes and places, to touch on the wider political issues of the 'white Australia' policy, to see to what extent a nineteenth-century view of relations between the sexes persisted, and to enquire into the preservation of wildlife.

On the question of wildlife, Jock Gibb warned Government House in Canberra that Elspeth 'has something almost amounting to mania over this question of animal preservation ... She needs to know the true facts over cropping and not be swayed by the emotion which crowds press reports.'[31] Norah Smallwood congratulated him on his foresight, which would prevent tears later, but stressed that although Elspeth must have her say she was ultimately humble-minded about her writing, and that if one suggested a view was overstated or inartistic, or that over-emphasis threatened to invalidate the whole, she did as a rule accept this.

Elspeth flew to Sydney on 10 January 1965, was whisked straight to Government House in Canberra, and then embarked on her Australian travels. Everything was very rushed and expensive, and the hectic life soon began to tell, though she wrote to Ian Parsons that 'no one ever thought of this in terms of a rest cure', and 'we old and tough troopers take it . . . in our stride'.[32] She was astounded to find that at parties all the men stood at one end of the room and all the women at the other. She havered over a title for the book, wondering if 'Wallaby Stew', from an old bush song,* would do; or 'They Call no Biped Lord or Sir', from Henry Lawson's 'Shearers'; or 'Their Shining Eldorado', from 'The Roaring Days', also by Lawson:

> Their Shining Eldorado
> Beneath the southern skies
> Was day and night forever
> Before their shining eyes.[33]

It was the last of these that was chosen. At the launch party in London in May 1967 a telegram from two prominent Australian civil servants was read out, wishing success to Elspeth's brilliant and perceptive book, which could not fail to promote a better understanding of Australia and its people. Far from being brilliant, *Their Shining Eldorado* is rather dull, with an emotional aridity that comes from Elspeth's evident lack of engagement with her subject. A somewhat pedestrian travelogue covering major cities, sheep and cattle farms and the question of culling kangaroos, it only comes to life in the section on the Aborigines, with whom she clearly empathises:

---

* 'Stir the wallaby stew,/Make soup of the kangaroo tail,/I tell yer things are pretty crook/ Since Dad's been thrown in jail.'

The Western and the aboriginal outlooks are not merely different, they are contradictory. The good Westerner who plans
ahead, husbands his resources and takes thought for the morrow accumulates possessions; his father-figure is a man of
property. The nomad turns this upside down. He who accumulates is a villain. In any case there is nothing to accumulate –
no houses, no furniture, not even crops or skins. And what
could be said of a man who found a well in the desert and
kept it secret? Who guzzled on wallaby while others starved?
Fair shares among tribesmen is not an ideal, it is the norm.
And what an irony that our own society whose religion teaches
this ideal should, in the name of progress, so totally extinguish
the only human societies on our planet that have achieved it!
The tribesmen reproach us, perhaps, with their success.[34]

Elspeth makes the point that human beings are the most adaptable
creatures on earth, for as individuals they can change their diet and
habits – but communities cannot, and disintegrate into individuals
who adapt. Assimilation would put an end to Aboriginal culture.
Elspeth is also gently critical of the 'white Australia' policy which
restricted immigration from Asian countries.

Chatto printed nearly 10,500 copies of the book, but it did not
do as well as had been hoped. British readers were not particularly
interested in Australia, a safe, white land unlikely to erupt into
violence and overthrow its government, while in Australia there
was a feeling that Elspeth was an outsider without a deep understanding of the country. Jock Gibb had foreseen this possibility,
recognising that, famous writer though Elspeth was, people were
bound to ask how she could write a book about Australia when
she had only been there three or four months.

The *TLS* review (25 May 1967) said that what interested Elspeth
about Australia could be predicted from her African background –
the terrain, the native people, the birds and the beasts: 'Certainly
only by a much more searching look at idiosyncratic Australian
suburbia (even at the expense of the Speckled Drongo and the
Native Companion) could the characteristics of modern Australia
be described. But Mrs. Huxley frankly disowns any claim to a

balanced point of view, and it might have been better if the Australian wild life, which really hogs the book, had been allowed to have the lot.' She was further criticised for some gaffes, like getting names wrong, which Australian reviewers swooped upon, particularly her assertion that gambling was illegal in New South Wales. The very idea was enough to foster revolution.

But what the book really lacked was what Laurens van der Post recognised in Elspeth's African work:

> It is not only because she is born and raised both to her subject and role that Mrs Huxley catches the swift and startled reality of Africa so brilliantly on the wing as she does in these sketches [*Forks and Hope*], but also because at heart she cares so truly. And this is the most important thing of all today: that we should go on caring, as she does, no matter how confusing, unpalatable or even hopeless the shift of pattern in Africa at any given moment may appear to be.[35]

Meanwhile, Nellie had arrived in Portugal with her friend Dorothy Powell to find a Portuguese family occupying Quinta dos Passarinhos, the farmhouse in the Algarve she had bought. They had to be evicted and the place made habitable, so it was not until 1 May 1966 that Nellie and Dorothy could move in. The first winter proved to be far colder than they had expected, although a visit from Cockie cheered them. Nellie found Dorothy inept, lacking initiative, depressed, miserable and temperamental – 'I have to spend a lot of time trying to be less irritating unto her.'[36] She then decided poor Dorothy was sly – 'Once people are SLY with me, I get rough.'[37] When Dorothy returned to Kenya to look after her mother, the idea of her living in the quinta with Nellie was quietly forgotten, and thenceforth Nellie was alone.

She busied herself taking Portuguese lessons and entertaining many visitors: Sally, wife of the Duke of Westminster, who had settled annual payments on Nellie; Joan Grigg; Daisy Balfour; Kathini and Donald Graham, ex-Kenya farmers now settled in England; Elspeth's son Charles and his girlfriend Frederica; and Cockie, disregarding a leg semi-paralysed by polio, who came regularly. Dolly Miles came too, though when she coincided with Cockie she would be sedated with two glasses of white port in the morning, to prevent her displaying her more irritating traits. Rose Cartwright was turned away at the airport because she did not have a visa, although she would return, insomniac and depressed by the political situation in Kenya but adamant she would never leave it. Ingrid Lindstrom's granddaughter Ingrid, Nellie's godchild, lost her husband David Matthews in a car accident a few months after her marriage and came to stay, as did many other Kenya friends.

Nellie had hoped that by moving nearer England she would be able to see Elspeth more often – perhaps for a month twice a year – but this was not to be. Elspeth did come for three weeks in March 1966 and invited her mother back to Woodfolds that summer, but Nellie flatly refused the invitation: 'Anyone sleeping more than a night or two irks you. The dream of Portugal being so close to "home" is just a bust dream, and my only friends remain – wisely – in Kenya.'[38] On 4 March 1967 Elspeth and Gervas came to stay, but the two women irritated each other, quarrelling much of the time. Nellie, who was on edge because she did not know whether her annuity would continue after the recent death of Gerald, Duke of Westminster, thought Elspeth was overwrought with work and lacking in the holiday spirit. Elspeth as usual chided Nellie for being on a different wavelength from herself. Perhaps she had some justification – Nellie's comment on the current hostilities in the Middle East was: 'If Hitler had *really* made a job of the Jews, all this wouldn't have happened.'[39] This may have been said in jest, but Nellie had always been anti-Semitic.

When Elspeth proposed that she visit Portugal for a week later that year, Nellie was still so deeply hurt about what had occurred in March that she told her daughter not to come and see her out of a sense of duty: 'It is only a short time ago that you wrote to me (I thought with exemplary primness) – "I have neither time nor money to visit you". No word of regret mit [Nellie often used the German word for "with"] the statement . . . I really should be unhappy at the thought of your spending so much money . . . on such an undeserving cause.'[40] However frosty their relationship at times, Nellie and Elspeth always wrote lengthy, newsy letters to each other at least once a week, and often more frequently. For Elspeth's birthday Nellie suspended the feud to send her a bottle-opener made from the tooth of a lion Jos had shot in Rhodesia in 1903. She took the opportunity to ask Elspeth to send her a caponiser to castrate cockerels and a mill to grind nuts. Both these items were for new enterprises she was undertaking. She also started to keep rabbits, but they succumbed to myxomatosis. Perhaps even more incorrigible than ever in her old age, she was still experimenting with one money-spinning scheme after another, and would continue to do so until her death, never making an escudo from any of them.

Elspeth and Gervas went to South Africa that winter, instead of to Portugal. The trip was intended to improve Gervas's ailing health – although, with her tendency to become gruffly unsympathetic when confronted by distress she could do little about, Elspeth was of the opinion that his problems were 90 per cent psychological. In the past few years, since the loss of his job, Gervas had occupied his time by writing books, with modest success. In order to study documents for his latest book, on Lady Elizabeth Grosvenor, Gervas had frequently stayed with Gerald, Duke of Westminster, and his wife Sally at their seat, Saighton in Cheshire, and he and Elspeth got to know the Westminsters well. After *Lady Elizabeth and the Grosvenors* was published by Oxford University Press in 1965, the Duke asked Gervas whether he would like to do a study of his grandfather, the first Duke, a politician, philanthropist and race-horse owner and breeder who had died in 1899. Having found he greatly enjoyed historical research, Gervas fell in with the suggestion, producing *Victorian Duke*, published (again by OUP) in 1967.

Now it was time for a rest from his labours and Gervas's first long journey with Elspeth since the end of the Second World War. Laurens van der Post, originally a South African himself, gave the Huxleys the names of contacts in South Africa and they embarked on the *Edinburgh Castle* early in January 1968, into the strange, unreal world of the ocean liner, where everything was thirty years out of date, even the tunes the orchestra played. The average age of the passengers was the same as the temperature of the swimming pool – seventy-eight to eighty. They spent their time dodging the author Sir Philip Magnus, an inveterate name-dropper, 'ineffably self-esteemed and married to a lady as broad as the acres she owns in Shropshire. He is like one of those missiles that can always find its target.'[41] When they reached their destination they spent a leisurely two months at various places including Constantia, the Stellenbosch Hotel, Mount Nelson and Swaziland. They also stayed on farms and with the Maggs family, from whom they borrowed a car for three glorious days in the Kruger National Park. Both of them arrived back home well rested.

Gervas then began writing his autobiography, *Both Hands*. In it he says of his writing career: 'I had found it highly flattering to my ego to be published and well-reviewed. I never had the slightest belief, however, that I had missed my vocation or that I could ever have rivalled Elspeth's professionalism which my own amateur efforts only made me respect the more.'[42] He was a clear, honest writer, unable to match his wife in facility and beauty of expression, but a good historian, proficient at bringing his subjects, including himself, to life. *Both Hands* was published by Chatto & Windus in 1970. It may be unfair to say that the firm's loyalty to Elspeth coloured its decision to publish the book, but it is unlikely that such a work would find a publisher today.

The Huxleys' son Charles was awarded a third-class degree in Philosophy, Politics and Economics from Oxford in 1965. Gervas, believing that the atmosphere and tempo of the United States, so very different from that of Oxford, would be beneficial to his son, wrote to two American colleagues he had come to know well while he was marketing tea. They found a job for Charles with the Madison Avenue advertising agency Ogilvie & Mather, as an advanced trainee. Charles liked the American way of life and stayed in New York for eighteen months, but he was ultimately compelled to return to England in March 1967 to avoid the draft for the war in Vietnam, for which, as the holder of a Green Card, he was eligible.

Elspeth asked Ian Parsons to pull strings to get Charles a job in London, and when he landed one parental anxieties were stilled for a while.

In America Charles had met Frederica Huxley, daughter of David Huxley, Aldous and Julian's half-brother who had married an American. She came to England in August 1967 and the pair went to stay with Nellie in Portugal. At first Nellie was unsure about the relationship, but Elspeth and Gervas were in favour of Frederica. She and Charles spent almost every weekend at Woodfolds. They even persuaded Gervas and Elspeth to accompany them to the musical *Hair*, the first show to display nudity on the British stage.

Charles and Frederica were married on 10 August 1968 in a simple ceremony at Marloes Road Register Office in Kensington, where Elspeth and Gervas had been married thirty-seven years before. Frederica's brother-in-law George Darwin and Gervas were the witnesses. The Registrar was astounded not only that he was marrying a Huxley to a Huxley, but that the witnesses were a Darwin and a Huxley. Elspeth and Gervas held a party for family and friends at Woodfolds the next day, and Charles and Frederica bought a house in Lambeth, London.

With Gervas unwell much of the time, and the anxieties about her mother, the late 1960s were not easy for Elspeth. She had Middle Gaer to distract her, but her loss of form in *Their Shining Eldorado* was an indication not so much of declining powers as of being overwhelmed by too many responsibilities. While writing the book she consistently claimed that she was being rushed. Whereas this had been a stimulus in former days, now it was a distinct hindrance to the free flow of thought and pen, and her prose became anaemic. She was also troubled by the ending of her friendly relationship with Chatto & Windus. Norah Smallwood, increasingly crippled by arthritis, had handed over the care of Elspeth's books to other people – for example, Ian Parsons exclusively dealt with *Their Shining Eldorado* – and they were not as skilled in handling her. Elspeth's habit had been either to ask Chatto whether a book was worth doing, or to embark on one without a word to them. In either case, she never produced a synopsis or signed a contract until the first draft of the book had been accepted. Then, relying heavily on the opinions of Chatto's readers and Norah, she extensively altered that first draft. This was not a practice welcomed by Chatto's new young men Hugo Brunner and George Trevelyan. They tended to treat her first drafts as the finished product, being hypercritical and failing to provide the detailed guidance she had come to expect.

The cosy and productive relationship with Norah had gone for ever. Realising this, Elspeth appointed London Management as her literary agency, and one of its employees, Herbert van Thal, began to look for other work and other publishers for her. She was, however, still locked into an arrangement with Chatto to give them first option on any substantial book she wrote. Some of the work she undertook at the beginning of the 1970s could not be classed as 'substantial' and therefore did not have to be submitted to Chatto. Thus Elspeth drifted away, perhaps not altogether deliberately, into the arms of Weidenfeld & Nicolson. She had, however, one last fling with Chatto in 1968 – with the third volume of her fictional reminiscences, *Love Among the Daughters*.

The book deals with Elspeth's departure from Kenya for university at Reading and Cornell. During vacations she stayed either with Aunt Vera or with Aunt Blanche, Nellie's sister, and her three daughters of the work's title. *Love Among the Daughters* is a delightful book, a jolly, witty and immensely charming romp through the swinging 1920s of England and an American campus. The daily routine of the dotty Aunt Madge (Aunt Blanche), whose sulks last up to three weeks, and her typical English squire of a husband Jack (Uncle Jim Holford) are regularly disturbed by the unpredictable and the chaotic. Though no one lacked for food, warmth or shelter at Nathan's Orchard in Devonshire (in reality Cherry Orchard in Dorset), aunt and uncle could not keep up with the County and did not try.

This is Elspeth at her finest: perceptive and funny, distorting characters to best advantage while still writing with love. The daughters Gertrude (Peggy) and Kate (Constance) are emancipated 1920s girls, looked upon with awe by their rustic colonial cousin, who has no idea what people are talking about, having to feel her way as if through a minefield. Any reference to Africa is a conversation-stopper, particularly with Uncle Jack, who thinks the continent should be left to 'elephants and niggers. Sooner or later the sun's actinic rays rot the cells of the brain.'[43] His daughter Kate, a true Bohemian, is particularly admired. Elspeth makes her suffer the same fate as had befallen herself in real life – she is expelled from school for betting on horses.

Elspeth had to make some changes to the book because two of her cousins were still alive, as was Aunt Blanche. Cousin Peggy, who had left Oaksey to live in Wales, hardly featured in the book and made no objections, but Cousin Joan (Joanna in the book) also had to be consulted. Joan had had an exciting youth which she did not particularly want her own daughter, who had a very respectable boyfriend, to know about. She asked Elspeth if cuts could be made to passages about drugs and other unsavoury subjects. Perhaps a short-cut would be to have Gertrude as Peggy and Kate as Constance, and give herself a cradle in the nursery corner. Elspeth rewrote the offending passages, omitting an illegitimate baby and an abortion, and invented many adventures for Kate, while allowing Joanna, whom readers might equate with the real Joan, to live a fairly blameless life. This entirely satisfied Joan, and the book was submitted to Chatto. Cecil Day Lewis found some slack in the dialogue, and thought some incidents went on longer than their interest justified. Elspeth took his advice and made some cuts. She suggested the unfortunate 'All Bitches Fight' as a title, but Morrow, the American publisher, refused to countenance it. Thankfully Ian Parsons came up with *Love Among the Daughters*.

The book came out in September 1968, in an edition of 7,500. The magazine *Queen* published an extract, 'At the Thé Dansant', on 11 September, and eight instalments were read on BBC's *Woman's Hour* from 12 March 1969. Foyle's Quality Book Club brought out an edition of three thousand in March 1969. Elspeth had not shown the book to Nellie before publication, and now received a tart letter: 'You can't expect me to enjoy all the miseries and tragedies of my nearest (and erstwhile dearest as regards Blanche) being exposed to the world and it certainly was a shock to find you had brought in about poor Jim and the conviction, and about Blanche and Perce. So we won't talk about it.'[44] Nellie was referring to Elspeth's mention of Jack being committed to Wormwood Scrubs for pawning jewels which he had on approval from a jeweller, which was based on a true incident. As a result Madge came to rely heavily on her farm manager, Perce, though Nellie hints that there was something more than reliance involved. Her reaction was characteristic of her relationship with Elspeth at the time – critical, edgy, yet mutually interdependent.

The critics as one found *Love Among the Daughters* a delightful book. An American reviewer described it as 'witty, intimate and charming ... the prolific Mrs. Huxley's *thé dansant*'. The *Irish Times* (3 January 1969) thought that 'Mrs. Huxley is clearly one of those electrically charged beings who set off explosions in their vicinity when contacts are made,' while Selina Hastings in the *Daily Telegraph* (26 September 1968) said that 'her quiet wit and accuracy of perception keep one continually amused. She has a rare talent for spotting the ridiculous and for visualising the absurd, which is as entertaining as it is salutary.'

Soon Elspeth was to suffer great upheaval. Gervas's illness had provoked her into actively imagining a future alone. How this was to be financed caused her puzzlement. She told Nellie that Gervas's income would die with him, but this is hard to believe, unless she meant that she would be left with a reduced pension, as is usually the case. The Huxleys had one large asset – Woodfolds, which was now too big and cold for them, even though a huge oil-fired central-heating boiler had been installed in Cleggy's old room – and in 1970 they made the decision to sell it and move into Green End, the cottage at the end of the driveway which Cleggy had been going to occupy before she succumbed to her brain tumour.

The move was postponed when a watertank in Woodfolds' roof overflowed and demolished several ceilings, but by the summer the house was on the market. Meanwhile the Huxleys began to renovate and enlarge the cottage, doing away with a lethal staircase. A possible sale of Woodfolds fell through, preventing the Huxleys from moving to Green End for fear that they would be liable to pay Capital

Gains Tax. The house was eventually sold to Duncan and Biddy Mackintosh in November, and Elspeth and Gervas moved in to the cottage in January 1971. It was just the right size for them, with three bedrooms and a large sitting room. Elspeth was pleased to have moved, finding the cottage snugger and easier to manage than Woodfolds, even if the garden required attention, looking as it did like a First World War landscape after bombardment.

The sale of Woodfolds, for just over £20,000, provided a reasonable sum for investment to provide an income. Middle Gaer could be offered for holiday lets to boost funds, and journalism, broadcasting and the writing of books would add to them. Elspeth's appearances on *The Critics* had dried up in 1961, though she continued to contribute to *The World of Books* until 1967. She also talked on *Woman's Hour* on several occasions throughout the 1960s, but she made no broadcasts at all between September 1969 and March 1975. As for journalism, she continued this throughout the late 1960s, having found the topic of nature conservation, which much engaged her, popular with readers. Yet in 1970 there was a marked drop in her output, almost as if she were allowing herself to retire; she was, after all, sixty-three, and most women of the period retired at sixty. Other matters, too, were distracting her.

TWELVE

Bereavement

Nellie had settled into her Portuguese quinta with a bustle uncharac-
teristic of the retired. She acquired a married couple to help her,
the husband in the garden and the wife in the house, bought a
donkey and devoted herself to farming once again. Her novel
scheme was to grow for sale strawberries of the Redgauntlet variety,
but the water supply from her well was erratic because the pump
was always breaking down. Needless to say, the strawberries failed.
Nellie's ebullience and wit soon earned her many friends, mostly
British expatriates, some of them ex-Kenya settlers. Daisy Balfour,
who had bought her the quinta, was a frequent visitor. She neatly
sidestepped the question of Nellie having to repay her by giving
the quinta to Charles as a wedding present, to go to him on Nellie's
death. When the British government restricted the amount of
money that could be taken abroad, Daisy smuggled currency into
Portugal interleaved with the pages of her Bible. This bought Nellie
a car, so she was mobile. Nellie found a bootlegger from whom she
could buy cheap gin, and the empty bottles came in handy as candle
holders during the regular electricity cuts. Sally, dowager Duchess
of Westminster, funded an order for the *Daily Telegraph*, which
kept Nellie *au fait* with British life and politics. Ingrid Lindstrom
and Nellie kept in touch by sending each other tapes, Nellie's an
hour long. Elspeth offered to pay Nellie's fare to Kenya for Ingrid's
eightieth birthday party,* but Nellie strenuously declined with the
words, 'NO, I couldn't bear to go to Kenya again.'[1]

---

* Ingrid lived to the age of ninety-three. She died in Nairobi.

Nellie did not go to England for Charles and Frederica's wedding, but they stayed with her in Portugal a fortnight later. The person Nellie most wanted to see, her daughter, came infrequently due to pressure of work, sometimes only once a year, while Nellie came to Woodfolds a couple of times a year. Meeting her at the airport on one occasion, Elspeth was almost toppled when she made the mistake of picking up a suitcase which proved to be full of bottles of bootleg gin, prudently packed by Nellie in order to avoid the overpriced English variety. On her English visits Nellie usually spent a fortnight with Elspeth before going to other friends such as Cockie or Daisy. Eighty-five years old in 1970, Nellie was now almost completely reliant on a hearing aid. Moreover, she had continual trouble with her feet, and developed sores on her legs which sometimes ulcerated. She would not allow infirmity to cramp her style, though, and after her quinta withstood an earthquake in March 1969 she was able to bustle about collecting clothes and doing good works for the afflicted in the vicinity. She was at her best with challenges like these.

But Nellie was deeply distressed when her silver was stolen in a burglary at Charles and Frederica's London home: 'I regret my poor silver deeply. What a sad end to it after 66 years.'[2] Also taken was Jos's gold watch, which Nellie had given to Charles: 'One wishes Charles could have been wearing Pa's gold watch. It spent a year once in the thatch of a boy's hut after having been stolen.'[3] This incident had occurred at Kitimuru in 1920. An outbreak of plague on the farm meant that all the African workers and their families had to be vaccinated. The operation went smoothly until two African children ran away at the sight of the needle – they later died of plague. Their families' huts had to be pulled down and burnt, and tucked away in the grass roof of one of them was a gold watch Jos had lost before the war. Clearly it had been stolen and concealed there. A repeat of such good fortune could not be expected, and the watch and silver were never seen again.

Nellie's visitors failed to compensate for not seeing her daughter as often as she wished. She said she would have loved 'family cosiness', but that seemed impossible. She wrote to Elspeth: 'Looking back over so many years of muddle and failure, I realise what a shocking mum I've been, contributing absolutely nothing and taking all.'[4] As for Gervas, he paid only one visit to Portugal. He did not like the quinta, so he said – what he probably meant was that he did not want to hear the constant, tiresome bickering between Elspeth and Nellie. In any case, he was unwell, and Elspeth could not leave him by himself for long. His earlier operation for a stomach ulcer had failed, and he still suffered pain on eating. He tried to solve the problem by consuming very little, and as a result grew even thinner than before. Elspeth was very worried. Gervas had been gassed in the trenches of the First World War and this had affected his lungs, which meant that any cold he caught could develop into bronchitis – as indeed happened in February 1971, shortly after the move to Green End.

Elspeth's concern for Gervas made her bossy and irritable with him. Now seventy-five and enfeebled by lack of food, he took to his bed and would not come downstairs. His heart had been troubling him for many years – Elspeth told Margery Perham that his problem was the weakening of arterial muscles in the heart. Gervas grew worse, and developed an accumulation of fluid in his legs – what used to be called dropsy – an indication that his heart and lungs were not working adequately. He began to become depressed, losing hope of recovery after several years of discomfort. Life no longer seemed worth living. He wrote a letter to Charles in which he said what a good life his had been, and that he was happy its end had come.

Facing his death with composure and a practical compassion for the feelings of others, Gervas asked Elspeth to help him die. As a member of the Voluntary Euthanasia Society she had foreseen this, but it must have been a painful decision for her. They had had many discussions on the subject over the years, Elspeth maintaining how stupid human beings were not to organise painless injections for themselves, as they allowed to animals. She never hid her views on euthanasia, once writing to Barbara Gough, her former Weidenfeld editor who had left publishing to become an osteopath:

While of course you'll be doing a great service in alleviating the pain etc. of diseases of old age like arthritis, I do implore you to do nothing to *prolong* life even further than it's already being prolonged, past the stage that nature has intended and when one has reached Shakespeare's seventh age. I think this extraordinary passion of some doctors simply to keep people non-dead at all costs, even hobbling feebly about deaf and incontinent and totally dependent and probably gaga, is revolting. In the last stages, if you don't look out, they end up keeping you strung up to the ceiling with tubes and pumps and drips and horrible machines just to prevent nature taking its merciful course. To show they are cleverer than nature in my opinion.[5]

She urged her friend Mary Lovell to join the Voluntary Euthanasia Society, whose bills were habitually thrown out of Parliament by 'pro-life' opponents: 'I am pro Life but not pro suffering, misery, indignity and keeping alive people who want to die, and think those are wicked who are.'[6]

As Elspeth reckoned right and proper, Gervas died at home by his own hand, with her assistance. He had fallen into a coma, waking briefly to ask Elspeth not to recall Charles from a trip he was taking with Frederica, and died on 2 April 1971. When Charles returned from his trip the farewell letter from his father was on the mat of his London home, with the rest of the post. Some of Elspeth's friends knew how Gervas had died. In later years her old friend the anthropologist Audrey Richards, now almost blind from cataracts, wrote to ask her how Gervas had 'managed it. You once told me he had been so efficient and considerate. You had better burn this or you might find yourself in a prison cell next to that queasy old Exit man with his paper [sic] bags.'[7]

Elspeth was practical and matter-of-fact about the funeral, held on 16 April in the Church of All Saints, Oaksey. 'Gervas and I didn't go in much for these ceremonials,' she wrote to Norah Smallwood, 'but I think this rounded off a well-spent life. I'm glad the flowers were so gay and the singing lusty – and a lot of people seemed to be there.'[8] The rousing hymns were 'To be a Pilgrim' and William

Blake's 'Jerusalem', and a passage was read from Shakespeare's *Cymbeline*:

> Fear no more the heat o' the sun
> Nor the furious winter's rages;
> Thou thy worldly task hast done,
> Home art gone and ta'en thy wages.
> Golden lads and girls all must
> As chimney-sweepers, come to dust.

Robert Louis Stevenson's poem, 'If I have faltered more or less/ In my great task of happiness', preceded the final hymn. Later, Gervas's ashes were scattered by the roses in the front garden at Green End.

Elspeth wrote to her friend Kit Taylor that she had enjoyed wonderful companionship and faithful love for forty years, and had hated seeing Gervas having to struggle to keep going as his heart grew weaker. In reply to a letter of sympathy from Peter Scott, she wrote: 'Gervas enjoyed everything so much that it is bleak when all that zest for life and enthusiasm is extinguished. I'd love to come over again one day to Slimbridge, which as you say continues in sun and storm and the birds never despair. But oh, dear, the humans!'[9]

After the funeral Elspeth went to Portugal to spend a week with her mother. On her return she did not want coddling, but Charles and Frederica regularly spent weekends at Green End in the coming months. Only when she had visitors did Elspeth turn on the central heating. When alone she huddled over a small Calor-gas heater, in order to economise. Elspeth always had great difficulty in expressing feelings other than irritation, believing firmly that rather than wear our hearts on our sleeves they should be invisible. Five years earlier Nellie had written that she was grateful for 'the definite anti-self-pity expression you've taught me over the last few years'.[10]

Years later Elspeth wrote to comfort a friend on the death of her partner. She described how things had been after the death of Gervas: 'I think at first one is sort of numbed, and this only wears off gradually but one *does* come to terms. Which doesn't mean forgetting the person, that can never be and one wouldn't want it to. But feeling, as it were, more companionable with their shade. Gervas was a lot older than me and almost of a different generation because he grew up before the First World War (and took part in it from the beginning). He had an outlook and a set of values that has gone . . . But of course it is lonely, we were married nearly 40 years. But one gets used to it as to everything in time.'[11]

In June Elspeth was greatly sustained in her grief by the news that Frederica was pregnant. She felt she should get on with life, despite facing an empty space of huge dimensions. This complicated and clever woman, unable to reveal her inner strife, struggled to write again. Nellie warned her against resuming creative work until she had rid herself of mental fatigue, and it is true that Elspeth's usually strong and restless imagination seems to have deserted her. Gervas's death had affected her profoundly, far more than she had imagined it would. To Margery Perham, who enquired solicitously about her work, she wrote:

> Writing. No, only a few odd articles. In the blood perhaps but as I get older, the daily round takes longer. I get slower and incredibly doddery and forgetful . . . I have so little to say. To whom? And what about? . . . I never had enough original imagination to become a good writer of fiction. [Margery Perham wrote NO! in the margin.] Poor and indifferent fiction writers are legion and should be suppressed. I have no time and facilities for research and can't afford it, it takes ages, yields little and no one pays while it goes on. Besides, there is a whole army of far more skilled researchers than I. Nor do I speak the modern idiom. . . . Basically one has accumulated all that one is ever going to in one's bank. I think I have drawn from it most of what is useful. There is, of course, the economic incentive, but that does not generate enthusiasm and ideas. One writer I know cut his throat because he had run out of ideas and quite a lot of others have given up by less gruesome methods.[12]

Margery asked Elspeth to come and stay with her in Oxford, but inertia had set in:

I've been trying to establish a small garden. I am doing virtually no writing. I'm much slower and even more muddled than I used to be (Parkinson's Law coming into play). Also I've lost touch with African matters and feel I have nothing of use or interest to say. It's a different world and it is useless to write about it unless one goes there and travels. And I've no wish to do so. I can't afford to earn nothing, so pick up a little here and there, and perhaps the time will come when I will hit on something I really want to write about ... What hundreds of thousands of irrelevant words have been written about Rhodesia. We – the British – find it impossible to realise that we have no gunboats any longer. Not even anchored off Belfast. I expect the fall of the Roman Empire was very much like this, don't you?[13]

Many years later there was a symposium at Oxford about Margery Perham and her work. Elspeth at first accepted an invitation to attend, but changed her mind and did not go, with the explanation, 'Yesterday's politics can be as stale as the day before yesterday's ham sandwich.'[14]

To the enquiries of friends about what she was writing now, she would sourly reply, 'Cheques.' Elspeth did, however, rouse herself enough to take out an annuity to try to give herself some financial security. She advised Margery Perham not to sacrifice herself to the resolve to leave as much as possible to her heirs, and to emulate her by taking out an annuity which repaid the full capital sum in ten years.

In October 1969 Elspeth had agreed to supply 30,000 words for one volume of a heavily illustrated series of seventeen about the world's explorers, for Aldus Books. She thought it would be an easy, hack job, but it was more arduous and time-consuming than she expected. Called *The Challenge of Africa*, the book was published in 1971. Towards the end of 1970 Elspeth's agent Herbert van Thal, of London Management, suggested she do an anthology of the writings of Charles Kingsley for a new series Allen & Unwin was producing. 'As I can't summon time or energy to launch out on anything original at the moment, this seems a good idea,' she told Norah Smallwood. 'The Canon [Kingsley] seems himself to be an engaging figure, but how he does go on about God.'[15] The great advantage of the project was that the material would come to her rather than she having to go to it. She included in the book Kingsley's brothers George and Henry, a writer of Australian bush tales, and hoped to insert a few excerpts from the work of their niece Mary Kingsley, one of her favourite African writers, but lack of space forbade this. *The Kingsleys* was published in 1973.

Norah Smallwood attempted to win Elspeth back to the Chatto fold. Elspeth, however, felt that she had no ideas that would stand up to close scrutiny, or that were worth imparting to the world – 'just as the world has too many people, so it has too many books'.[16] But, goaded by Norah, she put forward three possibilities – a life of David Livingstone's wife Mary, a book on big-game hunters, and a life of Benedict Arnold, the eighteenth-century American traitor. Departing from her usual habit, to satisfy Chatto's new partners Elspeth sent brief synopses of 'Benedict Arnold' and of what she called 'The Killers' (big-game hunters of the past such as F.C. Selous, Arthur Neumann, Karamoja Bell, A.J. Hunter and Bror Blixen, in tandem with modern 'croppers'). At Chatto the newcomer George Trevelyan favoured 'The Killers', Norah Smallwood Mrs Livingstone and John Charlton, another new face, none of Elspeth's ideas. They asked their sales manager, then travelling round Africa, to put the two African ideas to booksellers there, and back came the answer – 'The Killers' was what they wanted.

Now forced to think more deeply about the project, Elspeth began to have doubts. She thought Livingstone's description of big-game hunters as itinerant killers was nearer the mark than Ernest Hemingway's hair-on-chest approach, and there was something nauseating about the hunters' descriptions of the endless slaughter of frightened animals who could strike back only occasionally. Many of the hunters also lost her sympathy by being either American millionaires or businessmen making a profit from ivory trading or taking maharajahs on safari. There was also little useful material on these men of action, whose way of life precluded much analysis of motive, even though they wrote scores of books describing in tedious detail the action of the hunt. 'Perhaps I'm just a little bored with Africa, and their bites and boils and bowels, and all those gorgings of raw flesh including the offal,' she told Norah.[17] She began making notes in a dilatory way, distracted by plotting a possible detective story and by a far more momentous event – the birth of a grandson.

Josceline Grant Huxley was born on 15 February 1972. When Frederica entered hospital Elspeth went to look after her son, but she left when mother and baby came home. She told Norah Smallwood that her grandson was born with a Napoleonic will and an athlete's lungpower – he was a true Huxley, 'fidgety, imperious and demanding'.[18] In truth, this was a more pertinent description of the Grants, Nellie and Elspeth, than of Gervas and his kin. Elspeth stepped fairly smoothly into a grandmotherly role – though she never changed a nappy – perhaps glad to have a distraction from the difficulties of writing when her heart was not in it, perhaps anxious to compensate for the inadequacies of her raising of Charles. She even had charge of Jos (she took him to Cousin Peggy's, where the family nanny was in attendance) for seventeen days in September–October 1972 while his parents went to stay with Nellie in Portugal. At the same time she was in charge of the affairs of the eighty-nine-year-old Aunt Vera, Robin's widow, whose domestic arrangements had broken down. Elspeth took her into Green End while she searched for an old people's home in the vicinity. After a home was found, Elspeth visited Vera regularly and shouldered the responsibility of managing her finances, gaining power of attorney once Vera was unable to make her own decisions. Elspeth's letters of the time display a calmness and acceptance of inevitability that had never been there before. Gone are the complaints about the interruptions to her writing schedule, the difficulties of combining the routines of a household with a life of the mind.

A year after Gervas's funeral Elspeth endured a further blow. She adored dachshunds, as did her mother, and had had several. She was taking the last of these, Honey, for a walk when a greyhound slipped its collar and began to attack her pet. She lifted Honey high into the air above her head, but the greyhound continued to savage her, and also bit Elspeth. Honey was so badly injured that she had to be put down. Charles and Frederica tried valiantly to give Elspeth another dog, but she utterly refused. The greyhound was owned by the local butcher in Oaksey, and the incident rankled for a long time.

At almost ninety, Nellie too needed greater care, and came more frequently to Oaksey, while Elspeth herself paid more regular visits to Portugal. The desire to write took a back seat for a while, and there was none of the panicky, sometimes slightly selfish, guarding of her writing time that there had been in the past. A year and a half after the birth of Jos, in September 1973, Frederica produced non-identical twin boys. Thereafter Charles's whole family descended on Green End almost every weekend, and the two-year-old Jos was occasionally left in Elspeth's sole care. He howled on the stairs for attention in the mornings, but she resolutely refused to get up. Sometimes Nellie would come over from Portugal, still tremendously mentally alert and wanting to see relatives and friends all over the country. Her cataracts, weepy eyes (such a nuisance at funerals, she said, because they gave the wrong impression), corns, rickety knees and leg ulcers were but little inconvenience and did not deter her from rushing about like 'a human dynamo' or 'time-bomb', as Elspeth described her. As for Elspeth herself, approaching seventy years of age, her eyesight was not as good as it had been, and she was becoming forgetful. She left little notes about the house in likely places, as reminders of things to be done, which she then could not read. She found the garden at Green End a struggle to maintain, but became as passionate about it as Gervas had been about his at Woodfolds. Every year she planted another tree in a little wood she was creating.

She was still, however, forced to write to augment her income. And she had to give money to Nellie, now almost penniless despite a legacy from Dolly Miles, who had died in 1971. Nellie had raged about Dolly for years, putting up with her visits with bad grace. But when she died she wrote to Elspeth, 'we all, for some unknown reason, have had a basic real affection for Dolly dating from many, many years ago. I feel remorse for all my beastliness to her.'[19] The death of her friend caused Nellie to take practical steps about her own future. She persuaded her neighbour Mr Batchelor, a surgeon, to make the arrangements for her to buy a burial plot at nearby St George's cemetery in Bensafoein for £75, 'the cost of dying having gone up like the cost of living'.[20] For three centuries British residents of Portugal had been buried there, under the ilex trees.

It was Elspeth who paid for the plot, though Nellie still had hopes of earning a living – this time by preparing dried flowers. Elspeth was detailed to get gutta percha, borax, silicon gel and other paraphernalia for the enterprise, as before she had patiently bought equipment for other money-spinning plans. Then Nellie's beloved dachshund Rosie, one of the reasons for her settling in a Portugal free from quarantine laws, died. 'I am quite, quite definite,' she told her daughter, 'no more heart-tearing to bits, no more dogs of my own.'[21] As always Nellie's misery was relieved by action, and she bought lace to make christening robes for Charles and Frederica's twins. She wondered whether one robe would do, with a baby popped in at each end.

Elspeth was deeply troubled by Nellie's refusal to live in England near her. Even when Nellie did visit she insisted on sleeping in the separate stone extension Elspeth had built as a playroom for Charles's boys. Both women had mellowed, and they might have been able to live together if Nellie had agreed to do so. Nellie suggested living in a caravan in Elspeth's field – 'it could be tucked away out of sight of the sitting room. We could invite each other to meals. I'd be entirely self-supporting and very cosy and you could go away with an easy conscience about mum.'[22] She finally conceded that Elspeth could look around for an old people's home for her, though 'we aged *hate* giving up independence and loathe being a nuisance'.[23] She was not yet ready to die.

She asked Elspeth to send her cookery books and set out to make herself a cordon bleu cook, one of her specialities being Irish stew, because ever since she had had it at the Ritz with Evelyn Waugh she had considered it a luxury. Cockie continued to visit Nellie regularly, and Elspeth now wrote twice a week so that the postman would have to call more than once, and could report any untoward event. Nellie had to be brought over to England for a cancerous growth on her face to be removed, and when back at the quinta she developed an ulcer on her leg which would not heal. Her lack of mobility annoyed her, particularly as she was still maintaining that 'I have a gypsy urge.'[24] She thought she could make ends meet if she had a paying guest, but conceded that she would be able to tolerate only a deaf mute. Her maid Perpetua, who came each day to care for her, cost £40 a month, a lot of money for Nellie, so Elspeth continued with her injections of cash.

Nellie had something to look forward to when Ingrid Lindstrom arranged to visit her in July 1976. Her old friend arrived frail and deaf and troubled with impaired vision, but Nellie was wonderfully patient with her ailments. 'Ingrid is a desperately unhappy soul,' she said. 'She is a born fighter, and now has nothing left to fight for, except her vision and deafness which she can't win and knows it. Mentally she is marvellously alert and her excellent radio . . . goes on dawn to dusk and during the night. She longs for a job and constantly asks to help . . . I am so deeply sorry for her . . . I do wish I had the guts to say goodbye to everything.'[25] When Ingrid left to return to her daughter Viveka in England, it was the last time the two old ladies saw each other.

By July 1977 Nellie's ulcer was preventing her from walking and her maid came every day, even Sundays. Perpetua got her out of bed and dressed her, lifted her on to her chair, and left at 7.30 p.m. after putting her to bed. 'IF I depart this life,' Nellie wrote to Elspeth, 'don't worry. It will be no case of suicide, I haven't the guts. I really would sooner get over and done with it all, a horrid time clearing up etc I know, so don't *grieve* unduly, see?'[26] Cockie offered her a home, but Nellie refused. Her last written words to her daughter, on 30 July 1977, were 'God bless you and *all* love. Did you have a nice birthday?'[27] On 1 August, when it was clear that Nellie needed twenty-four-hour care, Elspeth flew to Portugal to pack up her belongings and bring her back to England. The night before they were due to fly, Nellie lapsed into a coma. Elspeth took her to the British Hospital in Lisbon, where she died on 21 August 1977, aged ninety-two. She was buried in St George's cemetery, as she had desired. Hers had been a life well spent. She had not acquired material goods or accumulated substantial property, but she had given immense pleasure to other people by her very existence. Rooms came alive when Nellie was there, with her flashing wit and wisdom. Elspeth was deeply affected by her mother's death. Nellie had had a good span of years, and the longer people live the more their death can surprise us, because we have come to think of them as immortal. To help her cope with her grief, Elspeth began to contemplate a book to commemorate her mother.

In 1972, the year after Gervas died, Elspeth had treated herself to an Aegean cruise, fulfilling a long-held ambition. Immediately after her return Weidenfeld asked her to write for their Great Explorers series a 40,000-word biography of David Livingstone, the centenary of whose death would be in 1974. Thinking that this would not involve much work and could be done from home, Elspeth agreed. She was now beyond the stage of travelling across the world for copy. Norah Smallwood, still attempting to woo Elspeth back to Chatto, counter-suggested that she write a book on the Black Prince, son of Edward III. Confessing ironically to 'a certain rustiness in my medieval French', Elspeth turned down a project she said she would have jumped at twenty years before.[28] 'The flame of ambition has burnt rather low,' she admitted.[29] She kept turning down ideas from other publishers, even an offer from America of $2,000 plus all expenses for five thousand words on racial tensions, to be written after a tour of African countries – 'I'd lose my specs in the first country, my passport in the second, my currency in the third etc,' she told Norah.[30] Norah wanted Elspeth to write another novel because no one wrote such witty letters as her, but Elspeth confessed she could think of no setting, motive or method with any spark of originality. In any case, she was busy with Dr Livingstone, who was 'gradually sinking into the swamps of Lake Bangweolo, bleeding as ever from the bowels* and writing letter after letter with no Post Office for 2,000 miles. It is all very sad.'[31]

Norah then suggested a country autobiography, a book about herself which could include moving home, stories about her grand-children and her experiences as a magistrate, something like E.M. Delafield's *Diary of a Provincial Lady* (1930). Elspeth was tempted, but saw immediate pitfalls, the most serious of which was that whatever one wrote about living people inevitably gave offence, especially if the writer was trying to be mildly funny, and 'one has to caricature a bit as you know'.[32] She also claimed to have an awful memory and to have forgotten everything that had happened. This was far from the case with *The Flame Trees of Thika* and *The Mottled Lizard*, but in both books Elspeth had relied for much of the content on letters and notebooks provided by Nellie, whom she had urged to put her African experiences on paper. And, as it happened, Elspeth had just agreed to write another short biography for Weidenfeld, this time on Florence Nightingale. She had enjoyed doing Livingstone, a regurgitation job which required no original research, and looked forward to Nightingale, which would be the same type of book.

None the less, Elspeth promised Norah she would 'try some autobiographical brooding, but I haven't had an interesting life, and couldn't do the soul-stripping that perhaps one ought to do'.[33] She was always self-conscious about her intellect, brushing off enquiries about her books and steering conversations round so that she could hear about the news and lives of those she talked to. And it was her habit to eschew profound self-analysis, for she abhorred the self-indulgence of feeling sorry for oneself. Her sensitivity about her intellectual credentials stemmed from her inadequate education, and she always claimed she was not 'academic'. This overflowed into a reluctance to examine her own motives. In fact her autobio-graphical works reveal a deeply sensitive person, free of bigotry and

---

* She was referring to Livingstone's haemorrhoids, for which modesty and a dread of publicity about his embarrassing complaint had prevented him seeking treatment when on a visit to England. He eventually died from anaemia caused by bleeding piles.

stereotyping, with a sense of wonder at nature and her fellow human beings. Her absence of sentimentality in no way inhibited her understanding and compassion. In April 1974 she quietly began a book on her daily life in the form of a diary.

Instead of 40,000 words, Elspeth's Nightingale typescript came to 200,000. Rigorous cutting reduced it to 60,000, which Weidenfeld accepted. Elspeth had run out of ideas about what to do next. Weidenfeld suggested a third biography and produced a list of five possible subjects. Elspeth chose Scott of the Antarctic, and was offered a generous advance of £4,500. For the moment, however, she was busy writing her village diary, which combined a quotidian account of events in Oaksey with aspects of the history of the village and its inhabitants. She sent a preliminary draft of the six months from April to October 1974 to Norah, who said she greatly enjoyed it and that Elspeth should definitely continue. Norah wanted to sign a contract at once, but Elspeth refused – to her later disadvantage. In April 1975 the diary for the whole year was sent to Chatto by Herbert van Thal of London Management – the first time Elspeth had used him in her negotiations with her main publishers. On Elspeth's instructions he tried to get the advance of £1,000 offered by Chatto raised to £3,000, the minimum she would accept.

When Norah Smallwood and her colleague Hugo Brunner read the typescript they were uneasy. Norah said she enjoyed the book immensely, and made suggestions for its improvement – she said that she and Hugo had felt at times the book was too sketchy, which was a pity when Elspeth was capable of fine, polished work. She was, she added, sure that Elspeth planned to eliminate unnecessary repetitions, and said there was a bewildering number of names. 'If you could introduce a little more of yourself in the diary it would gain immeasurably,' she advised.[34] Hugo Brunner thought Elspeth could be more selective about the dollops of history, perhaps only using them when they gave texture to the book. There was nothing in this criticism that Elspeth did not accept, and she polished and altered her manuscript accordingly. But times had changed for her, and she would not accept the terms offered. Her refusal caused the directors of Chatto to look closely at the work.

'We all think,' said Hugo Brunner in a memo, 'that while it bears the marks of a first-rate author whose books will sell to some degree on her name alone, it lacks the penetration of village life that is such a mark of *Akenfield** ... £1,500 is the maximum we should advance.'[35]

The other directors proposed that the book be refused, but Norah said this was a 'preposterous suggestion'. She said she would give the manuscript to others in the firm to read, because a revised offer would require everyone at Chatto to be behind the book. She then went into hospital for an operation. While she was away Hugo Brunner wrote to Elspeth that Norah 'would regret very much there should be a disagreement of this sort over one of your books after so many years of happy collaboration'.[36] He told Herbert van Thal that Chatto were bowing out because of the gap between their offer and the author's expectations. This would never have happened if Norah had been in the office rather than in hospital. Elspeth was deeply hurt by the rejection of her book. An anonymous little rhyme that had caused amusement was now only too true:

> Take it like a trooper
> Your MS missed the bateau.
> Windus thought it super
> But not so Mr Chatto.

Elspeth wrote to Hugo Brunner:

I feel very sad that after thirty-six years our association should come to an end, particularly over a disagreement about money. In the past when Gervas was alive and I was earning more than half my income from journalism, this was not of such predominant importance as it has since, inevitably, become, now I've given up journalism and have to cope with inflation on an annuity and a few dwindling dividends. I have to sell my wares to the best advantage. £1,000, which would have seemed reasonable ten years ago, is negligible by today's standards – about four months' salary for a good secretary. Ten years ago I received an advance three times as much as the

* By Ronald Blythe, published in 1969.

one you have just offered. You haven't got confidence in the book's future. You may be right, but it is discouraging to the author. My regrets are deep and genuine, especially as Norah gave me such encouragement over this book in the early stages.[37]

When Norah returned to the office the deed had been done, and there was nothing she could do about it. Her power at Chatto was waning as new blood came into the firm. A year later she wrote to Elspeth that she missed their regular exchanges and so much that was good in the past. A friendship cemented by Norah's regular visits to Woodfolds and Elspeth's cadging of a bed in Norah's London flat was now destabilised. Both women regretted the break.

As regards *Gallipot Eyes*,* as the village diary was called, it was accepted by Weidenfeld on far better terms than those offered by Chatto, and published in 1976. Yet Hugo Brunner was right – the book is not a success. It is too much a gallimaufry of Elspeth's present life, bits of village history, descriptions of some of Oaksey's four hundred inhabitants and their ancestors and tedious genealogical background. It is neither interesting nor perceptive, and almost seems afraid to look too deep. Elspeth found it difficult to write after the deaths of her husband and mother. Yet there are parts of the book which rise above the ordinary. There is a moving tribute to the cheerful, nimble, seventy-five-year-old Dolly Jennings, Elspeth's home help for the last thirty years who still came three times a week on her bicycle. She had never missed a day. Most of the rest of the book, however, appears to have been written by someone whose senses had been numbed, as Elspeth's were when Gervas died.

In 1975 there appeared the first American edition of Elspeth's and Margery Perham's *Race and Politics in Kenya*, first published in Britain in 1944. Margery Perham – who had always thought Elspeth's

---

* The title comes from a description by John Aubrey of north Wiltshiremen: 'Their persons are generally plump and feggy; gallipot eyes, and some black; but they are generally handsome enough.'

prose was Swiftian, whereas she was a carthorse by comparison – had asked Elspeth to help her correct the book, but she refused, saying she had never reread any of her work and did not intend to begin now: 'There's quite enough to do these days I feel without correcting mistakes made thirty-five years ago.'[38] She advised Margery not to put on that hairshirt and to leave it to the publisher, Greenwood Press, to do the work. But Margery persisted, and found many misprints.

After finishing *Gallipot Eyes*, Elspeth busied herself preparing for publication by the Folio Society an abridgement of *Travels in West Africa* (1897) by her heroine Mary Kingsley, the nineteenth-century adventurer. She was in her element doing an exercise such as this which could be undertaken without stirring from her own hearth, and she made a good job of it. Already familiar with the family from *The Kingsleys*, she described this niece of Charles Kingsley's as travelling like

> a lone she-wolf. She had no base, no armed guards, no network of African agents, no means of transport, no equipment beyond a black bag, a small portmanteau and some collecting boxes, and practically no money ... This very austerity gave her the key to the African mind and way of life. Officials and missionaries lacked this key because they did not live and eat and sleep and learn to think as Africans did, uninsulated, without European skills and tools for subduing the environment. Like Africans she lived with the environment without attempting to change it, or to avoid its rigours.[39]

Mary Kingsley insisted on wearing stiff Victorian dress in Africa, stoutly maintaining that it would prevent her body from being pierced by spikes if she fell into a game pit. She gave the impression that trudging through the jungles of the Congo was no more arduous than an afternoon stroll in Hyde Park. There was something of Nellie and Elspeth herself in this very amusing and courageous woman who cared not a fig for missionaries and colonial officials, and who thought gin an excellent article of trade because it did not lose its value from rust or mildew. Mary Kingsley also possessed

Elspeth's appreciation, at once sensual and intellectual, of African nature.

Norah Smallwood had not abandoned her attempt to regain Elspeth's trust. She suggested that writing the life of another woman African pioneer, Olive Schreiner, author of the famed *The Story of an African Farm* (1883), might interest her. Elspeth was wary, and still unforgiving: 'Let's see how we feel at the end of next year.'[40] She was also rather enjoying her growing grandsons, now they had left babyhood. The three exuberant, noisy and hungry boys who seemingly required no sleep came often to Oaksey with their parents at weekends, causing Elspeth to moan proudly, 'If it wasn't for frequent recourse to the bottle I might well give in. The aggressive instinct in the human male has not been sapped by the degeneracy of our fin de civilization era. Potential mercenaries every one.'[41]

She was also busy with her biography of Robert Falcon Scott. This time she branched out and did original research once more, which she thoroughly enjoyed. There were frequent visits to the Scott Polar Research Institute in Cambridge, where she grew to know and like the archivist, H.G.R. King. She spent a whole month there doing the initial research, and this break from home reinvigorated her. Thereafter she spent shorter periods at Cambridge, returning home more frequently. The experience of writing a book entirely her own once again was heady, and helped her to cope with the death of her mother that summer.

Elspeth's friend Peter Scott told her he was glad she was doing a book on his father, and said she could come to Slimbridge at any time to read what papers of his father's, mostly letters, were there. Elspeth drove over and was very excited to see how much material there was. She saw that her task would be eased by the proximity of Slimbridge, and began to commute daily to read the documents. Peter Scott lent her several books on polar exploration and gave her a letter of introduction to the Royal Geographical Society in London, which eased her path to the papers held there. She also consulted the Scott material at the Public Record Office and the Royal Naval College at Greenwich.

The research proceeded slowly, largely because of the immense amount of material available, although Weidenfeld's wish that the book should not be too academic meant Elspeth avoided having to keep detailed source references – a considerable time-saver. She began the research in September 1975, and continued it through 1976, except when she visited Nellie and spent a fortnight in Poland in August with an Australian friend, the cousin of the Australian Ambassador in Warsaw, where a car and driver was provided for them to visit Cracow and Gdansk. She was reluctant to hurry because another biography, of both Scott and Roald Amundsen, the Norwegian who beat him to the South Pole, was being written at the same time by Roland Huntford. Elspeth thought Huntford's book was bound to precede hers, and that a year should elapse between the two. She contacted Huntford, a very thorough researcher, and gradually became aware that such was his meticulousness that her book would be ready first. In the event, Huntford's book did not appear until 1979.

'I spend at least half my writing time,' Elspeth told H.G.R. King, 'on hunting through my notes to find bits I vaguely remember but can't locate; I wish I was more methodical'[42] – a common lament of historians. King gave Elspeth a great deal of help, not least with her confusion over geographical and statute miles and the location of the South Magnetic Pole. When the manuscript was finished in May 1977 he read it before it was sent to the publisher. He picked up some mistakes, and told her the book was 'a sympathetic and mature account and your lightness of touch is a welcome relief after the stodge that is sometimes put before us'.[43] Many years later he still remembered it: 'Elspeth Huxley wrote so well. I liked her book, because it was very fair. She was also a delightful person.'[44]

Elspeth was embarrassed about the book's lack of references, telling King she had meant to identify the source of each quotation as she went, but that there was too much rush (which was not true): 'This is unscholarly of course but then I am not a scholar (alas). I hope this won't strike you as a hamstringing defect.'[45] She was unable to rectify the fault because Weidenfeld suddenly decided to bring the book out before Christmas instead of the following spring. Such was the speed of the production that even Birdie

Bowers, a member of the doomed five-man Polar party, was left out of the index. The book's editor was absent at a critical time in August, handing it over, as Elspeth wrote to H.G.R. King, 'to someone called Sappho who perhaps was too much taken up with songs about the Isles of Greece to notice'.[46] Elspeth failed to mention, as was typical, that her mother had died in August and that she had been out of the country dealing with Nellie's affairs. She never courted sympathy.

Something of the triumph following the publication of *The Flame Trees of Thika* followed that of *Scott of the Antarctic*, despite another book on the explorer, *Scott's Men* by David Thomson, having been published at the end of June. The Scott Polar Research Institute lent a splendid display of Scott artefacts and manuscripts to Heffers bookshop in Cambridge, where Elspeth signed copies of the book – 'What a formidable place Heffers is. I felt like a polar bear in that pit, expecting to have a fish thrown down to me from the balcony. There are too many books in the world.'[47]

Elspeth was now seventy years old, a little world-weary, complaining of having a bad memory and without her former energy – 'there is so much to do, most of it futile'.[48] A small, thin, hunched figure, generally in trousers and baggy cardigan, she was occasionally left in sole charge of her twin grandsons, and once had all three boys while Charles and Frederica were away. She found them very tiring, on the go from 6 a.m. to 8 p.m., and perhaps realised how lightly she had been let off with her own son, kept out of her way by Cleggy. She struggled away in her kitchen, making cottage pies and apple crumbles for the boys and elaborate dishes for guests – by force of will she made herself into a good cook late in life. Elspeth also took on Charles's three cats when his family was away from home. She had never been a cat person, but now she clearly enjoyed looking after them – she even went to Oxford to rescue the Burmese cat of a friend who had died suddenly.

Elspeth was now feeling that writing was more of an effort than before, as age began to affect her brain – not in a serious way, but enough to make finding the right word a struggle rather than an easy pleasure. 'I'm beginning to feel,' she wrote to Norah Smallwood, 'I've had enough of putting one word after another and would like to stop but have few (if any) other skills.'[49] Others, too, were contemplating Elspeth's old age. *The Times*'s obituary editor asked Margery Perham to write an advance obituary of Elspeth. She demurred, saying that while she and Elspeth got on well, their attitudes to Africa did not coincide. Considering Laurens van der Post too mystical for the task, *The Times* approached Norah Smallwood to ask whether Elspeth's friend James Lees-Milne would be suitable. Instead Norah suggested John Buxton, until recently a don at New College, Oxford, who had known Elspeth for years.

Elspeth was not lonely, having as she did her son's family, and often staying with Cousin Peggy, now living in Suffolk. Her Aunt Bridget, Uncle Eddie Grant's wife, was also a good friend. And of the many East African friends who had now retired to England, a surprising number had settled within easy driving distance of Oaksey. In summer 1978 she visited Scotland for the first time since the early 1960s, staying for one week in an ancient castle and for another in a perfect little bungalow that had arrived from Sweden in two lorries and been put together on site.

To cope with her continuing sorrow at Nellie's death, Elspeth reread her mother's letters, all of which she had kept carefully since 1933. Nellie had written once or twice a week, by lamplight or erratic electricity in the evenings, detailing the minutiae of farm life at Njoro or her Portuguese adventures. They were very lively letters, telling of her farm's tragedies (many) and triumphs (very few), and full of indiscreet remarks about human beings, a species the reader might conclude that Nellie generally disliked, if she was to be believed. Only Rose, Cockie and Ingrid (and sometimes Njombo, Mbugwa, Muchoka and Karanja) were exempted from her scorn and disappointment with her fellow man. Yet so many people who knew her throughout her life said Nellie was a kind woman that she clearly hid her feelings everywhere except in her letters to her daughter.

As she reread them, it occurred to Elspeth that her mother's letters might be of interest to others, and wondered whether extracts from them could be published, if some of the more derogatory remarks were eradicated. Although she knew Nellie would have been furious at the prospect of her letters being published, Elspeth asked her editor at Weidenfeld, Barbara Gough, to spend a weekend at Oaksey in October 1978, and showed her the letters and the outline of a plan. 'Her heart was definitely in that project,' said Barbara.[50] Elspeth's declared intention was to give a day-by-day account of what trying to farm in the Kenya highlands was really like by one who had done it, 'an amazing personality, undefeated by all the slings and arrows etc. to the end. And so generous-hearted.'[51]

Barbara Gough was not sure that Weidenfeld would be interested in the book, but her fears were groundless, and *Nellie: Letters from Africa* passed smoothly to publication in 1980. The first ninety-four pages contain a memoir of her mother by Elspeth, a charming evocation of Nellie and her ancestors and a sympathetic portrayal of Jos. There is no inkling of the eventual breakdown in the relationship between husband and wife, or of the friction between mother and daughter. Elspeth herself tells of the early years at Kitimuru and Njoro, and then lets Nellie take over in 1933, the year in which the extracts from her letters begin. Thereafter Elspeth's voice is heard only in linking passages explaining some of the events mentioned in the letters, but otherwise Nellie is allowed to speak alone. The reviews all commented on the remarkable person who had written the letters, a woman of great resilience and courage – true features of the pioneer.

By comparing the printed extracts of the letters with their originals in Rhodes House, Oxford, the reader can see not only how much of them was cut, but also how frequently Elspeth felt it necessary to alter her mother's wording. This was a most unscholarly thing to do, but Elspeth had done it before when quoting from original documents, and clearly felt it was no sin. In trying to protect her mother, a prudent and laudable aim, she sometimes distorts the story. None the less, *Nellie: Letters from Africa* became a favourite book both of those who had known Nellie and those who had not. All Nellie's sprightliness of thought and tongue are

there, as is her wit. Elspeth captures Nellie excellently in one anec-
dote in the memoir section:

> The single tap and a proper bath, not a tin tub, were all the
> amenities [at Kitimuru]. To visitors from England, accustomed
> to indoor sanitation, Nellie would say primly, in the language
> of the day, 'Now I expect you would like to see the geography
> of the house.' She would open a door leading to the outside
> world and announce, 'You have all Africa before you.' Actually
> there was a path leading to a clump of bushes about fifty
> yards away which concealed the 'garden house' with a deep
> pit latrine. This little hut was inhabited by centipedes, spiders,
> beetles and other creatures who sometimes alarmed visitors,
> but so far as I know never did them any harm.[52]

Elspeth ends the book with the words, 'Naturally I received many
letters [after Nellie's death], and the one I think she would have
enjoyed most ended, "Dear, dear Nellie, I am sure she won't want
to Rest in Peace; she will invent a new way of stringing harps." '[53]

THIRTEEN

Final Years

'Man,' said Elspeth, 'is the most destructive creature of all; we are like a cancer, there are too many of us and we are destroying everything.'[1] As she grew into middle age Elspeth, like her mother, had become a passionate supporter of animals, both wild and captive, even hedgehogs and frogs. She had displayed this concern in her book *Brave New Victuals* (1965), and she belonged to many animal preservation societies, among them the Council for the Preservation of Rural England, the Wiltshire Trust for Nature Conservation, the Malmesbury Civic Trust, the World Wildlife Fund, the Royal Society for the Protection of Birds, Fauna and Flora International and the Fauna Preservation Society. Among the magazines to which she subscribed were *Wildlife*, and she bought Christmas presents from the WWF catalogue. She was one of the Friends of the Serengeti, and was not afraid to criticise animal preservation societies if she believed they were working at cross-purposes to the WWF. In fact she disliked the bureaucracy of conservation, being more of a protectionist herself.

Peter Scott, a powerful figure in the world of animal conservation, fully appreciated Elspeth's way with words. Early in their friendship he asked her to put into a 'pithy piece of prose' an appeal he was launching on the Stock Exchange. She obliged, and also sent him a copy of *Forks and Hope*, in which she points out the danger to Kenyan wildlife posed by encroaching African farmers. Scott much appreciated what she said in the book, 'though the arrangement of the chameleon's toes' worried him in Jonathan Kingdon's illustrations. After one memorable evening at Scott's home at Slimbridge Elspeth wrote to thank him: 'I'll *never* forget that sunset, the lake and the sunlight and floodlights mingling, the atmosphere of serenity, and before that the geese and the peregrine thrown in for good measure ... and the waterfront and the peace and quiet, a complete escape from the idiotic stress and fuss.'[2]

Her interest in wildlife led Elspeth to question whether it was right to breed wild animals in captivity for reintroduction to their natural habitat. But she came to support it unequivocally after studying the topic while preparing *Whipsnade: Captive Breeding for Survival,* which she was asked to write to commemorate the zoo's fiftieth anniversary in 1981. The aim was to combine a history of Whipsnade with an investigation of its (and other zoos') purposes, one of which was captive breeding to ensure the survival of endangered species. Although on the whole opposed to the practice of enclosing animals in zoos, Elspeth acknowledged zoos' importance in biological study, and approved of their reintroduction programmes and their educational intent, which she hoped would persuade people of the urgency of nature conservation. As well as giving a history of early menageries, zoos in general and Whipsnade in particular, Elspeth covered in her book subjects as wide-ranging as animal and human behaviour and personalities; zoo architecture; animal extinction and zoos' breeding successes; feeding, research, collecting and illegal sales of animals; the effects of captivity; national parks; and animal health and diseases.

While writing *Whipsnade* Elspeth corresponded with Joy Adamson. They had known and written to each other for years, and Elspeth and her mother had stayed with Joy more than once at her camp near Isiolo. On one occasion Elspeth and Joy's car had suffered a breakdown near Nakuru. During the night of waiting they became much closer, confiding to each other their real opinions of men. Joy had also come to Oaksey, delivering as ever, in a thick Austrian accent, her breathless monologues about animals, at fast-forward speed. At least in England she could not share her bed with her animals, as she did when a guest in other people's houses in Kenya. Unsurprisingly, many a host and hostess took a dim view of this, especially when Joy's animals urinated during the night. Joy was also notorious for making passes at men – Billy Collins, head of the publishing firm, with whom she had an affair, once returned to England with (he claimed) the jealous lioness Elsa's scratches all down his back.

While regarding Joy as an impossible woman, always having a fight with someone, Elspeth had a soft spot for her, as she glimpsed the sensitivity and accomplishment behind the abrasive personality. She described her as 'a proper bitch ... all the same I admired her,'[3] and said, 'Yes, she was maddening, but I don't think you get things done, let alone change attitudes, without being a battering ram.'[4] Joy suffered loneliness and isolation in the bush, particularly when her husband George could tolerate her no longer. Usually dressed in white vest and baggy shorts, occasionally she would put on a bra and dress and defrizz her hair to try to get him back. But in 1970 he left her for Kora, an isolated camp, where he studied lions. Elspeth described Joy and George's marriage as 'a strange one – they remained emotionally involved with each other despite a great gulf in temperament and character'.[5]

Mervyn Cowie, director of Kenya's national parks, found Joy a trial but liked George:

> Joy was a strange woman, and very difficult. She came into my office and asked if she could release Elsa in Tsavo. I said no, Elsa will walk into a tourist camp and be shot. Joy was furious. She threw a fit and rolled on the floor. The dentist came in from next door to see what I was doing. We had to escort her out. She was a funny person. We adored George – we tried to stop him being entangled with her. George liked a drink, but Joy wouldn't keep it in the house. So George kept some with Jerry Dalton, my chap at Isiolo, and some at his work-shop in a bottle labelled turps. One night he took the wrong bottle, which was rust remover, and he burnt his mouth.[6]

When George left her, Joy was confirmed in her belief that man was an inferior species to animals, and became increasingly undiplomatic and more than ever inclined to be weepy, especially when talking of her beloved Elsa and of Billy Collins, both now dead. She worried about George, who might end up in hospital 'due to a lion kiss'.[7]

Joy hoped to turn Shaba, where she camped, into a breeding reservoir of rare and endangered animals. But her leopard Penny's first litter miscarried, causing Joy great anxiety – 'In my own case I had three miscarriages and no children afterwards despite three husbands.'[8] It was a needless worry, for came the day when Penny proudly led Joy to her two new cubs under an overhanging rock: 'Can you understand how happy I am? Much love and please help to keep the leopards protected and on the list of endangered animals=because there is a war on between the USA Shikar Club who wants them to be taken off again.'[9] This letter, written in May 1979, was Joy's last to Elspeth. She was murdered a few months later by a disaffected former employee. Her cremation in Nairobi was attended by only a handful of people. George was there, the only one to seem genuinely grieved. He collected the ashes and spread them over the secret grave at Meru where they had buried Elsa.

Elspeth had written an introduction to Joy's autobiography, which greatly pleased the lonely woman. But she refused to write a film script based on Joy's phenomenally best-selling book about Elsa, *Born Free*, because she 'smelt a rat'. The proposal, however, was genuine enough, the film was a huge success (though Elspeth disliked it), and she lost an opportunity to make some real money.

After Elspeth's Whipsnade book was finished, another idea was put to her. Despite claiming 'I have been the subject of a high-level attack by Collins [who published *Whipsnade*] and have been more or less railroaded into taking on a very dubious proposition for an exceedingly inadequate reward,'[10] Elspeth viewed with favour a proposal from Philip Ziegler of Collins that she collaborate with Hugo van Lawick, a Dutch wildlife photographer living in Tanzania, on a coffee-table book about the Serengeti national park. She had always been interested in Kenya's national parks, so this study of one in Tanzania would coincide with her interests. Kenya's national parks had arisen from the Game Rangers' Department, formed to ensure that hunters kept to the restrictions of their licences and thus deeply involved in game preservation. As a child Elspeth had known the game rangers Blayney Percival and R.B. Woosnam. 'Woosnam was a terror,' said Lord Cranworth, 'to those who committed indiscriminate slaughter, either through sheer brutality and bloodlust or for the sake of profit.'[11] The flamboyant and glamorous Archie Ritchie, always deeply sunburnt and with a mane of white hair bleached even whiter by the sun, was for many years Kenya's chief game warden. Expert at dalliance and the breaking of hearts, he even made a pass at Margery Perham. A splendid custodian of animals, he began the policy of establishing national parks, the first of them a small area on the outskirts of Nairobi which became Nairobi National Park in 1946.

Tsavo National Park soon followed, due to the persuasion of Mervyn Cowie, Ritchie's successor, supported by Peter Scott and Julian Huxley. Cowie's long and bitter battle against poaching for ivory and rhino horn had caught Elspeth's imagination. African hunters set out from their villages and crept into national parks with bows and poisoned arrows, to kill elephants and rhinos wherever they could find them. From 1958 onwards Elspeth wrote several newspaper articles drawing the world's attention to the slaughter, and the need to preserve Africa's animals.

Philip Ziegler introduced Elspeth and Hugo van Lawick at a lunch in London. The plan was for her to fly to Tanzania and spend a month with Hugo in the bush, no easy journey for a woman of seventy-four. Yet Elspeth had regained her vigour and the *joie de vivre* snuffed out by Gervas's death, and looked forward to the great adventure. She landed at Arusha on 15 February 1981, to be met by Hugo and taken to Ngare Sera lodge. She immediately noticed the change in pace, which was here so gentle and so much more real. In Africa time was regulated by nature, not by man. Elephants ambled about peaceful and relaxed, putting their trunks into the mouths of companions as a greeting and sucking their own trunks, like humans their thumbs, for reassurance. Two rhinos played, and pelicans, so clumsy on the ground, soared into elegant and graceful flight to nest in thorn trees.

Hugo and Elspeth went on to Lake Manyara and then down into that animal Eden, the Ngorongoro crater. There were wildebeeste as far as the eye could see over a vast plain, two million of them with silvery-white backs and white beards. Just beyond Ndutu lodge, across the tip of Olduvai gorge, was Hugo's camp. It consisted of eight tents in a row, one of them the dining room. The longdrop lavatory overlooked Lake Ndutu, crimsoned with flamingos, a view not conducive to expediting one's business.

Always intensely interested in people, Elspeth talked to Hugo of his life and family over the campfire in the evenings. He told her the story of his birth in Indonesia, his escape with his mother just before the Japanese marched in, his year in Australia and his education in England and Holland, where he began to photograph wildlife. In 1960 he joined the documentary film-makers Armand and Michaela Denis in Nairobi as their assistant photographer. Louis Leakey then arranged for him to go to the Gombe stream chimpanzee project in Tanzania, to photograph chimps. Hugo and Leakey had argued about whether man started as a hunter or a scavenger. Leakey thought the latter, because man's early tools were incapable of butchering antelope or other large prey. But Hugo maintained that man was a hunter, for chimps caught antelope and ate them by tearing them apart. Hugo had been married twice, first to Jane Goodall, the chimp expert, who bore him a son, and secondly to the vivacious red-haired Terry, who disliked bush life and from whom he was at present getting an amicable divorce.

An abstemious perfectionist and a fiercely independent loner, Hugo no longer took animal photographs unless the subject was doing something interesting and hitherto unrecorded, or there were unusual and striking light conditions. He used his camera as an artist uses his brush and paints. There was an oriental patience in him that made him always aware. Once Elspeth pointed out a hoopoe on the road, lit up by the morning sun, but Hugo declined to take a picture because a feather was missing from its crest. He could be so still that a bird once perched upon his hand which was cupping his chin, gazed at him, then plucked two hairs from his head as nesting material. His vehicle would make alarming and erratic swerves to avoid a lizard or chameleon or sandgrouse, and his compassion extended to the five African staff at the camp, who were treated as friends.

Hugo showed Elspeth a kopje where two mother Thomson's gazelles stood beside their newly born, wet and wobbly fauns. It was a prehistoric place, with holes for bao, the Maasai game of skill and chance, scooped from the rock, and all around were chips of obsidian left from making arrowheads thousands of years before. Elspeth watched the birth of a wildebeeste and the tiny calf's wretched attempts to get to its feet and stay there. Once it did so the mother walked away and the calf followed; from birth to mobility had taken only six minutes. Hugo and Elspeth got within thirty yards of a group of sixteen lions, dozing with soft and pliant limbs, the essence of laziness. But their true character was evidenced by the skulls and skeletons all around. At sunset a thorn tree full of vultures was outlined against the red and orange sky. They watched the wildebeeste migration across a lake, where confusion reigned, mothers becoming separated from their calves who called for them with soft and moaning cries. Several lost calves galloped up to the Land Rover, and one lay down in the shade beneath the vehicle, grinding its teeth as it slowly died. Elspeth wanted to gather it up and take it back to camp to feed it with a bottle, but Hugo would not let her.

They went to Olduvai gorge to visit Mary Leakey, whose discoveries had first made probable the notion that man had originated in East Africa. She took them to her small museum to show them casts of her most exciting find, footprints made by human ancestors walking upright four million years before.

After a month with Hugo, Elspeth was taken back to Arusha, with its avenue of flame trees planted by German colonists so many years before. She wrote to Norah, 'My Serengeti trip went better than I had with my customary gloom expected. Hugo turned out to be rather a friendly chap – I think he could be difficult if one had cause to disagree with him, but I more or less sat at his feet which I feel was the right attitude.'[12] It had been a happy time, with Elspeth back where she belonged, in Africa, watching the sunsets and the dawns, free from the tyranny of time, among the animals and Africans she loved. The book she wrote, which was a sparkling return to form for her and made lovely by Hugo's photographs, she called *Last Days in Eden*. It was published by Harvill Press, and distributed by Collins, in 1984. Elspeth felt ill-served by Collins, who sat on the text for nearly two years after she submitted it in June 1981, then demanded a further 20,000 words from her. Gone were the days when her books were seen smoothly through the press by the efficient Norah Smallwood at Chatto & Windus.

Before Elspeth wrote *Last Days in Eden* she embarked on a novel, a form she had abandoned after *The Merry Hippo*, almost twenty years before in 1963. Her confidence restored, she described her new book as 'a very silly novel, a farce really', and sent early chapters to Norah, now forgiven and whom Elspeth knew from past practice was likely to encourage her.[13] This proved to be the case, and Norah's 'kind words on the phone *greatly* boosted my morale. I'll try to battle to the end of the book.'[14] Norah was invited back to Oaksey, and Elspeth to Norah's new London flat in Vincent Square. The novel, entitled *The Prince Buys the Manor*, was finished by October 1981 and published by Chatto in October 1982, described on its cover as 'an extravaganza'. In it Elspeth poked fun at hunt saboteurs, international terrorists, Save the Badger campaigners, a bearded guru and his chanting followers, and the bemedalled figure of General Mkubwa (the Swahili word for 'big'), the New Commonwealth ADC to the Royal Prince of Britain, who wishes to buy a manor in the smartest part of the Cotswolds. The book is dedicated to Norah, 'silken spur, incisive counsellor, and warm-hearted friend'.

Norah tried to interest Elspeth in writing the life of another of her authors, Richard Hughes, but the project fell through. *The Prince Buys the Manor* was the last time Elspeth and Norah were to work together, for Norah was persuaded to retire from Chatto in 1982. Now frail and arthritic and dependent on an ebony walking stick, with her legs often swathed in bandages, some colleagues felt she had become inflexible and had failed to keep up with the changing face of publishing. She had always been difficult to work with, and Chatto & Windus was now losing money every year. To her work colleagues formidable and intransigent, but to her favourite authors cheerful, strong and loyal, Norah was mourned by Elspeth when she died in 1984.

Elspeth's stay with Hugo van Lawick in Tanzania was not the first time she had revisited East Africa after her mother left Kenya. There was a flying trip in February 1974 to examine the situation of the elephants in Tsavo National Park, for an article for the *Guardian*. On that occasion she stayed with Rose Cartwright in the Rift Valley and at Pam Scott's (daughter of Lord Francis Scott)* house Deloraine at Rongai, as well as with Anne Joyce (Frank Joyce's daughter) at Kilima Kiu. She found time to go to Kilifi and Malindi, but it was a visit to her mother's Njoro farm that brought back most memories. All the old hands were there – even Karanja Mukoro the former herdsman, whom Elspeth reckoned must be almost a hundred. The school Nellie had started now had thirteen teachers and three hundred pupils, while next door Ingrid Lindstrom was still on her farm, undecided whether to sell or not.

Elspeth also used her brief time in Kenya to look at a collection of pioneers' memories she had been asked to edit for the East Africa Women's League. This eventually appeared in 1980, co-edited by Elspeth and Arnold Curtis, as *Pioneer's Scrapbook*. It was similar to the EAWL's earlier *They Made it Their Home* (1961) and their later *Memories of Kenya* (1986), for which Elspeth wrote the introductions.

Elspeth's subsequent visit to Kenya was in 1980, for the filming of *The Flame Trees of Thika* for television. The idea of a *Flame Trees* film had first been mooted in 1968, when Paul Radin, producer of the film of *Born Free*, approached Chatto & Windus for an option on *Flame Trees*. The agent Peggy Ramsay, who dealt with Chatto's film rights, organised the drawing up of an elaborate legal disclaimer to be signed by Nellie, the only living person accurately described

---

* Pam Scott stayed on in Kenya after independence and wrote a book about the country, *A Nice Place to Live* (1991). Elspeth was instrumental in getting it published.

in the book, even though Elspeth said her mother would not bring any legal action unless she was depicted as a drunken nymphomaniac or drug-peddler. The lawyer's bill of £80 was charged to Elspeth, but she refused to pay more than half of this. As for Nellie, when faced by the multi-claused, inordinately long disclaimer, she said it would have been far simpler had she herself written a letter saying she promised not to take any legal action. In the event Paul Radin could not raise enough capital to make the film.

Matters lay more or less dormant until 1978, when John Hawkesworth, the producer of *Upstairs, Downstairs* and other successful television series, went to see Elspeth in Oaksey to talk about filming *Flame Trees* in Kenya. This time the project took off, although the negotiations were not handled by her usual agency, and Elspeth got a very poor deal: only £5,000, with no repeat fees. With typical frugality, born of her lifelong insecurity about money and fear of being poor, Elspeth spent some of this on solar heating for Green End. She also became a script consultant – not because she wanted to interfere (her duties were nil), but in order to get a free trip to Africa. The filming began in September 1980, and Elspeth spent one week in a Nairobi hotel, going daily to the film set twenty-five miles away, and another week seeing old friends.

She took the opportunity to revisit her parents' first farm, Kitimuru at Thika. The old landmarks had gone; now everything was well developed and cultivated. At the end of a track through marching lines of coffee bushes a sign said 'Kitimuru House'. The flame trees leading to the door were no more, but there before her, now almost dwarfed by mature trees and shrubs, was the stone bungalow the Grants had built in 1912, with its curly Dutch gables and its steps up to the front door. Of the original grass and thatch house there was no sign – a coffee-drying plant now occupied its site. But the coarse lawn sown in front of the house by Nellie, on which Elspeth's pet duiker Twinkle had grazed, remained, though the stables had been replaced by sheds containing farm machinery. The vlei was there, unchanged. The house was now lived in by an old colonel named Merritt, who invited Elspeth in and gave her tea in the sitting room formerly occupied by Nellie's upright piano and revolving bookcase. Elspeth asked if her parents' coffee bushes were still alive, and was assured that they were. She was taken to the spot where she had watched the labourers dibbing in the seedlings seventy years before. Now it was part of a large, French-owned plantation of thousands of acres of coffee bushes. Elspeth keenly felt the ghosts around:

> The small white community that had cleared bush and planted the first coffee here had been young and hopeful, laughing off their troubles, charged with optimism, believing in themselves and in the worth of their task. All are dead ... my father's bones lie in Kenya. The seeds my parents, and others like them, planted and tended have not perished. Others have reaped the crop, but that is often so. Could they return, I think they would be satisfied.[15]

Elspeth spent a week on the film set watching the relaxed and witty Roy Ward Baker direct. For the purposes of the story Nairobi station was moved to Konza, south-east of the capital on the Mombasa line and still undeveloped enough to represent the early days, and filming took place around Lukenya, standing in for Thika; several 1913-style houses sprang up, containing furniture borrowed from descendants of pioneer settlers. The Nairobi Railway Museum provided old carriages, and a small track was laid. An ancient locomotive that ate eucalyptus logs and spat sparks was unearthed in a shunting yard and commandeered, while from somewhere else an old ox-wagon was found and refurbished. The film-makers took great trouble to get small details right, but they drew the line at naked breasts, which had been the norm among African women in 1912. They also refused to kill a single animal, and when a dead one was required they sent to London for a skin, which was then stuffed. A duiker was found in the national park orphanage to play Twinkle, but it grew so fast that two more youngsters had to replace it.

The filming lasted eighteen weeks. If rain was needed for a sequence the skies remained obstinately dry, and the Nairobi fire brigade was called to play water over the set. The local Africans, observing the scene, thought the film-makers were mad to waste the water. As for the flame trees, so necessary in the story, they were very temperamental. Flame trees are awkward at the best of times, going in and out of flower haphazardly just as they like, and now they stubbornly refused to blossom. When word of this got out, calls came in from all over Kenya whenever a flame tree was seen in flower, and a cameraman would be despatched to capture the phenomenon on celluloid. Christopher Neame, the co-producer, estimated that four thousand miles were travelled to photograph the wayward trees.

By the time Elspeth arrived in the first half of November, the cast's spirits were flagging. Her presence gave them all a psychological boost. She approved of what they were doing and did not mind her story being changed to suit the script, or even that her character was advanced in age from six to eleven, for 'reality is often ugly, untidy, and above all uncomposed'.[16] After all, she had herself manipulated truth for the purposes of her book, and even if she had attempted to be faithful, 'Memory always distorts, and memories of childhood, tinged inevitably with nostalgia, distort most of all. You remember women lovelier, men nobler, houses loftier, horizons wider than they really were.'[17]

Hayley Mills played Tilly (Nellie) and David Robb was Robin (Jos), while Elspeth as a child was played by Holly Aird, who had been chosen from five hundred hopefuls and was specially taught to ride for the film. Elspeth described her as 'a really superb small girl, aged 11, who was amazingly unself-conscious, natural and a born actress'.[18] One day there turned up on the set an old man, one Kamante – the same Kamante who had been rescued as a young boy by Karen Blixen and treated for a leg ulcer. He was invited to play a small part as one of the elders of an African village near the Grants' farm.

On 21 July 1981 Elspeth was invited to a press show in London to launch the film for Thames TV. It was shown in six episodes, and was very successful. Penguin sold 40,000 copies of the book almost immediately and had to rush through a reprint of 15,000, while Chatto reissued *The Mottled Lizard*. Argentina, Australia,

Greece, Hong Kong, Jordan, Ireland and New Zealand all bought the series, and it was shown on PBS in the United States, introduced by Alistair Cooke. It was so well received that it was repeated a few weeks later.

In October 1981 Elspeth appeared on *Desert Island Discs*, a sure sign that she had 'arrived'. The eight pieces of music she selected to take to the island with her were Cole Porter's 'Anything Goes', Dvořák's New World Symphony, Gershwin's 'Rhapsody in Blue', Grieg's piano concerto, Charles Trenet singing 'La Mer', Beethoven's Pastoral Symphony, 'Jupiter' from Holst's *The Planets* and the theme tune from the television adaptation of *Flame Trees*. As her book she picked a P.G. Wodehouse novel, but when she chose a dachshund as her luxury she was told that it must be something inanimate. With typical verve she argued that Malcolm Muggeridge had been allowed to take a hive of bees, but the presenter Roy Plomley countered that you could not make a companion of a bee. Elspeth chose instead a camera and film-developing equipment.

The success of *Flame Trees* on television prompted Norah Smallwood's successors at Chatto & Windus to issue an illustrated *Flame Trees* in 1987, with photographs of Elspeth's childhood in Kenya, an enterprise which earned her £6,000 from the print run of 20,000. In the same year Chatto held a luncheon at the Garrick Club to celebrate Elspeth's eightieth birthday. Apart from those who came from the world of books, such as Andrew Motion, then working at Chatto and later Poet Laureate, Elspeth had seven guests: Heather Jeeves (her agent at London Management following the retirement of Herbert van Thal), James and Alvilde Lees-Milne, Charles and Frederica, and John and Hyacinthe Hawkesworth. Hawkesworth described Elspeth as one of the most talented, worthwhile and modest people he had ever met.

The year 1987 was also notable for the publication of Elspeth's excellent book *Out in the Midday Sun* in Penguin paperback. Chatto had brought it out two years earlier in hardback. The book is a study of Kenyan settlers in the period between the First and Second World Wars, 'elderly ... period pieces ... and now that they are obsolete and therefore harmless, a certain indulgence has crept into the general attitude towards them, softening the disdain in which they were previously held'.[19] Elspeth had observed a significant change of opinion about Europeans in Kenya – 'far from being black-hearted villains, they are becoming nostalgic old things deserving of affection rather than abuse, like steam railway locomotives',[20] and had decided to write *Out in the Midday Sun* when James Fox's *White Mischief*, a re-examination of the circumstances of Joss Erroll's murder at Karen in 1941, appeared in 1983. Elspeth felt a great deal of *White Mischief* was exaggerated, and some of it untrue. Elspeth was determined to show that the disreputable Happy Valley crowd whose antics were described in *White Mischief* were not typical Kenya settlers. Michael Blundell said that Fox's approach seemed to him like 'someone who has enlarged the wart on a beautiful girl's face, ignoring the otherwise incomparable features'.[21] Pam Scott called Fox 'the Dung Beetle', and was furious with the writer and journalist Xan Smiley for handing over his grandmother Lady Francis Scott's diaries to him. *White Mischief* provoked Sir Humphrey Slade, a right-wing Kenyan politician prominent in the 1950s, to write to Elspeth:

> This beloved country owes an inestimable debt to that particularly fine type of settler who laid such firm foundations for its development (including excellent race relations between white and black) and displayed such courage and endurance during the awful years of economic slump, drought and locusts, and later during the years of war.[22]

Elspeth's grandson Hugh remembers watching the 1987 film of *White Mischief* with her, and Elspeth repeatedly exclaiming, 'That is *so* wrong.'[23] Elspeth believed Joss Erroll's murderer was indeed Jock Broughton, whose wife had been having an affair with Erroll, and who had been tried for the crime but acquitted. She thought, however, that the jury had been right to acquit him, because evidence had been muddled and there was 'reasonable doubt' – but she was convinced they knew he was guilty. According to Cockie, most of the wives of the local men on the jury had been seduced by Erroll, whom they thought 'had it coming to him'.

To gather information for *Out in the Midday Sun* Elspeth went to Kenya in 1983 to interview anyone who could be of use. Michael Blundell met her at the airport and put her up while she did the Nairobi interviews. Among the people she saw there were Rose Cartwright, now blind and living in an old people's home, and Charles Markham, Glady Delamere's son by her first husband and always a mine of delicious gossip. Elspeth found a Kenya in which much had changed since independence in 1963. Every inch of land along the road from Nairobi to Naivasha was cultivated – there were thousands of little plots of maize, clumps of bananas, gum trees and coffee bushes. The road was disintegrating under the huge tankers and container trucks on their way to and from Uganda, and Lake Naivasha was now ringed with houses. Her journey took her across the floor of the Rift Valley, a great sheet of land shimmering from the silver corrugated-iron roofs of Africans' houses. The round mud huts of former times had disappeared.

Elspeth went on to Njoro and her mother's old farm. She had rung beforehand to ask if she could visit, and the phone was answered by Benson, the son of Karanja the former cook. He said that of course she could, and that he had seen the *Flame Trees* series. As she wound up the still appalling road to the farm, past the huge complex of Egerton College on the right, there was no longer any sign of the twin thorn trees that she had loved so much. Benson Karanja had built himself a new house of cedar and planks, with a tin roof. Inside, a video of an English football match was playing on the television. Benson had begun his education at Nellie's school, and now sent his own children to a private school. His father, Karanja Kinoko the cook, smartly dressed in striped shirt and jeans, was building a wheat store and poultry house, and also made money from trading. He often lunched as a member at Njoro Club, where Nellie's name was still on a board on the wall.

When Elspeth arrived the old men gathered round on the floor of a wheat shed, on wicker chairs and benches – Karanja Kinoko, Karanja Mukoro, Manthi, Mbugwa and three others. Mbugwa spoke up first, with his eager and intelligent face, to ask when Nellie had died and where she was buried. Elspeth told them, and they were pleased to have the news. She asked them if they were happy now, and Mbugwa delivered a prepared speech. They were very grateful for Nellie's gift of the land. No other settlers in the district had let their former squatters stay on the land when the farms were sold. Many were turned away and had nowhere to go. Here, they stayed where they were and had land and security, and thus they were all very grateful to Nellie Grant. They honoured her memory, for everyone envied them. Elspeth wished Nellie was there to hear the words. They also remembered Charles and Gervas and asked after them.

Njombo's daughter and Mbugwa's half-sister, Esther Wambui, born on Nellie's farm, had joined the Kenyan army, had trained in England at the Staff College, Camberley, and was now head of Kenya's Women's Army. Elspeth went to see her in her Nairobi office, and told her that her mother would be very pleased that a pupil who had spent four years at her farm school had done so well.

Nellie's old Njoro farmhouse was now altogether dilapidated, its red roof rusty, its mantling creepers gone and no vestige left of the lovely garden. This was not surprising, thought Elspeth, for you cannot eat roses and delphiniums. The Africans had let what remained of the house, and Elspeth was not invited in. A glimpse showed holes in the floor, filth and goats within. One old olive tree remained outside, but other trees had gone. Nellie's irrigated area was abandoned and her bore unused, its pump long broken. As Elspeth sadly looked around she saw a lovely cinnamon-chested bee-eater and heard an ibis screeching.

She also had a look at the rest of Njoro. In the old Clutterbuck stables, where Beryl Markham had groomed her father's horses, African women were busy spinning and weaving on hand looms. The rugs and jackets they made were stored in the little cottage Clutterbuck had built for Beryl. There was an old man there with a peg leg made for him by Clutterbuck when he lost his own in the timber mill.

As Elspeth turned away down the hill from Njoro she must have wondered whether she would ever see Nellie's land again.

She motored on through Thomson's Falls, renamed Nyahururu, to Nanyuki, Naro Moru and Timau. Her purpose was to interview on tape as many old-timers as she could before they died. She acquired a recording of Will Powys, who had died two years before, reminiscing about his early days as a manager on Galbraith Cole's farm, and went to Powys's farm to see his paintings, always finished by his house servant as he grew older and his sight began to fail.

Among those Elspeth taped were Rose Cartwright, who told her of stalking the rare bongo antelopes in the forests of the Aberdares and how she knew the split between Karen Blixen and Denys Finch Hatton was inevitable because Denys told Rose he could not tolerate Karen's possessiveness; Cecily Hinde, who described the strangeness of her father Raymond Hook, who preferred camping on the slopes of Mount Kenya to living with his family; and Rachel Chilson, a Quaker missionary born at Kaimosi mission whose father went out to convert the heathen on a Harley Davidson motorcycle. Cockie, interviewed in England, told Elspeth of the abortion she arranged for Beryl Markham when Beryl told her she was having Denys Finch Hatton's baby.

Robin Wainwright told of times when he was DC in Lamu and Kisii, and how the 'goat bag' eased the official lot. Africans paid tax in the form of goats, which were used to feed King's African Rifles garrisons. The goat skins were dried and sold, and the proceeds went into the goat bag, from whence they were quietly dispensed to get DCs out of many a tight corner without the government knowing. Wainwright recollected the death of Hugh Grant, DC at Narok, whose grave lies near Denys Finch Hatton's in the Ngong hills. The Maasai had no respect for Grant, who was eccentric in many ways and whose Swahili was bad. During the Second World War they had agreed to provide stock for the abattoir at Athi River to feed the troops, instead of supplying men as soldiers. When the tribal elders ordered one young man to donate a bullock, he refused. Grant sent askaris to his boma, and they took his favourite bull. He went to Grant and asked to swap it for another. When Grant refused the young man ran his spear right through him.

From Dorothy Vaughan Elspeth heard much of her father Powys

Cobb and his extraordinary experiences of farming on the Mau escarpment, with two traction engines at opposite ends of the field pulling disc ploughs between them. A man of big ideas, who failed to think them through in detail, Cobb went bankrupt twice. One of his plans was to start a school on a boat to teach children geography by taking them round the world. He cheerfully told people how he put God on the horns of a dilemma by planting two different crops – one needed rain badly, but the other would not survive if it rained. He always called his wife 'the GAM', which stood for the General Arable Manager.

Sir John Hewett told Elspeth of his days in the East African Mounted Rifles in the First World War, when he marched to Nyasaland in pursuit of the German General von Lettow Vorbeck, and of his fifty-three years farming at Naivasha. He once had to walk 120 miles to a dentist. From Barbara Nightingale she heard how her father had been pulled into a harvester by his cardigan and slit open at the chest. Dr Burkitt had kept him alive by stationing an African beside him to pump up his one remaining lung every two hours with a bicycle pump. Burkitt's favourite soups were made from puff adders and frogs.

Charles Markham told her of growing up in the Delamere household, and of Roy Whittet's MC earned for flying a plane to Russia. Leslie Whitehouse recounted in his high and rapid voice his early days in Mau Narok and threw in for good measure an account of when he was Jomo Kenyatta's jailer at Lodwar in the 1950s. A fellow prisoner, Paul Ngei, had attempted to knife Kenyatta, who was working in the kitchen, but the future president's life was saved by a warden. As president, Kenyatta had to work with Ngei because he needed the support of his Wakamba tribe. In later years Whitehouse met Kenyatta at a cocktail party, and Kenyatta introduced him to the Prime Minister of Trinidad as 'my old jailer'. 'Was he a model convict?' asked the distinguished guest. 'He was, he was,' Whitehouse replied.[24]

Michael Blundell went into great detail about his years in politics. He told of giving a speech to Nandi warriors on the lines of 'we must all work together, European and African', when an old man stood up and said, 'Do not believe the white man. See what the white man did to me.' He threw off his blanket and revealed that he had no genitalia. They had been shot off in 1905, during the fracas with Meinertzhagen when the laibon was killed. The African chairman whispered to Blundell, 'Take no notice. The man has a grievance.'[25]

As Elspeth drove along the road to yet another interview, on the right rose Mount Kenya, dark blue that day. She wrote in *Out in the Midday Sun*:

> Although I was loyal to my childhood home at Njoro I think this was my favourite region, because of its wildness, its sense of freedom, the feeling that you could see to the ends of the earth and beyond, and the wild animals still there in abundance, whereas in the settled areas round Njoro most of them had gone. Above the plains the great brooding presence of Mt Kenya rose not abruptly but gently, like a swelling breast, to its twin white nipples; even when it was concealed by cloud you always knew that it was there. Something of its spirit seemed to permeate the air, a spirit ancient and impassive, indifferent to all human concerns and yet charged with unvoiced secrets.[26]

The wide-ranging book that emerged from these researches was written with nostalgia by Elspeth, who would not allow the struggles and disappointments of the men and women who introduced new farming methods into Kenya, and the hopes and frustrations of the young officials who battled to administer regions as vast as small countries, to be forgotten. The reader accompanies her through Kenya on a historical and geographical journey, full of stops and starts and charming digressions. Those long dead are brought to life again in all their oddness, eccentricity and hope:

> The apparent prevalence of Earls and Old Etonians in Kenya's white society has created an impression that the settler population was drawn mainly from Britain's aristocracy. This was far from the case. Afrikaner transport riders, Scottish cattle traders, Italian mechanics, Irish garage-owners, Jewish hoteliers, and farmers drawn from the despised and mediocre

middle classes, were all there too, in much greater numbers. They did not make news, whereas errant Earls and dashing barons did. They were in a small minority.[27]

She wrote about the Powys brothers, talented and tall, and Powys Cobb, and Delamere the dauntless, the Cole brothers and Gilbert Colvile, Scotts, Elkingtons, Taylors, Longs and Lindstroms. Tich Miles smiles at us from a photograph, dwarfed by Denys Finch Hatton, hands in pockets and cigar drooping from lip, behind them eucalpytus trees, so widely planted by the pioneers to provide some shade. Lady Idina and Cockie, both possessors of many husbands, the Hill-Williamses and Hooks, Harrieses and Hoeys, Feys and Nightingales, Blixens, Ridleys, and Cowies, names now found on stones in graveyards overgrown with sodom apples and blackjacks, are lovingly described and given credit for what they did. The loneliness of the young men of the Colonial Service, hardly out of school, in bomas where they ruled surrounding lands and some took black concubines (their Somali mistresses in the Northern Frontier District were known as 'sleeping dictionaries'), is captured here. Michael Blundell told Elspeth how the older Africans remembered the Colonial Service with affection, as a fair and dedicated body. Africans are not ignored, though they feature less than whites, and it is a mellow Elspeth now, wise with age, who sees the hurt they suffered more clearly than before.

Mombasa and its dhows, Nairobi and its dust, Eldoret, the Northern Frontier District and Laikipia are among the places delightedly described. The Rift Valley, that deep wound slashing through the country, useless as grazing land when white farmers came, was gradually transformed into superb ranching country by correcting the mineral balance, and those who lost fortunes and livelihoods by the expense of experimenting are not forgotten. Life was often harsh and hard, and illness reigned. Malaria, blackwater fever, veld sores, attack by wild animals and sometimes suicide from sheer despair meant death was never far away. White settlers had to show courage during years of economic slump, drought and locusts, and in years of war when their wives took over the farms.

This depiction of Kenya between the wars, written by Elspeth late in her life, distilled the thoughts of decades. The whites of the time believed, however ridiculous it may seem now, that they were taking part in an exciting and noble enterprise, that they were doing something socially desirable, even patriotic, for Britain was still in the process of enlightening what it regarded as darkest Africa, converting the heathen, introducing the mechanised plough to land previously turned over only with a jembe (a digging implement), and governing people subdued for centuries by slavers. The meeting of the incomers' advanced material culture and the simple African way of life confirmed the invaders' feeling of superiority. People outside Kenya often condemned the settlers, but they themselves believed they were doing what was right, laying the groundwork for the building of a twentieth-century country. The white pioneers soon felt more attachment to their new country than to their old, and agitated for a settler government separated from Colonial Office control in the mother country. In this they followed the example of Southern Rhodesia, which achieved it in 1922, but in Kenya the hope was eliminated by the Devonshire White Paper of 1923, laying down the principle that Kenya belonged to Africans, for whose benefit it should be run.

What the pioneers could not understand was why the British government then encouraged more white settlers to go out to Kenya, with promises of security, grants of leases and loans of money. Of course the reason, never stated, was expediency, for Britain needed Kenya to establish an economy if it were not to be a constant drain on resources, and white farmers contributed 80 per cent of Kenya's exports. Another reason was the feeling that there was plenty of time. Europe had taken hundreds of years to reach its present stage of 'civilisation', and while Africa would not take that long, it would be many years and several generations before Africans would be able to run the show. Britain made a serious miscalculation here. People much prefer to govern themselves badly than to be governed by outsiders, and a person does not have to read or write to have political ideas. The British unearthed an idea to solve the growing discontent – multi-racialism. But the multi-racial ideal was like a bandage over the eyes, blinding the wearer to reality. The Africans did not want the whites to stay, and the whites left their adopted country often penniless, in hurt and bitterness, warning that Kenya would be governed by a tiny, self-seeking minority, that the ideals of Western democracy would be swept away and replaced by autocracy or military dictatorship.

With *Out in the Midday Sun*, which appeared in 1985, Elspeth was back to the form she had shown in *Flame Trees* and *The Mottled Lizard*. Robert Baldock wrote in the *TLS* (31 January 1986): 'Kenya has been lucky in its interpreters. If Karen Blixen is its most elegant, Elspeth Huxley is its most humane . . . It is a rambling and disorganized book, part collection of anecdotes, but warm, generous, humorous, wise and packed with life on every page.'

Elspeth was always at her best when writing about Africa, and *Out in the Midday Sun* did particularly well in paperback. The title was taken from Noël Coward's song 'Mad Dogs and Englishmen'. There were, of course, some criticisms of the book. Pam Scott told Elspeth she recognised several passages taken from her own manuscript *A Nice Place to Live*, which Elspeth was then trying to get accepted by a publisher. But this is not the case – Pam had merely lived through the events described in Elspeth's book. She was riled because Elspeth had poked fun at her mother and father: 'My parents were very fond of your parents, especially your mother, and I am a little sad that this does not appear to have been mutual. You imply that there was a distance between them, because of the way we lived and you seem very conscious of "social status" and somewhat in awe of titles!'[28] This was an odd thing to say about Nellie, the granddaughter of a Duke.

After completing *Out in the Midday Sun* Elspeth spent three weeks in Kenya, staying with Michael Blundell in Muthaiga. She made two short trips, one to Naro Moru, where she spent a day in the Samburu game park, and one to west Kenya, where she visited Kisumu, Kakamega and Eldoret, then travelled along a magnificent new road built with Israeli assistance that dropped into the Kerio valley and up the other side to Kabarnet, and so to Lake Baringo and back via the Rift Valley.

Following the appearance of *Out in the Midday Sun* there was a gap of five years before the publication of Elspeth's next book, *Nine Faces of Kenya* (1990), an anthology of writings about the country divided into nine sections: exploration, travel, settlers, wars, environment, wildlife, hunting, lifestyles, and legend and poetry. This was published by Harvill, now a division of William Collins, with whom Elspeth had a great deal of trouble. 'I've never liked dealing with Collins,' she wrote to her friend Mary Lovell, who had first contacted her for information on Beryl Markham, whose biography she was writing.[29] One great problem was that Collins never answered her letters: 'My so-called editor at Collins is I think a Trappist monk and his vow of silence extends also to the written word. Not a glimmer of interest let alone help on one or two matters.'[30] Elspeth's editor left Collins in 1989 and was not replaced, thus making matters even more difficult.

Elspeth described her method of preparing the book to Mary Lovell:

> I plod on with the anthology, it's really an overpowering task. So many books – I've scanned over 80 and feel I've only scratched the surface. Most of them no good, but one must travel hopefully. Then marking possible passages, then reducing these, then photocopying those retained, then sorting them into categories in a large filing cabinet, then assembling the passages and arranging them in some kind of order, then the linking passages which are terrible – trying to reduce a whole event (such as a war) into two sentences, then scissors and paste, then more corrections and re-arrangements, more photocopying – so it goes on. Books pour in from the library each with a date of return, generally 5 or 6 going at once.[31]

In March 1989 Elspeth delivered the book, but Collins tried to alter their agreement with her so that she would have to apply and pay for permission to use quotations, which she would not do. In August Adrian House of Collins went to see her with a mass of suggestions for improving the anthology, but she was not prepared to rewrite and recast it after so much delay. 'It would be hard to imagine,' she told Mary Lovell, 'greater indifference, inertia and sheer incompetence.'[32] Elspeth was furious with Collins's 'remarkable lethargy' in selling the book. As far as she could see, they did absolutely nothing to promote it, and it was practically impossible to buy, because the bookshops had never heard of it. She was being a little unfair, because an interview with her about the book appeared in *The Times*, and she was interviewed on the *Gloria Hunniford Show* on BBC Radio 2. But as far as Elspeth was concerned, no editor or publisher could ever match Norah Smallwood, whom Elspeth thought had been driven out of Chatto. Chatto themselves were now suffering from Elspeth's displeasure: 'My agent has written to them three times, with increasing ascerbity [sic], about reverting rights, without a whisper of reply.'[33]

Elspeth dedicated *Nine Faces of Kenya* to Michael Blundell, who was himself writing a book. He wrote to her: 'How silly can one be? You and I should sit quietly in the sun or before a fire sipping gin or ginger wine and warming ourselves with its alcohol and our own romanticised memories.'[34]

Nine Faces of Kenya's range is wide, its selections apposite. Its purpose is defined in Elspeth's preface:

> The Africa and its peoples encountered by the first agents of the West has vanished and will never come again. The wild animals in their amazing abundance and variety have also gone forever, save for surviving pockets in parks and reserves. So perhaps this is a good moment to try to draw together some of the strands that have united to form the sovereign state of Kenya today. I hope that the visitor will find something in these pages to remind him of a land of great beauty, beguilement, harshness and infinite variety; the native in the wider sense something to interest, entertain and even amuse. As Henry James observed – though he was thinking of cats and monkeys – 'all human life is there.'[35]

This was the last book about Kenya that Elspeth wrote. She was now in her eighties. Travel was becoming more difficult, and the words she needed came to her mind less readily. But a new opportunity arose when she was asked by Peter Scott's widow Philippa to write a biography of her husband, who had died in 1989. Elspeth replied, 'You do realise that I am 82, don't you? Are you prepared to risk it?'[36] Philippa was prepared to do just that, and Elspeth began to drive over to Slimbridge almost every day to consult papers. 'It was such fun having her here when she was writing and researching,' said Philippa. 'She used to make me laugh.'[37] Elspeth also enjoyed the experience, 'since most of the research has been carried out in Lady Scott's home, . . . [she] answering endless questions for about three years: a potentially abrasive situation which passed off with patience on her part and pleasure on mine'.[38] At Slimbridge Elspeth sat at a table overlooking one of the lakes, and ate her lunchtime sandwiches somewhere in the grounds where she could watch the birds.

There was a whole roomful of files on the World Wildlife Fund, which Scott had founded, and Slimbridge's loft contained so many papers that the ceilings had had to be strengthened. There were also seventy-two volumes of Scott's travel diaries. To help her with the mountains of paper Faber & Faber, the book's publisher, put aside £5,000 to pay an assistant for two years. Elspeth wrote to the Professor of English at Bristol University to ask if he could suggest a postgraduate for the task, and he found John Lee, a young researcher doing a Ph.D. at Bristol. This was the only time Elspeth ever used an assistant. He undertook much of the typing, transcribed about fifty tapes which Elspeth made, delved into the boxes at Slimbridge and did away-from-base assignments difficult for Elspeth to do. Although Lee admitted to knowing nothing of natural history, and had never heard of Peter Scott, Elspeth found him willing. He also got on well with Philippa Scott's collie, which was important. Elspeth battled on with the book – 'still the old mare will limp along as well as she can towards the ever receding finishing post'[39] – which involved some research expeditions: in September 1990 she spent three days at a lighthouse on the Wash which Scott occupied in the 1930s, where he started his bird collection, and at Oundle School, where he was educated.

In winter 1991 she went to ground to write up the book. One of her problems was that Scott 'was such a nice chap that I can't find the warts that, as Cromwell remarked, should always be painted in'.[40] She also felt that everyone at Slimbridge had been so kind and helpful that if she made the least hint of criticism of her subject it would seem like a stab in the back – one of the real perils of authorised biography. Her editor at Faber was Andrew Motion, formerly at Chatto, with whom she got on well. But by the time she delivered the manuscript in October 1992 Motion had left, and she found his replacement uninterested and bored with the project. Elspeth had no rapport with her, and when she asked about a publication date she was told that it would not be until spring 1994, because the autumn 1993 list was already full. Elspeth's agent Heather Jeeves was indignant, pointing out that the contract said Faber had to publish the book within twelve months of receiving the manuscript. Consequently it was brought out, in an edition of ten thousand copies, in October 1993.

Peter Scott: Painter and Naturalist is a sympathetic portrait of a versatile and complex personality, a man who possessed a combination of culture and physical toughness. Elspeth understood Scott well because he had similar interests to her own, and of course she had known him for years. 'Because of him,' said Sir David Attenborough in the book's introduction, 'people of every race and every faith on every continent are dedicated conservationists, believing as he did, that humanity has a moral responsibility towards the other forms of life on this planet.' Elspeth, who heartily shared such sentiments, tells the story of how this was done, how Peter Scott spread the notion of conservation when the word was scarcely known and the science in its infancy: 'He was a prophet and a pioneer, not only in delivering awful warnings but in trying to arrest and turn the tide of events that was leading, as he believed, to degradation of the planet and the impoverishment of mankind.'[41]

Elspeth was very hurt when one reviewer said she wrote as well as a Huxley. She always considered herself a Grant, not a Huxley. Her view of writing was that 'the object of the whole exercise is entertainment of the reader; instruction too of course but this needs to be concealed as far as possible, introduced by stealth as it were'.[42] She felt that a biographer should draw some conclusions about motivation, even if the subject had not spelled this out, but she understood that the task was difficult. She wrote to Mary Lovell, 'Don't you think that "nothing extenuate, nor set down ought in malice" is the perfect precept which a biographer should follow?'[43] She genuinely felt that a biography was helped if the writer was sympathetic to the subject rather than setting out to denigrate him or her. 'What matters,' she said, 'is whether the reader has been presented with a credible human being with faults and virtues who has aroused and held our interest.'[44] Consequently there was no need to fuss about every minor detail of the life.

Elspeth reckoned that if one wished to be taken seriously as a writer, one should not take on projects just for the money. That was the difference between a writer and a hack. She said she considered herself more of a hack, but this was false modesty: in reality she was proud of her style and of most of her books, and when Robert Cross and Michael Perkin prepared a bibliography of her works for publication, she did not like being reminded of the potboilers she had written simply to make money. She did not include her crime stories in this category. She had reservations about the bibliography: 'I really don't believe, without false modesty, that my books etc. rate such generous treatment. I've never been a "literary" sort of writer.'[45] But she was pleased with the final result when it was published in 1996: 'Thank you very much . . . for all the work you have put in on my literary life, which inflates an ego otherwise diminished by the regrets of old age.'[46]

The bibliography brought Elspeth face to face with the fact that she should have employed an agent earlier than she did. She realised that she should have made much more from the television series of *Flame Trees*, which had not been handled by London Management. Mary Lovell's agent John Belcher told Elspeth in 1986 that she should have made at least $100,000 from it, rather than the £5,000 she had accepted. He was also of the opinion that although Chatto was a good publisher, it had not done the best possible marketing job for Elspeth. Consequently Elspeth asked Belcher if he would represent her, and he tried to arouse interest in a TV film-script of her work by John Hawkesworth, entitled 'Out in the Midday Sun' or 'Return to Thika', which Thames TV had eventually turned down after having more or less undertaken to put up the money. But Belcher died suddenly on 1 April 1987. In February 1989 the whole of Heather Jeeves's unit at London Management was made redundant. Heather set up on her own, and Elspeth retained her as her agent for the rest of her life.

Elspeth's later life was spent at Green End. She still drove a car, a blue Peugeot 205, too fast and increasingly erratically and dangerously. She was badly shaken when she had an accident on the Tetbury–Cirencester road, which she privately admitted was her own fault. She made excursions to visit friends but seldom went to London now, preferring rather to meet the people who wanted to see her in her own home. She collected them from Kemble station in her car, gave them a lunch she cooked herself, and delivered them back to the station. After Cleggy died she made herself into an excellent cook, swapping recipes with her mother by letter. But in her last years she found it took about two days' work to have two or three people to lunch, what with the shopping beforehand, the preparation and the clearing up afterwards. Eventually cooking meals for guests became too much for her, and she took her visitors to the local pub, the Wheatsheaf, for lunch instead.

Now that she had finished her Peter Scott book, Elspeth had to adjust to having plenty of leisure time. Initially she found it very pleasant. She sorted out the thousands of photographs she had taken over the years and gave them to the new British Empire and Commonwealth Museum in Bristol. She enlisted Joan Considine, secretary of the East Africa Women's League, to help sell most of her remaining books on East Africa, and donated the proceeds to the Benevolent Fund of the League. She also made an effort to come to terms with the new computer technology, and in 1994 even enrolled at a secretarial college in Cirencester for a word-processing course, but found it took longer to correct her mistakes on the word processor than to douse everything with white correcting fluid on her manual typewriter. One day, walking to the college, she slipped on the pavement in Cirencester, cut her head and broke her arm near the shoulder. She was taken to hospital and, though stoical about the pain, took a long time to recover. She reckoned that breaking her arm made her 'very tottery and . . . slow'.[47]

After her accident Elspeth never returned to the course. Even though she bought an electronic word processor/typewriter she did not use it, and reverted to her manual Olivetti – 'it's neck and neck between this old machine and myself, which wears out first'.[48] As she aged her typing became more inaccurate: 'Please excuse appalling typing and spelling,' she wrote to her bibliographer Robert Cross. 'Am quite sober, just running down like an old battery.'[49] The impact of computers and television led her to believe that 'the printed word, though it will not vanish, has past [sic] its peak as a method of propagating ideas, arousing emotions and appealing to the imagination'.[50]

Elspeth had made Green End into a comfortable home. The sitting room had highly polished floors with rugs that took off under the unwary. A Van Dyke painting inherited from the Grosvenors hung there, uninsured because the premiums were too high. The room also contained a trolley of indoor plants and the beautiful furniture made for her by Robin Wainwright. The curtains in the dining room were kept closed to keep the light off the water-colours hung on the walls. When she had guests the curtains would be opened and the covers of the pictures lifted so the visitors could enjoy them while eating. The house was generally cold, and Elspeth huddled at one little stove when by herself. One visitor said his knees knocked together, so cold was the room. Elspeth also had an office, which she kept neat, and she was a tidy cook, unlike her mother. The mess Nellie made in the kitchen would infuriate Elspeth, which was one of the reasons they snapped at each other. Although Elspeth was amused by Nellie, with her untrained but clever brain, she was annoyed by her impracticality, disorderliness and inability to persist in her projects. However, according to Angela Watt, who took over the cleaning from Dolly Jennings when Dolly became too old to cycle up to the cottage on her ancient bicycle, Elspeth was not excessively houseproud or fussy about dust.

In old age Elspeth, who had inherited Nellie's looks and build, became rather bent and suffered from back pain and arthritis. She used a disability disc when she parked her car, having obtained it even before she broke her arm. From 1991 she had a frozen shoulder which kept her awake at night. The painkillers the doctor gave her made her feel odd and necessitated her giving up alcohol – a severe stricture for one who liked her evening whisky. In middle life Elspeth had indulged in dieting fads to reduce her weight and, in particular, the size of her bust and her broad hips. In old age she abandoned the struggle – there were few consolations in advancing years, she said, 'but one of them is not worrying about girth, make-up and all the rest, just letting nature take its ugly course'.[51] She had cereals and toast for breakfast, a late lunch of a sandwich, and a meal cooked by herself in the evening. Her small, five-foot-two-inch, wiry body would incline forward as she walked with quick steps, as if heading into a wind. She remained active until near the end, though her hearing began to fail. She acquired a hearing aid, but it was useless because her fingers, always fat, were too large to twist its tiny knob. It was consigned to a little velvet box on the mantelpiece. In her final year she lost all hearing in one ear. Without vanity, she wore clothes of muted colours, often tweeds, and liked brown jerseys. She usually wore trousers rather than dresses and her hair, for which she cared little, was cut short in a pudding-basin shape. It looked as if it had been cropped with sheep shears. In old age she never used make-up. Her friend James Lees-Milne rather unkindly described her arriving for lunch 'looking the spit of Iris Murdoch ... These lady novelists with fringe cut awry, wearing stained, untidy blouses, trousers and no attempt at dress or make-up.'[52] He did, however, appreciate her beautiful manners and her sweetness towards himself and his wife, 'yet she can be tart'.[53]

One of Elspeth's great pleasures in these years was gardening, in which she had never indulged when Gervas was alive because he was so much better at it than she was. She swapped a piece of her land for the field beside Green End, on which she created a woodland and orchard, planting three trees every year, including apples and plums. Her grandson Alexander, who had studied forestry, told her she was planting the trees too close together, 'but she wouldn't listen. She was always so independent and stubborn.'[54] When the calves from the neighbouring farm began to eat the bark of her cherished trees, an electric fence was erected to keep them out. Her lawn was mostly moss. She loved birds and spent a lot of time in the garden watching and feeding them. If she could, she would spray the cats from over the road with water when they trespassed. She bought herself a hedge-trimmer and towards the end of her life a Spanish gardener, Francisco, came one afternoon a week to help her.

Our friends and acquaintances all have different views of us, and Elspeth was no exception to this. One said she was a bit of a bully who would browbeat people and did not suffer fools gladly, that anyone who took liberties with her did so at their own risk, and that you would be unwise to argue with her unless you were sure of your facts for fear of encountering her dry, caustic humour. Another said she was sharp but fair about others, though very dismissive if she felt someone was showing off. She was a disciplined person who could be very critical of others and had a provocative, journalistic manner. Another friend described her as having great sparkle, able to be witty without being cruel, gracious, amusing and perspicacious. A great reader, she was opinionated, with a good vocabulary in conversation. She used her exceptional intelligence in practical ways: 'She saw the wrongs of the contemporary world, succinctly analysed them and doubted that they could be put right; but rather than giving in to lassitude, she encouraged the positive, drew out the very best in her friends and acquaintances, and derived pleasure from even the smallest nicety.'[55] She was kind to people she liked. Almost all her friends described her as amusing and charmingly interested in themselves, always peppering them with questions about their family and their interests.

Elspeth found the devout, church-going circle in the village amusing. Politically she tended towards conservatism, though she did not always vote Conservative. By 1994 she believed that neither

Labour nor the Conservatives would face up to the fact that the Welfare State had got out of hand, and that it was beyond the nation's means to sustain it. More than one person found her reserved, even shy. This was one of the reasons she disliked attending cocktail parties, or any sort of reception or party attended by a large number of people. 'I'm no good at addressing strangers,' she said, 'and barging in to other people's conversations, and I found one just hung about feeling idiotic, so gave it up altogether.'[56] Shyness was also the reason she hated public speaking. She regarded herself as very bad at it, and much too frightened to be a success – a handicap from the career point of view, she admitted. She told a friend she had never been ambitious, rather merely content to plod along. But this was not true: literary ambition as well as the need for funds drove her forward.

Always careful with money (she used teabags twice), Elspeth upset the village when she raised the rent for the cottages she owned, dwellings which she had always been parsimonious about updating and to which she had been slow to introduce modern conveniences. She justified the increases by explaining that she had to pay for her grandsons' education, which would go on for years.

At the end of the 1980s Elspeth was still making excursions and visiting friends. She and Mary Lovell paid a visit to Hilary Hook, one of the Kenya Hooks who had retired to England, but he died in September 1990. In 1987 he had privately published his autobiography, *Home from the Hill*, and it was so successful that Penguin republished it the following year. Every year Michael Blundell came over from Kenya and stayed a night or two with Elspeth, and they wrote to each other frequently. Elspeth made regular visits to Cockie in Edgecombe Nursing Home near Newbury. 'She longs to be [dead], and simply sits there waiting for visitors and preferably death,' she told Mary Lovell.[57] Mary and Elspeth contemplated writing a biography of Cockie, and Elspeth began to gather material, contacting people in France, Sweden and South Africa for information. Although Cockie had had two strokes and was nearly blind and rather deaf, her memory was unaffected and she was prepared to co-operate. Unfortunately the material was very thin, consisting mainly of anecdotes remembered by her friends, some of which were not as funny on paper as they were in real life. The project came to naught after John Belcher could only get Elspeth an offer of £5,000 for the proposed book. Cockie died in December 1988, at the age of ninety-six. At her funeral the guests were kept waiting for the arrival of the coffin, because Cockie had decreed that she wanted to be late for her own funeral. One of the lessons at Cockie's memorial service in February 1989 was the parable of Christ turning water into wine, which Elspeth considered most apt.

Elspeth gradually made fewer and fewer excursions. In the last two years of her life, her interests contracted. She regretted that she was 'idle and forgetful about keeping up with past friends and acquaintances',[58] though when her friend Vivcka Lindstrom died in March 1996 she made the effort to go to Putney crematorium for the funeral. That year she was visited by the photographer Robert Vavra, as part of his project to portray people of importance who had written about Africa or painted it, such as Elspeth, Laurens van der Post and the wildlife artist David Shepherd. When Vavra and his assistant Valerie Hemingway, Ernest Hemingway's daughter-in-law, came to Oaksey Elspeth was in fine form, full of interesting comments and suggestions. The book of photographs and interviews which resulted, *Remembering Africa*, is due to be published shortly.

In these years Elspeth spent Christmases with Charles and his family, often at Middle Gaer, the cottage in Wales, to which she would bring an enormous turkey or a loin of Gloucester Old Spot pig, a breed saved from extinction by the Rare Breeds Survival Trust. One year she tried to pluck a Christmas goose by rotating it over a pan of methylated spirit. She had never much liked Christmas, admitting to being glad when it was over.

Elspeth's grandsons were growing up and she saw them frequently, treating them with greater patience and understanding than she had shown her own son. She paid particular attention to Alexander, one of the twins, who had attention difficulties and always did things at his own speed and when he wished, to the frustration of his teachers and others. He failed to make the grade for Rugby School, attended by his father, elder brother Jos and twin Hugh, and went instead to Lackham Agricultural College in Chippenham, near Oaksey. Recognising his vulnerability, Elspeth frequently had him to stay for weekends, and they went for walks together, Elspeth pointing out and naming wild flowers and birds. She had a special rapport with the boy.

During the 1980s Charles Huxley, like many others in England at the time, found it difficult to keep a job for long. Elspeth worried about him constantly. He had had, of course, a difficult childhood, with his mother so often away, and even when she was there Elspeth had failed to encourage and praise him, causing him to find her inflexible and to feel he was never good enough for her. When Charles's wife Frederica was made redundant from her job in 1991 Elspeth came to the rescue financially. In 1996 Frederica and Charles divorced, to Elspeth's sadness.

Worries about her will dominated the last years of Elspeth's life. Fearful that Frederica would get half of what she left when she died, despite the fact that Frederica assured Charles several times that she would make no claim on Elspeth's estate, she changed her will, leaving everything to her grandsons. But after the divorce had gone through, Elspeth changed her will back into Charles's name. She would leave over a million pounds, much of it tied up in property or shares.

In 1995 Elspeth had been persuaded by Monty and Barbara Brown, friends who lived twenty miles from Nanyuki, to make what was to be her final visit to Kenya. She almost did not go after another fall on the pavement in January, but she had recovered by March and wanted to fulfil a promise she had made to her grandson Jos to take him to Africa if he obtained his degree from Brunel University. Charles decided he wanted to go too, so the three of them set off in the third week of March for a fortnight in Kenya. Unfortunately Jos was stricken with gastro-enteritis soon after his arrival, but his grandmother was up at dawn every day. She took him to see Kiti-muru, where they were greeted by the occupants, Roger and Carole

Hemmings. The house had been beautifully done up by the large French company, of which Roger Hemmings was group manager, that owned all Thika's coffee. The young couple loved living there and commented on the good workmanship of the original Indian builders. All the teak cupboards installed before the First World War were still in excellent working order. Thika had grown into a small city, surrounded by immense fields of pineapples destined to end up in Del Monte tins.

Elspeth, Charles and Jos drove with the Browns through Nanyuki, with its vast second-hand clothes market, to the Browns' tile-roofed bungalow on the Nanyuki river. Elspeth wrote: 'Sitting at breakfast on the veranda with a view of the great mountain [Mount Kenya] sharp against a soft-blue sky, Eden does not seem far away. There is birdsong and sunlight, delicious ripe pawpaw, acacia honey from the bush ... A pair of jewel-bright starlings, resplendent in their metallic blue plumage and rufous breasts – so rightly called Superb – settle on the lawn.'[59] They spent a couple of days at Larsen's Camp in the Samburu game reserve and a night in the Ark (a Treetops-style hotel) near Nyeri. Charles and Jos did a quick climb as far as Mackinder's Camp on Mount Kenya and had three days in the Masai Mara while Elspeth stayed in the Nanyuki area and saw a few friends.

'I don't think I'll try any more scribbles,' Elspeth had said after she delivered *Peter Scott* to Faber in October 1992. However, she carried on writing till the end of her life, though she found she was much slower than before. She forgot how to spell quite simple words, and had to search painstakingly for others which used to spring straight to mind. She was approached by Rhodes House library in Oxford, where the Oxford Colonial Records Project had its headquarters, and asked if she would be willing to donate her papers to the project. Elspeth maintained that she agreed to this request in self-defence against American academics who pestered her for information about her life and writings. Mary Bull was detailed to catalogue the papers, and was made to feel instantly at home by Elspeth when she visited Green End. Having surrendered her papers, Elspeth also abandoned the buying of books, instead relying on the mobile library which visited Oaksey every other week, and which would order for her any book she wanted to read.

Desultorily, she began another crime novel to fill the long winter evenings, a murder mystery whose hero was a young policeman called Pike. Joan Considine volunteered to type it for her, and was sent the first three chapters in November 1995. Michael Macoun, an old friend from East Africa, found Elspeth an adviser on police matters, the former Detective Chief Superintendent of Devon and Cornwall Police, whom she bombarded with technical questions. She found concentration difficult to maintain: 'I have to keep on looking up words in the dictionary or thesaurus and feel an almost irresistable [sic] desire to potter about, see how things are getting on in the garden, read my library books and just drift along.'[60] She continually forgot what she had written, and rather than go back and reread the typescript she ploughed on, either repeating or contradicting what she had said before.

In January 1996 Elspeth sent the first hundred pages to her agent Heather Jeeves, whose advice was that she should definitely pursue the project, tentatively entitled 'The Black Prince Murders'. It was a classic 'cosy' crime story, set in an English village, Chipping Bowden, in the 1960s. Elspeth made slow progress, partly because of writer's block and partly because she found it took a lot of her time merely to exist. She felt the characters were rather dull and insufficiently romantic, and wished she had made the women into raving beauties. She laid the book aside for the summer of 1996, picking it up again as winter drew in. By now she was 'increasingly slow, muddled and idle', unable to concentrate for more than two or three hours a day. Elspeth had been in pain for some time. Since the spring she had stopped drinking whisky in order to take painkillers, so she must have been in considerable discomfort. Angela Watt, her cleaning lady, normally went to Green End on Mondays and Thursdays, but by December she was calling in every day, and Ros Taubenheim from the village went in to cook for her.

Elspeth had only three chapters left to write when the pain increased in severity and she sought medical advice. In the week before Christmas she went for an x-ray and a scan. She was told that she had terminal cancer of the liver, and had only three months to live. Elspeth was due to spend Christmas with Charles and his new partner at their home in Somerset, but instead she spent it in Malmesbury Cottage Hospital. She was now reliant on morphia, as she explained to Joan Considine in a letter of 27 December, in which she said she would be unable to finish the crime novel Joan was typing for her. She admitted to having had from the beginning a feeling that she might not complete the book.

> One has got to die of something at the age of nearly 90, the doctor & district nurse are being very good and helpful and say that pain can be kept under control these days. I may go into a nursing home, although they seem determined to keep one going in one's home if possible.[61]

Elspeth did not like the Malmesbury hospital because there was no single room available. She also required better pain control, so she moved to Dorothy House, a hospice in Bradford on Avon, near Charles's house. The hospice only kept patients for a week to a fortnight, and when that time was up Elspeth moved to Ilsom House, near Tetbury. She did not want to see anyone, but on 10 January 1997 Carolyn Bateman, an Oaksey friend, went to visit her, to be received with annoyance by the proud and independent old woman. Elspeth was lucid, lying in bed, and demanding to see a doctor. She did not look near to death. Her friend Freddie Burnaby-Atkins also went to see her that day, and she told him to get her a doctor. He too did not think she was near death – she was sitting in a chair, being very awkward. Both visitors were most surprised to hear that Elspeth died that night. Given her views on euthanasia, it is not impossible that she hastened her own death, because she was worried about the cost of being ill and was ready to go.

All the obituaries published within the next few days recognised the importance of *The Flame Trees of Thika*. *The Times* wrote: 'Her books are, at their best, distinguished with a clarity of exposition and incisiveness ... [They] reveal a personality too rigorous and outspoken always to have time for the social refinements of gentleness and tact. Nevertheless she was an excellent hostess and a welcome guest . . . She was not only a talented writer but an out-standing personality.' The *Financial Times* commented that 'there was nothing sentimental in her writing', while the *Economist* called her childhood recollections 'triumphs of the genre – funny, unpre-tentious, moving. Whatever the politics of the white families caught up in the last spasm of British imperial expansion (and they were far from uniform), they were brave and resourceful people. In Mrs Huxley they found a fitting memorialist.'

Elspeth was cremated at a private ceremony, and a memorial service, which she herself had planned, was arranged at All Saints' church, Oaksey, for Saturday, 8 March 1997. Sarah Foster in Kenya obtained some flame tree blooms from the avenue at Kitimuru (not the one her mother had planted, but one which had replaced it), and Kathini Graham received them from the plane, kept them in her bath, and put them on the altar before the service. At the ceremony three rousing hymns – 'Lord of all Hopefulness, Lord of all Joy', 'O Worship the King' and 'Mine Eyes have Seen the Glory of the Coming of the Lord' – were sung, and Elspeth's son Charles read 1 Corinthians 13, 'Though I speak with the tongues of men and of angels'. Her grandson Hugh read from Ecclesiastes, chapters 11 and 12, which include the verse, 'Remember now thy Creator in the days of thy youth, while the evil days come not, nor the years draw nigh, when thou shalt say, I have no pleasure in them', and his twin brother Alexander read a poem he had written for the occasion, 'Traveller, to where do you head?'. It contained the lines:

> To tales of Kenya
> In the midday sun,
> In the nine faces
> I see only one . . .
> So where do you head now:
> Is it back to Africa
> In spirit form, to re-trace a path
> So very well worn?

Their elder brother Josceline read the poem 'The Scribe', by Walter de la Mare, the final verse of which is:

Ere unto Z
My pen drew nigh;
Leviathan told
And the honey-fly:
And still would remain
My wit to try –
My worn reeds broken
The dark tarn dry,
All words forgotten –
Thou, Lord, and I.

Canon R.T. (Bobby) Miles, nephew of Tich and Daisy Miles, gave the address to a packed church. Mary Lovell noticed, as she went up to the altar after the service with Valerie Hemingway and Robert Vavra to look at the flame tree blooms, that a beautiful butterfly flew on to the flowers, hovered there for a few seconds, then fluttered out of the window. 'It was rather eerie – like a messenger. I think we may have laughed (the way one does) and said something like "Oh, I see Elspeth was here, then!"'[62] Afterwards those who had brought daffodils and irises in pots planted them in the orchard Elspeth had created at Green End, where her ashes had been strewn. Everyone repaired to Woodfolds for the wake, and talked about the woman who had touched them in so many different ways.

Conclusion

Elspeth Huxley is best known for her writings on Africa. Yet as a young woman she was excessively impatient to get away from her parents' farm there. The world beckoned, she answered the call, and she never returned to live in the continent of her childhood. But Africa had cast its spell on her and tugged her back for almost annual extended visits. She watched keenly the unfolding political and human drama as the British Empire in Africa disintegrated. She lyrically reminded her readers of the trials the colonists had faced, the human and financial investment they had made, their sorrows and triumphs, hopes and failures.

Elspeth saw the white man as a sort of tin-opener, who prised up the lid of a sealed continent to reveal what was beneath. He also came as a packet of yeast – he brought change and a thousand ideas which began to froth and bubble. But two world wars, a social revolution and the decline in Christianity caused the whites to lose faith in themselves, while Africans gained faith in themselves, coming to feel they had learned enough and would rather make their own mistakes and be their own masters.

When a correspondent wrote to Elspeth in 1988 to say he thought her work was undervalued, she replied that there were reasons for this. One was that she was a colonial, and colonials were thought, with some justification, to be ill-educated and culturally boorish, which caused them to be ignored and denigrated.

Also: in so far as I attempted to defend white settlement in Africa I gave offence to academics, intellectuals and other British natives who . . . have for the last fifty years . . . subscribed to the liberal, anti-establishment, left-wing dogmas. Whites were . . . in the context of Africa, considered to be morally black, and blacks to be without blemish. If you espouse an unpopular cause, you can't expect to be popular.[1]

A third reason, she maintained, was her own fault. Those who wrote books should do their best to sell them, and this involved giving talks and lectures, attending literary luncheons, publishers' parties and other events at which people from the literary world, especially reviewers, gathered together. She had either been incompetent at this or had avoided it altogether: 'I am a very bad public speaker and detest it, and hopeless on committees, which always include a few thrusters who leap in with their opinions and leave me tongue-tied.' For the last fifty years she had avoided London as much as possible: 'By my own choice I have been a country-dweller and have been milking cows and feeding pigs when, had I been trying to make a mark in the literary world, I should have been attending cocktail parties and inviting reviewers, radio and TV producers and literary agents to lunch.' She added that she thought she was in fact lucky to have got as much recognition as she had, and that she did not eat her heart out for praise and rewards.

Elspeth sometimes had doubts about the value of the colonial incursion in Africa, wondering if all there was to show for it was traffic lights, teapots and trousers:

Very often one doubts it [the overall good], realising that we merely drove one lot of devils out of the window to let in another lot by the door, and that human beings are the same whatever their colour and level of so-called civilisation – that is to say, on balance, bloody . . . All the same, rereading accounts of slavery makes one realise that pre-colonial Africa was not the Garden of Eden many people think it was.[2]

In some quarters today it is regarded as politically incorrect to talk of African slavery, and the part Arabs played in it, often with the complicity of African warlords or entrepreneurs; but there is no doubt that for centuries it caused great misery and faction in the African interior.

As for the British introduction of democracy into African states, Elspeth was not convinced that this would succeed. She felt democracy was not the answer in countries where loyalty lay to the tribe rather than to the nation. In fact she was puzzled about what would be the most effective system of government, because the alternative to democracy was dictatorship in one form or another. 'So what *is* the answer?' she wrote to Mary Lovell in 1992. 'The Second Coming, I suppose.'[3] With these words she summed up the rest of the world's puzzlement about the future of Africa, the quandary of whether to assist the Africans or leave them to their own devices. It was a subject she investigated all her life, and to which she found no solution.

Elspeth's elegant, rhythmic style of writing was one of her greatest accomplishments. Even her critics appreciated her prose. She was, moreover, a writer with great clarity of vision. She did not hesitate to point out gently that life would not necessarily be easy under African rule. She was sometimes unpopular for doing so, but no one doubted the penetration of her analysis or the judiciousness of her opinions. She was honest, though never brutally so; wise, but not obtrusively; and she made complex subjects easy to understand.

As a chronicler of colonial Kenya Elspeth was criticised for writing mainly about the whites – though this was far from the case with *Red Strangers, The Sorcerer's Apprentice, A New Earth* and *Forks and Hope* – but it was the whites she knew best. She began by accepting the contemporary view of the 'civilising' (and the word had no inverted commas in her day) influence of the British, but later accepted that Africans would prefer to govern themselves. She would not, however, allow the role of the white settlers to be ignored for the sake of political correctness. In the 1960s and 1970s, the years after African countries had gained their independence, it was unfashionable to like her work, but later her position in colonial literature was recognised. It was accepted that with *The Flame Trees of Thika* she had written a book to rank with Karen Blixen's *Out of Africa*.

Those two books are often condemned by African writers such as Ngugi wa Thiong'o, who regards Elspeth Huxley as a liberal apologist for white settlement. In her books, he says, 'the African character remains fundamentally a child at the mercy of irrational forces. He has no vital relationship with his environment, with his past. He does not create; he is created.'[4] On the contrary, it is precisely this relationship of Africans to their past and environment that is discussed in *Red Strangers* and *A Thing to Love*. It is true that Elspeth originally had an intellectual allegiance to the British Empire, but she soon recognised the inevitability of the Empire's demise. In the 1950s she was not one of those who cautioned delay until the so-called beneficent effect of the Empire upon Africans became more obvious; instead she knew that the Empire would soon be destroyed by those it was supposed to be helping, and by a British government that found it an expensive anachronism in a new liberal age. But she never succeeded in cutting her emotional bonds to Kenya, to the delight of her readers, who revelled in the stories she told about a land she loved, whether it be in white or black hands.

REFERENCES

ABBREVIATIONS
C&W papers – Chatto & Windus papers
CUL – Cambridge University Library
EH – Elspeth Huxley
GH – Gervas Huxley
NG – Nellie Grant
PRO – Public Record Office, London
RH – Rhodes House, Oxford University
RU – Reading University Library
WAC – BBC Written Archives Centre, Caversham

PREFACE
1 Elspeth Huxley, ed., *Nine Faces of Kenya*, Collins Harvill, 1990, p.xxv
2 *Africana*, vol.6, no.1, 1976, pp.25–7

CHAPTER 1
1 Elspeth Huxley, *The Flame Trees of Thika*, London, Chatto & Windus, 1959, p.159
2 Elspeth Huxley, RH, E. Huxley Add. Mss, Box 2
3 Elspeth Huxley, 'Africa – no Place for the White Man', RH, Mss Afr.s.2154, 25/6
4 *The Flame Trees of Thika*, pp 5–6
5 Ibid., p.37
6 NG's reminiscences of her early years, RH, Mss Afr.s.2154, 13/4. This was probably a transcription from tape
7 Ibid.
8 Nellie's black notebook, RH, Mss Afr.s.2154, 14/4
9 *Nine Faces of Kenya*, p.xxv
10 NG, Thika 1913–14, in a letter to EH, 18 January 1935, RH, Mss Afr.s.2154, 12/1

11 EH's Kenya book, RH, Mss Afr.s.2154, 12/1
12 NG, Thika 1913–14, in a letter to EH, 18 January 1935, RH, Mss Afr.s.2154, 12/1
13 *The Flame Trees of Thika*, p.11
14 NG to [unknown], 13 November 1913, RH, Mss Afr.s.2154, 13/2
15 NG to EH, 14 April 1956, RH, Mss Afr.s.2154, 3/9
16 NG, Thika 1913–14, in a letter to EH, 18 January 1935, RH, Mss Afr.s.2154, 12/1
17 NG to [unknown], 2 October 1913, RH, Mss Afr.s.2154, 13/2
18 Elspeth Huxley, *The Mottled Lizard*, London, Chatto & Windus, 1962, p.115
19 NG to [unknown], 1 April 1914, RH, Mss Afr.s.2154, 13/2
20 Ibid.
21 Nellie's 1914 diary, RH, Mss Afr.s.2154, 14/1
22 Elspeth Huxley, *Love Among the Daughters*, London, Chatto & Windus, 1968, pp.195–6

CHAPTER 2

1 Nellie's 1914 diary, RH, Mss Afr.s.2154, 14/1
2 NG, Thika 1913–14, in a letter to EH, 18 January 1935, RH, Mss Afr.s.2154, 12/1
3 Nellie's 1914 diary, RH, Mss Afr.s.2154, 14/1
4 Brian Havelock Potts to EH, 12 March 1980, RH, Mss Afr.s.2154, 15/5
5 *The Mottled Lizard*, p.15
6 NG, Thika 1913–14, in a letter to EH, 18 January 1935, RH, Mss Afr.s.2154, 12/1
7 *The Flame Trees of Thika*, p.224
8 NG, Thika 1913–14, in a letter to EH, 18 January 1935, RH, Mss Afr.s.2154, 12/1
9 *The Mottled Lizard*, p.319
10 NG's reminiscences of her early years, RH, Mss Afr.s.2154, 13/4
11 Elspeth Huxley, *Nellie: Letters from Africa*, London, Weidenfeld & Nicolson, 1973, pp.55–6
12 *Love Among the Daughters*, p.34
13 Ibid., p.25
14 NG's reminiscences of her early years, RH, Mss Afr.s.2154, 13/4.
15 NG, Thika 1913–14, in a letter to EH, 18 January 1935, RH, Mss Afr.s.2154, 12/1
16 Nellie's black notebook, RH, Mss Afr.s.2154, 14/5
17 EH to Tobina Cole, no date, in private hands
18 *Sunday Times Magazine*, 26 April 1987
19 J.H.C. Grant, election manifesto, RH, Mss Afr.s.782, 2/2
20 Ibid.
21 Elspeth Grant to Robin Grant, 18 February 1921, RH, Mss Afr.s.2154, 7/3
22 Elspeth Grant to Robin and Vera Grant, 1 March 1921, RH, Mss Afr.s.2154, 7/3
23 Ibid.
24 Elspeth Grant to Robin Grant, 1 November 1921, RH, Mss Afr.s.2154, 7/3
25 Ibid.
26 Elspeth Grant to Vera and Robin Grant, 30 January 1922, ibid.
27 Elspeth Grant to Vera Grant, 1 August 1922, ibid.
28 NG to Vera Grant, 17 November 1922, RH, Mss Afr.s.2154, 7/1
29 NG to Robin Grant, 14 March 1923, ibid.
30 NG to Robin Grant, 1 February 1923, ibid.
31 Typed sheet by NG, RH, Mss Afr.s.2154, 13/1
32 *Nellie: Letters from Africa*, p.78
33 Elspeth Grant to Vera Grant, 27 November 1923, RH, Mss Afr.s.2154, 7/3
34 *The Mottled Lizard*, p.94
35 Elspeth Grant to Vera and Robin Grant, 30 January 1922, RH, Mss Afr.s.2154, 7/3
36 *Kenya Sunday Times and Sporting News*, 22 October 1922 and 17 September 1923
37 *East African Observer*, 1 March 1923
38 *The Mottled Lizard*, p.291
39 *East African Annual*, 1958–59, p.60
40 Taped interview with Kit Taylor, 26 November 1984, in private hands
41 EH to Margery Perham, 4 August 1966, RH, Perham Papers 336/1
42 *The Flame Trees of Thika*, p.197
43 Elspeth Huxley, *White Man's Country*, 2 vols., London, Macmillan, 1935, vol. 1, p.285

CHAPTER 3

1 *The Mottled Lizard*, p.246
2 Ibid., pp.15–16
3 Ibid., p.324
4 Ibid., p.335
5 *Love Among the Daughters*, pp.9–10
6 Ibid., p.142
7 Ibid., p.189
8 Ibid., p.198
9 Ibid., p.203
10 I'll Tell the World! Impressions of an American University', *Tamesis*, vol. xxvi, no. 1, pp.11–13

11 *Love Among the Daughters*, pp.243–4
12 Ibid., pp.200–1
13 Elspeth Grant to Vera Grant, 31 December 1927, RH, Mss Afr. s.2154, 7/3
14 Jos Grant to Vera Grant, 12 January 1928, RH, Mss Afr.s.2154, 7/4
15 Elspeth Grant to Vera Grant, 31 December 1927, RH, Mss Afr.s.2154, 7/3
16 Nellie's cobbler notebook, RH, Mss Afr.s.2154, 14/5
17 GH, quoting a letter from Trudie Denman, in his *Lady Denman, GBE*, London, Chatto & Windus, 1961, pp.143–4
18 Michael Davie (ed.), *The Diaries of Evelyn Waugh*, London, Weidenfeld & Nicolson, 1976, pp.346–7
19 Gervas Huxley, *Lady Denman, GBE*, p.147
20 Ibid., p.149
21 Elspeth Huxley, 'Professor in the Hills', *Homes and Gardens*, April 1963, p.76
22 EH to Robert Cross, 14 September 1993, in private hands
23 Gervas Huxley, *Both Hands* (autobiography), London, Chatto & Windus, 1970, p.156
24 *The Mottled Lizard*, p.229
25 Rose Hodson to EH, 12 November 1982, RH, Mss Afr.s.2154, 15/5
26 Unpublished memoirs of Sir Charles Markham (Glady's son), and Sir Charles Markham to the author, 10 December 2000
27 Lord Altrincham (Grigg), *Kenya's Opportunity: Memories, Hopes and Ideas*, London, Faber & Faber, 1955, p.73
28 Elspeth Huxley, *Out in the Midday Sun*, Chatto & Windus, 1985, p.21
29 Notes by EH, RH, Mss Afr.s.2154, 12/1
30 *The Mottled Lizard*, p.264
31 EH to Vera Grant, 5 April 1933, RH, Mss Afr.s.2154, 7/3
32 NG to EH, 20 July 1933, RH, Mss Afr.s.2154, 1/1
33 *The Flame Trees of Thika*, p.45

34 EH's interview with Powys Cobb, 1933, RH, Mss Afr.s.782, 1/5
35 EH's interview with General Smuts, 21 August 1933, RH, Mss Afr.s.782, 1/5
36 The machinations of the Colonial Office are in the Public Record Office, Kew, CO 533/439/11
37 Eric Dutton, 'The Night of the Hyena' (unpublished ms). Kipling later published this as a verse of his poem 'The Proconsuls'
38 Edward Grigg to EH, 4 June 1935, RH, Mss Afr.s.2154, 10/1
39 W.C. Bottomley to EH, 5 June 1935, RH, Mss Afr.s.2154, 10/1
40 Margery Perham in *Spectator*, 14 June 1935
41 NG to EH, 14 November 1934, RH, Mss Afr.s.2154, 1/2
42 Preface to 1968 edition of *White Man's Country*, London, Chatto & Windus, 1968
43 EH's introduction to Eric Dutton, 'The Night of the Hyena' (unpublished ms)

CHAPTER 4
1 NG to EH, 20 February 1935, RH, Mss Afr.s.2154, 1/3
2 NG to EH, 15 August 1934, RH, Mss Afr.s.2154, 1/2
3 *Out in the Midday Sun*, p.39
4 Notes by NG on Louis Leakey, no date, RH, Mss Afr.s.2154, 7/4
5 EH to GH, 29 December 1936, ibid.
6 EH to GH, 6 January 1937, ibid.
7 EH to GH., 2 February 1937, ibid.
8 EH to GH, 17 February 1937, ibid.
9 EH to GH, 19 January 1937, ibid.
10 Elspeth Huxley, *Red Strangers*, London, Chatto & Windus, 1939, p.xvi
11 EH to Robert Cross, 12 March 1994, in private hands
12 EH to GH, 13 April 1938, RH, Mss Afr.s.2154, 8/1
13 *Red Strangers*, p.222
14 Letter quoted in Robert Cross and Michael Perkin, *Elspeth Huxley: A*

Bibliography, Winchester, St Paul's Bibliographies, 1996, p.16

15 Notes by Julian Huxley and Lord Hailey, RH, E. Huxley Add. Mss, Box 2

16 Jan Smuts to EH, 15 May 1939, RH, Mss Afr.s.2154, 10/3

17 Margery Perham to Chatto & Windus, 24 September 1943, C&W papers, RU, Elspeth Huxley 1938–54

18 EH to GH, 17 February 1937, RH, Mss Afr.s.2154, 8/2

19 EH to Tobina Cole, no date, in private hands

20 EH to GH, 28 February 1937, RH, Mss Afr.s.2154, 8/2

21 Elspeth Huxley, *Murder at Government House*, London, Methuen, 1937, p.68

22 Elspeth Huxley, *Murder on Safari*, London, Methuen, 1938, p.160

23 Elspeth Huxley, *Death of an Aryan*, London, Methuen, 1938, p.27

24 Ibid., pp.3–4

25 EH to Harold Raymond, RU, C&W papers, E. Huxley, 1938–54

CHAPTER 5

1 EH to GH, 24 March 1937, RH, Mss Afr.s.2154, 8/2

2 EH to GH, 13 April 1938, RH, Mss Afr.s.2154, 8/1

3 Elspeth Huxley, *Gallipot Eyes*, London, Weidenfeld & Nicolson, 1976, preface

4 EH to GH, 28 February 1937, RH, Mss Afr.s.2154, 8/2

5 EH to GH, 5 March 1937, ibid.

6 Internal BBC memo by H. Hoggan, 23 March 1938, BBC WAC, RCONT 1, Talks, E. Huxley, File 1, 1935–41

7 OEPEC Paper no. 82, Joint Broadcasting Committee, 27 September 1939, PRO, T162/858

8 EH to Robert Cross, 19 September 1994, in private hands

9 Schools feedback, BBC WAC, RCONT 1, Talks, E. Huxley, File 1, 1935–41

10 Internal memo by Evelyn Gibbs, 6 November 1941, BBC WAC, RCONT 1, Copyright, E. Huxley, File 1, 1938–43

11 F.N. Lloyd Williams to EH, 24 July 1941, BBC WAC, RCONT 1, Talks, E. Huxley, File 1, 1935–41

12 Memo by Controller, Overseas Services, on the CIO Liaison Officer, 26 July 1943, BBC WAC, R49/339

13 Memo by Ryan, Controller (News), 27 July 1943, BBC WAC, R34/305

14 T.I.K. Lloyd to EH, 2 October 1943, RH, E. Huxley Add. Mss, Box 2

15 NG to EH, 30 January 1941, RH, Mss Afr.s.2154, 2/1

16 NG to EH, 6 February and 23 June 1941, ibid.

17 Hans Stjernswärd to EH, 21 February 1979, RH, Mss Afr.s.2154, 13/5

18 NG to EH, 19 January 1938, RH, Mss Afr.s.2154, 1/6

19 EH to Tobina Cole, no date, in private hands

20 NG to EH, 19 August 1944, RH, Mss Afr.s.2154, 2/6

21 Tobina Cole to the author, 16 November 1999

22 Pamela Taylor to EH, 4 September 1962, RH, Mss Afr.s.2154, 10/3

23 NG to EH, 25 September 1944, RH, Mss Afr.s.2154, 2/6

24 NG to EH, 24 July 1944, ibid.

25 NG to EH, 19 August 1944, ibid.

26 NG to EH, 20 November 1944, ibid.

27 Margery Perham, *East African Journey*, London, Faber & Faber, 1976, p.35

28 Lord Lugard to Margery Perham, 25 March 1943, RH, Perham Papers 290/1

29 Lord Lugard to EH, 26 May 1943, RH, Perham Papers 290/1

30 EH to Margery Perham, 30 May 1976, RH, Perham Papers 44/6

31 Elspeth Huxley, *African Dilemmas*, London, Longmans Green, 1948, p.21

32 NG to EH, 11 September 1944, RH, Mss Afr.s.2154, 2/6

33 EH to J. Grenfell Williams, 11 April 1944, BBC WAC, R49/339

34 NG to EH, 1 October 1944, RH, Mss Afr.s.2154, 2/6

35 NG to EH, 20 November 1944, ibid.
36 EH to Tobina Cole, no date, private collection
37 EH to GH, 10 October 1945, RH, Mss Afr.s.2154, 8/3
38 EH to GH, 27 October 1945, ibid.
39 Charles Granston Richards, 'No Carpet on the Floor, Recollections and Reflections on the Work of Forty Years . . . in the Development of Literature and Publishing', RH, Mss Afr.s.2280
40 EH to GH, 10 November 1945, RH, Mss Afr.s.2154, 8/3
41 EH to GH, 3 January 1946, ibid.

CHAPTER 6

1 EH to GH, 1 November 1945, RH, Mss Afr.s.2154, 8/3
2 EH to GH, 22 November 1945, ibid.
3 EH to GH, 7 December 1945, ibid.
4 EH to GH, 26 December 1945, ibid.
5 EH to GH, 15 November 1945, ibid.
6 NG to EH, 25 February 1946, RH, Mss Afr.s.2154, 3/1
7 EH to GH, 14 November 1946, RH, Mss Afr.s.2154, 8/4
8 NG to EH, 13 October 1946, RH, Mss Afr.s.2154, 3/1
9 Elspeth Huxley, *Forks and Hope*, London, Chatto & Windus, 1964, p.171
10 EH to GH, 12 January 1947, RH, Mss Afr.s.2154, 8/5
11 EH to GH, 11 February 1947, ibid.
12 *Out in the Midday Sun*, pp.204, 206
13 Elspeth Huxley, *The Sorcerer's Apprentice*, London, Chatto & Windus, 1948, p.33
14 Ibid., p.46
15 Ibid., p.331
16 Ibid., p.122
17 Ibid., p.268
18 Ibid., p.365
19 Ibid., p.36
20 EH to GH, 4 March 1947, RH, Mss Afr.s.2154, 8/5
21 EH to GH, 12 April 1947, ibid.
22 NG to EH, 5 September 1948, RH, Mss Afr.s.2154, 3/3

23 EH to GH, 23 April 1947, RH, Mss Afr.s.2154, 8/5
24 *The Sorcerer's Apprentice*, p.290
25 Ibid., p.273
26 Lord Francis Scott to EH, 17 August 1944, RH, Mss Afr.s.2154, 10/3
27 EH to GH, 27 April 1947, RH, Mss Afr.s.2154, 8/5
28 EH to GH, 12 April 1947, ibid.
29 EH to GH, 16 April 1947, ibid.
30 NG to EH, 28 December 1947, RH, Mss Afr.s.2154, 3/2
31 Harold Raymond to EH, 6 January 1947, RU, C&W papers, E. Huxley 1938–54
32 Elspeth Huxley, *The Walled City*, London, Chatto & Windus, 1948, p.15
33 Ibid., p.16
34 Ibid., p.24
35 Ibid., p.26
36 Ibid., p.56
37 Ibid., p.68
38 Ibid., p.69
39 Ibid., p.71
40 Ibid., p.82
41 Ibid., p.103
42 Ibid., p.230
43 Ibid., p.318
44 EH to Miss Barker, 6 October 1948, BBC WAC, RCONT 1, Talks, E. Huxley, File 2, 1942–9
45 EH to GH, 21 January 1948, RH, Mss Afr.s.2154, 8/6
46 EH to GH, 31 January 1948, ibid.
47 EH to Harold Raymond, 4 July 1948, RU, C&W papers, E. Huxley 1938–54
48 EH to Norah Smallwood, 1 November 1948, ibid.
49 *The Sorcerer's Apprentice*, p.99
50 EH to Harold Raymond, 28 March 1949, RU, C&W papers, E. Huxley 1938–54
51 Elspeth Huxley, *I Don't Mind if I Do*, London, Chatto & Windus, 1950, p.95

CHAPTER 7

1 NG to EH, 11 February 1949, RH, Mss Afr.s.2154, 3/4
2 Negley Farson, *Last Chance in Africa*,

London, Victor Gollancz, 1949, pp.62, 65

3 NG to EH, 16 January 1948, RH, Mss Afr.s.2154, 3/3

4 NG to EH, 26 December 1948, ibid.

5 EH to Norah Smallwood, 27 April 1949, RU, C&W papers, E. Huxley 1938–54

6 NG to Ingrid Lindstrom, 15 October 1949, RH, Mss Afr.s.2154, 13/2

7 EH to Norah Smallwood, 27 April 1949, RU, C&W papers, E. Huxley, 1938–54

8 Notes (probably by NG) in a notebook entitled 'Shetland', RH, Mss Afr.s.2154, 13/1

9 Quote from letter from Nellie to Ingrid Lindstrom, no date, in Notes by EH, RH, Mss Afr.s.2154, 23/1

10 EH to Harold Raymond, 13 September 1949, RU, C&W papers, E. Huxley 1938–54

11 EH to Norah Smallwood, 29 September 1949, ibid.

12 NG to Ingrid Lindstrom, 15 October 1949, RH, Mss Afr.s.2154, 13/2

13 Robert Bridges, 'I Love All Beauteous Things', in John Wain (ed.), The Oxford Library of English Poetry, vol. 3, Oxford, Oxford University Press, 1986, p.251

14 EH to Harold Raymond, 23 February 1950, RU, C&W papers, E. Huxley 1938–54

15 BBC WAC, Advisory Committees, R6/29/2, General Advisory Council Meetings, 1945–54, Minutes of Meeting 27 October 1947

16 EH to D.F. Boyd, 15 May 1950, BBC WAC, RCONT 1, Talks, E. Huxley, File 3, 1950–62

17 EH to Arthur Langford, 10 September 1950, ibid.

18 EH to Norah Smallwood, 19 July 1950, RU, C&W papers, E. Huxley 1938–54

19 EH to Norah Smallwood, 18 October 1949, ibid.

20 Norah Smallwood to EH, 29 March 1951, ibid.

21 EH to Norah Smallwood, 30 March 1951, ibid.

22 Elspeth Huxley, Four Guineas, London, Chatto & Windus, 1954, p.196

23 EH to Harold Raymond, 13 March 1952, RU, C&W papers, E. Huxley 1938–54

24 Ibid.

25 EH to Norah Smallwood, 25 August 1952, ibid.

26 Elspeth Huxley, 'Mine Own Exchequer', Punch, 19 June 1963

27 Ibid.

28 Ibid.

29 EH's Notes on Mau Mau, 1953, RH, Mss Afr.s.2154, 11/3

30 NG to EH, 18 February 1953, RH, Mss Afr.s.2154, 3/6

31 EH to Norah Smallwood, 18 May 1953, RU, C&W papers, E. Huxley 1938–54

32 Harold Raymond to EH, 10 June 1953, ibid.

33 Four Guineas, p.93

34 EH to Harold Raymond, 7 March 1954, RU, C&W papers, E. Huxley 1938–54

35 NG to EH, 1 April 1953, RH, Mss Afr.s.2154, 3/6

36 NG to EH, 22 June 1953, ibid.

37 EH to GH, 9 November 1953, RH, Mss Afr.s.2154, 8/7

38 EH's Notes on Mau Mau, 1953, RH, Mss Afr.s.2154, 11/3

CHAPTER 8

1 EH to GH, 19 October 1953, RH, Mss Afr.s.2154, 8/7

2 EH to GH, 25 October 1953, ibid.

3 Interview with Vera Tugwell (née Norris), 31 August 1999

4 EH to Harold Raymond, 30 January 1954, RU, C&W papers, E. Huxley 1938–54

5 EH to GH, 9 November 1953, RH, Mss Afr.s.2154, 8/7

6 EH to GH, 23 November 1953, ibid.

7 EH to GH, 11 December 1953, ibid.

8 A Thing to Love, London, Chatto & Windus, 1954, p.16

9 Ibid., p.125

10 Ibid., p.189

11 Ibid., p.193

12 Ibid., p.103

13 EH to Terence Gavaghan, 4 November 1993, in private hands

14 EH to Norah Smallwood, 29 September 1954, RU, C&W papers, E. Huxley 1938–54

15 EH to Norah Smallwood, 10 March 1955, RU, C&W papers, E. Huxley 1955–62

16 NG to EH, 3 January 1954, RH, Mss Afr.s.2154, 3/7

17 NG to EH, 5 December 1954, ibid.

18 NG to EH, 12 December 1954, ibid.

19 NG to EH, 26 December 1954, ibid.

20 Harold Raymond to W.H. Clarke, 3 May 1954, RU, C&W papers, E. Huxley 1938–54

21 EH to Betty Rowley, 19 January 1953, BBC WAC, RCONT 1, Talks, E. Huxley, File 3, 1950–62

22 Elspeth Huxley, *Kenya Today*, London, Lutterworth Press, 1954, p.4

23 Ibid., p.7

24 Ibid., p.29

25 EH to Harold Raymond, 8 January 1956, RU, C&W papers, E. Huxley 1955–62

26 EH to Norah Smallwood, 1 April 1956, ibid.

27 EH to Norah Smallwood, 7 June 1956, ibid.

28 Elspeth Huxley, *The Red Rock Wilderness*, London, Chatto & Windus, 1957, p.90

29 Ibid., p.249

30 Ibid., p.28

31 NG to EH, 31 July 1955, RH, Mss Afr.s.2154, 3/8

32 NG to EH, 14 January 1956, RH, Mss Afr.s.2154, 3/9

33 NG to EH, 25 March 1956, ibid.

34 NG to EH, no date but between 14 and 27 April 1956, ibid.

35 EH to Norah Smallwood, 29 April 1956, RU, C&W papers, E. Huxley 1955–62

36 EH to GH, 9 October 1956, RH, Mss Afr.s.2154, 9/1

37 EH to GH, 2 November 1956, ibid.

38 EH to GH, 30 October 1956, ibid.

39 EH to GH, 10 November 1956, ibid.

40 EH to Norah Smallwood, 30 November 1956, RU, C&W papers, E. Huxley 1955–62

41 EH to GH, 24 October 1956, RH, Mss Afr.s.2154, 9/1.

42 Notes on Njoro, RH, Mss Afr.s.2154, 3/1

43 EH to GH, 9 December 1956, RH, Mss Afr.s.2154, 9/1

44 EH to GH, 13 December 1956, ibid.

45 EH to Norah Smallwood, 19 March 1957, RU, C&W papers, E. Huxley 1955–62

46 F.T. Holden to EH, 3 July 1957, RH, Mss Afr.s.2154, 3/4

47 Michael Blundell to EH, 1 March 1991, RH, E. Huxley Add. Mss, Box 2

48 EH to Norah Smallwood, 24 October 1957, RU, C&W papers, E. Huxley 1955–62

49 Gervas Huxley, *Both Hands*, p.241

50 EH to Harold Raymond, 12 July 1953, RU, C&W papers, E. Huxley 1938–54

51 Telephone conversation with Charles Huxley, 6 June 1999

52 NG to EH, 2 February 1957, RH, Mss Afr.s.2154, 3/10

53 Joan Grigg to NG, 5 February 1957, ibid.

54 NG to EH, 6 April 1957, ibid.

55 NG to EH, 18 April 1957, ibid.

56 NG to EH, 13 January 1957, ibid.

57 *Forks and Hope*, p.87

58 Tobina Cole to the author, 19 July 1999

59 Ibid.

60 EH to GH, 15 January 1958, RH, Mss Afr.s.2154, 9/2

61 *Sunday Times*, 16 March 1958

62 EH to GH, 1 February 1958, RH, Mss Afr.s.2154, 9/2

63 EH to Norah Smallwood, 22 February 1958, RU, C&W papers, E. Huxley 1955–62

64 EH to Norah Smallwood, 30 March 1958, ibid.

65 EH to Norah Smallwood, 8 August 1958, ibid.

66 EH to Norah Smallwood, 22 February 1958, ibid.

67 *Sunday Times*, 2 March 1958
68 EH to GH, 23 February 1958, RH, Mss Afr.s.2154, 9/2
69 EH to GH, 26 January 1958, ibid.
70 EH to GH, 28 January 1958, ibid.

CHAPTER 9

1 Karen Blixen, *Out of Africa*, 1st publ. 1937, many editions, e.g. Penguin, London, 1954, pp.329, 332
2 NG to EH, 2 January 1938, RH, Mss Afr.s.2154, 1/6. In her previous letter of 28 December 1937 Nellie gives it as her opinion that it was true that Karen Blixen took drugs, 'but she may have given it up'. (1/5)
3 EH to Norah Smallwood, 29 June 1958, RU, C&W papers, E. Huxley 1955–62.
4 EH to Norah Smallwood, 24 November 1958, ibid. By 1987 Elspeth had relented, because she selected a few photographs from her childhood for the illustrated version which appeared that year
5 Norah Smallwood to EH, 7 July 1958, RU, C&W papers, E. Huxley 1955–62
6 *The Flame Trees of Thika*, p.130
7 Ibid., p.7
8 Ibid., p.284
9 Ibid., pp.18–19
10 Ibid., p.8
11 Ibid., pp.45–6
12 Ibid., p.145
13 Ibid., p.276
14 NG to EH, 4 July 1958, RH, Mss Afr.s.2154, 3/11
15 Edward Rodwell to EH, 6 March 1978, RH, Mss Afr.s.2154, 16/2
16 EH to Norah Smallwood, 9 September 1959, ibid.
17 NG to EH, 7 July 1957, RH, Mss Afr.s.2154, 3/10
18 NG to EH, 12 December 1959, RH, Mss Afr.s.2154, 4/1
19 NG to EH, 10 August 1957, RH, Mss Afr.s.2154, 3/10
20 NG to EH, 9 November 1958, RH, Mss Afr.s.2154, 3/11

21 EH to GH, 25 January 1959, RH, Mss Afr.s.2154, 9/4
22 Diary written as notes for *A New Earth*, RH, Mss Afr.s.2154, 4/1
23 EH to GH, 8 February 1959, RH, Mss Afr.s.2154, 9/4
24 Elspeth Huxley, *A New Earth*, Chatto & Windus, 1960, p.9
25 Ibid., p.66
26 EH to GH, 4 November 1958, RH, Mss Afr.s.2154, 9/3
27 EH to GH, 5 February 1961, RH, Afr.s.2154, 9/6
28 EH to GH, 17 February 1959, RH, Mss Afr.s.2154, 9/4
29 Gervas Huxley, *Both Hands*, pp.246–7
30 EH to GH, 12 March 1959, RH, Mss Afr.s.2154, 9/4
31 Elspeth Huxley, 'My Kind of Life', *Daily Telegraph*, 29 September 1986
32 EH to Peggy Barker, 7 November 1959, BBC WAC, RCONT 1, Talks, E. Huxley, File 3, 1950–62
33 GH to Norah Smallwood, 17 February 1960, RU, C&W papers, E. Huxley 1955–62
34 EH to GH, 3 April 1960, RH, Mss Afr.s.2154, 9/5
35 EH's Monckton Commission Diary, entry for 23 April 1960, RH, Mss Afr.s.2154, 11/4
36 Ibid., entry for 18 February 1960
37 EH to Peter Calvocoressi, 5 December 1959, RU, C&W papers, E. Huxley 1955–62
38 Elspeth Huxley, *The Merry Hippo*, London, Chatto & Windus, 1963, p.10
39 Ibid., p.22
40 Ibid., pp.143–4
41 Ibid., pp.60–3
42 I.J. Bligh to EH, 25 April 1962, RH, Mss Afr.s.2154, 10/2
43 EH to Isa Benzie, 11 June 1962, BBC WAC, RCONT 1, Talks, E. Huxley, File 3, 1950–62
44 Sir Richard Turnbull to EH, 3 June 1962, RH, Mss Afr.s.2154, 10/3

CHAPTER 10

1 EH to Norah Smallwood, 27 September 1960, RU, C&W papers, E. Huxley 1955–62

2 EH to GH, 17 February 1961, RH, Mss Afr.s.2154, 9/6

3 EH to GH, 29 January 1961, RH, Mss Afr.s.2154, 9/6

4 EH to Norah Smallwood, 28 January 1966, RU, C&W papers, E. Huxley 1963–6

5 EH to GH, 13 March 1960, RH, Mss Afr.s.2154, 9/5

6 EH to Ian Parsons, 1 July 1961, RU, C&W papers, E. Huxley 1955–62

7 NG to EH, 20 January 1962, RH, Mss Afr.s.2154, 4/4

8 EH to Norah Smallwood, 28 January 1962, RU, C&W papers, E. Huxley 1955–62

9 NG to EH, 6 October 1962, RH, Mss Afr.s.2154, 4/4

10 NG to EH, 27 October 1962, ibid.

11 NG to EH, 24 August 1963, RH, Mss Afr.s.2154, 4/5

12 EH to GH, 10 April 1960, RH, Mss Afr.s.2154, 9/5

13 EH to GH, 1 February 1961, RH, Mss Afr.s.2154, 9/6

14 EH to Norah Smallwood, 22 September 1962, RU, C&W papers, E. Huxley 1955–62

15 EH to Ian Parsons, 16 January 1964, ibid.

16 NG to EH, 13 September 1959, RH, Mss Afr.s.2154, 4/1

17 Transcription from tape of August 1963, in private hands. There is also a transcription in RH, Mss Afr.s.2154, 15/6

18 NG to EH, 1 January 1961, RH, Mss Afr.s.2154, 4/3

19 NG to EH, 25 February 1961, ibid.

20 *Forks and Hope*, p.192

21 EH in *Listener*, 6 September 1962, pp.342–3

22 NG to EH, 25 September 1963, RH, Mss Afr.s.2154, 4/5

23 EH to Margery Perham, 22 December 1961, RH, Perham papers 350/4

24 NG to EH, 24 June 1963, RH, Mss Afr.s.2154, 4/5

25 NG to EH, 22 August 1964, RH, Mss Afr.s.2154, 4/6

26 *The Mottled Lizard*, p.264

27 Ibid., p.235

28 Ibid., p.330

29 Ibid., p.50

30 EH to A.T. Matson, 24 May 1962, RH, Matson papers, Mss Afr.s.1792, 1/1/3

31 EH to Ian Parsons, 23 June 1961, RU, C&W papers, E. Huxley 1955–62

32 *The Mottled Lizard*, pp.184–5

33 Ibid., p.322

34 Ibid., pp.18–19

35 EH to Norah Smallwood, 1 July 1961, RU, C&W papers, E. Huxley 1955–62

36 Diary of East African travels, 1963, RH, Mss Afr.s.2154, 11/5

37 *Forks and Hope*, p.65

38 Diary of East African travels, 1963, RH, Mss Afr.s.2154, 11/5

39 *Forks and Hope*, p.119

40 Diary of East African travels, 1963, RH, Mss Afr.s.2154, 11/5

41 EH to Cecil Day Lewis, 7 September 1963, RU, C&W papers, E. Huxley 1963–6

42 Jomo Kenyatta to EH, 19 February 1964, RH, Mss Afr.s.2154, 10/2

43 Diary of East African travels, 1963, RH, Mss Afr.s.2154, 11/5

44 *Forks and Hope*, p.256

45 Ibid., p.76

46 Ibid., p.272

47 Ibid., p.193

48 EH to Norah Smallwood, 14 July 1963, RU, C&W papers, E. Huxley 1963–6

49 EH to Norah Smallwood, 18 May 1963, ibid.

50 Elspeth Huxley, *A Man From Nowhere*, London, Chatto & Windus, 1964, p.73

51 Ibid., p.283

52 Ibid., p.292

53 Ibid., p.26

54 Ibid., p.298

CHAPTER 11

1 EH to Norah Smallwood, 4 January 1963, RU, C&W papers, E. Huxley 1963–6
2 EH to Norah Smallwood, 30 January 1964, ibid.
3 EH to Peter Calvocoressi, 6 February 1964, ibid.
4 EH to Norah Smallwood, 12 May 1962, RU, C&W papers, E. Huxley 1955–62
5 EH to Norah Smallwood, 19 August 1962, ibid.
6 Elspeth Huxley, *Back Street New Worlds*, London, Chatto & Windus, 1964, p.9
7 Ibid., pp.66–7
8 EH to Norah Smallwood, 14 November 1965, RU, C&W papers, E. Huxley 1963–6
9 Elspeth Huxley, *Brave New Victuals*, London, Chatto & Windus, 1965, p.154
10 Ibid., p.121
11 Ibid., p.122
12 James Lees-Milne reporting a conversation with Elspeth in his *A Mingled Measure: Diaries 1953–1972*, London, John Murray, 1994, pp.208–9
13 *The Mottled Lizard*, p.265
14 *Dear to My Heart*, programme on West of England Home Service, 29 October 1956, transcript in RH, Mss Afr.s.2154, 25/11
15 EH to Mary Lovell, 13 July 1986, in private hands
16 *The Mottled Lizard*, p.240
17 EH to Norah Smallwood, 1 March 1964, RU, C&W papers, E. Huxley 1963–6
18 EH to Norah Smallwood, 2 January 1966, ibid.
19 EH to Margery Perham, 4 August 1966, RH, Perham papers, 336/1
20 EH to Norah Smallwood, 28 January 1966, RU, C&W papers, E. Huxley 1963–6
21 EH to Norah Smallwood, 2 March 1966, ibid.
22 EH to Norah Smallwood, 25 June 1965, ibid.
23 Gervas Huxley, *Both Hands*, p.244
24 EH to Norah Smallwood, 11 May 1965, RU, C&W papers, E. Huxley 1963–6
25 EH to Norah Smallwood, 14 October 1965, ibid.
26 EH to Norah Smallwood, 15 May 1962, RU C&W papers, E. Huxley 1955–62
27 EH to Norah Smallwood, 14 February 1964, RU, C&W papers, E. Huxley 1963–6
28 EH to Norah Smallwood, 1 November 1964, ibid.
29 EH to Ian Parsons, 2 June 1964, ibid.
30 EH to Ian Parsons, 7 September 1964, ibid.
31 Jock Gibb to Colonel William Crowder, no date but end of October 1964, ibid.
32 EH to Ian Parsons, 27 November 1964 and 28 March 1965, ibid.
33 EH to Ian Parsons, 16 May 1965, ibid.
34 Elspeth Huxley, *Their Shining Eldorado*, London, Chatto & Windus, p.270
35 Norah Smallwood to EH, quoting van der Post's letter, 5 February 1964, ibid.
36 NG to EH, 12 November 1965, RH, Mss Afr.s.2154, 5/1
37 NG to EH, 21 August 1966, RH, Mss Afr.s.2154, 5/2
38 NG to EH, 31 July 1966, ibid.
39 NG to EH, 31 May 1967, RH, Mss Afr.s.2154, 5/3
40 NG to EH, 20 September 1967, ibid.
41 EH to Norah Smallwood, 7 January 1967, RU, C&W papers, E. Huxley 1967–70
42 Gervas Huxley, *Both Hands*, p.238
43 *Love Among the Daughters*, p.18
44 NG to EH, 6 September 1968, RH, Mss Afr.s.2154, 5/4

CHAPTER 12

1 NG to EH, 23 October 1970, RH, Mss Afr.s.2154, 5/6
2 NG to EH, 13 November 1968, RH, Mss Afr.s.2154, 5/4

3 NG to EH, 5 January 1969, RH, Mss Afr.s.2154, 5/5
4 NG to EH, 12 July 1969, ibid.
5 EH to Barbara Gough, 3 January 1982, in private hands
6 EH to Mary Lovell, 23 September 1990, in private hands
7 Audrey Richards to EH, 23 February 1982, RH, Mss Afr.s.2154, 16/2
8 EH to Norah Smallwood, 19 April 1971, RU, C&W papers, E. Huxley 1971–4
9 EH to Peter Scott, 26 May 1971, CUL, Peter Scott papers, M1286
10 NG to EH, 28 January 1966, RH, Mss Afr.s.2154, 5/2
11 EH to Mary Lovell, 19 March 1988, in private hands
12 EH to Margery Perham, 7 August 1971, RH, Perham papers, 27/1
13 EH to Margery Perham, 14 December 1971, ibid.
14 EH to Alison Smith, 12 April 1989, in private hands
15 EH to Norah Smallwood, 28 August 1970, RU, C&W papers, E. Huxley 1969–70
16 EH to Margery Perham, 31 December 1971, RH, Perham papers, 27/1
17 EH to Norah Smallwood, 9 November 1972, RU, C&W papers, E. Huxley 1971–4
18 EH to Norah Smallwood, 8 April 1972, ibid.
19 NG to EH, 12 December 1971, RH, Mss Afr.s.2154, 5/7
20 NG to EH, 6 August 1972, RH, Mss Afr.s.2154, 6/1
21 NG to EH, 30 March 1973, RH, Mss Afr.s.2154, 6/2
22 NG to EH, 1 February 1975, RH, Mss Afr.s.2154, 6/4
23 NG to EH, 18 August 1974, RH, Mss Afr.s.2154, 6/3
24 NG to EH, 27 November 1975, RH, Mss Afr.s.2154, 6/4
25 NG to EH, 11 and 22 July 1976, RH, Mss Afr.s.2154, 6/5
26 NG to EH, 9 July 1977, RH, Mss Afr.s.2154, 6/6
27 NG to EH, 30 July 1977, ibid.
28 EH to Norah Smallwood, 9 November 1972, RU, C&W papers, E. Huxley 1971–4
29 EH to Norah Smallwood, 26 November 1972, ibid.
30 EH to Norah Smallwood, 7 January 1973, ibid.
31 Ibid.
32 EH to Norah Smallwood, 8 September 1973, ibid.
33 Ibid.
34 Norah Smallwood to EH, 26 June 1975, RU, C&W papers, E. Huxley 1975–7
35 Director's memo by Hugo Brunner, 4 August 1975, ibid.
36 Hugo Brunner to EH, 7 August 1975, ibid.
37 EH to Hugo Brunner, 27 August 1975, ibid.
38 EH to Margery Perham, 19 December 1974, RH, Perham papers, 290/1
39 Introduction by EH to Mary Kingsley, *Travels in West Africa*, London, The Folio Society, 1976
40 EH to Norah Smallwood, 28 December 1976, RU, C&W papers, E. Huxley 1975–7
41 Ibid.
42 EH to H.G.R. King, 15 October 1976, Scott Polar Research Institute, Cambridge, 655.52:001.85
43 H.G.R. King to EH, 1 June 1977, ibid.
44 Conversation between the author and H.G.R. King, 15 February 2000
45 EH to H.G.R. King, 6 May 1977, Scott Polar Research Institute, 655.52.001.85
46 EH to H.G.R. King, 12 November 1977, ibid., 069.41 (Huxley, E.)
47 Ibid.
48 EH to Norah Smallwood, 26 September 1976, RU, C&W papers, E. Huxley 1975–7
49 EH to Norah Smallwood, 8 December 1978, RU, C&W papers, E. Huxley 1978–81
50 Barbara Gough to the author, 19 November 1999

51 EH to A.T. Matson, 29 June 1981, RH, Matson papers, Mss Afr.s.1792
52 *Nellie: Letters from Africa*, p.41
53 Ibid., p.314

CHAPTER 13
1 Interview with EH by Robin Page, *Sunday Telegraph Magazine*, 9 March 1980
2 EH to Peter Scott, 6 January 1965, CUL, Peter Scott papers, M1047
3 EH to Adrian House, 5 October 1992, in private hands
4 EH to Cherry Palmer, 25 March 1996, in private hands
5 EH to Adrian House, 10 November 1989, in private hands. Elspeth thought House's biography of the Adamsons made Joy out to be more unpleasant than she really was
6 Interview with Mervyn Cowie, 1983, in private hands
7 Joy Adamson to EH, 4 June 1978, RH, Mss Afr.s.2154, 16/2
8 Joy Adamson to EH, 28 January 1979, ibid.
9 Joy Adamson to EH, 28 May 1979, ibid.
10 EH to Barbara Gough, 13 December 1980, in private hands
11 Lord Cranworth, *Kenya Chronicles* London, Macmillan, 1939, p.71
12 EH to Norah Smallwood, 18 March 1981, RU, C&W papers, E. Huxley 1978–81
13 EH to Norah Smallwood, 2 February 1981, ibid.
14 EH to Norah Smallwood, 13 February 1981, ibid.
15 Elspeth Huxley, 'Going Back', *Observer Magazine*, 30 August 1981
16 Ibid.
17 Ibid.
18 EH to Barbara Gough, 13 December 1980, in private hands
19 *Out in the Midday Sun*, p.ix
20 EH to Kit Taylor, 29 October 1979, in private hands
21 Michael Blundell to EH, RH, E. Huxley Add. Mss, Box 2
22 Sir Humphrey Slade to EH, 13 December 1982, RH, Mss Afr.s.2154, 15/5

23 Interview with Hugh Huxley, 30 March 2000
24 EH's interview with Leslie Whitehouse, 1983, tape in private hands
25 EH's interview with Michael Blundell, 8 December 1983, tape in private hands
26 *Out in the Midday Sun*, p.123
27 Ibid., p.132
28 Pam Scott to EH, 18 December 1985, RH, E. Huxley Add. Mss., Box 2
29 EH to Mary Lovell, 15 January 1988, in private hands
30 EH to Mary Lovell, 19 May 1988, in private hands
31 EH to Mary Lovell, 19 March 1988, in private hands
32 EH to Mary Lovell, 16 August 1989, in private hands
33 EH to Robert Cross, 16 October 1993, in private hands
34 Michael Blundell to EH, 4 September 1989, E. Huxley Add. Mss, Box 2
35 *Nine Faces of Kenya*, p.xxv
36 Philippa Scott to author, 3 December 1999,
37 Ibid.
38 Elspeth Huxley, *Peter Scott: Painter and Naturalist*, London, Faber & Faber, 1993, acknowledgements
39 EH to Mary Lovell, 20 March 1992, in private hands
40 EH to Mary Lovell, 15 September 1991, in private hands
41 *Peter Scott*, p.303
42 EH to Mary Lovell, 13 July 1996, in private hands
43 EH to Mary Lovell, 9 March 1991, in private hands
44 EH to Mary Lovell, 23 May 1986, in private hands
45 EH to Robert Cross, 26 August 1995, in private hands
46 EH to Robert Cross, 23 August 1995, in private hands
47 EH to Joan Considine, 20 December 1994, in private hands
48 EH to Mary Lovell, 22 February 1989, in private hands

49 EH to Robert Cross, 21 April 1991, in private hands
50 EH to Viveka Lindstrom, no date, in private hands
51 EH to Mary Lovell, 23 April 1992, in private hands
52 James Lees-Milne, *Deep Romantic Chasm: Diaries 1979–1981*, London, John Murray, 2000, p.14
53 James Lees-Milne, *Ancient as the Hills: Diaries 1973–1974*, London, John Murray, 1997, p.46
54 Interview with Alexander Huxley, 24 October 2000
55 Chryssee Bradley Martin to the author, 26 November 1999
56 EH to Mary Lovell, 28 April 1988, in private hands
57 EH to Mary Lovell, 20 August 1987, in private hands
58 EH to Joan Considine, 16 May 1966, in private hands
59 Elspeth Huxley, 'The Flames Still Burn', *Daily Telegraph*, 24 June 1995
60 EH to Joan Considine, 1 November 1995, in private hands
61 EH to Joan Considine, 23 December 1996, in private hands
62 Mary Lovell to the author, email, 22 May 2000

CONCLUSION

1 EH to Martin ... [illegible], 10 April 1988, RH, E. Huxley Add. Mss, Box 2
2 EH to Margery Perham, 15 March 1970, RH, Perham papers 352/5
3 EH to Mary Lovell, 20 March 1992, in private hands
4 Ngugi wa Thiong'o, *Homecoming*, London, Heinemann, 1972, p.42

BIBLIOGRAPHY

BOOKS BY ELSPETH HUXLEY
There is a full list of Elspeth's Huxley's works, journalism and broadcasting in Robert Cross and Michael Perkin, *Elspeth Huxley: A Bibliography* (Winchester, St Paul's Bibliographies, 1996).

White Man's Country: Lord Delamere and the Making of Kenya, London, Macmillan, 2 vols, 1935
Murder at Government House, London, Methuen, 1937
Murder on Safari, London, Methuen, 1938
Red Strangers, London, Chatto & Windus, 1939
Death of an Aryan (US title: *The African Poison Murders*), London, Methuen, 1939
East Africa, London, Penns in the Rocks Press and William Collins, 1941
The Story of Five English Farmers, London, Sheldon Press, 1941
Atlantic Ordeal, London, Chatto & Windus, 1941
English Women, London, Sheldon Press, 1942
Brave Deeds of the War, London, Sheldon Press, 1943
Race and Politics in Kenya (with Margery Perham), London, Faber & Faber, 1944
Colonies: A Reader's Guide, Cambridge, Cambridge University Press, 1947
The Walled City, London, Chatto & Windus, 1948
Settlers of Kenya, London, Longmans, 1948
African Dilemmas, London, Longmans, 1948
The Sorcerer's Apprentice, London, Chatto & Windus, 1948
I Don't Mind if I Do, London, Chatto & Windus, 1950
Four Guineas, London, Chatto & Windus, 1954
A Thing to Love, London, Chatto & Windus, 1954
Kenya Today, London, Lutterworth Press, 1954
What Are Trustee Nations?, London, Batchworth Press, 1955

The Red Rock Wilderness, London, Chatto & Windus, 1957

No Easy Way, Nairobi, East African Standard, 1958

The Flame Trees of Thika, London, Chatto & Windus, 1959

A New Earth, London, Chatto & Windus, 1960

The Mottled Lizard (US title: *On the Edge of the Rift*), London, Chatto & Windus, 1962

The Merry Hippo (US title: *The Incident at the Merry Hippo*), London, Chatto & Windus, 1963

Forks and Hope (US title: *With Forks and Hope*), London, Chatto & Windus, 1964

A Man from Nowhere, London, Chatto & Windus, 1964

Suki: A Little Tiger (photographs by Laelia Goehr), London, Chatto & Windus, 1964

Back Street New Worlds: A Look at Immigrants in Britain, London, Chatto & Windus, 1964

Brave New Victuals, London, Chatto & Windus, 1965

Their Shining Eldorado, London, Chatto & Windus, 1967

Love Among the Daughters, London, Chatto & Windus, 1968

The Challenge of Africa, London, Aldus Books, 1971

The Kingsleys: A Biographical Anthology, London, George Allen & Unwin, 1973

Livingstone and his African Journeys, London, Weidenfeld & Nicolson, 1974

Florence Nightingale, London, Weidenfeld & Nicolson, 1975

Gallipot Eyes: A Wiltshire Diary, London, Weidenfeld & Nicolson, 1976

Scott of the Antarctic, London, Weidenfeld & Nicolson, 1977

Nellie: Letters from Africa, London, Weidenfeld & Nicolson, 1979

Pioneer's Scrapbook (ed., with Arnold Curtis), London, Evans Bros, 1980

Whipsnade: Captive Breeding for Survival, London, William Collins, 1981

The Prince Buys the Manor, London, Chatto & Windus, 1982

Last Days in Eden (with Hugo van Lawick), London, Harvill Press, 1984

Out in the Midday Sun, London, Chatto & Windus, 1985

Nine Faces of Kenya (anthology), London, Collins Harvill, 1990

Peter Scott: Painter and Naturalist, London, Faber & Faber, 1993

GENERAL BIBLIOGRAPHY

Altrincham, Edward Grigg, Baron, *Kenya's Opportunity: Memories, Hopes and Ideas*, London, Faber & Faber, 1955

Archer, Sir Geoffrey, *Personal and Historical Memoirs of an East African Administrator*, London, Oliver & Boyd, 1963

Aschan, Ulf, *The Man Whom Women Loved: The Life of Bror Blixen*, New York, St Martin's Press, 1987

Beard, Peter Hill, *The End of the Game*, New York, Viking, 1965

Berman, Bruce, *Control and Crisis in Colonial Kenya*, London, James Currey, 1990

Best, Nicholas, *Happy Valley*, London, Secker & Warburg, 1979

Binks, H.K., *African Rainbow*, London, Sidgwick & Jackson, 1959

Blixen, Karen (as Isak Dinesen), *Out of Africa*, New York, Random House, 1937

Blixen, Karen, *Letters from Africa*, London, Weidenfeld & Nicolson, 1982

Blundell, Michael, *A Love Affair with the Sun*, Nairobi, Kenway Publications, 1994

Boyes, John, *John Boyes, King of the Wakikuyu*, London, Methuen, 1911

Buxton, M. Aline, *Kenya Days*, London, Edward Arnold, 1928

Carman, John A., *A Medical History of Kenya*, London, Rex Collings, 1976

Carney, Michael, *Britain in Pictures: A History and Bibliography*, London, Werner Shaw, 1995

Carney, Michael, *Stoker: The Life of Hilda Matheson*, Llangynog, privately printed, 1999

Carson, J.B., *Sun, Sand and Safari*, London, Robert Hale, 1957

Carson, J.B., *Pages from the Past – Kenya*, Braunton, Merlin Books, 1990

Churchill, Winston S., *My African Journey*, London, Hodder & Stoughton, 1908

Clark, Ronald W., *The Huxleys*, London, Heinemann, 1968

Clough, Marshall S., *Fighting Two Sides*, Niwot, University Press of Colorado, 1990

Corfield, F.D., *The Origins and Growth of Mau Mau*, Colony and Protectorate of Kenya, Sessional Paper no. 5 of 1959/60

Coupland, Sir Reginald, *The Exploitation of East Africa*, London, Faber & Faber, 1939

Cowie, Mervyn, *Fly, Vulture*, London, Harrap, 1961

Cranworth, Lord, *A Colony in the Making*, London, Macmillan, 1912

Cranworth, Lord, *Kenya Chronicles*, London, Macmillan, 1939

Curtis, Arnold (ed.), *Memories of Kenya*, Nairobi, Evans Bros, 1986

Dower, Kenneth Gandar, *Abyssinian Patchwork: An Anthology*, London, Frederick Muller, 1949

East Africa Women's League, *They Made it Their Home* (intro. by Elspeth Huxley), Nairobi, East African Standard, 1962

East African Annual, Nairobi, published annually during the 1950s by the *East African Standard*, Nairobi

Eliot, Sir Charles, *The East Africa Protectorate*, London, Edward Arnold, 1905

Evans, Tenniel, *Don't Walk in the Long Grass*, London, Bantam Press, 1999

Farrant, Leda, *The Legendary Grogan*, London, Hamish Hamilton, 1981

Farrant, Leda, *Diana, Lady Delamere and the Lord Erroll Murder*, Nairobi, privately published, 1997

Farson, Negley, *Last Chance in Africa*, London, Gollancz, 1949

Fey, Venn, *Cloud Over Kenya*, London, Collins, 1964

Foran, W. Robert, *A Cuckoo in Kenya*, London, Hutchinson, 1936

Foran, W. Robert, *The Kenya Police*, London, Robert Hale, 1962

Fox, James, *White Mischief*, London, Jonathan Cape, 1982

Gann, L.H., and Duignan, Peter, *The Rulers of British Africa, 1870–1914*, London, Croom Helm, 1978

Gavaghan, Terence, *Of Lions and Dungbeetles*, Ilfracombe, Arthur H. Stockwell, 1999

Gillett, Mary, *Tribute to Pioneers*, Oxford, privately published, 1986

Githae-Mugo, Micere, *Visions of Africa*, Nairobi, Kenya Literature Bureau, 1978

Goldsmith, F.H., *John Ainsworth, Pioneer Kenya Administrator*, London, Macmillan, 1955

Gregory, J.R., *Under the Sun*, Nairobi, The English Press, no date

Hardy, Ronald, *The Iron Snake*, London, Collins, 1965

Harlow, Vincent, and Chilver, E.M., *History of East Africa*, vol. 2, Oxford, Clarendon Press, 1965

Harris, Michael, *Outsiders and Insiders*, New York, Peter Lang, 1992

Hayes, Charles, *Oserian, Place of Peace*, Nairobi, Rima Books, 1997

Hemsing, Jan, *Then and Now: Nairobi's Norfolk Hotel*, Nairobi, Sealpoint Publicity, 1975

Hill, Mervyn, *Permanent Way*, Nairobi, East African Railways and Harbours, 1949

Hill, Mervyn, *Planters' Progress: The Story of Coffee in Kenya*, Nairobi, East African Standard, 1956

Hobley, C.W., *Kenya, from Chartered Company to Crown Colony*, London, H.F. and G. Witherby, 1929

Hook, Hilary, *Home from the Hill*, Harmondsworth, Penguin, 1988

Huxley, Gervas, *Talking of Tea*, London, Thames & Hudson, 1956

Huxley, Gervas, *Endymion Porter: The Life of a Courtier, 1587–1649*, London, Chatto & Windus, 1959

Huxley, Gervas, *Lady Denman, GBE*, London, Chatto & Windus, 1961

Huxley, Gervas, *Lady Elizabeth and the Grosvenors: Life in a Whig Family 1822–1899*, London, Oxford University Press, 1965

Huxley, Gervas, *Victorian Duke: The Life of Hugh Lupus Grosvenor, 1st Duke of Westminster*, London, Oxford University Press, 1967

Huxley, Gervas, *Both Hands*, London, Chatto & Windus, 1970

Jackson, Sir Frederick, *Early Days in East Africa*, London, Edward Arnold, 1930

Kenyatta, Jomo, *Facing Mt Kenya*, London, Secker & Warburg, 1938

Lees-Milne, James, *A Mingled Measure: Diaries 1953–1972*, London, John Murray, 1994

Lees-Milne, James, *Deep Romantic Chasm: Diaries 1979–1981*, London, John Murray, 2000

Lewis, Jeremy, *Kindred Spirits*, London, HarperCollins, 1995

Leys, Norman, *Kenya*, London, Hogarth Press, 1924

Leys, Norman, *The Colour Bar in East Africa*, London, Hogarth Press, 1941

Lipscomb, J.F., *White Africans*, London, Faber & Faber, 1955

Lipscomb, J.F., *We Built a Country*, London, Faber & Faber, 1956

Livingstone, David, *Missionary Travels and Researches in South Africa*, London, John Murray, 1857

Lonsdale, John, *Politics in Kenya*, Edinburgh, Edinburgh University Centre for African Studies, 1992

Lovell, Mary S., *Straight on Till Morning: The Life of Beryl Markham*, London, Hutchinson, 1987

Lugard, Frederick D., *The Rise of our East African Empire*, London, Blackwoods, 1893

McDermott, P.L., *British East Africa or IBEA*, London, Chapman & Hall, 1893

Macdonald, J.R.L., *Soldiering and Surveying in British East Africa*, London, Edward Arnold, 1897

Maciel, Mervyn, *Bwana Karani*, Braunton, Merlin Books, 1985

Markham, Beryl, *West With The Night*, London, Harrap, 1942

Meinertzhagen, Richard, *Kenya Diary, 1902–1906*, London, Oliver & Boyd, 1957

Miller, Charles, *The Lunatic Express*, London, Macdonald, 1971

Mitchell, Sir Philip, *African Afterthoughts*, London, Hutchinson, 1954

Money, Roger Noel, *Ginia, My Kenya Coffee Shamba 1918–1939*, Perth, privately printed, 2000

Morell, Virginia, *Ancestral Passions: The Leakey Family*, Simon & Schuster, 1995

Mphahlele, Ezekiel, *The African Image*, London, Faber & Faber, 1962

Mungeam, Gordon, *British Rule in Kenya*, Oxford, Clarendon Press, 1966

O'Shea, T.J., *Farming and Planting in British East Africa*, Nairobi, Newland & Tarlton, 1917

Paice, Edward, *Lost Lion of Empire: The Life of 'Cape to Cairo' Grogan*, London, HarperCollins, 2001

Patterson, J.H., *The Man Eaters of Tsavo*, London, Macmillan, 1907

Perham, Margery, *Lugard: The Years of Adventure*, London, Collins, 1956

Perham, Margery, *East African Journey*, London, Faber & Faber, 1986

Playne, Somerset (ed. F. Holderness Gale), *East Africa (British): Its History, People, Commerce, Industries and Resources*, Foreign & Colonial Compiling and Publishing Co., 1908–09

Pollard, John, *African Zoo Man: The Life Story of Raymond Hook*, London, Robert Hale, 1963

Powys, Llewelyn, *Black Laughter*, London, Grant Richards, 1925

Preston, R.O., *Oriental Nairobi*, Nairobi, Colonial Printing Works, 1938

Prince, Vivien Schapira, *Kenya: The Years of Change*, New York, Carlton Press, 1987

Reece, Alys, *To my Wife – 50 Camels*, London, Harvill, 1963

Rodwell, Edward, *The Mombasa Club*, Mombasa, The Mombasa Club, 1988

Rosberg, Carl G., and Nottingham, John, *The Myth of Mau Mau*, New York, Hoover Institution, 1966

Ross, W. McGregor, *Kenya From Within*, London, George Allen & Unwin, 1927

Rotberg, Robert, *Joseph Thomson and the Exploration of Africa*, London, Chatto & Windus, 1971

Salvadori, Cynthia, *Two Indian Travellers*, Mombasa, Friends of Fort Jesus, 1997

Scott, Pamela, *A Nice Place To Live*, Wilton, Michael Russell, 1991

Seaton, Henry, *Lion in the Morning*, John Murray, 1963

Sorrenson, M.P.K., *Origins of European Settlement in Kenya*, London and Nairobi, Oxford University Press, 1968

Stapleton, James W., *The Gate Hangs Well*, London, Hammond, Hammond & Co., 1956

Thiong'o, Ngugi wa, *Homecoming*, London, Heinemann, 1972

Thurman, Judith, *Isak Dinesen: The Life of Karen Blixen*, London, Weidenfeld & Nicolson, 1982

Tignor, Robert, *The Colonial Transformation of Kenya*, Princeton, Princeton University Press, 1966

Trench, Charles Chenevix, *The Men who Ruled Kenya*, London, Radliffe Press, 1993

Trzebinski, Errol, *The Kenya Pioneers*, London, Heinemann, 1985

Trzebinski, Errol, *The Lives of Beryl Markham*, London, Heinemann, 1993

Trzebinski, Errol, *The Life and Death of Lord Erroll*, London, Fourth Estate, 2000

Waugh, Evelyn (ed. Michael Davie), *The Diaries of Evelyn Waugh*, London, Weidenfeld & Nicolson, 1976

Youé, Christopher P., *Robert Thorne Coryndon*, Gerrards Cross, Colin Smythe, 1986

Young, Francis Brett, *Marching on Tanga*, London, Heinemann, 1917

INDEX

Index

Index

Index

Index

Snow, C.P. 264
Society for the Propagation of Christian Knowledge 151
Society of Authors 239
Somalia 282
Somaliland 159, 162
Somerville, Mary 152
Sorcerer's Apprentice, The (EH) 192–7, 200–1, 207–8, 216, 222, 227, 271, 442
South Africa 9, 52, 101, 114, 115, 259, 304, 324, 343, 370–1
South Cerney 145
Southampton Zoo 356
Soviet Union 272, 281, 282, 306, 310
Spectator 111
Spiers, Len 270
Stalbridge, Lord, *see* Grosvenor, Lord Richard de Aquila
Stapledon, Prof. George 91–2, 93
Sterling Lord 344, 350, 357
Stewart, Neil 140
Stjernswärd, Hans 160, 164
Story of an African Farm, The (Schreiner) 395
Story of Five English Farmers, The (EH) 151
Stott, Janette 212, 250
Such Darling Dodos (Wilson) 221–2
Suez crisis 272, 275
Suki: A Little Tiger (EH) 355–6
Sunday Telegraph 336
Sunday Times 192n, 238, 266, 277, 280, 299, 324
Swahili people 7, 24, 33
Sweden 146
Swift, Randall 31, 212–13, 289

Tabora, Tanzania 197
Talking of Books (BBC radio) 263
Talking of Tea (G. Huxley) 270, 272
Tallents, Stephen 93, 95, 148
Tamesis 85
Tanga, Tanzania 196
Tanzania (Tanganyika) 114, 122, 142, 176–7, 299; in EH's book 195–7, 208; federation proposed 107; as German East Africa 2, 40; groundnut scheme 197; Jos's land in 88–9; national parks 340, 404, 405–7; World War I in 53
Taubenheim, Ros 436
Taveta, Kenya 41
Taylor, Charles 17, 31, 34, 56, 72, 290
Taylor, Kit 72–3, 381
Tazama 178
Tennessee Valley Authority 115
Thames TV 412, 428

Their Shining Eldorado (EH) 366–8, 372
They Made it Their Home (East Africa Women's League) 409
Thika, Kenya (formerly Chania Bridge) 15–18, 29, 60, 273; Boers 23; branch railway 24–5; coffee plantations 36, 38; development 435; leaving of 76; renamed 54; *see also* Kitimuru farm
Thika, river 16, 20
Thika District Association 59, 70
Thing to Love, A (EH) 255–8, 443
Thiong'o, Ngugi wa 443
Thomson, David 397
Tilsley, Frank 275
Time and Tide 222, 243, 280, 284
Times, The 208, 424; EH's articles for 94, 99, 114–15, 123; EH's obituary 398, 437; EH/Perham letter to 329; reviews EH's books 110, 209, 300; van der Post's obituary 301
Times Literary Supplement 110, 137, 195, 208, 240, 300, 336, 344, 346, 351, 353, 367, 422
Tit Bits 94
Tompson, Alan 31, 36
Travel Talks (BBC radio) 149, 152, 153, 182
Travels in West Africa (Kingsley) 394
Treetops, Kenya 229n, 260
Trevelyan, George 373, 384
Trinidad Guardian 94
Troup Report (1952) 171
Tsavo National Park 340, 405, 409
Turkana, Lake 140
Turkana people 3
Turnbull, Sir Richard 299, 318
Turner, Walter 151

Uaso Nyiro river 25, 121, 139, 283
Uganda 339; EH's book on 195, 197–8; federation proposed 107, 176–7; railways 3; EH's trips to 19, 91, 123, 212
Uhuru 299
United Nations 196
United States 84–7, 91, 114–15, 146, 150, 153; African university ties 339; Dust Bowl 115, 149; EH's unfinished book on 155
United States and Ourselves, The (BBC radio) 153
USSR, *see* Soviet Union

Van der Post, Laurens 263, 301, 308, 368, 370, 398, 433
Van Lawick, Hugo 404, 405–8, 409
Van Rensburg, C.J. 343
Van Thal, Herbert 373, 383, 391, 392, 413

481